14/43

The English Marriage

Also by Maureen Waller

1700: Scenes from London Life

Ungrateful Daughters: The Stuart Princesses Who

Stole their Father's Crown

London 1945: Life in the Debris of War

Sovereign Ladies: The Six Reigning Queens of England

The
English Marriage

Tales of Love, Money and Adultery

MAUREEN WALLER

JOHN MURRAY

First published in Great Britain in 2009 by John Murray (Publishers)
An Hachette UK Company

1

© Maureen Waller 2009

A CIP catalogue record for this title is available from the British Library

ISBN 978-1-84854-054-5

Typeset in Monotype Bembo by Servis Filmsetting Ltd, Stockport, Cheshire

Printed and bound by Clays Ltd, St Ives plc

John Murray policy is to use papers that are natural, renewable and recyclable products and made
from wood grown in sustainable forests. The logging and manufacturing processes are expected to
conform to the environmental regulations of the country of origin.

John Murray (Publishers)
338 Euston Road
London NW1 3BH

www.johnmurray.co.uk

For Brian, the best of husbands

Contents

Acknowledgements

I am particularly grateful to my publisher, Roland Philipps, for his patience, kindness and enthusiasm. Others I should like to thank are my agent, Jonathan Lloyd at Curtis Brown; Helen Hawksfield and the rest of the team at John Murray; Morag Lyall for her scrupulous copy-editing; and Juliet Brightmore for her kind assistance with the illustrations. I should also like to thank the staff of the London Library for their courtesy and wonderfully efficient service, which is so helpful to country members like me.

Above all, I wish to thank my husband, Brian MacArthur, for all his support. Looking over my shoulder occasionally as I worked on *The English Marriage*, he expressed all the most appropriate responses of shock, surprise, outrage and amusement at its revelations.

Introduction

FOREIGN VISITORS TO England were impressed by the status and freedom enjoyed by English wives and the courtesy shown them by their husbands. 'Now the women of England, who have mostly blue-grey eyes and are fair and pretty, have far more liberty than in other lands and know just how to make good use of it, for they often stroll out or drive by in very gorgeous clothes and the men must put up with such ways,' marvelled one sixteenth-century visitor, while another noted:

> Wives in England are entirely in the power of their husbands, their lives only excepted. Therefore when they marry, they give up the surname of their father and the family from which they are descended, and take the surname of their husbands . . . But although the women are entirely in the power of their husbands . . . they are not kept as strictly as in Spain or elsewhere. Nor are they shut up, but they have free management of the house and housekeeping. They are well dressed, fond of taking it easy, and commonly leave the care of household matters and drudgery to their servants. In all banquets and feasts they are shown the highest honour; they are placed at the upper end of the table, where they are first served . . . All the rest of their time they employ in walking and riding, in playing cards, in visiting their friends and keeping company, conversing with their equals (whom they term *gossips*) and their neighbours, and making merry with them at child-births, christenings, churchings and funerals; and all this with the permission and knowledge of their husbands, as such is the custom. This is why England is called the Hell of Horses, the Purgatory of Servants, and the Paradise of Married Women.

If England was a paradise for wives, it could only have been through the feistiness of the women. On her wedding day, a woman stepped into the same legal category as wards, lunatics, idiots and outlaws. She surrendered her rights as a *feme sole*, a single woman who enjoyed many of the same rights as men, for those of a *feme covert*, subject to a whole series of legal handicaps. As the legal commentator Sir William Blackstone described it: 'By marriage, the husband and wife are one person in law: that is, the very being or legal existence of the woman is suspended during the marriage, or at least is incorporated and consolidated into that of the husband, under whose wing, protection and *cover*, she performs everything.'

On marriage, a woman literally became her husband's property, but then marriage was very much about property, or had been since the Norman Conquest. England after 1066 was an intensely militaristic society, one in which those who could not fight – women – were allotted second place. The land of England had been parcelled out to the Conqueror's faithful retainers, who owed feudal service to their overlord in exchange for it. If a woman inherited property, it was considered only right that she should yield up all interest in it to her husband, who would render military service on her behalf. In return he was obliged to protect her and maintain her according to their rank and dignity.

For many centuries marriage was the single most important vehicle for the transmission of land in England. If the woman died, her husband was still entitled to receive the rents and profits from the land for the rest of his natural life, provided a child who breathed for even a few minutes had been born of the marriage. This was known as 'the courtesy of England'.

The superiority of men over women became part of the unchallengeable order of ideas, dovetailing neatly with the teachings of the Church. Christianity, after all, was basically an eastern religion and the subjection of the woman to the man was preached with conviction by its most important early convert, St Paul, and eventually permeated the law of marriage in England, which was essentially the Church's law, for many centuries.

The Church and the secular, Norman, authorities discovered a mutual interest in regulating marriage, which had previously been a more informal arrangement, with greater equality between the sexes. Monogamy was a central tenet of Christian marriage, while for the Norman ruling class marriage was the key to inheritance.

Unambiguous legitimacy was crucial, particularly since by the law of primogeniture, introduced by the Normans, an entire estate was invested in the eldest son. Everything hinged on property. The sexual double standard, which was at the heart of the marriage laws until women finally achieved equality before the law in 1923, came into existence to protect property: a man's infidelity was winked at, but a wife's severely condemned, since a man needed to be sure that his heir was his own. If legitimacy was crucial, what price a wife's chastity? As Dr Johnson said, 'Chastity in women is all important, because the whole of property is involved in it.'

It was to ensure an orderly system of inheritance that the ruling class was prepared to be subject to the jurisdiction of the Church and to allow the Church control over all marriage litigation through the ecclesiastical courts – a system that endured until the Divorce and Matrimonial Causes Act of 1857 transferred the business to the new, secular, Divorce Court in London. In taking control over matrimonial affairs from the Church it openly rejected the theological principle of the indissolubility of marriage.

It was not, however, the Divorce Act so much as the series of Women's Property Acts of 1870, 1874 and 1882, which finally restored to women full rights to own their own property, that had the most profound effect on the English marriage.

By the fourteenth century the Church had enjoyed a large measure of success in persuading the English people to marry in church and under its supervision. The fact that the common law stipulated that the bride's endowment – the confirmation of her dower before witnesses – had to take place 'at church door' proved a great incentive to a church wedding. Marriages took place at the church door, *in facie ecclesiae* – publicly, in the presence of the congregation or community – rather than in the body of the church. By the fifteenth century churches were building sumptuous porches – the wedding marquees of the late medieval period. This was not so much to protect the bridal party from the elements, as part of a move to relocate the noisy transaction of business from the great naves. Only after the exchange of vows had taken place before the priest and he had blessed the ring – believed to give it magical, protective powers – did the bridal pair move into the body of the church for the nuptial mass.

The Church's main purpose in taking control of marriage, beyond sanctifying it, was to make it as public as possible, so as to rule out subsequent questioning of its validity. To this end, banns were to be read in church on three successive Sundays or major feast days. Those who knew the couple were required to examine the past and report any impediment to the marriage. Impediments included pre-contract, whereby one or both of the parties had previously promised themselves irrevocably to someone else, or close kinship. People as distantly related as third cousins, godparents and in-laws all fell within the prohibited degree. The field was narrowed at the English Reformation, but it was not until the late Victorian period and after much debate that the ban on marrying a deceased wife's sister or a widow her brother-in-law was lifted.

For all its Herculean efforts to control and regulate marriage, the business of the ecclesiastical courts was almost entirely taken up with the consequences of members of the laity thinking they could dispense with the services of the Church and manage their own marital affairs. It invariably led to trouble and it fell to the ecclesiastical courts to untangle the mess of such irregular unions, particularly when a binding promise or contract had been made with one party, only for one of them to make a subsequent marriage with someone else.

Part of the problem was that the laws relating to marriage were so ambiguous and inconsistent that with the best will in the world many couples did not know whether or not they were legally married. There was confusion between the betrothal – a promise *pro verba de futuro*, that is, to marry in the future – and the actual marriage, when vows *pro verba de praesenti* were exchanged, preferably at the church door before a priest. The confusion arose because if the couple made the vows privately, they were still married, albeit illicitly, in the eyes of the Church.

Many believed that betrothal or 'spousals' was sufficient. Indeed, the Church regarded betrothed couples, 'spouses', as imperfectly married. A betrothal was a legally binding contract, precluding a subsequent valid marriage with someone else. Only gradually, over many centuries, did betrothal become simply an engagement that could be broken without penalty.

A promise to marry *per verba de futuro* followed by sexual intercourse

4

amounted to a marriage in the present. As far as many couples were concerned, such an exchange of promises meant they were married in the eyes of God, but the Church frowned on sexual intercourse taking place before the proper solemnization of the marriage in church. Indeed, one of the purposes of the Church in regulating marriage had been to harness sexuality. In *Utopia*, Sir Thomas More assumed that the major reason people married was that it was the only way to avoid fornication and ensure sex on demand. Women's sexuality, in particular, was seen as a dangerous force that must be kept in check.

For some inexplicable reason, the Church had neglected to specify an exact form of words for the vows *pro verba de futuro* and *pro verba de praesenti*, so that one of the main tasks of the ecclesiastical courts – as we shall see in the case of Margery Paston, who was brought before the Bishop of Norwich in 1469 – was to establish the actual words spoken in the thousands of cases of disputed contracts that came before them over the centuries to determine whether the contract was legally binding.

It could be said that those unencumbered by property really did not care too much whether the Church considered them legally married or not, as long as they themselves believed they were 'married in the sight of God'. One of the striking features apparent in the depositions is the impetuosity of so many marriages. For instance, Isabella Wakes and Thomas Walker 'in the month of August last past, in the year of 1609, were married together in a field near to the town of Ashton-under-Lyne, in the night time, by moon light, by one John Ward, clerk'. They had not had banns read or obtained a licence from the Bishop's court in their diocese *in lieu* of banns, but thought it was all right because they had three witnesses present. Subsequently they had 'lain together in one bed'. Also to the point, 'Thomas and Isabella are reputed for lawful man and wife amongst their neighbours.'

Indeed, when the vicar of Tetbury in Gloucestershire compiled a list of those living in his parish who were 'clandestinely married' – that is, living in a 'common law' marriage contracted by a private exchange of vows or celebrated by 'hedge priests' in private dwellings – he found that it comprised half the parish. He made the list in the late 1690s, no doubt to cover his back, since the government had recently imposed a tax on marriages and now had a vested interest in the proper solemnization of marriage by the parish priest because of the taxes it accrued from it. Taxes on marriage – and, incidentally, on bachelors – provided a further incentive for people to try to buck the system.

Along with this casual attitude to the forms of marriage was a marked moral laxity. In an upper-class marriage that involved property, a woman's virtue had to be guarded at all costs, but this was not true of those belonging to the lower levels of society. From the sixteenth to the nineteenth centuries, when Victorian notions of respectability filtered down to the labouring class, a high proportion of English brides were pregnant on their wedding day.

The Reformation in the sixteenth century would have been the perfect opportunity to iron out some of the inconsistencies and ambiguities of the English marriage laws. While Scotland and other Protestant states introduced divorce for adultery and Catholic Europe made marriage before a priest in church compulsory, ruling out all other forms of marriage, England seemed paralysed by inertia, clinging to the chaotic and contradictory laws of the medieval Church. The proposed reforms of the boy-king Edward VI's fiercely Protestant government were considered too radical, although it was during his brief reign that the Book of Common Prayer containing the beautifully worded marriage service was produced. Elizabeth the Virgin Queen was not particularly interested in the subject of marriage, for obvious reasons. England was left stranded – an island carrying an old Germanic legal system embodied in the common law, lying off a continent dominated by Roman law.

The system was ripe for exploitation and, indeed, between the late seventeenth and the mid-eighteenth centuries there was a boom in the clandestine marriage business. The irregularity of the proceedings and dubious nature of the paperwork encouraged abuse: the drugging, kidnapping and rape of heiresses by ruthless fortune-hunters, bigamy – as we shall see in the case of Con Phillips, who made a career out of it – even same-sex unions with one of the parties disguised as the opposite sex.

When Lord Hardwicke introduced his Bill for the Better Preventing of Clandestine Marriage in England in 1753 its primary purpose, typically, was to protect property. It was one of the most fiercely guarded preserves of English common law that marriage was solely a contract between two people. To be valid, like all contracts, it had to have the full, free and mutual consent of the parties – Cnut had stipulated that no woman should be married without her consent – but it was not, ultimately, a contract that required the agreement of others. Now, Hardwicke's Marriage Act sought to protect the children of the rich from unscrupulous fortune-hunters by putting a stop to the clandestine marriage business.

The Act inched English law for the first time towards the continental laws, by insisting that a marriage must take place before an ordained priest of the Church of England in the parish church of one of the parties, after the reading of banns or the production of a properly executed licence. No other form of marriage was valid. Not only did many fiercely resent this unwarranted intrusion into their private business, but the thousands of Nonconformists were torn between the dictates of their consciences and obeying the law in order to safeguard rights of property and inheritance. Foreign visitors had always been struck by the freedom young people in England enjoyed to mingle with the opposite sex and to conduct their courtships without too much parental control, contrary to European customs. Now, Hardwicke's Marriage Act stipulated that marriages of those under twenty-one were illegal without the consent of parents or guardians.

Ironically, the Achilles heel of the Act was that it did not extend to Scotland. For the next century a steady flow of eloping couples beat a path to the border to make clandestine marriages.

One of the most striking features of the English upper class was their passionate preoccupation with money. Their lives were alternately spent between schemes to acquire it and the startling speed with which they got rid of it again. Marriage was a sure way to make money. The early feminist Mary Astell cynically describes the upper-class marriage: 'What will she bring is the first enquiry? How many acres? How much ready coin?' The arranged marriage, knitting together two families for their political, social, economic and landed interests, was the norm for the aristocracy. It is surely no coincidence that many of the most sensational trials for adultery of the eighteenth

7

century feature such marriages, where the couple had barely met before they were married and there was no love, or even liking, between them.

Many who committed adultery might in modern times have simply divorced and remarried, but until 1857 divorce with permission to remarry was confined to the privileged few, who could afford to go through the long and expensive process of securing a private Act of Parliament to free them from an adulterous wife whose promiscuity was threatening to place the inheritance of a great estate in the rightful line in jeopardy. For the English as a whole, high rates of prostitution and adultery may have been the price they paid for the rigid marriage code.

Their modes of courtship and expectations from marriage were different from ours. People were more restrained in making overt expressions of love, but romantic love is certainly present in the private intimate letters between husband and wife, as well as inadvertently revealed in court depositions. 'Dear Heart, let me beg of thee to dispatch thy business quickly,' wrote Ralph Verney to his wife Mary when they were separated during the civil war, 'that thou may speedily return to him whose love daily increases, even beyond thy imagination.' Henry Oxinden was very badly smitten when he fell madly in love with his eighteen-year-old ward: 'I have tried to cure myself by labour, art and friendship . . . by exercise and diet and fasting . . . I have tried philtres . . . and all to such purpose as if I had run my head against a post.'

The automatic equation of marriage with happiness, in particular with individual happiness and self-gratification, is a modern concept. Indeed, the Royal Commission of 1956 identified as the single most important factor in marital breakdown the idealization of the individual pursuit of self-gratification and personal pleasure at the expense of a sense of reciprocal obligations and duties towards spouses, children and society as a whole.

In the past, love was by no means the sole basis for marriage: the passions were considered notoriously wayward. Sexual passion had little or no place at all in marriage; affection, compatibility and mutual interests were considered surer grounds. The couple had to work at their marriage because there was no easy escape, and the family unit was seen as a microcosm of society, a little commonwealth, whose good order would contribute to the whole.

John Milton laid great stress on the mutual comfort to be derived from marriage. Marriage, he argued, was created by God to abate the separateness, the loneliness of the individual. Men and women were similar yet sufficiently dissimilar to be complementary, remedying the other's defects. It was on the basis of these high ideals that he advocated divorce on grounds of incompatibility: if love and companionship were absent then the marriage should not be artificially prolonged. It was a radical concept, not taken up in law until the 1960s.

The companionate ideal was summarized in *The New Whole Duty of Man* in 1680:

> Men should maintain their wives as becomes partners; they are friends and companions to their husbands, not slaves, nor menial servants; and are to be partners in their fortunes: for, as they partake of their troubles and afflictions, it is just that they should share their fortunes. For when a husband falls into decay, or any sort of calamity, he involves his wife with him; they are inseparable companions in misery and misfortune.

Diaries of the middling classes, such as those of Samuel Pepys, Dudley Ryder and Thomas Turner, tell us their motives for marriage, their hopes, their joys, their disappointments and sorrows. Pepys himself had married spontaneously for love, but most do not enter marriage without careful thought and weighing up the pros and cons. Dudley Ryder confessed that he felt 'a strong inclination towards it, not from any principle of lust or desire to enjoy a woman in bed' but because it offered the prospect of 'a pretty creature being my most intimate friend, constant companion . . . always ready to soothe me, take care of me and caress me'.

A century later Charles Darwin jotted down the pluses and minuses under the headings 'Marry' and 'Not Marry', torn between having a 'constant companion' and 'friend in old age' and 'the expense and anxiety of children'. However, he did make the point that marriage is 'good for one's health'.

Few of the labouring class put pen to paper or thought to record their experience of courtship and marriage, although Francis Place's autobiography is an invaluable record of the stresses poverty puts on marriage in eighteenth-century London. Working and living in one room with his wife, theirs is a relationship of 'dogged comradeship', while it is indicative that Thomas Turner, a Sussex shopkeeper in the eighteenth century, puts 'very industrious' at the top of the list of attributes of his intended wife.

Perhaps as a mark of confidence in marriage, multiple marriages were common in the past when so many of them were cut short by death. As the widows of London and Westminster expressed it in a petition to the House of Commons in 1693: 'We that have had good husbands, are encouraged to try once more, out of hopes of meeting the same success; and we that have had bad ones, are not for all that deterr'd from matrimony, but hope to mend our hands in a second bargain.' Chaucer's Wife of Bath married five times, Bess of Hardwick four. In a Nottinghamshire parish at the end of the seventeenth century the rector noted that of the sixty-seven couples thirteen were on second marriages, three were third marriages, four were fourth marriages and one a fifth. Even so, few could hope to compete with the men of the malaria-infested Essex marshes encountered by Daniel Defoe in the early eighteenth century, who married more than twenty times.

Loneliness was the driving factor for many to remarry. It was very often a death that prompted an intimate insight into the feelings of the survivor for the lost spouse. Thomas Turner gives a poignant account of a man who has lost his 'other half', describing his late wife as his 'only friend . . . the centre of my worldly happiness', while Francis Place mourned a wife who was 'for ever my *friend* my long cherished *companion* in all my various changes of life, she who had my entire confidence, she who gave me hers, and had loved me most sincerely for thirty-seven years'.

The Church's insistence on the indissolubility of marriage was so deeply ingrained that marital breakdown was the rare exception rather than the norm. The support of family and 'friends', particularly when a marriage was in trouble, helped keep marriages together. Today's wife has to make up the rules as she goes along, but in the past a plethora of advice books set out what was expected of her.

Gentleness, respect, consideration, and just being nice to one's partner as to a friend are eternal verities which in the frantic haste of modern life and the obsession with sexual politics are perhaps overlooked.

There is a temptation to see all happy marriages as the same, but each unhappy marriage as unhappy after its own fashion. Today, marriage and divorce are often uttered in the same breath, but they are two separate subjects, not even two sides of the same coin. Yet it is the divorce records that tell us what the expectations of marriage and the standards of behaviour were. It is the broken marriages that come before the courts that prompt changes in the law.

This can be traced, for instance, in the changing definition of cruelty, which over the centuries has evolved from a man beating his wife to within an inch of her life to what is now termed 'unreasonable behaviour', which seems to encompass anything from a light tap to raising one's voice in an argument.

In the past, English society was brutal and a husband had almost unlimited power over his wife. He could demand sex as a right, chastise and beat her, subject her to life-threatening violence, dissipate her fortune, starve her, banish her from his house even if that house had been purchased with her money, forbid her to see her children, imprison her or incarcerate her in an asylum. *The English Marriage* highlights instances of all these manifestations of cruelty. The law is conservative, slow to catch up with society's needs and demands for change, but this does not take account of the flexibility of individual judgements in the courts, which gradually set precedents and changed the law.

The establishment of the new Divorce Court in London in January 1858 opened a window on to the private hell of many Victorian marriages. Heavy press coverage of the proceedings, together with an avid public hunger for the details, was a vital factor in stimulating changes in attitudes to marriage and setting new standards of what was acceptable or reasonable behaviour within marriage. Marriage would now be subject to public scrutiny and state regulation, while the threat of exposure in court was seen as a salutary deterrent to misconduct.

Patriarchal marriage met its greatest challenge in the nineteenth century, when reformers tackled the issues of child custody, divorce and married women's property. Hitherto, the mortality rate had been so high that few marriages endured more than ten or twenty years. The Divorce Act of 1857 fortuitously coincided with a decline in the mortality rates. The combination of higher emotional expectancy from the companionate marriage and the prospect of marriages lasting longer placed an added strain on marriage.

In 1857 most MPs simply could not conceive of a marriage in which husband and wife met as political and economic as well as social equals. John Stuart Mill maintained that there could be no true harmony in marriage until there was equality between men and women. Equating marriage with slavery, he believed a wife was denied any meaningful role in life except as 'the personal bodyservant of a despot'. Marital equality could only be achieved, he argued, if the laws governing marriage were changed and women given the franchise, equal education and employment opportunities. Human relationships between equals were of a higher, more enriching order.

As Mona Caird predicted in 1890, 'a glimpse of the end of the twentieth century might puzzle even those who are most prepared for change.' Two world wars in the twentieth century led to massive social disruption and had a profound effect on marriage. The emancipation of women and their emergence in the workplace, the erosion of religious belief and the sexual revolution of the 1960s have all placed strains on the traditional marriage, while one of the biggest challenges still facing modern marriage is adjusting to the equality so ardently advocated by John Stuart Mill and finding a new equilibrium between husband and wife.

Is it equality or the absurdly high expectation of romantic love which puts a strain on modern marriage?

And although their dispositions are somewhat licentious, I never have noticed anyone, either at court or amongst the lower orders, to be in love; whence one must necessarily conclude, either that the English are the most discreet lovers in the world, or that they are incapable of love. I say this of the men, for I understand it is quite the contrary with the women, who are very violent in their passions. Howbeit, the English keep a very jealous guard over their wives, though anything may be compensated in the end, by the power of money.

A Relation of the Island of England c.1500,
presented to the Venetian Senate

PART ONE
1465–1645

I

'Marry thy daughters in time lest they marry themselves'

IN THE WINTER of 1465 the Norfolk gentlewoman Margaret
Paston returned from a shopping trip to Norwich and sat down to
dictate a letter to her husband John in London. There was exciting
news. She had taken their daughter Margery to town and they had
called in on John's mother, Agnes. There, a fellow named Wrothe
saw Margery and was full of praise for her, saying she was 'a goodly
young woman'. Agnes asked him to find the girl 'one good marriage
if he knew any'. As it happened, he knew the perfect candidate: 'Sir
John Cley's son, who is chamberlain with my Lady of York', and
worth 300 marks a year. The young man was eighteen years old and,
if John agreed to the match, his 'mother thinks it should be got for
less money now than it should be hereafter, either that one, or some
other good marriage'.

This was often the way marriages were made, with relatives and
friends of the family putting out feelers and acting as go-betweens.
They would be looking for someone of equal rank, about the same
age, and with good financial prospects. On this last point, it was typical of the Pastons, particularly of John's indomitable mother, Agnes,
that they should immediately think of haggling. Marriage, after all,
was a business arrangement, one of the surest ways to make money
and advance a family's influence, and the *nouveaux riches* Pastons were
still rising in the world.

Nothing came of the idea, possibly because John, a lawyer, was too
embroiled in a long-running dispute over the legacy he had received
from his old patron, Sir John Fastolf, to give much thought to his
daughter's marriage. At seventeen, there was time enough to find
her a suitable match, although not for John. Only a few months later,
in May 1466, he died suddenly, aged forty-four. It fell to his sons,

John II and John III (inexplicably given the same Christian name) to continue the battles, legal and otherwise, for the family inheritance. It was while they were engaged in the defence of Fastolf's prize property, Caister Castle, that Margery took the matter of her marriage into her own hands.

The first hint of trouble appears in a letter from Margaret to John II, asking him to find alternative accommodation for his sister, 'for we be either of us weary of each other. I shall tell you more when I speak with you. I pray you do your devoir herein . . . for divers causes which you shall understand afterward'.

The reason for Margaret wanting Margery out of the house, and for her guarded tone in the letter, became clear shortly afterwards. Margery at twenty had so demeaned herself as to fall in love with the family's bailiff, Richard Calle. It seems that the relationship had been going on for two years and that the couple were now sufficiently sure of their feelings for each other to brave the family's inevitable wrath by seeking permission to marry.

The position of a woman depended entirely on marriage and yet she was powerless: she had to rely on her family to find her a husband. The alternative, especially for a girl whose father was unable to afford a dowry with which to secure her a husband, was either to enter a nunnery or become a burden on the family, trying to make herself useful in the guise of unofficial servant. Until her fate had been decided, she came under her mother's rule.

Margery might have been aware of the sad history of her aunt, Elizabeth Paston. Elizabeth was beaten so severely by her mother Agnes that a cousin remonstrated, urging John Paston to find his sister a husband quickly, lest in her misery she made some misguided choice of her own. Elizabeth was willing to accept any suitor, no matter how unappealing, in order to escape her mother and become mistress of her own household.

Finally, when she was twenty-eight, a marriage was agreed. Robert Poynings was a man whom she hardly knew, but whom she reported treated her kindly enough. The Pastons had obviously got the better of him in the marriage settlement and were slow in paying, and Elizabeth was reduced to pleading with her mother 'that my master, my best beloved, fail not of the hundred marks at the beginning of this term, the which ye promised him to his marriage, with the remnant of the money of father's will'.

Margery, who sounds as strong-willed as her mother, had probably grown impatient with her brothers' dilatoriness in finding her a husband. As with her aunt, offers had been made on behalf of young men she had never met, whose families typically opened negotiations by laying out the financial terms, such as this one made around 1468:

> *To my right worshipful and good Master, Sir John Paston, Knight.*
> Right worshipful Sir, after due recommendation, please it you to understand the cause of my writing is for a marriage for my Mistress Margery your sister; for my nephew John Strange would make her sure of forty pounds jointure, and two hundred marks by year of inheritance; and if ye and your friends will agree thereto, I trust to God it shall take a conclusion to the pleasure of God and worship to both parties.

It was nothing if not businesslike. Possibly Margery and John Strange would have liked each other well enough when they met, but no more is heard of the proposal. Not only were Margery's brothers too preoccupied elsewhere to think of her marriage, but the Pastons were chronically short of cash, and the Le Stranges would require a decent dowry in exchange for the jointure they were offering.

By 1468 Margery was already involved with Richard Calle. She must have known Calle, who came to work for the family in 1450, all her life. Until now, they had all been fond of him. Calle, who seems to have been considerably older than Margery, perhaps in his late thirties, was loyal, likeable, capable and efficient. He was an invaluable servant. But that was the problem: he was only a servant and came from a family of Framlingham shopkeepers.

The Paston family's gentility was too recently acquired to regard their sister's descent through the hard-won ranks with equanimity. Only a century earlier their great-grandfather Clement was a free peasant who 'followed the plough' out at Paston, a remote village on Norfolk's east coast. He had scraped together enough money to give his son William an education. He had become a brilliant lawyer. In his forties, his career established and fortune made, William had made a good marriage, to Agnes Berry, a knight's daughter, who had brought him three manors.

Thanks to the fortune accumulated through his father's hard work, their son John, a lawyer like his father working mainly in London, could afford to marry young, in order to produce sons to inherit the family properties and hopefully live long enough to see them grow up. The first we hear of his bride is in a letter from Agnes to William, simply announcing 'the coming, and the bringing home, of the gentlewoman'. She was a local heiress, Margaret Mauteby, whose lands in the north and east of the county would complement the Pastons'. The marriage had been arranged between the two families. William had probably known the girl for years, since he was a trustee of the Mauteby estates, but this was her first meeting with her future husband. 'And as for the first acquaintance between John Paston and the said gentlewoman,' Agnes continued, 'she made him gentle cheer in gentle wise, and said he was verily your son. And so I hope there shall need no great treaty between them.'

Fortunately, John and Margaret, even at eighteen, were as pragmatic as their parents. They knew the relationship had to work and they had a mutual interest in furthering the family fortunes. Love was seldom the criterion for marriage. They were compatible and affection, if not love, would surely grow in time. Three years after the marriage, when John lay sick in London, Margaret was all concern, touchingly revealing her feelings: 'Right Worshipful Husband,' she began, as she did all her letters, showing him due reverence and respect, 'If I might have had my will, I should have seen you ere this time; I would ye were at home . . . lever [rather] than a new gown though it were of scarlet.'

Margaret had been educated as befitted an heiress, who would be expected to manage a wealthy household and look after her husband's local interests during his many absences. Knowing something of the law and having a sufficient sense of authority through her birth and position, she was, in effect, his highly capable agent in Norfolk. In 1448, when after the birth of several sons she was pregnant with Margery, she and the children were forcibly driven out of Gresham Castle by Lord Moleyns. Undaunted, Margaret set up home in another Paston property on his doorstep, a constant reminder to the usurper of his unjust action. A relative of Fastolf of Agincourt fame, she sent urgently to John for crossbows and other weapons in order to defend herself.

In spite of the genteel birth and success of their womenfolk, the third-generation Pastons were still smarting from jibes that they were descended from serfs. So it was an uncomfortable reminder of their tenuous gentility when Margery declared her intention to marry Richard Calle. The normally easy-going John III was surprisingly angry, writing to John II to complain of Calle's presumption and 'our ungracious sister's assent'. If they thought that he approved the idea of marrying his sister into a family of shopkeepers they were very much mistaken, for they would 'never have my good will for to make my sister to sell candle and mustard in Framlingham'.

The family separated the lovers, sending Calle to London, but not before they had secretly exchanged marriage vows. We do not know what words they used, but simply to say, 'I, Margery, take thee, Richard, for my husband', and for Richard to do the same would have made the contract valid in the eyes of the Church. If they promised to marry each other some time in the future but consummated their love, the marriage was equally valid, although the Church frowned on fornication between the contract and the solemnization of marriage. A mere promise to marry in the future, a betrothal, amounted to a valid contract that could not be broken. It would be up to the Church to decide.

There is one surviving love letter from Richard Calle to Margery and in it he clearly believes they are irrevocably bound together. The fact that the letter survived and that she did not burn it as he instructed may indicate that the letter was intercepted by Margaret and that Margery never read it.

'Mine own Lady and Mistress, and, before God, very true wife,' he begins, 'I with heart full sorrowful recommend me unto you, as he that cannot be merry, nor nought shall be till it be otherwise with us than it is yet, for this life that we lead now is neither pleasure to God nor to the world, considering the great bond of matrimony that is made betwixt us, and also the great love that hath been, and as I trust, yet is betwixt us.' He loves her more than ever and deplores the fact that 'we that ought of very right to be most together are most asunder'. It seems a thousand years since he spoke to her and he wanted to be with her more than anything in the world. He knew how much she was having to suffer on his account and only wished he could bear the burden. 'I understand, Lady, ye have had as much sorrow for me as any Gentlewoman hath had in the world, as would God all that sorrow that ye have had had rested upon me.' It is 'death to hear that ye be entreated otherwise than ye ought to be'.

He goes on to say how loath he is to displease her mother, but suggests that perhaps it is time the family were told of their secret betrothal. They were married in the sight of God and surely the family would respect that and not endanger their souls by denying it. 'I suppose and ye tell them sadly the truth, they will not damn their souls for us; though I tell them the truth they will not believe me as well as they will do you, and therefore, good Lady, at the reverence of God be plain to them and tell the truth, and if they will in no wise agree thereto, betwixt God, the Devil, and them be it.'

Richard was clearly surprised and hurt at the vehemence of the Pastons' opposition, but neither he nor Margery needed their families' consent to marry. The Church required that the couple themselves must willingly give their consent, but the consent of parents, although desirable, was irrelevant. Provided the vows the couple had exchanged at their secret betrothal amounted to a contract, their union was valid and irrevocable. The prime task of the ecclesiastical courts was to defend and uphold marriages, rather than to dissolve them. In cases of disputed contracts – for instance, where one party claimed vows had been exchanged but the other denied it, perhaps going on to marry someone else – the courts had to establish what words the couple had used, in order to pronounce the marriage valid or otherwise.

Margery and Calle were summoned to appear before the Bishop of Norwich, as Margaret reported to John II. She and John's mother Agnes had been to see the bishop to ask him to delay the interview until Margery's brothers and the other executors of their father's will could be there, 'for they had the rule of her as well as I'. The bishop would brook no delay, however, insisting that Margery appear before him the next day. He very much hoped that he would find that the contract was not valid, for her mother's and grandmother's sake and that of her 'other friends', since he understood that 'her demeaning had struck sore at our hearts'.

The Church frowned on marriages made without parental approval. The bishop was clearly as disappointed by Marjory's choice, as were her family. He warned her that such a marriage would lose her the support of her family and friends and that she would be received nowhere, but Margery stood her ground. He asked her to repeat the vow she had made to Calle, 'that he would understand the words that she had said to him whether it made matrimony or not'. Margery 'rehearsed what she had said', adding boldly that 'if those words made it not sure . . . that she would make it surer ere than she went thence, for she said she thought in her conscience she was bound whatsoever the words were'.

Calle was then examined alone and 'her words and his accorded, and the time, and where it should have been done'. The bishop was still hoping for an excuse to deny the contract was valid and asked for a few days' grace before announcing his decision. Possibly he was hoping to discover some misdemeanour of Calle's, perhaps an earlier liaison. In the event, he could find none and the contract of marriage was proved and confirmed. Since Margaret was later to make a note on the back of one of her letters that the couple were subsequently married, it appears that their marriage was duly solemnized before a priest in church.

Meanwhile, Margaret was apoplectic when she heard how Margery had conducted herself before the bishop. 'I was with my mother, at her place in Norwich, when she was examined, and when I heard say what her demeaning was, I charged my servants that she should not be received in mine house . . . and I sent to one or two more that they should not receive her if she came.' It was left to the bishop to find some accommodation for Margery while she awaited his judgement.

Margaret assured her eldest son that although they were all very upset by Margery's behaviour, she was obviously flawed, and no loss to them. She 'were dead at this hour, she should never be at mine heart as she was'. But, as Calle had calculated, Margaret was God-fearing and she would not countenance a wrong. Possibly the family had hoped to pressure Margery into denying she had ever promised herself to Calle. Or perhaps they hoped to find or invent some impediment that would render the marriage invalid. Once the bishop had found in favour of the couple, however, Margaret would not endanger her soul by breaking a union blessed by God.

'As for the divorce that ye write to me of,' Margaret wrote to John II, 'I [understand] what ye meant, but I charge you upon my blessing that ye do not, nor cause none other to do, that should offend God and your conscience, for and ye do, or cause to be done, God will take vengeance thereupon.' Margery would reap her own reward: 'she shall full sore repent her lewdness hereafter, and I pray God she might'.

There is no evidence that Margery ever did repent or was unhappy with her choice of husband. At least she had the satisfaction of knowing that she had married for love, unlike her younger sister Anne. In an uncanny coincidence, Anne seems to have fallen for an older man in service to the family, John Pamping. Fearing the disgrace of another misalliance, the family quickly had Pamping removed, to work with John II in London and Calais. A marriage with a young man of equal rank was arranged for Anne, but clearly there was no question of love, since, according to John II, William Yelverton said, 'he would have her if she had her money, and else not'.

Marrying beneath her and without the family's approval, Margery received no dowry and Margaret cut her out of her will, although she did leave money to the eldest of Margery's three sons by Calle. Possibly Margery was already dead by that time, although Calle, who had become a man of property, was still living in 1503. Ostracized by the Pastons, Margery disappears from the story.

2

'Upon Friday is Saint Valentine's Day and every bird chooses a mate'

WITH THE ELDER John Paston reluctant to tie the knot, it was left to his younger brother, John III, to marry and continue the family line. A younger son needed to marry a rich wife, but such brides were hard to find. The family of a girl with a good dowry would want to marry her to the eldest son, who would inherit the bulk of the estate, even though her dowry or 'portion' might then be used as dowries for his sisters to attract good matches. Since on marriage everything a woman owned, except her 'paraphernalia' – clothes, jewels and ornaments suitable to her rank – became her husband's, she was powerless to stop her money being used in this way, as long as he maintained her at an adequate level.

The other option for a younger son was to find a rich widow; not surprisingly, they were highly sought after. Widows were in the happy position of being at their own disposal. Unlike married women, a widow, as a *feme sole*, had pretty much the same rights as a man: she could enjoy the use of her own property and wealth; she could conduct business, borrow and lend money, on her own account; she could sue and be sued; she could make a will. No wonder some widows were reluctant to remarry and lose all these advantages.

On the other hand, from the family's point of view, widows represented a drain on their resources. Under English common law, a widow automatically received one-third of her husband's estate for life, but if she had brought a good dowry, as Agnes and Margaret Paston did, her marriage settlement would reflect that by guaranteeing her more than a 'widow's thirds' in the form of a jointure. A jointure involved the setting up of a joint estate, held by husband and wife, within some part of the estate, to be theirs for their joint lives and for the remaining life of the survivor. In this way, both Agnes and Margaret Paston retained during their long widowhoods a valuable slice of the family estates, while John II was under pressure to make provision for his brothers and sisters from what was left of his inheritance.

After a number of possible wives for John III were raised and discarded – among them Alice Boleyn, the daughter of a wealthy London mercer who had bought Fastolf's manor of Blickling – John III's choice fell on the widowed Lady Walgrave. He left it to his elder brother to conduct negotiations, sending a ring as a token, but the response was not encouraging. 'She will in no wise receive, nor keep your ring with her, and yet I told her that she should not be any thing bound thereby.' His brother, he explained, only wanted her to have the ring so that she would be reminded of him. He would far prefer to be daily in her presence. It was no good. Lady Walgrave asked that his brother put her right out of his mind. After some sleuthing John II discovered the cause: the lady already had another man in mind for her second husband. No wonder she was so insouciant. It was a pity, he concluded, because she played the harp so prettily.

Fortunately for John III's self-esteem, another and rather more attractive proposition soon materialized. Margery Brews was the daughter of Sir Thomas Brews of Salle and Topcroft, a man of good standing in the county, and her mother Elizabeth was related to Margaret Paston. Not only was this an eminently suitable match, but Margery, in her late teens, and thirty-three-year-old John seem to have fallen headlong in love.

To marry merely for love, as Margery Paston had done, was unacceptable. But in an arranged marriage where all the other criteria – rank, money, age, compatibility – were met, it was recognized that the addition of love was a positive ingredient. Where Margaret Paston had been vehemently opposed to her daughter's marriage for love with a social inferior, she was positively purring over the love match of her younger son.

Both mothers were keen to promote the match. Dame Elizabeth wrote to her prospective son-in-law assuring him that 'I shall give you a great treasure, that is, a witty gentlewoman and if I say it, both good and virtuous; for if I should take money for her, I would not give her for a 1000l.' Nevertheless, as in any marriage among the gentry, it all came down to money. The Pastons were not about to allow John's heart to rule his head, while Sir Thomas was equally determined to drive a hard bargain.

John III wrote to his brother to complain that 'I am yet at no certainty; her father is so hard; but I [believe] I have the good will of my Lady her mother and her'.

Indeed, Elizabeth was busy keeping the romance alive. 'Ye have made her such an advocate for you,' she reported to John of her daughter, 'that I may never have rest night nor day, for calling and crying upon me to bring the said matter to effect.' She advised him to persevere with her husband, for 'it is but a simple oak that is cut down at the first stroke', and reminded him that 'upon Friday is Saint Valentine's Day and every bird chooses a mate'.

Margery was a determined young woman and used Valentine's Day as an excuse to prod John. 'Right reverend and worshipful, and my right well beloved Valentine,' she began. 'And if it please you to hear of my welfare, I am not of good hele [health] of body, nor of heart, nor shall be till I hear from you.'

As for the negotiations, she assured him that 'my Lady my Mother hath laboured the matter to my Father full diligently', but her father was immovable. She was really sorry about this, 'But if that ye love me, as I trust verily that ye do, ye will not leave me therefore.' If he would only accept what was offered, she told him, she would be the happiest girl on earth.

No doubt prompted by Margery, the family chaplain wrote to John to plead her case, assuring him that 'the young gentlewoman, she owes you her good heart and love'. Not only that, but she brought a good dowry of 200 marks and would have linen and clothing worth another 100 marks. 'And I heard my Lady say that . . . both ye and she should have your board with my Lady three years after.'

John in his thirties might have been less than thrilled at the prospect of living with his in-laws for three years after the marriage, but for a newly wed couple to receive free board and lodgings for a stipulated time with the bride's parents had become almost standard practice. In fact, by the terms of his father's will, John had his own manor of Swainsthorpe, but this was one of the sticking points. A mortgage of £120 had been taken out on Swainsthorpe. Margery's father objected to the fact that to redeem it would eat up almost all Margery's dowry, in which case, what would the couple have to live on?

Not impervious to the pleadings of his wife and daughter, Sir Thomas indicated that he would be willing to lend John III the £120, to be repaid on easy terms, but in return he expected the Pastons to provide a better jointure for Margery in the event of her being left a widow. This would typically come from rental income accrued from one or more of the Paston properties allotted to Margery as her jointure.

He wrote to John II, telling him in no uncertain terms that the marriage would not be concluded until he had satisfaction on this point. After all, he had three other daughters to provide for: 'And Cousin, I were right loath to bestow so much upon one daughter, that . . . her sisters should fare the worse.' And, 'whereas I had laid up an 100l. for the marriage of a younger daughter of mine, I have now lent the said 100l. and 20l. over that, to my cousin your brother'.

With John II dragging his heels, Margaret unexpectedly came to the rescue by offering the manor of Sparham from her Mauteby inheritance. This broke the deadlock, because Sir Thomas confirmed that in exchange for the manor of Swainsthorpe and 10 marks out of Sparham as jointure for Margery, 'I will depart with 200 marks in hand, and to give them their board free as for two or three years . . . or else 300 marks without their board, payable by 50 marks yearly, till the sum of 300 marks be full paid.' However, if the income from Sparham in its entirety were to be given to Margery as her jointure, then Sir Thomas would 'be agreeable to depart with 400 marks' for her dowry.

Needless to say, John II was less than pleased when he heard of this further depletion of his inheritance. It was not that he begrudged his brother and future sister-in-law the manor, but he felt that the matter had not been thoroughly considered. What if Margery were to die before her husband, leaving only a daughter? Any son of John III's by a subsequent marriage would lose this part of his inheritance. John felt that he should have been consulted before Margaret made her impulsive offer of Sparham and asked that she and his brother 'trouble me no more in this matter'.

The brothers had always been close and the *froideur* over the marriage settlement did not last for long. John Paston the younger and Margery Brews were married in the autumn of 1477. Nine months later, Margery gave birth to a son. John II was genuinely delighted, never having married and produced a legitimate heir of his own. A year later he died of the plague. He was only thirty-seven. The Paston inheritance passed to John and Margery. Sir Thomas Brews had indeed made a fine bargain for his daughter.

INTERLUDE

The Form of Solemnisation of Matrimony, Book of Common Prayer

The English Reformation, prompted by King Henry VIII's wish to rid himself of his first wife, left the marriage laws of the medieval Church virtually intact. Marriage ceased to be regarded as a sacrament, but it was still sacred and indissoluble. In 1549 Thomas Cranmer, Archbishop of Canterbury, produced the first Book of Common Prayer; a revised edition appeared in 1552 and a combination of the first and second editions in 1559, shortly after the accession of Elizabeth I. The Prayer Book contained the Form of Solemnisation of Matrimony used by the Church of England over succeeding centuries.

First of all, it asked for the reading of the banns in the parish of each of the parties three times; then:

At the day and time appointed for solemnisation of matrimony, the persons to be married shall come into the body of the Church with their friends and neighbours: and there standing together, the Man on the right hand, and the Woman on the left, the Priest shall say,
Dearly beloved, we are gathered together here in the sight of God, and in the face of this congregation, to join together this Man and this Woman in holy Matrimony; which is an honourable estate, instituted of God in the time of man's innocency, signifying unto us the mystical union that is betwixt Christ and his Church; which holy estate Christ adorned and beautified with his presence, and first miracle that he wrought, in Cana of Galilee; and is commended of Saint Paul to be honourable among all men: and therefore is not by any to be enterprised, nor taken in hand, unadvisedly, lightly, or wantonly, to satisfy men's carnal lusts and appetites, like brute beasts that have no understanding; but reverently, discreetly, advisedly,

soberly, and in the fear of God; duly considering the causes for which Matrimony was ordained.

First, It was ordained for the procreation of children, to be brought up in the fear and nurture of the Lord, and to the praise of his holy Name.

Secondly, It was ordained for a remedy against sin, and to avoid fornication; that such persons as have not the gift of continency might marry, and keep themselves undefiled members of Christ's body.

Thirdly, It was ordained for the mutual society, help, and comfort, that the one ought to have of the other, both in prosperity and adversity. Into which holy estate these two persons present come now to be joined. Therefore if any man can shew just cause, why they may not lawfully be joined together, let him now speak, or else hereafter for ever hold his peace.

And also, speaking unto the persons that shall be married, he shall say,
I Require and charge you both, as ye will answer at the dreadful day of judgement when the secrets of all hearts shall be disclosed, that if either of you know any impediment, why ye may not be lawfully joined together in Matrimony, ye do now confess it. For be ye well assured, that so many as are coupled together otherwise than God's Word doth allow are not joined together by God; neither is their Matrimony lawful.

If no impediment be alleged, then shall the Curate say unto the Man,
N. Wilt thou have this Woman to thy wedded wife, to live together after God's ordinance in the holy estate of Matrimony? Wilt thou love her, comfort her, honour, and keep her in sickness and in health; and, forsaking all other, keep thee only unto her, so long as ye both shall live?

The man shall answer, I will.

Then shall the Priest say unto the Woman,
N. Wilt thou have this Man to thy wedded husband, to live together after God's ordinance in the holy estate of Matrimony?

Wilt thou obey him, and serve him, love, honour, and keep him in sickness and in health; and, forsaking all other, keep thee only unto him, so long as ye both shall live?

The woman shall answer, I will.

Then shall the Minister say,
Who giveth this Woman to be married to this Man?

Then shall they give their troth to each other in this manner.
The Minister, receiving the Woman at her father's or friend's hands,
shall cause the Man with his right hand to take the Woman by her right
hand, and to say after him as followeth,

I, N., take thee N., to my wedded wife, to have and to hold from this day forward, for better for worse, for richer for poorer, in sickness and in health, to love and to cherish, till death us do part, according to God's holy ordinance; and thereto I plight thee my troth.

Then shall they loose hands; and the Woman, with her right hand
taking the Man by his right hand, shall likewise say after the Minister,
I, N., take thee N., to my wedded husband, to have and to hold from this day forward, for better for worse, for richer for poorer, in sickness and in health, to love, cherish, and to obey, till death us do part, according to God's holy ordinance; and thereto I give thee my troth.

Then shall they again loose their hands; and the man shall give unto
the Woman a Ring, laying the same upon the book with the accustomed
duty to the Priest and the Clerk. And the Priest, taking the Ring, shall
deliver it unto the Man, to put it upon the fourth finger of the Woman's
left hand. And the Man holding the Ring there, and taught by the
Priest, shall say,
With this Ring I thee wed, with my body I thee worship, and with all my worldly goods I thee endow: In the Name of the Father, and of the Son, and of the Holy Ghost, Amen.

Then the Man leaving the Ring upon the fourth finger of the Woman's
left hand, they shall both kneel down; and the Minister shall say,

Let us pray.

O Eternal God, Creator and Preserver of all mankind, Giver of all spiritual grace, the Author of everlasting life; Send thy blessing upon these thy servants, this man and this woman, whom we bless in thy Name; that, as Isaac and Rebecca lived faithfully together, so these persons may surely perform and keep the vow and covenant betwixt them made, (whereof this Ring given and received is a token and pledge,) and may ever remain in perfect love and peace together, and live according to thy laws; through Jesus Christ our Lord. *Amen.*

Then shall the Priest join their right hands together, and say,
Those whom God hath joined together let no man put asunder.

Then shall the Minister speak unto the people.
Forasmuch as N. and N. have consented to live together in holy wedlock, and have witnessed the same before God and this company, and thereto have given and pledged their troth either to other, and have declared the same by giving and receiving of a Ring, and by joining of hands; I pronounce that they be Man and Wife together, In the Name of the Father, and of the Son, and of the Holy Ghost. Amen.

After the reading of Psalms and prayers the couple and the congregation were reminded of the duties of man and wife: 'All ye that are married, or that intend to take the holy estate of Matrimony upon you, hear what the holy Scripture doth say as touching the special duty of husbands towards their wives, and wives towards their husbands.'

Saint Paul, they were told, urged, 'Husbands, love your wives, even as Christ also loved the Church, and gave himself for it.' Men ought 'to love their wives as their own bodies. He that loveth his wife loveth himself: for no man ever yet hated his own flesh, but nourisheth it and cherisheth it, even as the Lord of the Church.' For this cause 'shall a man leave his father and mother, and shall be joined unto his wife; and they two shall be one flesh'. Saint Peter, a married man, asked the husband to give 'honour unto the wife, as unto the weaker vessel'.

As for wives, Saint Paul said, 'Wives, submit yourselves unto your own husbands, as unto the Lord. For the husband is the head of the wife, even as Christ is the head of the Church . . . Therefore, as the Church is subject unto Christ, so let the wives be to their own husbands in every thing . . . Let the wife see that she reverence her husband.'

3

'My Lord hath complained that
he hath not lain with me'

ON 5 JANUARY 1606 the society wedding of the year took place at the Chapel Royal in the Palace of Whitehall. An exceptionally beautiful girl, fifteen-year-old Lady Frances Howard, married Robert Devereux, 3rd Earl of Essex, who had not quite reached his fifteenth birthday. If the young couple were put to bed together, as was traditional on the wedding night, it was only a token ceremony. Frances's father, the Earl of Suffolk, could be satisfied that he had secured for his daughter one of the best matches in the kingdom, while gaining some political advantage for himself. Since he had no wish to imperil his daughter's health by forcing her into motherhood too soon, it was agreed that the couple would live apart until after they had reached their eighteenth birthdays. As it turned out, consummation never took place, prompting the most sensational nullity case. This is a tale of impotence, adultery, passion and murder.

It was just the sort of arranged marriage, motivated by worldly considerations, the preachers deplored. 'For here is marriage for pleasure, and voluptuousness, and for goods, and so that they may join land to land, and possessions to possessions: they care for no more in England,' a disapproving Hugh Latimer had proclaimed in a sermon before Edward VI at the height of the English Reformation. If marriage was not about romantic love or, God forbid, sexual passion, all were agreed, both before and after the Reformation, on its three main purposes: it was for procreation, a remedy against fornication, and mutual help and comfort. In the Book of Common Prayer, Cranmer emphasized the 'mutual society, help, and comfort, that the one ought to have of the other, both in prosperity and adversity'.

At fifteen, Essex and Lady Frances were old enough to consent to marriage – the age of consent being twelve for a girl and fourteen for a boy – but not to consider the full implications of what they did. Not that it made much difference, since she would neither have had nor expected to have any say in her marriage. Essex was at least allowed to state a preference for Frances over her younger sister, Katherine, who being younger would have been more suitable. While he was sent abroad to complete his education, Frances, as a married lady of fifteen, had her first taste of the extravagant, dissolute and corrupt Jacobean court.

When Essex returned from his travels in 1609, he found a changed woman. Frances had lost the sweet innocence of her youth and affected the jaded, sophisticated air of the court. Having spent crucial years of their development apart, it quickly became apparent that they were incompatible. Essex had inherited neither the good looks nor the charm of his father – Elizabeth I's doomed last love – and he lacked the quick wit and repartee of the other men Frances had met at court. Although he later confessed, 'When I came out of France, I loved her,' he lacked romance. Frances found him both unappetizing and dull. To make matters worse, he was an outdoors man, who loved the country and country sports. For Frances, whose whole existence revolved round the court, its pleasures, its intrigues, its opportunities, a day in the country was the equivalent of a day in hell.

Not surprisingly, there were sexual problems. Four years later, Essex would tell the divorce commission that during the first year they lived together he 'divers times attempted' to consummate the marriage. As for Frances, he confessed that though on some occasions 'when he was willing to have carnal knowledge of her body, she showed herself ready thereunto . . . some other times she refused it'. Frances's lawyers claimed that 'desirous to be a mother . . . [she] again and again yielded herself to his power, and, as much as lay in her [power], offered herself and her body to be known, and earnestly desired conjunction and copulation'. Even so, Essex admitted that he had not been able to 'penetrate into her womb, nor enjoy her'. After a year of futile attempts, he stopped trying, although they continued to share a bed for another couple of years.

Frances maintained that she had done everything possible to help her husband overcome his difficulties. This might have been true at first, but gradually her evident disdain and disgust must have been seriously off-putting. Although Essex was to claim that he was impotent only with Frances, he seems to have had a low sex drive, never showing much interest in women. When some courtiers later put a woman in his bed, for a laugh, he refused to touch her. Evidently he preferred male company – 'he drinketh with his men', Frances once commented acerbically, as if this were habitual – although whether he had homosexual tendencies, or would have admitted it even to himself if he had, is a moot point.

A year or so after they had started living together, Frances must have decided that she did not want the relationship to be consummated. She had fallen in love with another man.

Robert Carr, Viscount Rochester, the court favourite, was one of the Scots who had accompanied King James VI and I to London. He was blond and good-looking with a fine figure. He was also beardless, wore his hair frizzled according to fashion, and dressed to kill – all attributes calculated to please the King, whose minion he was. In deference to divine monarchy, English courtiers fought hard to conceal their shock and disgust as their ungainly King fawned over handsome young men, hung on them with his arm familiarly round their necks, sat them on his knee, and planted slobbering kisses on their lips. One young man turned round and spat in disgust after James pressed his lips against his, but Rochester affected not to mind. As a gentleman of the bedchamber he slept in the King's room, supposedly on a truckle bed at the foot of the royal bed. What went on behind the bed curtains is anyone's guess, although Buckingham, a future favourite nicknamed Dog by James, once alluded to the time when 'the bed's head could not be found between the master and his dog'.

Frances's father, proud of his Howard lineage, didn't trouble to conceal his contempt for the lowly, poorly educated Scottish interloper with the thick accent. Hearing that the King was teaching him Latin, he remarked that it might be wiser if he tackled English first. He would have been amazed to discover that his own daughter, Frances, was the foremost of Rochester's admirers among the court ladies.

It seems that Rochester's interest in Frances began as a bit of a lark. None too bright himself, he relied on his friend Sir Thomas

Overbury to do his thinking for him, and it was Overbury who wrote romantic letters to Frances on his behalf. Frances was smitten, seizing the chance of love. Her eager response probably surprised and horrified Rochester. Desperate to ensnare him, Frances turned to her friend and confidante, Mrs Anne Turner, who introduced her to the astrologer, necromancer and physician, Dr Simon Forman. It was an era of superstition and Jacobean London was full of such 'cunning' men and women, wizards, fortune-tellers and the like. Frances begged Forman to weave a spell so that she might win Rochester's love. As it later transpired that Forman had supplied her with 'jellies' – either to stimulate desire in Rochester or deflect it in her husband – it would seem that Frances was now actively employing 'remedies' to prevent her husband from consummating the marriage.

In 1611 Essex took his wife to the country, having complained to her family that she was refusing to do her wifely duty, without admitting any fault of his own. Knowing that she was unhappy, but not the reason for it, the Howards urged Frances to make the best of her marriage, since there could be no escape from it.

Holed up for months with a man she loathed, Frances wrote a highly incriminating letter to Mrs Turner:

Sweet Turner,
I am out of all hope of any good in this world, for my father, my mother, and my brother said, I should lie with him; and my brother Howard was here, and said, he would not come from this place all winter; so that all comfort is gone; and which is worst of all, my Lord hath complained that he hath not lain with me, and I would not suffer him to use me. My father and mother are angry, but I had rather die a thousand times over; for besides the sufferings, I shall lose his [Rochester's] love if I lie with him [Essex]. I will never desire to see his face, if my Lord do that unto me . . . You may send the party [Forman] word of all . . . I am not able to endure the miseries that are coming on me, but I cannot be happy so long as this man liveth . . . Let him [Forman] know this ill news; if I can get this done, you shall have as much money as you demand, this is fair play – Yours sister, Frances Essex.

It seems that on her return to court, in the spring of 1612, Frances and Rochester became lovers. They found an unlikely ally in Frances's uncle, the wily Henry Howard, Earl of Northampton, who saw the affair as a means of increasing Howard influence by luring the favourite into their orbit. It only remained to persuade Suffolk to overcome his aversion to Rochester – and for Frances, always the keener of the two, to push Rochester into marriage.

The Essex marriage appeared to have reached a crisis. At a meeting with the Howards, Essex admitted that he had never managed to consummate the marriage, 'although he did his best endeavour, he never could'. The confession led Suffolk to conclude that 'the Earl had no ink in his pen, that himself had confessed he could not know a woman'. He was appalled to hear of the deprivation his daughter had suffered in her marriage and determined to end it.

At the beginning of 1613 he initiated a nullity suit on her behalf. At this stage Essex was willing to comply, provided he was not publicly humiliated. He was prepared to admit that he had not been able to consummate the marriage, but would not declare himself wholly impotent, not least because if he did so he would never find another wife. 'We all agreed to part fair,' Northampton noted with satisfaction.

However, it was not that easy.

Divorce as we know it – the termination of a valid marriage, enabling the partners to remarry – did not exist in England. At the Reformation, other Protestant states, including neighbouring Scotland, had legalized divorce on grounds of adultery and desertion, albeit with the proviso that only the innocent party was permitted to remarry. In England the Reformation allowed that marriage was not a sacrament. If it was not a sacrament, but merely a contract, some argued, surely adultery negated that contract, leaving the parties free to remarry. It was a debate that would continue for many centuries.

In post-Reformation England the effects of the debate on divorce were if anything to tighten rather than slacken the bonds of marriage. The efforts of the radical Protestants during the brief reign of Edward VI had culminated in the *Reformatio Legum Ecclesiasticarum*, which contained divorce proposals that would have brought England into line with other Protestant countries, but they came to nothing when the scheme as a whole foundered. Although one of the premier nobles among the Protestant ruling clique, Queen Catherine Parr's brother the Marquis of Northampton, snatched the opportunity to divorce his wife and make a second marriage of dubious legality, it is doubtful if such a dramatically sweeping revision of the law of divorce had much support, either among the clergy or the public at large.

The Church's insistence on the indissolubility of marriage and the relative stability of most marriages in actual practice meant that there was little demand for divorce, at least throughout the sixteenth and most of the seventeenth centuries. The exceptions tended to occur at the extreme ends of society. About 10 per cent of aristocratic marriages broke down, but these represented a tiny minority of the population. The poor tended to end unhappy marriages simply by walking away: a survey of the poor undertaken for the city of Norwich in 1570, which could be considered vaguely representative of the nation as a whole, indicated that about 8 per cent of wives had been deserted by their husbands.

The Church offered only two means of release from an unsatisfactory marriage. A separation from bed and board – *divortium a mensa et thoro* – could be granted on proof of adultery or extreme cruelty. It did not, however, give either of the separated spouses the right to remarry during the other's lifetime. It was also possible to secure an annulment if some impediment, such as a pre-contract, meant that the marriage had not been valid in the first place. In this case, the woman would have to surrender her dower and any children of the union would be bastardized. Crucially, as far as Essex and Lady Frances were concerned, a marriage could be annulled because of permanent frigidity or impotence.

According to a thirteenth-century papal ruling, if a husband testified under oath that he was impotent, and his wife confirmed this, their marriage could be considered void. The drawback was that it had to be permanent impotence: if the husband subsequently succeeded in having sex with another woman it would be taken as proof of perjury, and he would be obliged to take back his former wife. If he was not prepared to admit impotence, the wife's testimony alone was not sufficient to secure an annulment.

The problem here was that Essex was prepared to admit impotence with Frances, but only with Frances.

There was one tiny ray of hope. In the twelfth century Thomas

Aquinas had declared that witchcraft could make a man impotent with one woman while he remained virile with others. If a husband and wife lived together for three years without consummating their marriage, this could be taken as proof that the husband had been permanently disabled, at least as far as this particular woman was concerned. Such a marriage could be dissolved by judgement of the Church, leaving both husband and wife free to remarry.

The Howards' lawyers eagerly seized on this obscure doctrine, which seemed to offer honourable release for both parties. But would it convince the nullity commission?

George Abbot, Archbishop of Canterbury, who headed the party of ten commissioners who met at Lambeth in May 1613, was a highly principled man and a stickler for canon law. He would not be cajoled into granting an annulment if it ran counter to the laws of the Church. Not only had the canons of 1604 reaffirmed the Church's traditional ban on remarriage after a separation from bed and board, but they had also laid down stricter rules for the handling and determination of both separation and annulment suits by the ecclesiastical courts. Abbot intended to see they were followed to the letter.

Politically, he was diametrically opposed to the Howards, who were pro Spain and Catholic sympathizers. Instinctively, he didn't trust them. When he interviewed Lord Essex he thought him a nice, upright young man, whereas the more he saw and heard of Lady Frances, the less he liked or approved of her.

It could not have helped that just when her lawyers were presenting the witchcraft argument, Frances's involvement with a 'cunning woman' became public knowledge. Mary Woods was a particularly unsavoury character. She sold fraudulent potions and if her clients complained or asked for their money back, Woods would retaliate by telling them that if they went to the authorities she would claim they had consulted her because they wanted their husbands dead. Frances had invited Woods to Salisbury House. We do not know what services she was hoping to buy – perhaps a love potion, or something less innocent. At any rate, Woods demanded a down payment and Frances was foolish enough to give her a valuable diamond ring, which had been a gift from Essex.

Woods promptly sold the ring for a pittance and high-tailed it to Norfolk. Realizing that she had been cheated, Frances sent her servant Richard Grimstone in pursuit. Woods repeated her usual blackmail threat, claiming that Frances had come to her for a potion with which to poison Essex, but that having initially agreed to help her, Woods had thought better of it and gone home. Undaunted, Grimstone had her arrested and she was brought to London for further investigation. Fortunately for Frances, Woods had such a reputation for false accusations that her wild claims were dismissed. But Frances's reputation was besmirched by association and some wondered if perhaps there might just be a grain of truth in her willingness to rid herself of Essex by foul play.

Abbot and the other commissioners were being asked to believe that Essex was suffering from a highly selective form of impotence, a 'perpetual and natural impediment' which prevented him having intercourse with his wife. Abbot was concerned that there was no precedent in English law, where an annulment had been granted to a man recognized as impotent towards his wife but virile towards other women. He was reminded of the case of Henry VIII and Anne of Cleves, in which Henry had sought an annulment on the grounds that he was unable to consummate the union with this particular woman, although clearly he had not been impotent with other women. It proved no precedent, as the Church had resorted to the time-worn excuse of pre-contract – Anne had been formerly contracted to the Duke of Lorraine – to declare the marriage null and void.

Although the commission was satisfied that Essex and Frances were not colluding, or pretending non-consummation in order to have the marriage annulled – collusion ruled out any possibility of the Church granting a separation or annulment – Abbot remained sceptical. He dismissed the witchcraft theory and looked for a more rational explanation for the couple's problems. Why had they not sought medical advice and, if they really believed in supernatural intervention, why had they not turned to the Church for an exorcism? An unmarried man himself, it seemed to him that they had not consummated their marriage through lack of love, or a lack of will, and that they should work at it.

To make matters worse, when Essex appeared before the commission on 5 June, he had altered his stance, perhaps because he had already become the object of ridicule. Far from confirming that

Frances had repeatedly submitted herself to him in the hope of being penetrated, he told the commission that she had sometimes rejected his advances. When asked if Frances was *virgo incorrupta* he answered cryptically, 'She saith so, and is so for me.' What was that supposed to mean? Was he implying that she had been unfaithful?

Abbot might already have heard the rumours circulating at court that there was something going on between Rochester and Lady Essex. If there was any suspicion of adultery, the Church would certainly not agree to annul the marriage. Knowing that Sir Thomas Overbury loathed her, disapproved of her relationship with his friend and would do anything to prevent their marriage, Frances determined to get rid of him. In April she offered Sir David Wood, whose enmity Overbury had incurred, £1,000 to kill him. Wood was shocked, replying that he would not kill a man for all the gold in the world; however, he would beat him up. Frances then contrived through Northampton and with the connivance of the King and Rochester to have Overbury sent to the Tower on some flimsy charge and kept in close confinement. Six months later, in September 1613, Overbury died the most horrible death, silenced for ever – or perhaps not.

Various witnesses were brought before the commission to testify that they had seen Essex and Lady Frances 'in naked bed together as man and wife for divers nights', that is, for the three-year period the Church demanded in an impotency case. Frances Britten, who had known Frances all her life, testified that when she

> was at Hampton Court, after the Earl and Lady Frances were risen, the lady missing a pendant ruby that usually hung at a ring in her ear, desired this deponent to look for it in the bed. That thereupon she and the lady's chambermaid turned down the bedclothes, and there they saw the places where the Earl and Lady had lain, but that there was such a distance between the two places and such a hill between them that this deponent is persuaded they did not touch one another that night.

In medieval England, some courts had adopted the bizarre practice of subjecting an allegedly impotent male to the attentions of a group of women, whose task it was to try to excite his passion, but this was no longer the case. It is surprising, however, that Essex was not asked to submit to an examination by competent physicians, so that they could confirm that the condition of impotency actually existed and that there was no help for it. Instead, Bishop Neile of Coventry and Lichfield sought to clarify the position by questioning Essex more closely. He wanted to establish whether Essex had ever had an erection or experienced an emission of semen. Essex refused to answer and the other commissioners were too embarrassed to press the point. There was much hilarity at court at this latest revelation.

When the commissioners asked Essex whether he believed Frances was 'a woman able and fit for carnal copulation', he denied it, 'because he hath not found it'. Frances's lawyers had to refute the suggestion that she was somehow incapable of intercourse, while establishing that she was still a virgin. As was usual in such cases, Frances would have to undergo a gynaecological examination by a panel of midwives and matrons. It was a high-risk strategy, since Frances was almost certainly not a virgin.

The panel comprised six in all, including two midwives 'expert in the matter of marriage' and four God-fearing gentlewomen. It is possible that Frances attended the examination heavily veiled, supposedly to preserve her modesty, and that another young woman took her place. It is more likely, however, that the gentlewomen allowed the midwives to do the actual search by hand, relying on their supposed expertise and accepting their verdict. Either the midwives did not really know what they were looking for, which is highly likely at that time, or they had been 'tampered with'. The kindest explanation is that the panel erred on the side of caution. They pronounced Frances 'fit for carnal copulation and still a virgin'.

Vindicated, she appeared before the commission to testify that, despite all her efforts, her marriage had never been consummated:

> That since the Earl of Essex was 18 years of age, he and I have for the space of three years divers and sundry times lain together in naked bed all night. And at sundry of the said times the said Earl hath purposely endeavoured and attempted to consummate marriage with me, and to have carnal copulation with me for procreation of children: And I have at such times, as the said Earl hath attempted so to do, yielded myself willing to the same purpose. All which notwithstanding, I say and affirm upon my oath, that the said Earl never had carnal copulation with me.

Interestingly, she signed this statement 'Frances Howard', as if the annulment were already accomplished.

Not only did the earl refute Frances's claim always to have been available to him, but his lawyers contended that the verdict of the panel of midwives and matrons should be quashed, since the examination had not been thorough enough. Their request was ignored.

The commission was deeply divided. On one side there was Abbot, who was extremely uneasy – sceptical about the impotency claim and suspicious of Frances; on the other, commissioners who were deeply sympathetic, especially to the lovely young woman who would be imprisoned in a sexless marriage and denied the joys of motherhood if the annulment was denied.

The King now intervened, colluding with Rochester and the Howards against Essex. Some of the commissioners wished to recall Essex for further questioning, but James forbade it, possibly because Essex was likely to say something damning, which would ruin Frances's case. James ordered the commission to reach its verdict by 25 September. Abbot, under enormous pressure, was determined to do nothing against his conscience. He prepared a detailed report as to why he denied there was a case, but when it came to it, James insisted that each commissioner merely answered Yes or No, without giving reasons.

The verdict came in at seven for and five against the annulment. The sentence said that in view of the fact that 'some secret, incurable, and binding impediment' had prevented Essex from having carnal knowledge of his wife, the marriage was 'utterly void and none effect'. Both parties were declared free to remarry, with the proviso that it was up to their own consciences that they were, in all truth, entitled to do so.

It would be seventeen years before Essex married again and the indications are that his second marriage was no more successful than the first. The marriage broke down after only six years, when his wife committed adultery.

Essex was left simmering with resentment at the outcome of the nullity suit. Annulment entailed drastic legal and financial consequences. Normally a wife lost her dower rights. In this case, Essex had to return Frances's dowry of £6,000, which meant that he had to sell a considerable chunk of property and land to realize the cash.

No wonder that when it came to the great showdown between King Charles I and Parliament in the 1640s, he opted to lead the parliamentary army.

A grand wedding was planned for Rochester and Lady Frances. It took place in the Chapel Royal at Whitehall, the same venue as her marriage to Essex only seven years previously, on 26 December 1613, a spectacular event coinciding with the Christmas festivities at court. The King created his favourite Earl of Somerset, so that Frances might maintain her rank. Not only did James offer to pay for the wedding, but he lavished £12,000 worth of jewels on the bride. Defiantly, Frances went to the altar with her long hair loose, in token of virginity.

She was to enjoy only two years of marital happiness. In the summer of 1615 rumours began to circulate that there was something suspicious about the death of Sir Thomas Overbury. Could he have been poisoned? Lesser people such as Sir Gervase Elwes, Lieutenant of the Tower, and Richard Weston, Overbury's keeper – corruptible characters who owed their posts to the machinations of Frances's uncle, Northampton – and Mrs Anne Turner, Frances's faithful go-between who had procured poisons on her behalf, were quickly swept up, brought to trial and found guilty.

Frances, held under house arrest at Blackfriars pending the birth of her first child before being sent to the Tower, admitted her guilt. Certainly, she had sent jellies and cakes laced with poison into the Tower for Overbury. But had he been given them and, if so, did they kill him? There was no proof of it. Perhaps it was enough that Frances intended to kill him, to silence him for ever, lest he disclose her adultery and so give Archbishop Abbot the opportunity he was looking for to deny the annulment.

It was assumed that Frances, as a mere woman, could not have organized Overbury's murder herself and that she must have acted under her husband's direction. Yet Somerset, no longer the favourite since the King's eye had alighted on the exquisitely beautiful George Villiers, categorically denied any involvement in his former friend's death. Yes, he had contrived to have Overbury sent to the Tower and kept in close confinement – and here he pointed to the King's discreditable part in the affair – but only to get him out of the way while the nullity suit went through.

At Frances's trial, Lord Chief Justice Sir Edward Coke dwelt on her licentiousness, needlessly dragging her adulterous affair with Rochester while still married to Essex into the proceedings. The assumption was that a woman prepared to commit the heinous crime of adultery was capable of murder. Frances pleaded guilty and was condemned to death, but because she had admitted her guilt and thrown herself on the King's mercy, she was reprieved, although condemned to live away from court in obscurity.

Somerset never forgave her. Even though she had steadfastly refused to implicate him in her crime, he blamed her for his disgrace and downfall. He was filled with loathing, anger and distrust for what she had done. For the rest of their lives together, they occupied the same house as strangers. Frances had gambled everything for another loveless marriage.

In this fiercely patriarchal society, Frances came to represent the innate corruptibility of the female sex when not held in check. The ideal woman was passive and subservient. Frances was neither. She had taken steps to make her own happiness, and look at the chaos that ensued. It seemed only fitting to those who condemned Frances as a sexually voracious, adulterous murderess that she died in agony of cancer of the womb. She was only forty-two. Essex himself seemed to have derived some satisfaction from this, since a copy of Dr Mayerne's autopsy report was later found among his papers.

The one person Rochester still cared for was their daughter, Lady Anne Carr. When she fell in love with William, Lord Russell, son of the 4th Earl of Bedford, his father strongly disapproved. Seeing the couple so devoted, the uxorious Charles I encouraged the match, leaving Bedford no option but to allow it, but he demanded an unreasonably high dowry of £12,000. Determined to secure his daughter's happiness at any price, Rochester agreed. The marriage followed on a down payment of £1,000, but Rochester failed to produce the rest of the cash, embarrassing his daughter and embroiling him in a law suit with the Russells. At least her marriage turned out to be supremely happy.

INTERLUDE
William Gouge, *Of Domesticall Duties*

Before the Reformation advice books on marriage were written almost exclusively for the clergy's use, since they played an active role in resolving marital problems among their parishioners. With the expansion of printing such books began to be aimed directly at the laity. The clergyman William Gouge, an experienced family man – he and his wife had seven sons and six daughters – published *Of Domesticall Duties* in 1622 and dedicated it to his parishioners at St Anne's, Blackfriars. It ran to 693 pages, but the following outlines some of the salient points.

PARTICULAR DUTIES OF WIVES
1. Acknowledgement of a husband's superiority.
2. A due esteem of her own husband to be the best for her, and worthy of honour on her part.
3. An inward, wife-like fear.
4. An outward reverend carriage towards her husband, which consists in a wife-like sobriety, mildness, courtesy, and modesty in dress.
5. Reverend speech to, and of, her husband.
6. Obedience.
7. For fearing to do without or against her husband's consent, such things as he has power to order, as, to dispose and order the common goods of the family, and the allowance for it, or children, servants, cattle, guests, travel, etc.
8. A ready yielding to what her husband would have done. This is manifested by her willingness to dwell where he will, to come where he calls, or to do what he requires.
9. A patient bearing of any reproach, and a ready redressing of that for which she is justly reproved.

10. Contentment with her husband's present estate.
11. Such a subjection as may stand with her subjection to Christ.
12. Such a subjection as the Church yielded to Christ, which is sincere, pure, cheerful, constant, for conscience sake.

ABERRATIONS OF WIVES FROM THEIR PARTICULAR DUTIES

1. A conceit that wives are their husbands' equals.
2. A conceit that she could better subject herself to any other man than to her own husband.
3. An inward despising of her husband.
4. Un-reverend behaviour towards her husband manifested by lightness, sullenness, scornfulness, and vanity in her dress.
5. Un-reverend speech to and of her husband.
6. A stout standing on her own will.
7. A peremptory undertaking to do things as she wanted, without and against her husband's consent.
8. An obstinate standing upon her own will, making her husband dwell where she will, and refusing to go when he calls or to do anything upon his command.
9. Disdain at reproof, giving word for word [answering back] and waxing worse for being reproved.
10. Discontent at her husband's estate.

PARTICULAR DUTIES OF HUSBANDS

1. Acknowledgement of a wife's near conjunction or fellowship with her husband.
2. A good esteem of his own wife to be the best for him, and worthy of love on his part.
3. An inward entire affection.
4. An outward amiable carriage towards his wife, which consists in a husband-like gravity, mildness, courteous acceptance of her curtsey, and allowing her to wear suitable dress.
5. Mild and loving speech to and of his wife.
6. A wise maintaining his authority, and forbearing to exact all that is in his power.

7. A ready yielding to his wife's request, and giving a general consent and liberty unto her to order the affairs of the house, children, servants etc. And a free allowing her something to bestow as she sees occasion.

8. A forbearing to exact more than his wife is willing to do, or to force her to dwell where it is not meet, or to enjoin her to do things unmeet or against her mind.

9. A wise ordering of reproof, not using it without just and weighty cause, and then privately, and meekly.

10. A provident care for his wife, according to his ability.

11. A forbearing to exact anything which stands not with a good conscience.

12. Such a love, as Christ bears to the Church, and man to himself, which is free in deed, and truth, pure, chaste and constant.

ABERRATIONS OF HUSBANDS FROM THEIR PARTICULAR DUTIES

1. Too mean account of wives.

2. A preposterous conceit of his own wife to be the worst of all, and that he could love any but her.

3. A stoical disposition, without all heat of affection.

4. An unsuitable carriage towards his wife, manifested by his baseness, tyrannical usage of her, loftiness, rashness and niggardliness.

5. Harsh, proud and better speeches to and of his wife.

6. Losing of his authority.

7. Too much strictness over his wife. This is manifested by restraining her from doing anything without particular and express consent, taking too strict account of her, and allowing her no more than is needful for her own private use.

8. Too lordly standing upon the highest step of his authority, being too frequent, insolent and peremptory in commanding unnecessary things and against his wife's mind and conscience.

9. Rashness and bitterness in reproving and that too

frequently, on slight occasions, and disgracefully before children, servants and strangers.

10. A careless neglect of his wife, and niggardly dealing with her, and that in her weakness.
11. A commanding of unlawful things.
12. Such a disposition as is most unlike to Christ's.

4

'Teach her to live under obedience'

IN JULY 1617 'a notorious riot' took place at a country house near Weybridge in Surrey. Witnesses to the scene would have been treated to the sight of the former Lord Chief Justice of the King's Bench, Sir Edward Coke, the champion and proponent of the common law, prising open a downstairs window and squeezing through it, followed by his gang of amateur housebreakers. Running amok inside the house, he bellowed to the cowering inhabitants: 'If WE should kill any of your people it would be justifiable homicide but if YOU should kill any of us it would be murder.'

He met with no resistance. Searching every nook and cranny, he eventually alighted on his prey. Inside a little dark closet, clinging together and hardly daring to breathe, he found his wife and daughter. None too gently, he pulled the fourteen-year-old girl, weeping with fright, out of the closet. There followed an undignified tussle, as each parent held on to the girl, trying to wrench her from the other. Superior male strength won the day. Frances Coke was carried out of the house, mounted on horseback behind one of her half-brothers, and the party rode off into the night.

The girl's mother, Eliza, Lady Hatton, lost no time in hurrying to London to demand a warrant from the Privy Council to bring Sir Edward Coke before the Star Chamber on a charge of house-breaking. The ex-judge retaliated by summoning Lady Hatton, his estranged wife, on a rather more serious charge of conveying his daughter away 'clam et secrete' and of endeavouring to marry her to Lord Oxford 'without the consent of her father'. On the contrary, Lady Hatton told the court, it was Coke who had been 'intending to bestow her against her liking'. Frances had merely appealed to her mother to protect her from her father's 'ill usage'.

Lady Hatton had every right to feel aggrieved. Here was another battle to fight in her long war of attrition with her husband. She and Sir Edward had lived separate lives for years, although, contrary to the laws of the Church, they had not troubled to apply for a separation. Strictly speaking, the Church had the right to prosecute couples who took it upon themselves to live apart without procuring an order from the ecclesiastical court, but of course Lady Hatton and Sir Edward belonged to the class most prone to marital breakdown, yet least amenable to ecclesiastical control.

From the outset, they had been at loggerheads over money. Basically, he was mean. She had been a twenty-year-old widow when her family rushed her into marriage with Coke, who had promptly appropriated the fortune left her by her previous husband, leaving her perennially short of funds. In an age where deference to a husband was such that a wife did not even presume to address him by his first name, Eliza defiantly refused to take Coke's name, continuing to style herself Lady Hatton. Not content with helping himself to her money, Coke was now proposing to sacrifice their daughter Frances on the altar of his career, to marry her against her will and without even consulting her mother.

When the avaricious court favourite, George Villiers, Earl and later Duke of Buckingham, was casting round for lucrative marriages for his impecunious relations, he had selected Frances Coke as a likely bride for his elder brother, Sir John Villiers, a dull knight much older than herself, who was utterly repugnant to her and suffered from bouts of insanity. It was an unworthy match for Frances. Not only was she a most captivating girl – blonde, pretty, quick-witted and charming – but she stood to inherit her mother's fortune. When first approached by Sir John, Coke naturally spurned the proposal from the unprepossessing suitor. His subsequent disgrace over some other matter, however, brought Coke scurrying back to Buckingham as a supplicant. Perhaps he could worm his way back into royal favour by offering his daughter in marriage to the favourite's brother.

They wasted no time in thrashing out a settlement. 'Although I would have been pleased to have taken her in her smock, I should be glad by way of curiosity, to know how much could be assured by marriage settlement upon her and her issue?' Sir John began.

She would have her mother's fortune, Coke promised, which he would augment by his manor of Stoke Poges in reversion, a dowry of £10,000 down and an allowance of £1,000 a year. Buckingham disdainfully replied that this was insufficient, at which Coke retorted that he 'would not buy the King's favour too dear'. In the end, he just had to pay up.

When Lady Hatton discovered that her husband had arranged their daughter's marriage without consulting her – which he had every right to do, since in law both a man's wife and his children were his property, to dispose of as he wished – her fury knew no bounds. But no matter how much she argued, while Frances wept and wailed and begged her father not to marry her to a man so distasteful to her, Coke would not be moved.

Lady Hatton decided that the only way to save her daughter from a hateful marriage was to marry her to someone else. Henry Vere, Earl of Oxford, was a nice young man, but poor. He would be only too happy to marry Frances, especially as her mother was offering him two houses, an income of £3,000 a year rising to £6,000, and, ultimately, her fortune. The only problem was that when Lady Hatton approached him with the proposal, Oxford was travelling in Italy. To hurry things along, she forged a letter purporting to be from Oxford to Frances asking for her hand. Frances was pleased. Her mother had her write out an obligation, which she did willingly enough:

> I vow before God and take the Almyghtie to witnesse that I Frances Coke yonger daughter to Sir Edward Coke late lord chiefe justice of England doe gyve myselfe absolutely to wyffe to Henry Vere Erle of Oxenford to whom I plyghte my trothe and inviolate vows to keepe myselfe till death us do part: and if ever I brake the leaste of these I pray God damme mee bodye and soule in hell fire in the world to come: and in this world I humbly beseeche God the erth maye open and swallow mee up quicke to the terror of all faythe brakers that remayne alive. In witnesse whereof I have written alle theis with my owne hande and seald it with my owne seale which I will weare till your retourne to mayke this goode that I have sent you. And for further witnesse I here underneath set to my name. Frances Coke, in the presence of my deare Mother, Eliza Hatton, 10 July 1617.

The outcome of the Star Chamber hearing was that Frances was to return to live with her mother at Hatton House in Holborn, rather than at Stoke Poges with her father, but with the unwelcome proviso that the disagreeable Lady Compton and her son, Sir John Villiers, were to have daily access, so that he could woo her. Sir Edward followed up this minor triumph with a letter to the King, justifying his actions and appending a long list of the riches and estates Frances would inherit and bring to the marriage. Buckingham was satisfied and Coke moved a step closer to regaining royal favour. Oxford, meanwhile, had no wish to get on the wrong side of Buckingham and beat a hasty retreat.

Knowing that the redoubtable Lady Hatton would do everything in her power to impede the marriage, Coke had her removed. She was placed under house arrest at Alderman Bennett's on some flimsy charge. Frances was left to the tender mercies of the Villiers family and her half-siblings – her father's children by his first marriage to Bridget Paston – who threatened and bullied her to agree to the marriage. She wept and pleaded, to no avail, but she would not submit.

The Church required 'full, free and mutual consent' to a marriage, although it also enjoined children to respect the wishes of their parents. By the canons of 1604, children under the age of twenty-one had to obtain parental consent to a marriage, but in the illogical way of the Church, if they married without that consent, the marriage was still valid. While children did not need parental consent, therefore, parents had to have that of children. Children, however, were invariably subjected to influence and various degrees of pressure. The higher the social standing, and the more economic leverage the parents had, the more extensive the influence that was brought to bear, especially as children of the nobility and upper gentry tended to marry young. Obviously it was preferable if there was liking and compatibility, but instances of excessive force being used to pressure a daughter into consenting to a marriage desired by the parents were by no means unusual.

In this highly patriarchal society, a man was king in his own household and had 'power and dominion over his wife'. Sermons and conduct books emphasized the governing role of the male householder and the duty of his wife and children to submit to his superior judgement. Coke, the defender of the nation's liberties against the royal prerogative, was not going to give way to the whims of a fourteen-year-old girl. He demanded and expected filial obedience. Violence was always to hand when he was punishing offenders; it was, after all, a brutal age. So now he resorted to the last drastic measure to make his recalcitrant daughter submit.

Frances was tied to a four-poster bed and whipped. The inference is that she suffered this torture on more than one occasion before she screamed out for mercy and consented to the match.

Her father then dictated a letter for Frances to send to her mother. In words all too reminiscent of her father's autocratic style, she wrote:

> I resolve to be wholly ruled by my father and yourself, knowing your judgements to be such that I may well rely upon, and hoping that conscience and the natural affection parents bear to children will let you do nothing but for my good, and that you may receive comfort, I being a mere child and not understanding the world nor what is good for myself. That which makes me a little give way to it is, that I hope it will be a means to procure a reconciliation between my father and your Ladyship. Also I think it will be means of the King's favour to my father. Himself is not to be misliked; his fortune is very good, a gentleman well born . . . So I humbly take my leave, praying that all things may be to every one's contentment.

A postscript tellingly reads: 'Dear mother, believe there has no violent means been used to me by words or deeds.'

The wedding took place on Michaelmas Day 1617 at Hampton Court Palace before the whole court. There was a huge press of people, including all the Cokes and the Villiers. But Frances's mother was still under house arrest and her family, the Cecils, boycotted it. Coke gave his daughter to the King, who gave her to Sir John Villiers – a sacrificial victim in a travesty of a marriage. The next morning James I, who took a prurient interest in these things, visited the couple while they were still in bed, playing peek-a-boo between the bed curtains and rolling on the bed in a cringe-making display which utterly belied his pretensions to divine monarchy. Later that day Coke received his reward when he was restored to the Privy Council.

Now that Frances was safely sold in marriage, Lady Hatton was released. As she still held the key to her fortune, the Villiers were eager to placate her. Although Coke held her property as her husband and took the rents, he could not prevent her settling it on Frances – or rather, Frances's husband – now if she wanted to do so, and the Villiers family very much wanted her to do so. In anticipation of Lady Hatton handing over Corfe Castle and the Isle of Purbeck, they prevailed on the King to create Sir John Viscount Purbeck. Lady Hatton was not for one moment deceived by their greedy self-interest, but nor did she wish to make things difficult for Frances by falling out with her family.

The Villiers vented their frustration at Lady Hatton's ability to withstand their demands on Frances, whose life they made truly miserable. In due course, she found solace elsewhere. Robert Howard, fifth son of the Earl of Suffolk and brother to the notorious Frances, Countess of Somerset, was young, attractive, accomplished, and was to prove loyal and constant. He and Frances became friends. There was nothing more to it at first, but the Villiers seized on the relationship as a means of ridding themselves of Frances legitimately, while keeping her fortune. Although John was fond of his young wife, and was to remain so, his family separated them on the pretext of his mental disorder, which they claimed she was exacerbating by her bad behaviour. Lunatics fell into the same legal category as wives – they were powerless. In view of Purbeck's mental incapacity, his family were able to take control of his property and Frances's.

Frances protested loudly, but in vain, that husband and wife should not be forcibly separated. She asked for some financial provision. Practically everything her husband owned was hers and surely she was entitled to something to live on? Her home was dismantled, her clothes and jewels confiscated. They told her she had forfeited her right to anything and had her quite literally thrown into the street.

Frances adopted the role of the injured and faithful wife, writing to her cruel brother-in-law:

My Lord,
Though you may judge what pleasure there is in the conversation of a man in the distemper you see your brother in, yet the dutie I owe to a husband and the affection I bear him (which sicknesses shall not

diminish), makes me much desire to be with him to adde what com-
forte I can to his afflicted mind, since his onely desire is my companie,
which, if it please you to satisfie him in, I shall with a very good will
suffer with him, and think all but my dutie, though I think every wife
would not do so. But if you can so far dispense with the lawes of God
as to keep me from my husband, yet aggravate it not by restraining
me from his means and all other contentments, but which, I think,
is rather the part of a Christian, you especially ought much rather to
studie comforts for me than to adde ills to ills, since it is the marriage
of your brother makes me thus miserable.

For if you please but to consider not only the lamentable estate I
am in, deprived of all comforts of a husband, and having no means to
live on, besides falling from the hopes my fortune did then promise
me; for you know very well I came no beggar to you though I am
like so to be turned off. For your honor and conscience sake, take
some course to give me satisfaction, to tye my tongue from crying to
God and the world for vengeance for the unworthy dealing I have
received . . .

Lady Hatton appealed to the King, who hinted to Buckingham that
it would be better for his reputation to deal fairly with his sister-in-
law. Frances's household goods, clothes and jewels – the paraphernal-
lia which were a wife's personal property – were accordingly given
back and, in return for promising never to live with Purbeck again or
claim him for her husband, she was promised a stipend, which never
materialized. Naturally the Villiers family would keep her fortune.

Living in lodgings under an assumed name, Frances gave birth to a
son, who for some inexplicable reason she named Robert Wright. It
was all it took for the mother-in-law from hell, Lady Compton, and
Buckingham to have her hauled up with her lover before the spiritual
court at Lambeth to answer charges of adultery.

Adultery was seen as moral outrage, hateful to God, who might
bring down His wrath on the whole community. By threatening the
stability of marriage, adulterers and fornicators endangered the well-
being of the commonwealth. In an age where little distinction was
drawn between 'sin' and 'crime', the 'foul crime of adultery' drew
the full legal penalty. Not only must justice be done, but it must be
seen to be done by the community who had been wronged. Public

penance was the means by which the sinner was both punished and reconciled to God and the community; the sheer humiliation of it was to deter others.

Frances defended herself vigorously in court. She complained that she had been treated in a very cruel manner, deprived of the comfort of her husband's company, accused of infidelity, denied her subsistence, although endowed with a very great fortune, and reduced to such straits as hardly to have 'wherewith to buy herself clothes'. The occupants of the public gallery were all the more moved in that she 'had been married without her consent, to a man disordered in his senses, and the crime of infidelity urged against her'.

Claiming privilege of Parliament as an MP, Sir Robert Howard refused to testify, while Frances denied the allegations. Nevertheless, their excommunication – from the communion of the faithful, which also drew various civic disabilities – was proclaimed at Paul's Cross and they were thrown into gaol.

After petitioning the King, they were released, but Buckingham would not rest until his sister-in-law was vanquished. His main purpose was to have Frances's son declared a bastard, so that he would not inherit any Villiers property, which of course encompassed Frances's own inheritance. According to English law, a child is taken to be the legitimate offspring of a marriage unless the husband repudiates it. Frances was to be tried again for infidelity.

The trial, which opened in November 1627 with an impressive line-up of judges and bishops, was the *cause célèbre* of the day. Frances had adopted the attitude of innocence maligned and in distress and the public was largely sympathetic. She told the court that owing to the cruelty with which she and her husband were treated by his family they had been forced to live apart, but they had had the happiness to meet together when he was in his right senses, and that her son was his. They had concealed their meetings because of the fury the Villiers would be sure to unleash on them and she painted a touching portrait of the terror in which she lived, compelled to give birth in humble obscurity and afraid to let her baby out of her sight lest he was snatched by her brother-in-law. She demanded that her husband be brought to the court to corroborate her story, but Buckingham refused to produce him.

Frances was pronounced guilty. She was to pay an exorbitant fine of £500 and to undergo the humiliation of public penance by walking barefoot in a white sheet from Paul's Cross to the Savoy and stand at the door of the church there for all to see. If she failed to present herself the following Sunday she would be arrested and imprisoned until she had performed her penance.

The crowd who waited to watch the spectacle were doomed to disappointment. Frances had no intention of walking barefoot in a white sheet for anyone. Buckingham was determined to seek her out. He had the house where she was hiding surrounded. The ambassador of the Duke of Savoy, who lived next door, was politely asked if he would permit access through his garden. He demurred. At last he hinted that if Buckingham's men kept strict watch around dinner time, they would be rewarded. At noon a coach drew up and a blonde stepped briskly inside before it clattered away at breakneck speed with Buckingham's men in hot pursuit. They caught up with it in the Strand, where the fair-haired passenger turned out to be the ambassador's page-boy in female dress. A second coach, meanwhile, had arrived. Dressed as the page-boy and holding her son, Frances climbed aboard before it rushed off in the opposite direction.

Frances spent the next five years in obscurity, living with Sir Robert Howard at his property in Clun, Shropshire. It was only when the couple showed up in London again that they were arrested. Howard was sent to the Fleet and Frances to the Gatehouse Prison in Westminster. Archbishop Laud was determined that she would suffer the full humiliation of the female penitent. She was to be brought to the Church of St Clement Danes without Temple Bar on the following Sunday. Once more, Frances contrived to escape in male attire, making for the coast and voluntary exile in France. The French court was sympathetic to her plight, especially as she was a victim of the hated Buckingham, and resisted all Charles I's demands to have her repatriated. At some point after the outbreak of civil war in England, Frances returned quietly. She died in Oxford in 1645, in the company of Robert Howard, who was devoted to her until the end.

INTERLUDE

Henry Oxinden of Barham in love

Just as England was on the brink of civil war, Henry Oxinden of Barham in Kent fell in love. Katherine Culling was eighteen and his ward. Although this was Henry's second marriage, his family strongly disapproved. Katherine was not his equal in age, rank or fortune; indeed, her father, a neighbour, was a mere yeoman. But Katherine was seductive and manipulative and Henry was truly smitten, as he confessed to his cousin, Elizabeth Dallinson:

> I do now begin to be of Lady Oxinden's belief that marriages are made in heaven, and what is concluded there all the wit of man cannot hinder, and this I say, because though I ever loved my mistress, yet I endeavoured not to be in love with her, at least wise so as not to marry her . . . I have tried to cure my self by labour, art and friendship . . . by exercise and diet and fasting. I have endeavoured to hinder it in its first growing; in the bargain I have kept to a whole quarter of a year out of her company. I have endeavoured to call to mind the weakness of most women, their pride, their dissimulation, their uncertainty . . . I have tried philtres . . . and all to such purpose as if I had run my head against a post . . .

There was nothing for it but to marry. Elizabeth, in London, was asked to buy a diamond ring for the bride. Oxinden was rather hoping she would strike a bargain: 'I should think in these dead times such toys might be had at easiest rates,' he ventured. He also needed a new bed: 'We would willingly have of the latest fashion, for this is all the beds we are like to make in our time, and were it not, as I may say, a case of absolute necessity, we should not put ourselves to the cost of a bed, and now especially these turbulent and uncertain times.'

Whether the bed was a good investment when the country was about to embark on an orgy of destruction was indeed a moot point.

PART TWO
1642–1734

5

'Good men with good fortunes are very hard to be gotten'

WHEN SIR EDMUND Verney, the King's standard-bearer, was slain at Edgehill at the opening of the civil war, Lady Sussex wrote presciently to his son Ralph: 'I am afraid in these bad times you will not match your sisters as you desire.' Ralph, as the eldest son and heir to Claydon in Buckinghamshire and the Verney estates, had to assume responsibility for his five unmarried orphan sisters, ranging in age from nine to twenty-one, and to find the older ones suitable husbands in a world suddenly gone mad. The difficulty was compounded by the fact that at the end of 1643 Sir Ralph fell foul of the new regime and was forced into exile, leaving the young women to fend for themselves. No wonder he wrote urgently to Susan, cautioning her about marriage: 'I pray mistake me not, for this is the weightiest business that ever yet befell you, for in this one action consists all your future happiness in this world; therefore, do nothing rashly . . . good men with good fortunes are very hard to be gotten.'

Only Cary, the fourth of Sir Edmund's six daughters, had been provided for in marriage by her father. On the very eve of the war, fifteen-year-old Cary had been married from Sir Edmund's Covent Garden house to Thomas Gardiner, a young captain of dragoons, the eldest son of Sir Thomas Gardiner of Cuddesdon near Oxford. She had been made most welcome by his family. 'I must let you know how well I like this place,' she wrote to Ralph on her arrival. 'When I came my grandmother [it was the practice to refer to a husband's relations as one's own] bid me very welcome and made what entertainment she could, more a great deal than I expected, and Sir Thomas and my lady bid me very welcome to Cuddesdon and said they wished it might be my own and truly use me very civilly. . . All my sisters with a great deal of compliments did bid me very welcome.'

One of the most crucial lessons a young bride was taught, other than to love, honour and obey her husband, was to treat his family with respect. As Lady Peyton advised her newly married daughter, Anne Oxinden, 'Let no respect be wanting to your husband and his mother, with the rest of his friends, in this you shall gain yourself a good repute and show yourself a virtuous wife whose price is not to be valued.' Now Sir Ralph did likewise, writing to Cary: 'Those good people with whom you are now settled will still continue to love and kindness unless you fail in your due respects to them, which I am confident you. will never do.'

The idyll was quickly shattered by the war. In the summer of 1645 the recently knighted Thomas Gardiner was killed in a skirmish near Aylesbury. The previous year Cary had given birth to a boy, who did not live long, and now the eighteen-year-old widow was heavily pregnant again. Her position was precarious. The family's benevolent uncle, Dr Denton, wrote to Ralph, already in exile in France: 'When her husband died he left her not a penny in the house, her father and mother when I left her had not and I am confident will not contribute a penny towards her relief.' Everything hinged on the sex of the child. If it was a boy, Cary's position within the Gardiner family, as mother of the heir, would be assured. It was understandable, then, that when Henry Verney wrote to Ralph that 'my sister was brought to bed of a girl to all our griefs' the disappointment was intense. From being the daughter of an intimate of the King, the sister of a man highly respected in parliamentary circles, and the beloved wife of the gallant young Cavalier who was the eldest son of the family, Cary was suddenly nobody.

The Gardiners were no longer nice to her. To be fair, they were probably suffering similar financial difficulties to the Verneys and other families like them, the bulk of whose income derived from land. And they had lost not one, but two of their sons in the war. Nevertheless, they would not trouble to be kind to their daughter-in-law now that she had nothing to offer. They begrudged her board and made difficulties over the payment of her jointure. Cary with her sickly baby girl returned to her brother's house at Claydon, where her sisters were living, when they were not being boarded out with relatives, in equally straitened circumstances.

Tom Verney described their situation to Ralph: 'Since I am desired to write, I shall (with much brevity) declare in what a sad condition my sisters in general are now in, and how (with a little help of yours) they may be much bettered . . . They living at Claydon are subject to the affrights of rude soldiers rushing in at all hours both by day & night, and not a man there that dares show himself in their defence.'

Marriage was a woman's sole 'preferment', the whole purpose of her existence. It was the only option open to the Verney women, yet the civil war was making the business of finding a husband even more difficult than usual. Marriage negotiations had become more abrasive. Proposal after proposal was considered and dropped, with barely any attempt to conceal the fact that they were motivated by self-interest rather than affection. The Verneys' value on the marriage market was greatly diminished, owing to the fact that their portions were reduced, or currently unavailable. None of them was a great beauty, but in normal circumstances looks did not matter, as long as a girl brought a decent portion. Everyone looked to Ralph for money, but how was Ralph to supply them all with portions now that the whole financial structure on which they had depended had been exploded by the war?

During the war rents were slow in coming in, or they were not paid at all, while taxes rose. The income from land was further reduced by the depredations of armies, bribes in money or stock paid out to the military in order to avoid even greater losses from pillaging, and outright destruction of property. Not only debts, but annuities, jointures and marriage portions, calculated on previous income and payable under legal contract, had now to be paid from an income that was at best intermittent and unpredictable and at worst non-existent.

Banks had not yet been established in England, so that the usual method of placing money to raise interest was done privately, between individuals, very often members of the extended family or kin group. In this way, portions could be allotted and placed out at interest, until they were required. Margaret, for instance, had been given a gift of £1,000 as a portion by her aunt Eure, but unfortunately Ralph had lent the money to an MP, who was serving in the Long Parliament. His privileged status meant that he could take as long as he pleased to repay the money. The ordinary decencies no longer applied.

The matter of marriage was all the more pressing for Penelope, Margaret and Susan, since they were already in their twenties. Soon they would be considered too old and facing the dismal prospect, as unmarried women, of being a perpetual burden on the family. Annuities paid to unmarried women were considered dead money. The tie of marriage extended beyond the particular couple to embrace the whole family, so women who failed to marry lost the opportunity to expand the circle of family influence, for this was an age of patronage, when doing favours and reciprocating them was the way life worked. As it was, the sisters could barely manage on the reduced annuities they were receiving from Ralph. Penelope, who had only the clothes she stood up in after parliamentary forces destroyed the house in which she was staying, complained that she could not dress herself as befitted her father's daughter.

Margaret Cavendish, Duchess of Newcastle, opined that 'a bad husband is far worse than no husband', but the Verney women could not afford to take such a lofty view. They were each aware that they must reduce their sights. Susan, the eldest, found an unlikely spouse through her brother Tom, the black sheep of the family. As she described it, matter-of-fact, to Ralph: 'My brother Thomas has wished me to a gentleman who has a very good fortune for me, for he has at least 500 pound a year . . . All that knows the man gives him good commendations. He is a widower but has no child; his fortune is in his own hands; he has seen me, vows that it is the first time that ever he thought of marriage since his wife died, and if he fail of me it shall be the last.'

Richard Alport was a Cheshire squire with an estate of about £600 a year. He was also a prisoner in the Fleet, for a debt of £1,000, although this at a time when it was all too easy to find oneself in prison for debt did not perturb the family unduly. Brother Henry was very much opposed to the match, probably because Alport was so feckless with money, telling Ralph 'she is resolved to take him with all faults'.

The negotiations dragged on. Mr Alport, Susan told Ralph, 'is very ready to perform all things in ten days warning, so where the fault lyeth I know not, but I suffer extremely in the tediousness of it, both in my honour and purse'. She was living with her aunt and uncle off Fetter Lane and was greatly indebted to them for her subsistence 'although I know they do borrow it, and pawn for it', but she was determined not to leave town until the settlement was concluded.

Of course, Alport desperately needed Susan's portion to pay his creditors and get out of the Fleet, while Ralph, knowing this to be the case, was intent on extracting the last advantage out of the situation, pushing the dowry ever downwards. There was a suggestion that Susan and Alport had already been sexually intimate, so that as Ralph said, 'if she have him not she is a lost creature'. He was willing to let Susan have the material for three new gowns for her marriage, and she asked him to send her a little pair of French scissors, presumably so that she could make up the gowns. However, the money for the gowns was not to be forthcoming until after her jointure of £200 a year was agreed, which presumably meant that they would not be ready in time for the wedding. Susan was upset: 'Sure it would have been much handsomer for me to have had them before I had married . . . it may begat suspicion in his friends that I brought no clothes to my back and that he bought me those which you will give me.'

In April 1646 an offer of marriage was made for Margaret – Pegg to her family. It seemed almost too good to be true. Mr Elmes was a Northamptonshire gentleman with an estate of £1,000 a year, and he was offering Pegg a jointure of £500 a year on good security. Susan described her prospective brother-in-law as 'a pretty gentleman of a very great fortune'. The temptation was to have a joint wedding, but Susan demurred, because Pegg 'will have clothes like herself and I shall not, therefore it must not be'.

If Pegg had the better trousseau, Susan had secured the kinder husband. After the wedding, she admitted touchingly, 'I was never so happy since my father died as I am now.' Alport was still in the Fleet and Susan had joined him there. 'It is no prison to me,' she assured Ralph, 'I live as well here as ever I lived anywhere in all my life, and dare compare husbands with her that has the best.'

Soon she was reporting sadly to Ralph that 'poor Pegg has married a very humorsome cross boy . . . and she is very much altered for the worse since she was married; I do not much blame her for being so altered, because sometimes he makes her cry day and night.'

Even Henry was reporting that Elmes had a volatile temper and was jealous. He seems to have struck Pegg during an argument. Two years after the wedding, the couple took the highly controversial step of separating. Dr Denton, who tried to act as mediator, was shocked at the language they used to each other, saying he had not heard the like in Billingsgate. Ralph was concerned about the proprieties, writing to his brother Edmund: 'I wish with all my heart that they were reconciled again, but I doubt that cannot be done suddenly.' Pegg was to consult Dr Denton as to the best place for her to live. Country obscurity would be best, but with so much soldiery about, not advisable. She was to dress quietly, avoiding bright colours, and not 'to keep much company, for it is not fit for a person in her condition either to flaunt it in clothes or appear often in public at playhouses and taverns', even with her closest friends. Pegg was indignant: 'Now for my living a retired life, truly I do not know anything I have done should make me do so.' Besides maintenance of £160 a year, Ralph hoped that Elmes would give her enough 'good furniture for her chamber and a bed for her maid, with some linen for her bed and board'.

In September 1646 Penelope married her cousin, John Denton, for whom she had had feelings for years. There was no time to consult Ralph, nor did the bridegroom consult his parents. The extraordinary thing was that he was prepared to take Penelope without a dowry, trusting that it would be forthcoming eventually, but of course this also meant that no jointure had been settled on her. 'On my word,' Henry wrote to Ralph, 'I know not one in England would have made her his wife on the like conditions.' He assured Ralph that her failure to consult him was not out of disrespect, but 'had she stayed for your approbation she must have lost him'. Penelope was 'sensible her portion lay in a desperate condition, besides, she grew in years and was not to all men's liking; these reasons made her so ready to yield to his desires, having most of her friends' consent present.' It was important to have the consent of 'friends', if not of her eldest brother. Friends described those people – drawn from the wider kin group or employers – who could be helpful in advancing one's marriage prospects or career.

Henry had advanced his sister £30 for 'gownes and linnen', which he hoped Ralph would reimburse. He also asked Ralph to pay a debt of £10 which Penelope has incurred, 'that I may justly swear to her new father when we go that she is clad like a gentlewoman, and owes not in the world a penny'.

By their mid-twenties, most children of the middling and lower classes had been working away from home for several years; they were economically independent and, strictly speaking, did not need their parents' consent to marry, even supposing one or both of their parents were still alive by that time. If they sought it, it was merely out of courtesy. It was almost unheard of, however, for members of the gentry to marry without consulting parents. Ralph seemed surprisingly sanguine on the matter of Penelope's marriage to John Denton, 'for I believe the land is settled, and if they carry themselves wisely and with respect to him [Denton's father], a little time and good nature would procure an act of oblivion'. He was right to be optimistic, for Penelope's parents-in-law 'received her with great content and make infinite much of her' – at least for the moment.

When Ralph sent his wife Mary to England at the end of 1646 to treat with the authorities for the return of Verney property, which had been confiscated by Parliament, it was a relief to her to find the three eldest sisters married. ''Tis a very great blessing to us that they are all married,' she told him, 'for I did never in my life see or hear of so much indiscretion as is amongst them; truly, there is not one of them that hath any discretion.' Susan made the best wife, she reported, since she 'studies nothing but to please her husband' – as, indeed, a good seventeenth-century wife should. 'If you did but see him you would wonder how she could be so fond of him,' she continued, 'but I think he is very kind to her.' Poor Pegg 'hath so ill a husband that I cannot give you a character bad enough of him', while Penelope's husband 'is as fit a match for her as can be, though she outgoes him much in cunning, for she is deadly crafty'.

There remained only the two younger ones to settle – and civilize: Mary, who was 'as wild as a buck', and Betty, who is 'much the worst natured' and most wilful of them all, a 'pestilent wench' of a 'cross proud lazy disposition'. If they were to make good marriages, their reputations must be unblemished, but already Betty had been discovered sitting familiarly in the lap of one of the male servants.

Lady Verney had never been in the situation of her sisters-in-law, trying to secure a husband while handicapped by lack of money. Born Mary Blacknall, she was thirteen when her parents died of the plague in 1625, leaving her sole heiress to Misterton, an estate not far from Claydon. Until 1641 when Charles I surrendered this and other unpopular prerogatives to mollify his more moderate opponents, the custody of heirs under the age of twenty-one or unmarried heiresses of any age passed to the crown, which exploited their wardship as a source of revenue. Mary's wardship was eagerly purchased by Sir Edmund Verney, who in so doing became her guardian. Guardians had the right to profit from the marriage of their wards, provided the proposed match was without disparagement; that is, fitting in terms of age, rank, health and fortune. In fact, Edmund intended to marry Mary to his eldest son, Ralph, which was an eminently suitable match.

They were married young, while Ralph was still at Oxford, and their relationship grew into one of devotion and love. The success of their marriage may be attributed to the fact that they shared similar attitudes and values concerning the conduct and goals of married life.

This is not to say that Ralph was faithful in the sexual sense. While adultery was considered the most heinous crime in a woman, the sexual double standard prevailed. It was not done to make 'a whore' of one's wife and all advice books tended to concur with John Evelyn in warning against 'too much frequency of embraces'. Wives, who were almost constantly pregnant, tended to turn a blind eye to mistresses and it was quite common for men to satisfy their sexual appetite with their servants. A curious letter survives, written to Ralph in September 1646 by Mary's devoted uncle, Dr Denton, who was engaging a new English maid for the Verneys in France:

> Because you write me word that you were in love with dirty sluts, I took great care to fit you with a Joan that may be as good as my Lady in the dark, and I hope I have fitted you a pennyworth. I will while she stays [in England] take her into my house and observe what I can, but Luce [a former servant of the Verneys] is very confident she will match your cock, and she should know for they lived half a year together in one house.

Once they had produced the requisite heir and spare, upper-class women had little else to contribute to a marriage, but during the civil wars they proved extraordinarily useful, way beyond their normal pale of influence. They withstood sieges, petitioned for the release of their husbands, acted as spies, raised money and dealt with creditors, and, in the case of Lady Verney, appeared before the Committee for Compounding to plead on their husband's behalf for the repossession of their estates – in return for a large fine. As Dr Denton commented, 'Women were never so useful as now . . . their sex entitles them to many privileges.'

Even an upheaval of the magnitude of the civil war was not enough to reverse male opinion on the subject of women's innate inferiority – a notion reinforced by Protestantism, which upheld paternal authority through a patriarchal God – or to shake their confidence in the idea that women were silly, irrational creatures incapable of dealing with any matter of genuine importance. Sir Ralph and Lady Verney were a partnership, united in the ambition to preserve his patrimony for their children. But they were not equal partners, as she would be the first to acknowledge. He made all the decisions, she merely carried them out. She did so out of love for him and habitual obedience to his wishes. If he sent her to England on his behalf, it was with the cynical expectation that the male members of the committee would be more amenable to the feminine pleas of the helpless and incompetent creature before them than they would to him.

There is no question that Sir Ralph loved his wife and they missed each other terribly. 'I long for nothing more than to hear thou art safe at Blois,' she wrote, 'and wish for nothing in this world so much as to be with thee again', while he urged, 'Dear Heart, let me beg of thee to dispatch thy business quickly, before your friends' affections cool, that thou may speedily return to him whose love daily increases, even beyond thy imagination or the expression of thy most faithful Ralph Verney.'

Mary was an intelligent woman with a knack of getting on well with people, but Ralph treated her as a child, and sought to regulate her every activity, even her leisure hours, reminding her to practise her guitar. While Mary patiently lobbied and bribed Members of Parliament and their wives, paid tedious social calls and distributed gifts where it would help, entertained influential people, waited for appointments, eked out her living expenses in London in inferior lodgings and calculated whether or not she could afford to take a coach to a meeting, Ralph from a distance was urging her to hurry up, imposing additional tasks on her or complaining that she had failed to answer some point in one of his letters.

But she was ever loyal and devoted to him, always deferring to his 'superior' judgement. ''Tis only because you bid me do it, that I trouble you with my silly advice, for I am sure thy own judgement is much better, and what that leads thee to will please me,' she told him carefully, when she agreed to let him dispose of her property as he thought best. She could not bear to hear him criticized, especially by a member of the family. 'Believe me there is nothing puts me in so great choler as to hear thee taxed, that I know art so good and just to all.'

'As thou lovest me be careful of thy self, and let no business make you neglect your health,' Ralph urged. Mary was pregnant. There was a loving dispute between them over the name. 'I will be governed by thee in anything but the name if it be a boy, for to tell the truth I must have it have thy name,' she told him. Ralph was just as insistent that it must not. She had her way, but the boy, left with a wet nurse at Claydon, died without his father ever seeing him. Mary made a slow recovery and was depressed by the thought that 'I cannot see any hopes or likelihood of a sudden dispatch of my business.'

To add to her woes, her little daughter Margaret died of dysentery in France. Mary wrote painfully to Ralph:

My dearest heart, I was in so much affliction for the loss of my dear children . . . that I was not in a condition to write or do anything else and truly at present I am so weak that I am scarce able to go up and down my chamber but my trust is in my good God; for he gave them to me and he took them from me, and I hope, and I trust he will in his good time deliver me out of all my troubles and give my mind some quiet and bring me to thee for until I am with thee I cannot take any content in any thing in this world, for the truth is I would not to gain the greatest riches in this world be so long again from thee as I have already been, but as soon as I am able to go abroad I will follow thy business night and day.

Just over a year after Mary arrived in London, she succeeded in her business. The sequestration was removed from the estate, which meant that Ralph could begin to pay off his father's debts and put his finances back in order. Mary joyfully prepared for her return to France, taking Jack, the small son who had been left behind at Claydon at the beginning of the war, to join his father and elder brother. Ever protective, Ralph wrote warning her to wrap herself and the boy up 'extraordinarily warm', for 'that town [Calais] standing upon the seaside is subject to bitter weather'. The couple were reunited in the spring of 1648. Two years later, Mary, aged thirty-three, died of consumption.

In writing to his sister Margaret, Ralph paid Mary a tribute which was, perhaps, a recipe for a successful marriage:

> When I was most peevish she would be most patient . . . and studied nothing more than a sweet compliance. But perhaps you think I was a better husband than your own; alas, if that were so, 'twas she that made me so, and I may thank her silence and discretion for your good opinion of me, for had she (like so many other wives) divulged my faults, or in a proud disdainful way despised me for my pettish humours, 'tis ten to one I had been found more liable to censure than any other man.

Ralph had Mary's body embalmed and sent to Claydon for burial, where he would eventually lie beside her. He intended to travel in Italy, 'not to delight myself with anything there, for since my dear wife's death I have bid adieu to all that most men count their happiness'.

He remained a widower for the next forty-six years, devoted to her memory.

6

'Women must love silently'

> Let me ask you if you have seen a book of poems newly come out, made by my lady Newcastle. For God's sake if you meet with it send it to me, they say it is ten times more extravagant than her dress. Sure, the poor woman is a little distracted, she could never be so ridiculous else as to venture at writing books – and in verse too. If I should not sleep this fortnight I should not come to that.

The request for the latest book of verse by Margaret Cavendish, Duchess of Newcastle, was made by Dorothy Osborne in one of her secret letters to her beloved, William Temple. Dorothy had more in common with 'Mad Madge' than she realized. Both women, near contemporaries, were living in an age of revolution and they had both broken the mould, whereby a young woman's marriage was arranged by her family, to take the liberty of choosing her own husband. If Margaret shocked the world by publishing verse and plays, at a time when women were expected to be silent, Dorothy too was refusing to play by the rules, engaged as she was in a clandestine epistolary courtship in defiance of her family. The idea that young women of their class could choose whom they wanted to marry on the grounds of personal liking, even love, was considered tantamount to social anarchy.

It was the unique and shattering effects of civil war that broke the constraints of their lives. Both women came from royalist families of similar standing who had lost their fortunes in the maelstrom of war. If they seemed bold and eccentric, it has to be remembered that the 1640s and 1650s witnessed a ferment of debate in which the traditional relationships between King and people and husbands and wives were questioned, and radical notions about marrying for love or divorcing for incompatibility were aired. Not only did religious

Cril war
effect an marrage

sects such as the Levellers and the Quakers believe in total equality between men and women, but for the first time women were preaching and prophesying – emerging on the public stage, just as actresses were to do a generation later. All this represented a challenge to the traditional idea of the passive and subordinate role of women, who were supposed to be silent and obedient.

Margaret Cavendish, née Lucas, had had an unusual upbringing. Her father had died when she was small and her mother's attitude to her daughters' education was lax, even by the standards of the time. Margaret was taught to read and write by 'an old decayed gentlewoman' and otherwise allowed to run wild, read poetry, and indulge her love of dressing up in fantastic clothes of her own design. She later complained that 'for the most part women are not educated as they should be . . . for their education is only to dance, sing, and fiddle, to write complimentary letters, to read romance, to speak some language', so that they could never be men's equals and were only fit for the inferior position of wife, hardly better than beasts. Her childhood effectively ended when the rioting townspeople of Colchester broke into the Lucas estate and indulged in an orgy of destruction. Margaret never saw her home again. She elected to join Queen Henrietta Maria in exile in Paris as one of her maids of honour.

Here she met William Cavendish, Marquis of Newcastle, whose handsome presence, polished manner, high rank and reputation alone would have captivated most women. He was a connoisseur of beautiful women and could have had his pick of the court ladies, but he was drawn by Margaret's youth, undoubted physical attractions, and her studied aloofness. She had professed herself averse to marriage – too many dangers lurked there and too many people married imprudently, foolishly believing that they would be immune from its problems. 'A happy marriage is very happy, but an unhappy marriage is hell,' she later told her sister. 'Where there is doubt the best is to be mistress of yourself, which in a single life you are.' For a woman to think of remaining single was a bold and not very practical idea.

Only the strength of her love for Newcastle could persuade Margaret to put aside her doubts: 'though I did dread marriage and shunned men's company as much as I could, yet I could not, nor had not the power to refuse him, by reason my affections were fixed on him, and he was the only person I ever was in love with, neither was I ashamed to own it.' The fact that he was thirty years older meant that he could equally well play the father and lover, and she needed both. He was old enough and sophisticated enough to tolerate her idiosyncrasies and experienced enough to supply the want of confidence she felt in facing the world. She wonders that he should love someone so unworthy, 'but being as your choice makes it good, and so I shall value my self, which else I should not'.

And Margaret was very much alone in the world. Normally a young woman's courtship was closely monitored by her family, but Margaret had to conduct her affair without their protection or the benefit of their advice, surrounded by idle, backbiting, refugee courtiers, who would jealously slander her once they learned of her great prize. Margaret must occasionally have wondered if she could trust Newcastle, who courted her passionately, often with erotic verse. One mistake could so easily lead to the loss of her reputation. They resorted to a secret correspondence, with Margaret once complaining that she had had to read his letter by candlelight, it came so early, and that 'if you cannot read this letter, blame me not, for it was so early I was half asleep'.

It would be Newcastle's second marriage. He already had sons, but his avowed purpose in marrying a young woman, according to Margaret, was to have more. When someone spitefully revealed their relationship to the Queen she was furious, not just because of the couple's perceived duplicity, but because it was such an unequal match. Margaret herself was conscious that 'those that marry below their quality give respect and reputation to those they marry, but take it from themselves'.

Thanks to the war, she had lost the £10,000 dowry her father had left her; she was of gentle but undistinguished birth; she lacked useful political connections; and her shyness and eccentricity meant that she was unlikely to be a social asset. Newcastle's friends, Lord Widdrington and Endymion Porter, were very much against the marriage. Margaret was aware of this, writing, 'My lord, my lord Widdrington in his advice has done as a noble and true affectionate friend would do, yet I find I am infinitely obliged to you whose affections are above so powerful a persuasion.' Her friends, too, were slyly insinuating that Newcastle would let her down — that he had made promises to many but 'was constant to none'.

Uncomfortably aware that jealous courtiers believed she was in hot pursuit of Newcastle, she asked him to excuse her if he did not hear from her, 'for though I love you extremely well, yet I never feared my modesty so small as it would give me leave to court any man'. A woman's reputation was everything; Margaret thanked him for 'the fear you have of my ruin', telling him she was especially careful of her reputation because any blemish would reflect on him. Although it was impossible for her to avoid slanderous tongues, she could at least ensure that she gave them no ammunition.

And yet she could not help confessing her love. 'Though I give you all the love I have, yet it is too little for your merit.' Thinking that she had been too frank, the next day she wrote: 'I am a little ashamed of my last letter, more than of the others; not that my affection can be too large, but I fear I discover it too much in that letter, for women must love silently. But I hope you will pardon the style because the intention was good.'

In the summer of 1645, when Margaret was twenty-two, they became secretly engaged. 'There is nothing will please me more than to be where you are,' Margaret wrote. 'I begin to admire Paris because you are in it.' There is a suggestion that Newcastle wished to share her bed before all the formalities had been completed, but Margaret tactfully avoided this, telling him, 'There is a customary law that must be signed before I may lawfully call you husband.' Although a betrothal followed by consummation amounted to a valid if illicit marriage, it would have been only too easy for Newcastle to extricate himself by denying her version of events.

Later, in her play *The Bridals*, Margaret describes how Lady Coy dreads marriage and confesses she is 'afraid to lie with a man'. On the wedding night, her attendants beg her to undress, but she is reluctant; three times the bridegroom comes to the door of the bridal chamber for the bedding ceremony, only to be turned away. It may well have been autobiographical, although Newcastle's experience and sensuality would surely have overcome her reluctance.

For whatever reason, there seem to have been some last-minute doubts, because Margaret wrote offering to free him from their engagement:

> Pray, my lord, consider well whether marrying me will not bring a trouble to yourself; for, believe me, I love you too well to wish you unhappy and I had rather lose all happiness my self than you should be unfortunate. But if you be resolved, whatever day you please to send for me I will come . . . I understand the persuasion of some against your marriage; sure, they would not persuade you but for your good; but if you think you have done unadvisedly in promising yourself to me, send me word and I will resign all the interest I have in you, though unwillingly.

They were married towards the end of 1645 in the chapel of Sir Richard Browne, the English Resident at the French court. Margaret's family could hardly object to such a splendid match, even if the young woman did take the unusual liberty of arranging it herself. Elizabeth Lucas wrote to her new son-in-law to thank him for honouring her daughter by marriage 'and thereby made her extremely happy: for oftentimes these come not together, but by yourself she hath attained to both'. She could only apologize that 'the state of the kingdom is such yet that her brother cannot give unto her that which is hers' – a dowry.

The Newcastles were to continue in impoverished exile for the next fifteen years. 'I desire nothing so much as the continuance of your affection,' Margaret assured him, 'for I think myself richer in having that than if I were a monarch of all the world.' Touchingly, he never begrudged the money spent on publishing her literary works, although many other men would have been embarrassed to have had so radical a wife as a published author, whose heroines were anything but submissive.

Three years after Margaret married Newcastle, twenty-one-year-old Dorothy Osborne met William Temple on a journey to France. Dorothy's father, Sir Peter Osborne, a royalist, was old, unwell, newly impoverished and in exile. William's father, Sir John Temple, a parliamentarian, had sent his son abroad to complete his education and avoid the fighting at home. They would never agree to a marriage between their children. The young people spent a month in each other's company at St Malo and vowed never to marry anyone but each other. For the next seven years their love survived long periods of separation and constant family harassment, even emotional blackmail, to marry more suitably. Through the memory of her beauty, and the intelligence and wit displayed in her letters, Dorothy maintained her hold on a handsome, highly sexed young man, who had all the freedom that her sex denied her.

A young woman was not meant to enjoy the society of anyone of the opposite sex, except through the contrivance of her family, whose priorities were to guard her honour and secure an advantageous marriage for her. It was defiant, to say the least, for Dorothy and William to carry on a secret courtship through their correspondence. 'I will write every week, and no miss of letters shall give us any doubts of one another, time nor accidents shall not prevail upon our hearts,' Dorothy promised.

Through their letters they explored each other's feelings and ideas, particularly about marriage, and indulged in dreams of a future together. 'Can there be a more romance story than ours would make if the conclusion should prove happy?' she asks. Like Margaret, Dorothy was rather more forward than a young woman of her time was expected to be: 'I am apt to speak what I think; and to you have so accustomed myself to discover all my heart, that I do not believe 'twill ever be in my power to conceal a thought from you.'

The Osbornes compounded for their estate, Chicksands Priory near Bedford, paying Parliament a fine of £10,000 – at least a million in today's money. It meant that they could return home, albeit with an income reduced from £4,000 to £400 a year. It was all the more imperative, therefore, for Dorothy to make a good match, to repair the family fortune. Suitor after suitor was brought forward. She pretended to consider, prevaricated and declined. Like William, she was conventional enough not to disobey her family openly by marrying someone they disapproved of and she had too much filial love and respect for her father to upset him:

> I can never think of disposing myself without my father's consent; and
> though he has left it more in my power than almost anybody leaves a
> daughter, yet certainly I were the worst natured person in the world
> if his kindness were not a greater tie upon me than any advantage he

could have reserved. Besides that, 'tis my duty, from which nothing can ever tempt me, nor could you like it in me if I should do otherwise, 'twould make me unworthy of your esteem; but if ever that may be obtained, or I left free, and you in the same condition, all the advantages of fortune or person imaginable met together in one man should not be preferred before you.

The couple were aware that to marry without the consent of parents and the approval of their 'friends' – in the seventeenth-century meaning of the term – would mean financial and social ruin and the loss of suitable career opportunities for William.

Nevertheless, Dorothy defied her family covertly by thwarting all their plans for her to make a marriage of their choice. She kept William entertained by mercilessly disparaging her suitors and despatching them without a qualm. 'I had no quarrel to his person or his fortune, but was in love with neither, and much out of love with a thing called marriage,' she recalled of an earlier suitor, who had had to flee after a duel. Another wanted a larger dowry than her father was prepared to offer. 'Yet he protested he liked me so well, that he was very angry my father would not be persuaded to give £1000 more with me; and I him so ill, that I vowed if I had £1000 less I should have thought it too much for him.'

If she could not marry William, Henry, second son of Oliver Cromwell, would 'be as acceptable to me as any one else'. Lucy Hutchinson describes Henry as 'a debauched ungodly Cavalier', which indicates that he was no dour Puritan, but more charming, light-hearted and courteous than others who featured in his father's regime. It is not known how he and Dorothy met, but they certainly liked each other. 'If I had been so wise as to have taken hold of the offer made me by Henry Cromwell, I might have been in a fair way of preferment, for, sure, they will be greater now than ever,' she teased William, when Oliver Cromwell became Lord Protector. Henry, serving in Ireland, sent her a gift of 'two of the finest young Irish greyhounds that ere I saw', but eventually he married someone else.

Dorothy was doubtful that in an arranged marriage love would follow in time. 'I find I want courage to marry where I do not like . . . And though I easily believe that to marry one for whom we have already some affection will infinitely increase that kindness, yet I shall never be persuaded that marriage has a charm to raise love out of nothing, much less out of dislike.'

Nor would she find it easy to conform to someone else's requirements. 'I have lived so long in the world, and so much at my own liberty, that whosoever has me must be content to take me as they find me, without hope of ever making me other than I am.' When her brother said of one of her suitors that 'any woman that had wit and discretion might make an ass of him and govern him as she pleased', Dorothy could not deny it, but she would not do it.

She described the sort of man she would not want to marry. 'He must not be so much a country gentleman as to understand nothing but hawks and dogs, and be fonder of either than his wife', nor must he be 'a town gallant, that lives in an tavern or an ordinary, that cannot imagine how an hour should be spent without company unless it to be sleeping, that makes court to all the women he sees, thinks they believe him, and laughs and is laughed at equally'. The man she married 'must not be a fool of no sort, nor peevish, nor ill-natured, nor proud, nor covetous'. Above all, 'he must love me and I him as much as we are capable of loving'. Without love, it did not matter how rich he was, she would not marry him.

Many of the letters observe other people's marriages. 'What an age do we live in, where 'tis a miracle if in ten couples that are married, two of them live so as not to publish to the world that they cannot agree.' She particularly disapproved of the Countess of Sunderland's marriage to plain Mr Smith. 'I think I shall never forgive her one thing she said of him, which is that she married him out of pity.' It was a 'contemptible' thing to say and 'though he be a very fine gentleman and does more than deserve her', she treated him disdainfully. 'With what reverence he approaches her, and how like a gracious princess she receives him,' Dorothy noted tartly. 'She has lost by it much of the repute she had gained by keeping herself a widow,' she concluded, adding witheringly, 'But we are all mortal.'

Another of her acquaintance had 'broke loose from an old miserable husband that lived so long; she thinks if she does not make haste she shall not have time to spend what he left'. Dorothy had a wry sense of humour in observing the way of the world. 'She is old and was never handsome, and yet is courted a thousand times more than the greatest beauty in the world would be that had not a fortune. We could not eat in quiet for the letters and presents that came in from people that would not have looked upon her when they had met her if she had been left poor.'

Of her own brother and sister-in-law, she commented: 'He loves her, I think, at the ordinary rate of husbands, but not enough, I believe, to marry her so much to his disadvantage if it were to do again; and that would kill me were I as she, for I could be infinitely better satisfied with a husband that had never loved me in hopes he might, than with one that began to love me less than he had done.'

She considered the radical notion that 'all such as intend to marry should live together in the same house some years of probation; and if, in all that time, they never disagreed, they should then be permitted to marry if they please; but how few would do it then!'

Isolated at Chicksands, rarely able to see William, Dorothy had moments of doubt and despair. 'You undo me by but dreaming how happy we might have been,' she wrote, 'when I consider how far we are from it in reality. Alas! How can you talk of defying fortune; nobody lives without it, and therefore why should you imagine you could?' William took advantage of her brother's brief absence to visit her at Chicksands to persuade her that their love could prevail. He had heard a rumour that she was betrothed to someone else, but she assured him it was not so, 'that you have still the same power in my heart that I gave you at our last parting; that I will never marry any other; and that if ever our fortunes will allow us to marry, you shall dispose of me as you please; but this, to deal freely with you, I do not hope for. No; 'tis too great a happiness, and I, that know myself best, must acknowledge I deserve crosses and affliction, but can never merit such a blessing.'

She was wrong. Dorothy's father died in March 1654 and she was required to move out of Chicksands by her elder brother and his family. From being the daughter who had loyally looked after her ailing father, she was now an impoverished twenty-eight-year-old unmarried woman whose presence was an inconvenience and yet whose life her family still felt they had some jurisdiction over. On the day of her father's burial, she told her brother bluntly that she would marry no one but William Temple. Fortunately, William's father, at last understanding the depths of his son's feelings for Dorothy, relented.

Just as they abolished Christmas, the Puritans banned church weddings. The Marriage Act of 1653 introduced civil marriage into England for the first time. It required the names of those wishing to be married to be posted on the door of the common meeting-house, otherwise known as the parish church or chapel, for a period of three weeks, after which the couple, accompanied by two witnesses, were to go before a magistrate to exchange the simplest of vows. Taking the woman by the hand, the man said, 'I, A.B., do hereby in the presence of God take thee C.D. to my wedded wife, and do also in the presence of God, and before these witnesses, promise to be unto thee a loving and faithful husband.' Then the woman promised to be a 'loving, faithful, and obedient wife' and the magistrate pronounced them man and wife.

At the time Dorothy had expressed qualms about the Act, saying that 'it will fright the country people extremely, for they apprehend nothing like going before a Justice', yet 'they say no other marriage shall stand good in law'. Needless to say, Dorothy thought 'the old one is better; and for my part I am resolved to stay till that comes in fashion again'.

After seven years, it would be madness to let a little thing like a civil marriage ceremony stand in the way of their happiness. Dorothy and William were married in London, early in 1655, and seem to have done what so many other couples did, follow the compulsory civil ceremony by a quiet religious service at St Giles in the Field. They were happily married for forty years, the only blight on their happiness being that they outlived all their children.

INTERLUDE

Hannah Woolley, *The Gentlewoman's Companion or, a Guide to the Female Sex*

After the Restoration of the monarchy and the patriarchal Anglican Church in 1660 there was a concerted effort to re-establish the status quo as it had existed in 1642. To question the family, the place of women, or any other part of the social order was to flaunt nature, reason and the will of God. Wives must be submissive to their 'lawful superiors' (husbands), otherwise there would be anarchy and chaos. Each household was a society in miniature and the well-being of the commonwealth depended on the good management of families. Hannah Woolley's conservative conduct book, *The Gentlewoman's Companion or, a Guide to the Female Sex* (1675), gave some practical tips:

1. There are these two essentials in marriage, superiority and inferiority. Undoubtedly the husband hath power over the wife, and the wife ought to be subject to the husband in all things.

2. The more particular duties of a wife to a husband are first, to have a greater esteem for him than any other person and . . . to have a settled apprehension that he is wise and prudent. She is to give honour, respect, and reverence to her husband . . . with reverence she is to express her obedience in all lawful things; and apply and accommodate herself to his humour and disposition.

3. Honour and obey and love no man's company better than his.

4. Be quiet, pleasant and peaceable to him, and be not angry when he is so; but endeavour to pacify him with sweet and

winning expressions; and if casually you should provoke him to a passion, be not long ere you show some regret.

5. Be careful to keep your house in good order, and let all things with decency be in readiness when he comes to his repast; let him not wait for his meals, lest by so staying his affairs be disordered or impeded. And let whatever you provide be so neatly and cleanly dressed, that his fare, though ordinary, may engage his appetite, and disengage his fancy from taverns, which many are compelled to use by reason of the dissatisfactions they find at home.

6. Show respect and kindness to what friends he brings home with him, but more especially to his relations; for by this means he will find your love to him by your respect to them; and they will be obliged to love you for your own as well as his sake.

7. It is your duty to hide his faults and infirmities, and not detect them yourself, or suffer them to be discovered.

8. Breed up your children in as much or more obedience to him than yourself; and keep them in so much awe that they show no rudeness before him, or make any noise to his disturbance. Make them show him all aweful regard, and keep them sweet, clean and decent, that he may delight himself in them.

9. Be careful to manage what money he trusts you with . . . abuse not the freedom you have of his purse, by being too lavish; and pinch not the guts of your family at home, that you may pamper yours abroad; or throw away money in buying trifles.

10. Suffer not your expenses to exceed the receipt of your husband's income.

7

'Lay long in bed, talking and pleasing myself with my wife'

WINTER MORNINGS WERE cold and, if he was not in a desperate rush to get to the office, Samuel Pepys liked to lie in bed 'talking and sporting' with his wife. On this particular January morning of 1663, however, Elizabeth awoke and began pestering him yet again to let her have a companion. Gone were the days when the newly married couple were content with each other's company in a Whitehall attic and Elizabeth had made the coal fires and washed his dirty clothes with her own hands. Pepys was now a man of consequence in the Navy Office, steadily accumulating the fortune he dreamed would one day buy him an estate. Elizabeth had servants to do all the work and her husband was out at the office all day making money and often in the evenings too. He prided himself that 'we have been for some years now, and at present more and more, a very happy couple, blessed be God', but Elizabeth was not altogether happy. Childless, she was bored and lonely and wanted someone to keep her company.

Last October she had written out the whole story of her discontent in a letter she had sent to him at the office. Pepys burned it unread. Elizabeth had carefully kept a draft of it, however, and she now sent for Jane the maid to bring the keys of her trunk so that she could retrieve it from a bundle of papers, which included his love letters to her, and read it aloud to Pepys. It 'was so piquant and most of it true, of the retiredness of her life and how unpleasant it was', that Pepys lost his temper. Perhaps he felt a twinge of guilt, but of more immediate concern was that the letter was written in English. Anyone could have read it – the private details of their marriage. Angrily, he demanded that she tear it up immediately. She refused. He snatched the whole bundle of papers from her, leapt out of bed and stuffed them into the pockets of his breeches, so that she could not get them. He then hastily began to dress, fumbling with his 'stockings and breeches and gown', before he began the business of destruction:

> I pulled them out one by one and tore them all before her face, though it went against my heart to do it, she crying and desiring me not to do it. But such was my passion and trouble to see the letters of my love to her, and my Will, wherein I had given her all I have in the world when I went to sea with Lord Sandwich, to be joined with a paper of so much disgrace to me and dishonour if it should have been found by anybody.

Even in his fury, Pepys was sufficiently methodical to save their marriage licence and one or two other important documents. He tore up the will, however, and burned the rest.

He records the episode in microscopic detail, looking at himself and the scene objectively and not hesitating to describe how ridiculous a figure he cut as he grabbed the papers and pushed them into his breeches then groped for his clothes in his haste to dress. He does not modify his disproportionate fury in the report or deny his wife's tears to put himself in a better light. He had worried that the letter might be read by others, and yet here he is, in a diary that he left quite deliberately for posterity, revealing in all its entirety one of the most shameful scenes of his marriage. It is the very honesty and humanity of the diary with all its emotional intensity that gives it its power. Where most seventeenth-century diaries were spiritual or concerned with political events, and certainly did not disclose sexual intimacies, Pepys presents a candid portrait of his marriage and infidelities which is almost unique for any time.

Pepys was also pretty unique, for an aspiring career man, in that he had married for love. One has to admire him for that, although his contemporaries would have thought him a fool. He was an avid reader of Francis Osborne's popular work, *Advice to his Son*, in which the pundit states: 'The best of husbands are servants, but he that takes a wife wanting money, is a slave to his affection, doing the basest drudgeries without wages.' Unfortunately, the book was published three years after Pepys had married Elizabeth, so that he was not able to benefit from its advice, even if he had wanted to. Although there were moments when he flung the insult 'Beggar' at Elizabeth, reminding her of her dowerless state, it is doubtful if he ever really regretted his impetuosity. He loved his wife, for all her little faults.

He was twenty-two when he wooed and won Elizabeth, the fourteen-year-old daughter of a French émigré, Alexandre Le Marchant, who called himself Sieur de St Michel, the son of a noble family of Anjou who had disinherited him when he turned Huguenot. He had come to England in 1625, as a gentleman carver in the train of Queen Henrietta Maria. Dismissed from court after a fight over religion, he had become a soldier of fortune, trying his luck in Ireland. Here he married a well-dowered widow, a knight's daughter with family connections in Devon. He promptly lost his wife's money in a fruitless attempt to regain his French inheritance. By the time Pepys met the feckless Le Marchant and his wife, they were living in penury, although they maintained their pretensions to gentility. To Pepys, the son of a City tailor, Elizabeth's background was sufficiently different to give her an exotic appeal. She had lived in Paris, spoke French and seems to have had the refinement of a lady; he was also proud of her looks, which won her much admiration and which reflected well on him. But she brought him no money or worthwhile family connections. There was no question of a marriage settlement on either side.

They were married on 10 October 1655, two weeks before Elizabeth's fifteenth birthday, according to the rites of the Church of England. He gave her a thin gold ring and she wore a new gold-laced petticoat. Afterwards they had a small wedding dinner at a tavern on Fish Street Hill, although whether their socially incompatible parents attended is unknown. According to the laws of republican England, a church ceremony was banned and the ring was another sign of popish superstition; a second, civil, ceremony presided over by a city magistrate therefore took place at St Margaret's, Westminster, on 1 December. After the religious ceremony on 10 October Pepys had taken his bride back to the servant's attic room he occupied above his master and distant cousin Edward Montagu's lodgings at Whitehall and there consummated the marriage. It was the day the couple always celebrated as their true wedding anniversary.

The chief purpose of marriage was procreation, but the second was to act as a curb on lust. The ideal husband and wife were expected to yield 'due benevolence one to another', so that fornication should be unnecessary. When Elizabeth and Samuel were first married, the Commonwealth Act of 1650, by which a woman caught in adultery could suffer the death penalty and fornicators were imprisoned for a first offence and executed for a subsequent one, was still in force. If a wife failed in her duty towards her husband she could not complain when he sought pleasure elsewhere. Elizabeth's reluctance in the marriage bed left Samuel open to the 'temptation of lust', although, given the inhibitions that the Puritan regime imposed, it was some years before he actually did more than fantasize.

Almost immediately after their marriage Elizabeth began to suffer from a sore on 'the lip of her *chose*'. Its cause was a mystery, but since she seemed to suffer worse after intercourse she naturally attributed it to that, with predictable consequences. She was suffering from a condition in which the glands to the entrance of the vagina become blocked and a cyst is formed, producing abscesses that are not only painful but make penetration virtually impossible. The condition would flare up and then seem to disappear, only to return. While doing what he could to help, Pepys admitted that he was troubled by it – 'and not a little impatient'. In October 1660 he noted: 'My wife hath been so ill of late of her old pain that I have not known her this fortnight almost, which is a pain to me.' Had Pepys been as insensitive as many husbands he would have possessed his wife when he wanted to, indifferent to her pain, moods and feelings, but he was too considerate to demand his rights from a wife who was unwilling or indisposed.

Even after the Restoration and the laxer moral climate brought in with the monarchy and a dissolute court, timidity and good taste prevented Pepys from resorting to a brothel like some of his colleagues. One day in August 1661 his friend Peter Luellin, a clerk of the Privy Council, coaxed him into a 'pitiful alehouse in Bartholomew Fair', where 'a dirty slut or two come up that were whores'. Pepys, always fearful of venereal disease, found them disgusting and hurried away as quickly as possible for fear of being seen in their company.

He liked nothing better than to be in bed with his wife and had she been able to give him sexual satisfaction he might never have strayed. But occasions of connubial bliss were increasingly few and far between. If it wasn't the old recurring problem of the 'sore on her *chose*', Elizabeth had taken to bed with period pains, no doubt disappointed that yet again she had failed to conceive. Marital sex was too infrequent for a man of Pepys's ardent disposition. Without it, he grew restless and unhappy and looked at other women with lascivious eyes.

His sexual frustration built up over a summer of bachelorhood in 1662, when they had the builders in to their new Seething Lane house and he had sent Elizabeth to the country to avoid the dirt and chaos. One morning he arrived at the office early to find the doorman's maid sweeping out, and 'God forgive me!' he wrote. 'What a mind I had to her, but did not meddle with her.' He heard that his neighbour Sir William Penn's maid Betty had left. 'I was in hopes to have had a bout with her before she was gone, she being very pretty,' he noted regretfully. He also confessed he had 'a mind' to his own maid, Jane Birch, 'but I dare not for fear she should prove honest and refuse and then tell my wife'. Jane remained a constant temptation. 'Dined at home and can hardly keep myself from having a mind to my wench, but I hope I shall not fall to such a shame to myself.' A few years later he appeared to have lost these inhibitions, because he routinely fondled the breasts of his maid, Mary Mercer, every morning 'when she dresses me, they being the finest that I ever saw in my life'.

Fortunately, Elizabeth returned in late September and Pepys 'was very pleased to see her; and after supper, to bed and had her company with great content – and much mutual love'.

Elizabeth's condition, his own barely suppressed itch for pleasure, and the changing moral climate all conspired against his vow to be a good and faithful husband. Pepys tended to take his morals from his surroundings and the court's licentiousness had already influenced him more than he realized. Even his patron Edward Montagu, now Lord Sandwich, once a good upstanding Puritan and loyal supporter of Cromwell, was rumoured to have a wench in Chelsea. At the theatre Pepys saw plays dealing with sexual intrigues, seductions and rapes, while in the pit the whores paraded openly soliciting custom. The restrained black clothing of the Puritans had given way to dangerously low-cut gowns and inviting petticoats that could be artfully raised to reveal an ankle; it pleased him that Elizabeth actually wore drawers for modesty, which was rare. He himself was obsessed with the royal whore, Lady Castlemaine, relishing the sight of her lacy underwear hanging up to dry in the privy garden. The unattainable Castlemaine was his idea of sexual heaven, the focus of his erotic fantasy.

There were other tensions in the Pepys' marriage. Very soon after the wedding Samuel discovered that his girl-bride had a temper and a will of her own and that unless he asserted his authority his wife, 'who ought in right reason to serve and obey', would command. Many of their quarrels resulted from her attempts to get her own way. Pepys hated to resort to violence, although it did not trouble other husbands, but sometimes he had to strike her or pull her by the nose to enforce obedience. 'At night to bed,' he reported of one such battle of wills in 1660, 'and my wife and I did fall out about the dog's being put down into the cellar, which I have a mind to have done because of his fouling the house; and I would have my will. And so we went to bed and lay all night in a quarrel.'

Once when she bought a pair of earrings costing twenty-five shillings he was furious, not so much because of the frivolity, but because she had presumed to do so without first consulting him. He scolded her and she resorted to every weapon in her well-stocked arsenal, using foul language and taunting him with his jealousy. But he stuck to his guns and issued an ultimatum: take the earrings back to the shop or see them destroyed. She sent her maid with the earrings, but Pepys intercepted her and returned them to his wife, satisfied now that she acknowledged his authority to let her keep the trinkets.

There was a perpetual conflict between Pepys's frugality and Elizabeth's perceived extravagance, although it has to be said that he selfishly spent far more on his own clothes than on Elizabeth's. Jemima, Lady Sandwich, had to shame him into buying a fitting wardrobe for his wife and Elizabeth was well practised in extracting a new item of clothing as a means of his making amends after a quarrel.

Whenever he came to audit Elizabeth's jumbled housekeeping accounts at the end of the month, there was sure to be a quarrel. 'I find she is very cunning, and when she least shows it has her wit at work; but it is an ill one.'

Elizabeth's untidiness offended him. 'I went up to put my papers in order, and finding my wife's clothes lie carelessly laid up, I was angry with her.' She was a good cook when she made the effort and could lay on a successful dinner party, but they often quarrelled about her 'sluttish' housekeeping: 'Home to dinner; and there I took occasion, from the blackness of the meat as it came out of the pot, to fall out with my wife and the maids for their sluttery; and so left the table.' Elizabeth failed to manage the servants, invariably quarrelled with even the most loyal and steadfast of them, and there was a constant turnover. 'Lay long in bed, talking with my wife,' he reported one Sunday in October 1662, 'and among other things, fell out about my mayde Sarah, which my wife would fain put away, when I think her as good a servant as ever came into a house, but it seems my wife would have one that could dress a head well.'

On the morning of 19 December 1664 he rang for the maids. There was such confusion as they stirred themselves that Pepys rebuked his wife for failing to command her servants properly. 'Thereupon she giving me some cross answer I did strike her over the left eye such a blow as the poor wretch did cry out and was in great pain, but yet her spirit was such as to endeavour to bite and scratch me.' He felt sorry afterwards, particularly as he had given her a black eye for all the servants to see.

Both of them were afflicted by jealousy. After the row about Elizabeth's need for a lady's companion in January 1663, Elizabeth took a further month to wear him down before he conceded. They engaged Mary Ashwell, the daughter of one of Pepys's old associates when he was an Exchequer clerk. Mary was a pretty girl, eager to please, good at all fine work such as embroidery, played the harpsichord well, and taught them card games. She was altogether 'a merry jade' and, with a pretty, intelligent girl to talk to and amuse him, Pepys found his home more attractive, while Elizabeth was able to go out more, playing the great lady with Ashwell at her side.

In April Elizabeth started dancing lessons. Dark, handsome Mr Pembleton, the dance tutor, came to the house daily and the room above Pepy's study became a dance hall as the two ladies practised their steps. Elizabeth was so absorbed with her new interest that Pepys had to scold her for 'neglecting the keeping the house clean'. She gave him a pert reply, at which he taunted her for being 'a beggar' because of her lack of dowry, to which she responded 'Pricklouse!' – referring to his origins as the son of a tailor. Clearly, she was getting out of hand. The next day there was another quarrel, because Pepys would not break off a pleasant chat with Ashwell to pay her attention. 'She reproached me that I rather talk with anybody than her – by which I think she is jealous of my freedom with Ashwell – which I must avoid giving occasion of.'

Pepys, too, soon had cause to be jealous. One day he came home in the late afternoon and went upstairs and found his wife and Pembleton alone 'not dancing but talking'. It all seemed to have gone to her head – the lady's companion, the hours spent with Pembleton. She was failing to show him the respect due to a husband, answering him scornfully 'before Ashwell and the rest of the world'. Once he would have struck her for less. 'So that I fear, without great discretion, I shall go near to lose too my command over her; and nothing doth it more than giving her this occasion of dancing and other pleasure, whereby her mind is taken up from her business and finds other sweets besides pleasing of me, and so makes her that she begins not to take pleasure in me or study to please me as heretofore.'

His suspicions were further aroused when Elizabeth took to attending church twice on a Sunday. Pepys soon thought he had discovered the reason. 'I espied Pembleton and saw him leer upon my wife all the sermon . . . and I observed she made a curtsey to him at coming out, without taking notice to me at all of it.' The sooner these dancing lessons came to an end and he sent her off to the country the better, he decided.

On the morning of 26 May he 'lay long in bed, talking and pleasing myself with my wife', before leaving for the office. He did not stay long, however, and when he nipped back home it was to find Pembleton there 'and I am led to conclude that there is something more than ordinary between my wife and him'. All through a business lunch that day, he could not get the idea of Elizabeth and Pembleton out of his head, especially as it was his wife's intention to give all the servants the afternoon off. 'This is my devilish jealousy, which I pray

God may be false, but it makes a very hell in my mind.' He returned to the office but could not concentrate, so went home. Sure enough, there was Pembleton 'with my wife and nobody else in the house, which made me almost mad'. He did not confront them, however, but returned briefly to the office. He left early to find Pembleton still there, which led him to conclude that 'if they had any intentions of hurt, I did prevent doing anything at that time'. He stayed in his study, fuming, until Pembleton left. For good measure, he went up to the bedchamber 'to see whether any of the beds were out of order or no, which I found not; but that did not content me'.

He slept badly and at three o'clock in the morning woke up and 'took occasion by making water to wake my wife'. He began to 'tax her discretion over yesterday's business'. She told him not to be absurd, 'knowing well enough it was my old disease of jealousy, which I disowned, but to no purpose'. It developed into a row, until he was satisfied that although she had been indiscreet, she had not been unfaithful. 'I caressed her and parted seeming friends, but she crying and in great discontent.'

He had not heard the last of it. He came home the following night to find Elizabeth 'in a musty humour'. She embarrassed him by announcing in front of Ashwell that Pembleton had come, but that she would not admit him to the house unless her husband was there. Later, Pembleton returned and Pepys made the best of it by joining the lesson and inviting him to take supper with them, in a vain attempt to show he was not jealous. He put on a show of merriment, but was only too aware that Elizabeth had made a fool of him by exposing his jealousy.

On 15 June it was time to wave Elizabeth and Ashwell off to the country. Pepys carefully gave Ashwell one kiss and Elizabeth several. That night he practised on the violin for a while and then went to bed without supper: 'sad for want of my wife, whom I love with all my heart, though of late she hath given me some troubled thoughts'.

A summer bachelor again, he lost no time in making an assignation with Betty Lane, a buxom wench who ran a stall in Westminster Hall. He took her to a private room in a nearby wine-house, where he ordered lobster and wine, and did 'towse her and feel her all over, making her believe how fair and good a skin she has, and indeed she has a very white thigh and leg, but monstrous fat'. Someone from the street saw them, which 'vexed me – but I believe they could not see my towsing her; and so we broke up'. Pepys furtively left by the back way.

A month later, after chatting up little Betty Howlett, who reminded him of his wife at the same age – 'I could love her very well' – he took Betty Lane to the Crown Tavern in Palace Yard, where they enjoyed a cosy dinner and a bottle of wine. She allowed him 'full liberty of towsing her and doing what I would but the last thing of all'. A few weeks later and they were at it again. 'I did so towse and handle her! But could get nothing more from her though I was very near it; but as wanton and buxom as she is she dares not adventure upon the business, in which I very much commend and like her.'

Elizabeth came home from the country. She had quarrelled both with Pepys's father and with Ashwell, whom she insisted on dismissing. Pepys had no real choice but to let her go.

Elizabeth's abscess was now so bad that the surgeon, Thomas Hollier, wanted to operate, but she was too terrified at the thought of the knife to agree. He decided that a 'fomentation' would suffice, although slower. Elizabeth was a semi-invalid through November and December 1663, insisting that Pepys nurse her, lest the servants thought she had some unmentionable disease. He dined at her bedside, relaying the news and gossip, and reported how pleased they were with one another's company.

When he heard that Betty Lane was married and was now Mrs Martin, it gave him hope. It was always safer to dally with married women in case of unwanted pregnancies – not that Pepys seemed able to father a child. 'I must have a bout with her very shortly, to see how she finds marriage.' He did so at her lodgings the next day, kissing and caressing her, and met her new husband, 'a sorry, simple fellow', a ship's purser. Betty was keen to set up another assignation with Pepys, so that on the following Saturday he took her over to the King's Head Tavern near Lambeth Marsh, where he plied her with food and drink, kissed and 'towsed' her at will, and finally had his 'pleasure of her twice'.

Gradually Pepys was finding sexual independence and growing away from his wife. He still loved her and occasionally desired her,

but with her moods and her various ailments she had become unde-
pendable as a bed-mate. What he wanted from women was not so
much consummation as erotic play and merriment and easy companionship. His pleasure came from being wanton and being wanted.
He felt justified in taking erotic pleasure away from home, perhaps
mindful of the immortal words of Francis Osborne: 'Strangers are
taken for dainties, wives as physick.'

He was growing bolder and not above taking advantage of his
position. A Mrs Bagwell visited him at the office to ask for a small
favour for her husband, a ship's carpenter. A few months later he
journeyed to Deptford to visit the Bagwells, ate and drank wine with
them, and promised Bagwell promotion. Three months later she
came to the office again. He took her into his private office and kissed
her so ardently that she appeared to be offended and rebuked him,
but of course she knew exactly what she was about. She came again a
few weeks later for more of the same and Pepys made an assignation
with her at a tavern. If she was not a fool she must have guessed at
the price of her husband's preferment.

Early in November they met at the Royal Exchange and she
followed him up to a tavern in Moorfields for a meal. That night
he reported in his diary: 'I did there caress her, but though I did
make some offer did not receive any compliance from her in what
was bad, but very modestly she denied me, which I was glad to
see and shall value her the more for it, and I hope never tempt her
to any evil more.' Famous last words! Two weeks later they were
back at Moorfields and he was able to report: 'I did arrive at what I
would, with great pleasure.' On a subsequent occasion he visited the
Bagwells again at Deptford, sent the husband out on a fool's errand,
and coaxed Mrs Bagwell up to the marital bed. Mr Bagwell returned
after 'a decent interval'.

When he encountered Betty Martin again in Westminster Hall,
she was 'great with child' but not *hors de combat*, and he did 'what
he would with her' to his content. No doubt she hoped he would
do something for her husband, although unlike the more calculating
Mrs Bagwell, Betty liked a romp for its own sake. Pepys fell into a
pattern of visiting Betty about twice a month. Probably he was not
her only lover.

Then there was the other Betty, little Betty Howlett, who by now had grown up into 'a handsome wench' and married. Unfortunately for Pepys, Mr Michell the husband was the jealous type and he had to tread carefully. He took the Michells under his wing, as it were, inviting them to his home to dinner. Whenever they went out in the coach together, sometimes even in the company of Elizabeth or Mr Michell, Pepys would take Betty's hand under his cloak and have her touch him, although not to the extent of orgasm. Presumably it was dark. At first she snatched her hand away, but then conceded, although with such reluctance that she evidently found it distasteful. Eventually, she plucked up the courage to tell him she did not like 'touching'.

On another occasion he called at the Michells' spirit shop in Thames Street and persuaded Michell to allow his wife to meet him and Elizabeth that day at the New Exchange. Of course, when Betty arrived there was no Elizabeth. He took Betty across the river, where he spent twenty shillings on a dressing box for her, and was flattered when the shopkeeper took the pregnant Betty for his wife. The whole business took so long that Pepys feared that Michell would send round to Seething Lane for Betty and discover the ruse. He delivered Betty within a short walk of the Thames Street shop and rushed home, just as Michell's servant reached the door, so heading her off from alerting Elizabeth. Whether Michell grew suspicious or Betty only pretended he was, it was all the excuse she needed to put a stop to Pepys's advances.

Although he liked to record his conquests, Pepys was never confident with women. He listened with awe at the sophisticated banter of the *beaux* he encountered at court or the theatre. He was under the illusion that the women he chased enjoyed his attentions, when in reality most of them were probably just enduring it. Few people have ever described their triumphs and reverses in the sexual field as openly and honestly as Pepys.

So far Elizabeth was happily ignorant of her husband's infidelities. Her antennae were more attuned to any perceived signs of husbandly neglect. By the late 1660s they appeared to have reached a *modus vivendi*. He had learned that whenever they fell out to restrain his temper and let her have her way, whenever he could do so without loss of authority. As long as she obeyed him, lived thriftily and discreetly, and attended to her wifely duties, he was content; he made few other demands on her. In return Elizabeth was content as long as she had her share of outings and parties, new clothes and the occasional treat, such as the £80 pearl necklace which he had long promised and finally bought her.

In the autumn of 1667 this tenuous balance in the power play of husband and wife was violently overturned by the arrival of Deborah Willett, who joined the household as a new companion for Elizabeth. She was pretty and petite, a seventeen-year-old orphan straight out of boarding school. Both the Pepys were fond of her, indulging her like a daughter. When Pepys began to make his usual advances, starting with a kiss, she did not resist. After all, she must have reasoned, Mr Pepys had been kind to her and she liked him. Elizabeth noticed his interest and Pepys feared 'she is already jealous of my kindness to her, so that I begin to fear this girl is not likely to stay long with us.'

It was normal for one of the 'family' to help with washing and dressing, so that one night at the end of March 1668 when Pepys was going to bed and Deb 'undressed me', he took the opportunity to kiss her and 'yo did take her, the first time in my life, sobra mi genu and did poner mi mano sub her jupes and toca su thing, which did hazer me great pleasure; and so did no more, but besando-la went to my bed.' Pepys loved to resort to foreign-speak when he was describing a sexual encounter; on this occasion he had placed his hands up her skirts and touched the girl's private parts, which gave him much pleasure.

It was one thing to have the odd grope with the maids, Jane Birch or Mary Mercer. That was the hazard servants routinely ran and many a mistress turned a blind eye. It was quite another to seduce the wife's companion, an innocent young woman of only seventeen living under one's own roof. Towards the end of October 1668 Elizabeth finally caught Samuel *in flagrante delicto*. He admits the incident 'occasioned the greatest sorrow to me that ever I knew in this world'. After supper Pepys had gone upstairs to have his head combed by Deb. He was embracing the girl and had his hand up her skirt − 'endeed, I was with my main in her cunny' − when Elizabeth silently appeared. The couple were struck dumb and it was a while before a shocked Elizabeth found her voice and started screaming.

They went to bed, but Elizabeth could not sleep and about two in the morning woke him. She told him she was secretly a Roman Catholic, which in the fiercely anti-papist London of 1668 was guaranteed to fill him with horror. The trouble was that as she rambled on Pepys could not be quite sure just what Elizabeth had seen. Wisely, he kept his mouth shut. After she had cried and reproached him 'with inconstancy and preferring a sorry girl before her, I did give her no provocations but did promise all fair usage to her, and love, and foreswore any hurt that I did with her – till at last she seemed to be at ease again'. Just before daybreak he managed to snatch some sleep, before rising wearily and going to the office, his mind 'mightily troubled for the poor girl, whom I fear I have undone by this, my wife telling me that she would turn her out of the door'.

When he returned home that night after a demanding day's work, it was to find his wife and Deb on frosty terms. Yet again, Elizabeth woke him in the small hours to hurl accusations at him, confirming that she had seen him hug and kiss the girl. Ah! So that was all, then. Smoothly, he admitted the first and denied the latter. The following night he had to prepare for an important meeting with the Duke of York, but once again Elizabeth kept them awake half the night 'in a mighty rage from some new matter that she had got in her head, and did most part of the night in bed rant at me in most high terms, of threats of publishing my shame'. In Restoration London broadcasting a husband's infidelity would have made about as much impact as throwing a goldfish into the Atlantic. He did regret his indiscretion with the girl, or, more correctly, he regretted being caught. He did not want to lose her, but he was more concerned that 'the poor girl should be undone by my folly'.

By the beginning of November Pepys admitted ruefully to himself that it would be better if the girl were gone, 'for my wife's peace and mine; for she cannot but be offended at the sight of her, my wife having conceived this jealousy of me with reason'. He hardly dared look at Deb, Elizabeth had become so vigilant. Night after night his sleep was disturbed by Elizabeth's ranting. One day he managed to pass a note to Deb advising her that he had denied he had ever kissed her, so that she could confirm the same; she nodded to him and returned the note. It was just as well they were singing from the same hymn sheet, as Elizabeth was determined to extract a confession from the girl.

On 12 November Elizabeth had Pepys dismiss Deb, which troubled him greatly, not least because 'I have a great mind for to have the maidenhead of this girl, which I should not doubt to have – but she will be gone and I know not whither.' He wanted to slip her some money on the last morning, but Elizabeth was watching him like a hawk. The only compensation for the whole business was that Elizabeth had shown more sexual interest in him than she had done for at least a year and they had made love 'with more pleasure to her than I think in all the time of our marriage before'.

In the wake of Deb's departure Elizabeth was far too jealous to allow Pepys out of her sight 'for fear of my going to Deb'. He denied it, but of course he was frantically looking for her. Finally, on 18 November he tracked her down. He invited her into his coach and 'yo did besar her and tocar her thing, but ella was against it and laboured with much earnestness, such as I believed to be real; and yet at last yo did make her ener mi cosa in her mano, while me mano was sobra her pectus, and so did hazer her with great delight.' In plain English, she held his penis in her hand while he placed his hand on her private parts and so brought them both to pleasure. Afterwards he gave her a stern warning to guard her honour, fear God and suffer no man to do with her what he had just done. The hypocrisy of it! To top it all, he gave her twenty shillings, as if she were a whore.

Elizabeth knew just what had happened and there was a mighty row. He confessed all, enduring her 'threats and vows and curses all the afternoon'. She swore that she would slit the girl's nose and demanded a few hundred pounds 'to buy my peace, that she might be gone without making any noise, or else protested that she would make all the world know of it'. He was never to go out alone again, but always be accompanied either by Elizabeth or the faithful Will Hewer. It was the afternoon from hell for Pepys. That night he and Elizabeth made love, despite the fact that she had not washed for the duration of the Deb turmoil, and he prayed to God to make him faithful to his wife, there being 'no curse in the world so great as this of the difference between myself and her'.

Deb was the one girl Pepys did fall in love with and it took him a long time to get her out of his system. He glimpsed her once walking in a group. She winked.

The year 1668 ended with 'mutual peace and content', however, and Pepys vowed never to repeat his folly. There was an equally serious concern now that his eyesight was failing. The Duke of York agreed he should take a long leave to give his eyes a rest. This is where the diary ends. He decided to give Elizabeth her longed-for wish, by taking her back to France for a holiday. It was on their return journey to London that she began to feel unwell. She went straight to bed at Seething Lane and became feverish. It was probably typhoid fever. She died three weeks later on 10 November 1669. She was only twenty-nine.

Three nights later, she was laid to rest under the chancel at St Olave's. No doubt remembering her beauty and his love for her, and lamenting his shortcomings as a husband, Pepys grieved, before resuming life. He did not join her there for another thirty-four years.

INTERLUDE

Henri Misson on English marriage customs

The Frenchman Henri Misson, visiting London in the late 1690s, was a keen observer of English customs, especially marriage:

> And when bed time is come the bride men pull off the bride's garters, which she had before unty'd that they might hang down, and so prevent a curious hand coming too near her knee. This done, and the garters being fastened to the hats of the gallants, the bride maids carry the bride into the bed chamber, where they undress her, and lay her in bed. The bridegroom, who by the help of his friends is undress'd in some other room, comes in his nightgown as soon as possible to his spouse, who is surrounded by mother, aunt, sisters, and friends, and without further ceremony gets into bed . . . The bridemen take the bride's stockings, and the bride maids the bridegroom's; both sit down at the bed's feet and fling the stockings over their heads, endeavouring to direct them so as that they may fall upon the marry'd couple. If the man's stockings, thrown by the maid, fall upon the bridegroom's head, it is a sign she will quickly be marry'd herself; and the same prognostick holds good of the woman's stockings thrown by the man.

When undressing the bride, the bridesmaids had to be sure to remove every pin and dispose of it. To keep one was very bad luck and meant that the culprit would not be married before Whitsuntide. Bride lace (ribbons) and knots (ribbon bows) were distributed as favours among the guests and worn on hats for several weeks. Gloves and scarves were also distributed as favours. Some brides wore gloves to bed, their removal symbolizing the loss of virginity. Finally, the bridal couple was given a posset – a potion made of milk, wine, egg yolk, sugar, cinnamon and nutmeg. They would try to swallow this as quickly as possible so as to 'get rid of the troublesome company'.

8

'The bargain was struck'

O N TUESDAY, 17 January 1707 the Yorkshire baronet Sir Walter
Calverley noted with relief in his pocket book: 'I was married
to Mistress Julia Blackett, the eldest daughter of Sir William Blackett,
in St Andrew's Church, in Newcastle, by Mr Thomlinson, before my
Lady, Sir William Blackett, Mistress Elizabeth Blackett, and Mistress
Frances Blackett, brother and sisters to the young lady, my nephew
Thompson Wade, Mr Wilkinson and others, about eleven in the
forenoon.'

The pocket book gives no inkling whatsoever of his feelings for his
bride; all Sir Walter's energies had been taken up with the settlement,
which had been negotiated over many months. For the upper classes,
whose marriages were arranged between respective parents and their
lawyers, there was little wooing. Playwrights of the age found fertile
ground for satire in the cold-blooded nature of the arrangements.
As Henry Fielding's Sir Positive Trap expressed it: 'I never saw my
lady . . . till an hour before our marriage. I made my addresses to
her father, her father to his lawyer, the lawyer to my estate . . . the
bargain was struck. What need have young people of addressing, or
anything, till they come to undressing?'

We do not know where Sir Walter met Julia Blackett. Perhaps it
was in London, which by now had established itself as the national
marriage market. The elite flocked to town for the season. Here their
marriageable children could mingle within a prescribed social circle
and meet potential marriage partners from outside their limited rural
confines. Or perhaps the couple met at one of the fashionable spas,
such as Bath or Buxton, or more locally, through the network of
'friends'.

The pocket book tells us only that in the summer of 1706 Sir

Walter made several trips over to Newcastle, where he 'dined and supped at Lady Blackett's'. It was not until the beginning of October that 'the match was agreed upon, and I signed proposals in order to a settlement for marriage'.

By the early eighteenth century the costs of marriage were spiralling and it was necessary to buy into marriage as never before. Money was the key. 'What will she bring is the first enquiry? How many acres? Or how much ready coin?' the early feminist Mary Astell noted sadly. Of course money was important, she argued, but it must not be the only consideration. Marriage should be based on a reasoned choice and, above all, on friendship. The dissenter Daniel Defoe deplored the absence of love: 'Ask the ladies why they marry, they tell you 'tis for a good settlement . . . Ask the men why they marry, it is for the money . . . How little is regarded of that one essential and absolutely necessary part of the composition, called love.' Making wedding vows before God to love each other when love was completely absent, he declared, made a travesty of marriage.

Mercenary marriages did not bring happiness, the *Spectator* warned, but encouraged vice and excess: 'Men rather seek for money as the complement of all their desires; and regardless of what kind of wives they take, they think riches will be a minister to all kinds of pleasures, and enable them to keep mistresses, horses, hounds, to drink, feast, and game with their companions, pay their debts contracted by former extravagancies, or some such vile and unworthy end.'

If only women received a better education, Astell reflected, they would not be caught in this marriage trap. As it was, a girl was taught that her only goal was to get a husband. The *Spectator* concurred:

> When a girl is safely brought from her nurse, before she is capable of forming one simple notion of any thing in life, she is delivered to the hands of her dancing-master and with a collar round her neck, the pretty wild thing is taught a fantastical gravity of behaviour, and forced to a particular way of holding her head, heaving her breast, and moving with her whole body, and all this under pain of never having a husband, if she steps, looks or moves awry.

Defoe describes men literally shopping for a wealthy wife, while, spurred on by their ambitious mothers and conscious of the fact that they could not afford to turn down too many suitors, there was fierce competition among young women to 'catch' a husband. With an inverse ratio of ten men to thirteen women, those without money were at a distinct disadvantage, as Defoe's fictional heroine Moll Flanders was quick to notice: 'The market is against our sex just now and if a young woman have beauty, birth, breeding, wit, sense, manners, modesty, and all these to extreme, yet if she hath not money, she's nobody, she had as good want them all, for nothing but money recommends a woman.'

In this money-driven society, marriage settlements had become more complex, with the terms drawn up and thrashed out as in any other business transaction. Portions had become dearer and settlements – the sum provided for a woman's maintenance if her husband should predecease her – were being driven down. Since on marriage everything a woman owned became her husband's to control as he pleased, clever lawyers were now taking steps, before her engagement, to convey at least a proportion of her property to trustees, so that it could be preserved for her use or that of her heirs. A married woman could not write a will, but this did not apply to property held in trust.

Separate trusts were a first, very tentative step towards a married woman's property law. Needless to say, they were not well received. There are innumerable cases of husbands mistreating their wives in order to force them to rescind a trust. As one eminent judge later remarked, 'he had hardly known an instance where the wife had not been kissed or kicked out of any such previous settlement'.

There was also the vexed question of pin-money, a small allowance allotted to a wife as her spending money. For many men, this was the thin end of the wedge.

'Separate purses between man and wife are as unnatural as separate beds,' thundered the *Spectator*. 'Furnishing a man's wife with pin-money is furnishing her with arms against himself.' Women were becoming like generals who never engage in battle without securing a retreat, arguing 'that it is but a necessary provision they make for themselves, in case their husbands prove a churl or a miser, so that they consider this allowance as a kind of alimony, which they may lay their claim to, without actually separating from their husbands'.

Not only was pin-money seen as a threat, but also a disgrace. 'I could therefore wish, for the honour of my country women, that they had rather called it needle-money,' another contributor moaned, 'which might have implied something of good housewifery, and not have given the malicious world occasion to think that dress and trifles have always the uppermost place in women's thoughts.'

Many a marriage settlement foundered on the shoals of pin-money, but Sir Walter's negotiations moved slowly forward. In November he took Samuel Hemingway with him to Newcastle 'to assist about matters' and

> staid most of three weeks, and the draft was made very long, but not then fully agreed to, though we had counsel of both sides, and several meetings, both of Mr Wilkinson, Mr Thomlinson, and the counsel, and at some of them I was also present myself. They made use of Mr John Ord for drawing the writings, and Mr Barnes counsel for my Lady; and I had Mr John Cuthberts, the recorder of Newcastle for my counsel, but the matter was not concluded, upon account of some scruples about the young lady's portion, when it would be due and payable.

Lady Blackett had to send to London to take 'advice about the portion . . . and had opinion that it was payable upon marriage'. Mr Poley, however, raised the question of the interest payable if the portion was not immediately forthcoming. Mr Vernon 'seemed to advise for a decree to confirm matters', while Mr Thornton 'to make the payment more secure, advised two or three years time to be set for payment of the portion, with interest, and if not paid in that time, the settlement to be void'. By this, he meant not the entire marriage settlement, but the amount that had been agreed for Lady Calverley's jointure in the event of her widowhood. It was suggested that Lady Blackett 'obtain a decree for mortgaging', that is, take out a mortgage on her land in order to raise the cash portion immediately, 'but she would not consent to it'.

And so matters dragged on, until just before Christmas Sir Walter graciously decided to be satisfied with Lady Blackett's and Mr Wilkinson's promise alone for payment of the portion. The settlement, which had taken months and the expense of several lawyers to negotiate, amounted to over 10,000 words.

Sir Walter still had all the costs of the wedding to meet. He gave the clergyman Mr Thomlinson, for officiating and 'for the trouble also which I had given him, in lodging at his house for all the times before, and other kindnesses', a purse of guineas. 'My Lady was at cost of entertaining all friends and relations', but, as was customary, Sir Walter gave them all gloves. He also distributed 16 guineas to the servants. He and his mother 'were at cost of a fine set of dressing plate for my wife, came to £116 odd money. And I paid for a pair of earrings for her 130 shillings, and a bill for gloves bought at London, £15-6s 6d, and for a new coach £82-7s, and for velvet for lining it £30-7s.' The smart new coach had to have 'new coach mares' at a cost of £50. Finally, 'it cost me for my own wedding clothes and a long wig and liveries, etc, near £300.'

It was not until March that he set out 'with my wife in our own coach' for Yorkshire. On 18 December 1707 she fulfilled her duty and gave birth to a son.

9

'My circumstances were not proper at all for matrimony'

IN 1716 DUDLEY Ryder, the second son of a prosperous linen draper, was a law student living at home in London. He was already twenty-five and inevitably his thoughts ran on marriage, although he was not sure that 'the sorrows and cares and burdens to which it exposes a man' were sufficiently balanced by its 'joys and pleasures'. As he confided in his diary:

> I wish I could reason myself into an easy state of mind under the thoughts of being never married, but I feel a strong inclination towards it, not from any principle of lust or desire to enjoy a woman in bed but for a natural tendency, a prepossession in favour of the married state. It is charming and moving, it ravishes me to think of a pretty creature concerned in me, being my most intimate friend, constant companion and always ready to soothe me, take care of me and caress me.

Ryder had clear views about the qualities he desired in a wife, not least drawn from observing the behaviour of the women around him. He was concerned 'to see my mother so peevish and fretful, continually saying some ill-natured thing or other to my father or the maid. I will endeavour if possible not to have a fretful uneasy wife.' His sister was even worse. She was spoilt and petulant and constantly irritable, taking it out on her husband. 'I pity him,' Dudley wrote. 'Such a temper is the worst thing can be in a wife. I am resolved therefore to be very careful as to the temper of the woman I choose to be my wife. It is of the greatest consequence to my peace and happiness to have her of a meek, humble and modest one.'

Foreign visitors to England were amazed at the freedom of young people of the middling sort to mingle with the opposite sex. Indeed,

England was distinctive for its sexual *laissez-faire*. A Twelfth Day party attended by the sons and daughters of London tradesmen described in Dudley's diary of 1716 suggests a very free and easy atmosphere. They 'passed the afternoon and evening at cards during which we were very merry'. The young men kissed their partners 'very much'. Then they 'played at blind man's buff and puss in the corner' and 'more kissing' went on. Ryder envied his brother's way with women. 'His talk with them is prodigiously silly . . . by what I can perceive, though they despise him for his parts, they love his company because he is free with them and kisses and tumbles them about and makes a mighty noise with them.'

Kissing seems to have been as far as it went on this occasion, although bundling, or sexual play usually but not always stopping short of full intercourse, seems to have been accepted practice among a broad swathe of the middling sort, even up to the ranks of the minor gentry, and the poor. Where there was no question of an inheritance or little or no property involved, the attitude to premarital chastity was relaxed. After a betrothal or an exchange of verbal promises many couples tended to consider themselves 'married in the eyes of God' and anticipated the wedding night. Others might 'bundle' with several partners, which was one reason why so many were opting to marry by licence, rather than going through the humiliation of having banns read in their parish church to the titters of those friends and neighbours who knew of their previous sexual liaisons.

Up until the civil war, the authorities had been assiduous in forcing cohabiting couples to marry and discouraging sex outside marriage. During the Interregnum there had been an even more determined effort to enforce sexual morality. The Act of 1650 made adultery and incest felonies punishable by death, while fornication drew a three-month gaol sentence, but with the return of the monarchy the Act was allowed to lapse. In the sexually abandoned atmosphere of the Restoration, moral standards underwent a sharp decline, while the Church's 'bawdy' courts seemed to have lost their efficacy.

Between the Reformation and the dawn of Victorian respectability more than one in six English brides was pregnant before marriage; that is to say, baptism of their first child took place within nine months of the wedding. The incidence of premarital pregnancy rose steeply in the course of the eighteenth century, to about 40 per cent of all marriages. In most cases the pregnancy anticipated rather than precipitated the marriage. In a predominantly rural society, premarital sex was often regarded as a fertility trial: if the woman did not become pregnant, the couple went their separate ways.

Neither the Church nor the secular authorities condoned premarital pregnancy: the first because fornication was a sin which earned the humiliation of public penance, and the second because the upkeep of an illegitimate child would most likely fall on the parish. A close eye was kept on the dates of the wedding night and the arrival of the first child. In 1780 a Norfolk vicar even offered his female parishioners an incentive. If the birth of the first child occurred nine months *after* the wedding he would give the woman 'ten shillings for ye christening dinner and also a silver plate of ten shillings value to be worn upon her breast every Sunday when she comes to church, with this inscription – "The Reward of Chastity".'

Whenever Dudley and his male friends discussed sex, he sought out prostitutes in the streets: 'I was so raised with our discourse about women that I was extremely inclined that way and looked for a whore with a resolution not to lie with her but to feel her if I could.' He was always full of remorse afterwards, even if he never had full intercourse, and he had another worry:

> But there was one thing troubled me extremely and lay heavy upon my mind, and that was the apprehension I was under that I was not capable of getting my wife with child if I had one. I find myself not very powerful that way and it makes me very uneasy to think my wife should have reason to complain, that I could almost resolve not to marry, but I don't know how to conceive of being happy in this life without one.

In April 1716 he was riding beside his sister's coach on the first leg of her journey to Bath, when he spied Mrs Sally Marshall (Mistress was used as a courtesy title, denoting rank not marital status) inside the coach and was immediately taken with her appearance. It was particularly satisfying that every time he stole a look at Mistress Marshall he found her eyes 'turned upon me'.

He became so infatuated with her over the succeeding months that it was almost impossible to concentrate on his work: 'Read law all the morning till 10 o'clock,' he noted one morning in July, 'but my mind runs so much upon Mrs Marshall that I could scarce mind what I read or comprehend anything.' He rehearsed the proposal of marriage he would make to her, but it was all wishful thinking, for he knew very well that as a man hardly even on the threshold of his career, the circumstances were 'not proper at all for matrimony'.

Marriage represented the transition from irresponsible youth to adult maturity, when a man and his wife set up their own household, with all its privileges, burdens and responsibilities. Early marriage, Daniel Defoe argued in *The Complete Tradesman*, was improvident and a sure way to ruin. A man had to establish some 'bottom' before taking a wife. This meant that he had to be out of his seven-year apprenticeship – apprentices were forbidden to marry – or to have completed his studies, and to have set himself up in business or a career with some money behind him, before he could even think of marriage. He might be in his late twenties or early thirties and he would probably be looking for a wife ten years or so younger. Dudley Ryder, in his mid-twenties and a graduate of the universities of Edinburgh and Leyden (as a dissenter, he was excluded from the English universities), was beginning to realize the impracticality of his plans for marriage and echoed Defoe's sentiments: 'I thought my circumstances were not proper at all for matrimony at present. If she has but a small fortune it would ruin me to marry her, keep me low in the world and prevent my rise. And if she has a considerable fortune her father would never consent I should have her without a [proportionate] fortune.'

Sally Marshall was the daughter of a Highgate tailor of moderate means, but she had some pretty ambitious ideas as to what she expected from marriage: 'It gave me a great deal of discouragement in my love for Mrs Marshall that upon talking of charges of keeping house and living genteelly, she said that £400 or £500 a year would but just maintain a family handsomely in London. And I believe Mrs Marshall is one that will never marry unless she can be maintained genteelly and handsomely.'

A man of Dudley Ryder's social standing was free to make his own choice of marriage partner without parental interference; parents should be consulted, if only out of courtesy, but they recognized their children's right to choose whom they married. Money was important, but unlike in the arranged upper-class marriage, it was not paramount. Love, or at least a deep affection, and compatibility were the prime considerations in the 'companionate' marriage. Of course, this raised the stakes of what was expected of the marriage. Significantly, Dudley's father was willing to help if he was 'so deeply engaged in love as to interrupt my study or that I could not be easy without her', but he hardly had the means. He had already spent a considerable amount setting up his other son as a married man.

Dudley describes a painful meeting between his father and his brother's prospective in-laws, the sort of meeting that must have been repeated in so many homes of the middling sort:

> I enquired about what my father had done concerning brother William's marriage with Mrs Burton, for he had been to meet her yesterday at her son-in-law's, Mr Atwell. When he came they sat silent for a little while before anybody opened and then my father began. He put it upon this foot, that whatever fortune she had he would give his son equal, and desired to know what she had. They refused to tell that, but asked him what he had heard. He said £1000 or £1500. He said she had that, but this finished the conversation, only that Mr Atwell said the man ought to have double the woman's fortune . . . nothing at all was done and my father parted telling her that whenever she should think fit he should be glad to wait upon her.

In fact, Mr Ryder had decided that if 'she has £1500 he would settle £100 per annum in houses [from rent on property he owned] upon William and her instead of an estate in money equivalent, since her £1500 would be sufficient to employ in trade'. We are not told what William's employment was, but obviously London tradesmen preferred to have ready cash to employ in the business, unlike the gentry, who relied on the rents from land to make up their portions and pay their jointures.

Sadly for Dudley, William's settlement meant that their father would not be able to give him 'anything at all till after his death and after mother's death . . . this is what I cannot be pleased with at all, since it will quite destroy my prospect of marrying and keep me low as long as he and mother live.'

We do not know how long Dudley's parents lived. If Dudley was in his mid-twenties, their marriage had already lasted longer than the average seventeenth- or eighteenth-century marriage. We do know, however, that it was not until 1728 that Dudley met his ideal wife, Anne Newnham of Streatham, at a concert. He married her in 1734 when he was forty-three. By this time he was a successful lawyer and presumably needed no help from his family. He also had a more mature view of the purpose of marriage, writing to her: 'I look upon matrimony, as it really is, not only as a society for life, in which our persons and fortunes in general are concerned, but as a partnership wherein our very passions and affections, our hopes and fears, our inclinations and aversions, all our good and ill qualities are brought in one common stock.'

As Attorney-General, Sir Dudley Ryder introduced Lord Hardwicke's Marriage Bill into the Commons in 1753. The following year he became a Privy Counsellor and Lord Chief Justice of the King's Bench, but died the night before he was to receive a peerage.

The Church maintained that mutual consent was necessary to make a marriage, and no one else's permission was required. In 1753, however, parliament introduced a parental veto on the marriages of all children under 21. This was to prevent the children of the ruling class from making impetuous marriages with persons of inferior rank or fortune. The only option was to elope

. Feb. 1476-7. 16 Eiv.

Above: By February 1477 the negotiations for a marriage between Margery Brews and John Paston had reached a critical point. Margery seized the opportunity afforded by Valentine's Day to write to John. 'Right reverend and worshipful, and my right well beloved Valentine,' she began, urging him to settle with her father, as no more money would be forthcoming, 'But if that ye love me, as I trust verily that ye do, ye will not leave me therefore'

Middle: John Paston's sister, Margery, made a secret, irrevocable vow to marry Richard Calle, the family's bailiff, and subsequently received the blessing of a priest in church. The family disowned her for marrying beneath her

A Gentleman about 30 Years of Age, that says He has a Very Good Estate, would willingly Match Himself to some Good Young Gentlewoman, that has a Fortune of 3000 l. or thereabout, and he will make Settlement to Content.

VVhen it shall appear that I am Candid, and no otherwise concerned than in bringing two Elderly Persons to a Treaty; and the Nine Days VVonder and Laughter (usually attending new things) are over, and that no body shall know any thing of the matter, but where I shall reasonably believe they are in good earnest; then 'tis probable such Advertisements may prove very useful.

Left: Professional matchmakers were rare in England, but by the end of the seventeenth century a burgeoning newspaper industry was publishing agony aunt letters and lonely hearts columns. This is the first such advertisement

Right: This illustration from
Aphra Behn's satirical *The Ten
Pleasures of Marriage* shows
the moneymen still at the table
at the conclusion of the
settlement, the happy couple,
and the marriage feast
underway in the background

Below: A Fleet parson greets a
bridal couple. He will perform
a 'clandestine' marriage
ceremony – one which is
illicit, but valid in the eyes of
the Church. The irregularity
of a Fleet marriage
encouraged all sorts of abuses
and subsequently it could be
difficult to prove in court.
Note the market trader
symbolically selling rue

Above left: It was impossible to conduct an affair without the servants finding out. They were forever snooping, listening at keyholes and examining the bed sheets. Servants often testified against their employers in trials for adultery

Below left: An angry husband finds his wife committing 'the foul crime of adultery'. He may bring a case of criminal conversation against her lover, suing him for pecuniary damages for encroaching on his property (his wife)

Above right: The marriage contract is agreed; the haggling is over, the money has changed hands. The lawyers are busy in the background, while the betrothed couple reveal their utter indifference to each other

Below right: The notorious career of Teresia Constantia Phillips served to highlight the abuses in the marriage system. Like Hogarth's harlot, she found herself prey to the dishonest and unscrupulous. She spent much of her life mired in litigation and pursued by creditors. Here the magistrate arrives with a warrant

Violence, fuelled by high alcohol consumption, was commonplace among all sections of society. Servants or neighbours tended to intervene if the woman seemed to be in danger of her life

After clandestine marriage was outlawed in England in 1753 the trade moved to Scotland – Gretna Green being a popular venue – where such marriages could still be performed. They had to be conducted in haste, sometimes in a smithy – 'striking while the iron's hot' – to outrun parents or guardians who pursued the couple

Wife-sale was a popular form of self-divorce among the poor. A husband would put a halter about his wife's neck and auction her on a busy market day, just as he would a cow

This country wedding is simple, natural and joyous. The bridal procession was traditionally accompanied by musicians. Note the bride wears a hat rather than a veil

A girl must never appear clever or too well educated, which was deemed off-putting in the marriage market. What little education she received was totally with the aim of securing a husband: 'a girl is delivered into the hands of her dancing-master … the pretty wild thing is taught a particular way of holding her head and moving with her whole body, and all this under pain of never having a husband, if she steps, looks or moves awry'

The purpose of marriage was procreation. Contraception was frowned upon and most people were ignorant of it, at least until the late Victorian period when the rich, followed by the professional middle class, began to limit the size of their families. A married woman could look forward to a constant succession of pregnancies during the twenty years or so of fertility following marriage – that is, if she did not die in childbirth

IO

'Nothing but adultery can dissolve a marriage'

IN THE EARLY eighteenth century two couples locked in sexless marriages appeared before the courts. Neither had consummated their marriage. In one case, they could if they would; in the other, they would if they could.

In 1700 George Downing, aged fifteen, was married to thirteen-year-old Mary Forester. The marriage was arranged by parents and guardians — George's father was mentally incapacitated — and the couple had never seen each other before. After the ceremony, they were duly 'put to bed in the daytime, according to custom, and continued there a little while, but in the presence of the company, who all testify they touched not one the other; and after that they came together no more.'

Like so many young men of his social standing, George was sent abroad for the Grand Tour, while Mary remained with her parents. Three years later George returned to England. It was expected that he and Mary would start to live together as husband and wife. George adamantly refused, declaring that 'he would never complete the marriage'.

By 1715 the couple had 'contracted an incurable aversion to each other' and were 'very desirous to be set at liberty'. They wished to 'dissolve this marriage, and to give each party leave, if they think fit, to marry elsewhere'.

The Church would grant a divorce *a mensa et thoro* only on grounds of proven adultery and cruelty, and clearly this was not the case with the Downings. Besides, this did not mean divorce in the modern sense; it simply meant what later came to be termed a judicial separation, without permission to remarry. Another means of escape beckoned — a private Act of Parliament, which offered a divorce *a vinculo matrimonii*, allowing both parties to remarry – but the catch was that the applicants had to have first obtained a divorce *a mensa et thoro* from the ecclesiastical court.

Since England had the distinction of being the only Protestant country in Europe that had failed to offer some form of legalized divorce with permission to remarry, at least for the innocent party, the rich and powerful had devised their own means of escape: parliamentary divorce. It seemed to offer a precedent for the Downings.

In the 1660s John Manners, Lord Roos, heir to the Earl of Rutland, brought the first case before the House of Lords. He had married Anne Pierrepont, daughter and co-heiress of the Marquis of Dorchester, in 1658. John seems to have been a bit of a mother's boy, because soon after the marriage Anne's husband sided with his mother against her in a row over whether she should be wearing tight stays in the early stages of pregnancy. When she ignored their advice, they proceeded to spend Christmas at Belvoir without her, leaving her behind at Haddon with a handful of servants. She gave birth to a daughter, who died, and unable to tolerate the quarrels with her husband and mother-in-law and his debauched behaviour when in his cups any longer, she returned to her father's house, taking her jewels and plate, worth about £5,000.

The reason so many marriages held together was the support they received from a wide network of family and 'friends', who at the first signs of trouble banded together to iron out problems or effect reconciliation. With virtually no avenues of escape from an unhappy marriage, a couple's only option was to patch up their differences and make the best of it. After a formal reconciliation arranged between the two families, Anne returned to her husband's house, but her father, either as a precaution or out of greed, retained her jewels and plate. The Manners were furious and Roos – no doubt at the instigation of his mother – vowed that he would never get 'between the sheets' with his wife until the valuables were returned.

Somebody got between the sheets with her, however, because Anne was soon pregnant again. She claimed that Roos had come to her and proposed that if they had intercourse on the top of the bed, rather than in between the sheets, he would not be breaking his vow. Given that she usually had to rouse him by dressing up in boy's clothes, and that he was normally so inebriated that he could not perform, his sudden enthusiasm is questionable. Certainly Roos maintained that the child was not his and Anne did not help her case by taunting him in the heat of an argument, 'A better man than you got it. I will make you father it in this world, and let me answer for it in the world to come,' before exiting the room singing 'Cuckolds all in a row'.

During her pregnancy Anne was kept locked in a room without ink and paper and at her confinement Roos or his mother used the time-worn tactic of employing a midwife to interrogate Anne in her agony to reveal the identity of the child's father. She stoically gave nothing away, but Roos had his revenge by naming the child Ignotus.

Dorchester lobbied for his daughter's release and the couple were examined before the Privy Council. Since Anne's adultery could not be proved, a private separation was suggested, but before any agreement could be reached Anne became pregnant again. There could be no question of her adultery this time and John successfully obtained a divorce *a mensa et thoro* in the Court of Arches, with the proviso that he could not remarry during Anne's lifetime.

There remained the problem of Ignotus and his unresolved legitimacy. He stood to inherit the Rutland title and estates unless Roos succeeded in disowning him. In 1663 Roos introduced a private bill into the Lords 'for illegitimating of a child called Ignotus born of the body of Anne, Lady Roos'. Since Anne was pregnant yet again, the bill slid through without a murmur. But now Roos wanted Parliament to pass an enabling Act to allow him to remarry, in spite of the fact that he had given bond to the ecclesiastical court not to remarry. After all, a great estate was involved and it needed a male heir. If it concerned property, the Lords were interested. They sat up and listened.

The case prompted an intense debate in the Lords, with Bishop Cosin of Durham arguing for the adoption of the terms originally drafted by Cranmer in the *Reformatio Legum Ecclesiasticorum* – that is, full divorce on grounds of adultery, cruelty or desertion, with permission, at least for the innocent party, to remarry. He rehearsed the arguments of the sixteenth-century reformers, that adultery or malicious desertion broke the matrimonial bond. A mere separation from bed and board without permission to remarry only encouraged further adultery, bigamous unions and illegitimacy. He and his fellow conservatives did not go so far as to adopt the radical Puritan view, notably proposed by John Milton in his *Doctrine and Discipline of Divorce*, that mere incompatibility justified divorce.

This would have been the moment to bring the English divorce laws into line with the rest of Protestant Europe, but both the Lords and Convocation hesitated to open the floodgates. The idea that marriage was indissoluble was deeply ingrained. Instead, the Lords opted to pass private Acts for specific cases, where a wife's adultery placed a great estate in danger of being passed to 'spurious issue'. This completely illogical decision in favour of the elite in a society where divorce was otherwise prohibited was one of the anomalies of the English marriage.

With Charles II attending the proceedings and declaring the recounting of Lady Roos's promiscuous exploits as good as a play, Roos won his case. It was followed in the 1690s by the notorious Norfolk case. The duke wished to rid himself of his childless duchess. The fact that he was a Protestant supporter of the Glorious Revolution and she was a Catholic Jacobite and that the next Howard heir was also a Catholic gave these proceedings a political edge: heaven forbid that the premier dukedom should fall into Catholic hands. The duke must be free to remarry.

Unfortunately, the duke had not troubled to approach the ecclesiastical court for a separation *a mensa et thoro*, even though it had emerged that the duchess had discreetly taken a lover, John Germain, a Dutch officer rumoured to be the bastard half-brother of the new King, William III. Norfolk was so flagrantly unfaithful to his wife that he would have been hard put to convince the court of the veracity of his case. Neither the Church nor indeed the House of Lords wished to condone or reward adultery.

The Lords were split along political lines, since the Anglican Tory bishops and Tory, crypto-Catholic peers naturally supported the duchess, while the Whig bishops – among them Burnet, a strong advocate of the argument that adultery negated the marriage contract – and peers rallied behind Norfolk. Even so, his bill was defeated.

Given the mercenary nature of the age, a cuckolded husband was less likely to fight a duel than to bring a case of criminal conversation – 'crim.con.' – against his wife's lover in the court of King's Bench. In common law a wife was a man's property and he could sue anyone who encroached on that property for damages. It was tantamount to putting a price on a wife's virtue. An injured husband might demand damages so high that his opponent would languish in the debtors' prison for the rest of his life. In some cases, husband and lover would agree a price beforehand, simply as a means of facilitating a divorce, and the lover would return the money when the case was concluded. Or the defendant-lover might successfully argue that the wife's reputation was already so notorious as not to be worth much. The wife – who had no legal personality apart from her husband – could not defend herself in court; she could only stand helplessly by as her reputation was torn to shreds. Few men, other than perhaps her lover, would want to marry her now.

Norfolk sued Germain for £10,000, but probably because of his own scandalous reputation – the ladies of Norwich refused to attend a ball he gave in his palace there during Assizes Week, in case they were sullied by association – the jury awarded him only a derisory £66. Undeterred, Norfolk introduced another private bill into Parliament. By this time, two key witnesses, servants of Germain who had been spirited away to the Dutch Republic, had been tracked down and gave evidence for the duke. Either he was bribing them handsomely, or there was an element of collusion here, since the duchess and Germain wished to marry. Any hint of collusion would rule out a divorce.

As Norfolk had still not obtained a divorce *a mensa et thoro* from the ecclesiastical court, there was a great deal of disquiet about it. A champion of the double sexual standard, he argued that only a wife's adultery counted, as it jeopardized the transmission of property in the legitimate line of descent. Naturally this sentiment was echoed by most of the peerage. Even so, the bill passed only with the narrowest of margins. Divorce meant the unravelling of a marriage settlement and Norfolk had to return the duchess's £10,000 dowry, making Germain a rich man when she married him.

It had taken the best part of a decade for Norfolk to obtain his divorce, only for him to die the following year before he had had a chance to remarry. The dukedom passed into the hands of his Catholic heirs, where it has remained ever since.

If Sir George and Lady Downing were hoping to benefit from the precedents of Roos and Norfolk in jointly appealing to Parliament to dissolve their marriage in name only, they were destined to be disappointed. Private bills tended to present the petitioner as having no heirs or hope of any, but that was misleading. Parliament was already beginning to restrict the purpose of private bills to bastardizing the children of an adulterous wife and freeing the husband to remarry, in order to provide a legitimate heir to a title and estate.

In May 1715 the Downing case was hotly debated before the House of Lords, who decided against the dissolution of the marriage by two votes. The Lords found that the marriage, which had been performed according to the rites of the Church of England in the presence of witnesses and within the canonical hours, was perfectly valid. Each party had reached the legal age – fourteen for a boy and twelve for a girl – and had consented to the marriage. They were man and wife according to the law of God and the law of the land.

The case exposed the absurdity of forced or child marriages. As one lawyer argued, 'It seems so senseless and unreasonable to give our children the power of disposing of their persons for ever, at an age when we will not let them dispose of five shillings, without discretion and advice.'

Yes, the couple had given their consent, but had they really understood the full import of what they were doing? The Bishop of Ely made an eloquent plea on their behalf: 'My Lords, the children were entirely passive in the matter and very obedient to the orders of those that govern'd them; and would have given away their fortunes and their liberties, and everything they had, had they been bid to do so.' They had consented to 'give the use and the dominion of their bodies each to the other, as long as they both should live, without so much as understanding what they meant when they said so.'

Crucially, the Lords pronounced, 'since nothing but adultery can dissolve a marriage, and no adultery is pretended here, the marriage continues indissoluble.'

If the Downings had failed to complete their marriage by leaving it unconsummated, this was through lack of will, rather than impotence or inability, which would have earned them an annulment. But obtaining such an annulment was by no means straightforward either, particularly if one of the parties was reluctant.

In 1731 Lady Catherine Elizabeth Weld of Lulworth Castle brought a suit in the ecclesiastical court to dissolve her marriage because of her husband's impotence: 'The said Edward Weld is frigid, impotent, and insufficient, and not capable of knowing a woman carnally and the said Catherine Elizabeth Weld, alias Aston . . . doth refuse to live and cohabit with him, and doth now live separate from him.'

Poor Edward could not see why they should not continue to live together as brother and sister, but duly consulted the physicians. Initially they said there was nothing they could do to help him, 'nor could they cause any valid erection of his penis, whereby he might be able to penetrate, or have carnal knowledge of his wife, although he did often attempt it.' He told them that whenever he did so 'he was seized with a violent pain across his belly, which so contracted his privities, and put him in so great torture, that he was obliged to desist from such caresses.'

Meanwhile, three experienced midwives declared Catherine to be *virgo intacta* and that 'her parts of generation are in such a state as render her capable of conjugal embraces'.

They were convinced that she could have had no 'carnal conversation with a man', but Edward, desperately trying to save his marriage, maintained that 'he *believed* he had such knowledge of her twice within the first year'. Catherine's lawyer argued that 'if the gentleman could not swear *positively*, it looked as if he was not a competent judge'. The comment provoked much hilarity.

Edward consulted a surgeon, who had some success in 'strengthening his member, so as to render him more apt for coition', yet still he did not manage to consummate the marriage. Five eminent surgeons gave evidence that there had been some impediment, which had now been removed by their skill, while at the same time throwing doubt on the midwives' testimony.

There are obvious parallels with the Essex case in the early seventeenth century, except that this time there was no intervention from a partisan king. Impotence could not just be selective; it had to be a permanent disability. That had not been proved here. The judge warned that if the marriage should be annulled and the parties remarried and Edward managed to perform with the second wife, then his marriage with her would be declared void and he would be obliged to return to his first wife.

It seems there was to be no escape for Lady Catherine. The case, which went to appeal in the Court of Arches, was dismissed as not sufficiently proven. The court ordered Catherine to go home to her husband. Instead, she took her appeal to the next stage, to the King in the High Court of Delegates, where the original sentence was confirmed. She was condemned to spend the rest of her life in an apparently sexless marriage, denied the gratification of children.

INTERLUDE

Lord Halifax, *The Lady's New Year's Gift: or Advice to a Daughter*

Not long before she eloped with him, Lady Mary Pierrepont wrote to Wortley Montagu: 'I have seen so many of my acquaintance unhappy, and heard so many secret complaints of husbands, I have often resolved never to marry, and always not to sacrifice myself to an estate.' Given the weak and inferior position of wives in relation to husbands, it was an understandable reaction, but really not practical. Few women seriously contemplated not marrying. Perhaps if they were given a better education, Lady Mary's friend the feminist Mary Astell believed, more of them would opt not to marry or at least choose more wisely, for once married, a woman was totally in her husband's power. As it was, she could only advise resignation, for the married woman to acknowledge her husband's authority and make the best of it. For the next two centuries and more, therefore, all the advice books concentrated on how to 'manage' a husband.

Given this context, it is no surprise that Lord Halifax's *The Lady's New Year's Gift: or Advice to a Daughter* became a bestseller which ran to twenty-five editions in the eighteenth century. It was dedicated to his beloved daughter Elizabeth, who was twelve years old when it was published in 1688.

Marriage, he tells her, 'is too sacred to admit a liberty of objecting to it'. The good order of society depends upon it. 'You are therefore to make the best of what is settled by law and custom, and not vainly imagine, that it will be changed for your sake.'

First of all, let the adults choose a husband for you, for they know best. 'It is one of the disadvantages belonging to your sex, that young women are seldom permitted to make their own choice, their friends' care and experience are thought safer guides.'

Certainly there is inequality between the sexes, since men 'who were to be the law-givers, had the larger share of reason bestow'd upon them'. Nature, however, has restored the balance. 'You have it in your power not only to free yourselves, but to subdue your masters, and without violence throw both their natural and legal authority at your feet.' A woman could use her femininity. 'You have more strength in your looks, than we have in our laws, and more power by your tears, than we have in our arguments.'

If your husband is unfaithful, rise above it; do not take him to task over it. Nor should a wife 'blaze it to the world, expecting it should rise up in arms to take her part'. On the contrary, the world will laugh at her. Your silence will be the most effective reproof. 'An affected ignorance, which is seldom a virtue, is a great one here.' If nothing else, it will make him more yielding in other things.

If your husband is a drunk make sure he is 'received at home without a storm or so much as a reproaching look'. Otherwise he may be provoked into a rage.

A husband with a mercurial temperament needs to be observed carefully, 'so that by marking how the wheels of such a man's head are used to move, you may easily bring over all his passion to your party'. Such a man thinks he is diminished if he is opposed. 'You must in this case take heed of increasing the storm by an unwary word, of kindling the fire while the wind is in a corner which may blow it in your face.' You are 'dexterously to yield everything till he begins to cool, and then by slow degrees you may rise and gain upon him'. A kind smile will win him round, whereas a 'shrill and pettish answer' will provoke him. A little flattery will not go amiss, which 'by being necessary will cease to be criminal'.

If a husband is sulky and ill-humoured look out for 'the first appearance of cloudy weather' and wait till it passes.

If he is mean, find out if he has reason to be. There are far too many husbands being accused of avarice these days, he tells her, to ring true. 'There are wives who are impatient of the rules of economy, and are apt to call their husband's kindness in question, if any other measure is put to their expense than that of their own fancy.' A husband will resent a greedy, profligate wife.

If a husband really is a 'close-handed wretch', go along with him on the big things, 'by which you will have the better opportunity of persuading him in things where he may be more indifferent'. Few husbands are 100 per cent mean and usually 'there are opportunities to be exploited'.

If he is 'weak and incompetent', step into the vacuum. This gives you power, if you 'make right use of it'.

If your husband is 'an ass', you would be foolish if 'you did not take care he may be *your* ass'. But you have to go about this carefully. Never reveal his shortcomings in public. 'Your slighting him in company . . . may provoke the tame creature to break loose, and to show his dominion for his credit, which he was content to forget for his ease.'

Above all, you must hope you have a wise husband, for 'that by knowing how to be a master, for that very reason will not let you feel the weight of it; one whose authority is so softened by his kindness, that it gives you ease without abridging your liberty; one that will return so much tenderness for your just esteem of him, that you will never want power, though you will seldom care to use it.' To be married to such a man would be the equivalent of being ruled by a benign prince, which is 'to be preferred before the disquiet and uneasiness of unlimited liberty'.

The family you enter will generally expect that 'like a stranger in a foreign country you should conform to their methods'. You are to be very careful to get on well with your husband's 'friends'.

Do not be disappointed if his family do not love you as your own family does. 'The tenderness we have had for you, my dear, is of another nature, peculiar to kind parents, and differing from that which you will meet with first in any family into which you shall be transported.' However, 'your husband's kindness will have so much advantage of ours, that we shall yield up all competition, and as well as we love you, be very well contented to surrender to such a rival.'

PART THREE
1706–1780

Con Phillips
✓ *chapter melan*

II

'For ten guineas he should procure a man (who was already marry'd) that should marry her in another name'

I N 1748 a stunningly beautiful, notorious and litigious woman
– described as one of the great sexual man-eaters of history –
published her memoirs. Frustrated at every turn by money, lies and
legal chicanery to prove her one true marriage legal, she resorted to
naming, shaming and blackmailing the various men who had featured
in her busy marital and amorous career. The resulting *Apology* was so
hot that no publisher would touch it and she had to publish it herself.
As the house in Westminster where she was living was surrounded by
a bevy of constables, ready to seize and convey her to Newgate if she
so much as put a foot outdoors, she cheekily advertised that anyone
who wished to buy a copy should contact her servant, who would
hand it out of the window.

With so much advance publicity it is no surprise that the scandalous memoir was a publishing success running into four editions and
incidentally triggering off a whole spate of printed rebuttals and libel
suits. But its effect was more far-reaching than that. The author's ready
exploitation of the clandestine marriage system and candid admission
of a string of bigamous marriages, together with her tortuous journey through the courts in search of justice, exposed the defects in
the system and prompted her old enemy Lord Hardwicke, the Lord
Chancellor, to push through the most fundamental alteration in the
English marriage laws since the Middle Ages.

Teresia Constantia Phillips's story was as racy as anything invented
by Daniel Defoe. Con Phillips was born in January 1709, the eldest
daughter of a gentleman, a captain in the Grenadier Guards, of an
old Welsh family. Her mother was equally well connected. When
Lieutenant Colonel Phillips was discharged from the army after the
end of the war with France in 1713, he settled with his wife and five

children in London. Four years later, the family was in such dire financial straits that the children were farmed out among various relatives. Con was taken in by her godmother, the Duchess of Bolton, illegitimate daughter of the illegitimate Duke of Monmouth, who sent her to Mrs Filer's boarding school, where she acquired all the accomplishments necessary for a lady.

When Con's mother died in 1721 her father, whose fortunes had by now improved with a post in Portsmouth, brought her home. Unfortunately, he had married his late wife's maid, who was the wicked stepmother personified. Con returned to London to earn her living and support her younger sister, which she did by fine sewing. She spent Sundays at the house of a general's widow, who had been a friend of her mother's, and it was here she met Philip Dormer Stanhope, the eldest son of the Earl of Chesterfield, who had been ruined in the South Sea Bubble disaster of 1720 and was hiding from his creditors. In her memoirs Con revealed that the future Lord Chesterfield – he was a prominent statesman and moralist by the time they were published – had a taste for young virgins. Certainly he set out to woo the beautiful thirteen-year-old Con with a series of ardent letters, written under the assumed name of Thomas Grimes, promising her that she would be a great lady.

Grimes used an old procuress to insinuate herself into Con's confidence and wear down her resistance to his approaches. On the occasion of King George I's return from Hanover she was persuaded to watch the celebratory firework display from Grimes's lodgings. He got her drunk, came behind her, used a knife to rip the lace off her coat and divest her of her clothes, tied her to the chair, and raped her. 'Tears and prayers were all in vain. She was then in his power and he resolved to make use of it.' Afterwards he protested that 'though no ceremony had passed between them, he should always look after her as his wife, and would instantly make provision for her.'

Two months later, his interest waned, leaving her penniless. Con's lack of dowry already ruled out a marriage with someone of her own rank, while her refinement and ladylike education made her an unsuitable partner for someone of lesser rank, who would expect her to make a contribution to the marriage or work alongside him. In her memoir Con railed against the double sexual standard. Chastity was not the only virtue, she argued; moral integrity was just as valuable. The fact remained that with a ruined reputation, there was little prospect for her now in the marriage market.

The procuress lured her closer to prostitution by providing her with food and clothes in exchange for notes of hand for five times their value. Never good with money, in three months Con found herself £500 in debt and facing the prospect of arrest. Terrified at the thought of prison, she readily acceded to the procuress's suggestion that for ten guineas one Mr Morell of Durham Yard in the Strand 'should procure a man (who was already marry'd) that should marry her in another name, and that the ceremony should be performed before such witnesses as should when called upon, prove it, and by that means screen her from her debts'.

When a man married he not only acquired the woman's property, but he also became responsible for any debts she had incurred before marriage. There was therefore an incentive to marry to fob off creditors, particularly if it was a clandestine marriage with all its peculiar anomalies and irregularities and the man could conveniently disappear afterwards. All the woman had to do then was produce her marriage certificate to avoid arrest. It was even better if she happened to marry someone already in prison for debt, since clearly he could not be arrested twice.

Clandestine marriage – one conducted secretly, without the calling of banns or obtaining a legitimate licence from the Bishop's court, and performed outside the parish of residence – was valid in the eyes of the Church, provided the couple were of legal age, gave their free consent, and there were no impediments. Unlike the old contract marriage, or exchange of verbal promises between the parties, which had largely fallen into abeyance by the mid-sixteenth century, a clandestine marriage was performed by a clergyman using the service laid down in the Book of Common Prayer and in the presence of witnesses.

It need not take place in church. During the Interregnum Church of England weddings had been forbidden and the population had grown accustomed to the idea of marrying outside church or of being married furtively by some ejected Anglican minister. A clandestine marriage could just as easily be conducted in a private house, a prison, an ale-house or a brothel; rather than observing the canonical hours for marriage – eight in the morning to noon – it could take place at any time, even in the middle of the night.

Between 1694, when the state first became involved in marriage by trying to tax all marriages and then imposing stamp duty on marriage licences and certificates, and Lord Hardwicke's Marriage Act of 1753 thousands of such marriages – perhaps 15 to 20 per cent of the total – took place within the Rules of the Fleet Prison and other 'peculiars': churches such as St James's Duke's Place in London and some provincial centres that were outside diocesan jurisdiction.

Clandestine marriage was just as popular in rural society as it was in London. At the turn of the century the vicar at Tetbury in Gloucestershire recorded that almost half his parishioners were married clandestinely or cohabiting in some irregular union and he was having little success in persuading them to marry in his church. All classes of society resented the calling of banns, seeing it as an unwarranted interference in their private business, which is why at least a third of the population opted to be married by licence, either slipping quietly off to church early in the morning or having the ceremony conducted at home. Above all, they wanted privacy.

'To proclaim banns is a thing nobody now cares to have done; very few are willing to have their affairs declar'd to all the world in a public place, when for a guinea they may do it snug, and without noise,' noted Henri Misson, a keen observer of English customs, 'and my good friends the clergy are not very zealous to prevent it. Thus, then, they buy what they call a licence, and are marry'd in their closets, in the presence of a couple of friends, that serve for witnesses; and this ties them for ever.'

Licences, however, were expensive and many opted not to bother with them, or bought them from venal surrogates, who illegally obtained and sold blank documents from the Bishop's court, for some negligent clergymen to fill in the names with no questions asked. More often than not the licences and certificates lacked the official stamp, since the great majority would do anything to wriggle out of the tax. To make matters worse, the entries in the so-called marriage registers were scanty and liable to be tampered with, with erasures, insertions and back-dating all too common. A clandestine marriage was recognized in canon law and common law as legally binding and carried with it full property rights, but if it should founder, it could be difficult to produce the evidence to convince the courts of its existence, throwing any rights to dower or of inheritance into jeopardy. An exasperated Lord Hardwicke showed his contempt when he tore up some grimy marriage register in court as utterly worthless.

Given the ease with which clandestine marriage was carried out and the dubious nature of the paperwork, the whole seedy business was wide open to abuse. Many of the clergymen were defrocked or debtors themselves, glad of the money, and not inclined to make too close enquiries as to whom they were joining together. The Fleet and its surrounding marriage houses were a popular resort of the labouring poor from London and its suburbs, who, unencumbered by property, were not too bothered about the legality of their union. They just wanted something cheap, quick and convenient, with not too much spent on fees, nothing on taxes, and the bulk of the expense devoted to the rowdy celebrations to follow.

Clandestine marriage beckoned to couples of all classes with something to hide. It facilitated bigamous and incestuous unions, under-age unions without parental consent, and even same-sex unions with one of the parties disguised as the opposite sex. It invited young men still in apprenticeship to marry their pregnant girlfriends and widows to remarry without losing their privileges. Crucially, as far as Lord Hardwicke and his fellow peers were concerned, it was a means of enticing their children into unsuitable matches and encouraged the kidnapping and forced marriages of heiresses, who were drugged and raped by fortune-hunting strangers.

It was the obvious route for a desperate Con. Shuddering at the idea of placing herself in the power of a stranger, she was 'given to understand that it was only a mere matter of form that was to pass between them that the man should never know who she was or what she was'. Since he was already married, he was committing bigamy, which was a felony punishable by death, so that he was unlikely to hang around. Nor would he want to encounter Con's creditors.

True to form, the paperwork set out to mislead and confuse. The man's name was Francis Delafield, but the licence read Francis Deval. This was supposedly so that his wife did not find out, but one suspects she knew exactly how he was making extra cash. Con's name was misspelled Tresue and her age given as twenty-one. The venue was St Benet Paul's Wharf, where the bridal party was kept waiting for two hours, until Delafield turned up so inebriated that he had to be supported by his companions. The point of being drunk was so that 'he might not remember her, if by any accident he should get sight of her'.

After the ceremony, they adjourned to the Half-Moon Tavern in the Strand, where 'the business of the men was to keep our bridegroom so drunk that he was perfectly speechless – for there was another part of the ceremony yet unperformed, absolutely necessary, as they told her, in the proving a marriage, which is consummation.'

Delafield was conveyed in a chair to Morell's house, undressed and put to bed. Con lay fully clothed under the covers beside the comatose bridegroom, then 'all the people were let in that they might be able to swear to the consummation'. None of the usual jollities, such as taking the bride's garters or throwing the couple's stockings backwards across the bed, seem to have taken place. The farce over, Con got up and went home. It was not, however, her last encounter with Delafield.

Con judged it best to lie low in France for a few months, before returning to London. Her luck seemed to change now, because she met Henry Muilman, the son of a very rich Amsterdam merchant, who became absolutely besotted with her. She expected him to make her his mistress – 'in which case, she proposed to make the best bargain she could for herself' – but much to her amazement he proposed marriage instead. Judging it unfair to deceive her future husband, she decided to tell him the truth about her past. Con's father was consulted and both he and Muilman sought legal advice as to the validity of her phoney marriage. All agreed, correctly, that it had been no marriage and that Con was free to marry. Whenever she asked Muilman to have it officially declared null and void in the London Consistory Court, however, he refused, saying that it was unnecessary and that it would ruin the reputation on which his credit depended.

By some strange coincidence they were married in the same church by the same parson who had performed the previous ceremony. 'Mr

Cook recollected our young lady so well, as to give her his compliments.' Did he not think to question what had happened to her previous 'husband'? The couple took a commodious house in Red Lion Street, Clerkenwell. The marriage was made public and, according to custom, the newly weds embarked on a series of visits and receiving visitors. Everyone remarked on the young bride's 'beauty, politeness, and sweet behaviour'.

It seemed that Con had been rescued from a life of vice in the nick of time, but her good fortune was not to last. Bulwark, a fellow Dutch merchant, sniffed a scandal and seized the opportunity to discredit a rival. His intention was to go to Holland and spread the word that Muilman had 'contracted a base marriage with an extravagant abandon'd young creature, who would infallibly ruin him in a year's time'. The couple forestalled him by arriving in Amsterdam first. When Bulwark entered the Muilmans' house it was to find the family charmed by their son's bride. They had no suspicions about her past and their son had given them to understand that she had money. Bulwark decided to bide his time, while dropping hints to Muilman's father to go to England and look into his daughter-in-law's past.

Soon after Muilman's parents arrived in London, Con felt a growing coolness towards her on the part of her father-in-law and husband. At a dinner Muilman Senior publicly insulted her, much to the discomfiture of their guests. She asked him how 'she had had the misfortune to displease him'. He replied that he did not like her character. 'Pray, Sir, what part of my character is it, which has so greatly offended you?' 'Why,' he said, 'I am told you were a common whore before you married my son.'

Muilman Senior blamed Con for enticing his son into marriage and was determined to break it at all costs. Rifling through her husband's *escritoire*, Con found letters from his father ordering him to part from her under threat of disinheritance. Muilman had begun to mistreat her, hoping by that means to provoke her to leave or throw herself into the arms of another suitor. It was the standard method of ridding oneself of an unwanted wife.

One morning Con received a visit from one of Muilman's friends, who was 'too much a man of honour to deceive her'. He informed her that Muilman was planning to seize her jewels, clothes and papers that afternoon. Con called the servant to bring down a trunk and had her valuables removed to the vault of a bank in Fleet Street. At dinner, Muilman arrived with a group of ruffians, whom he invited to sit at table with them, making coarse jokes and innuendos. As soon as the meal was over, Muilman demanded her keys and at the lewd suggestion of one of the ruffians searched her person. They then proceeded to her bedchamber, only to find everything gone. Muilman started to threaten her, telling her that as she was not his wife he could have her arrested for theft and sent to Newgate, but she refused to reveal the whereabouts of the trunk.

Con repaired to Doctor's Commons – the London headquarters of the Province of Canterbury where the ecclesiastical courts sat – for the best legal advice and discovered that her husband had bribed Delafield to initiate divorce proceedings against her, on the plea that she was living in adultery with Muilman. Obviously her best plan was to answer the libel with a statement of the facts, and to serve an indictment against Delafield for bigamy. Delafield, of course, absconded – Con later learned that Muilman had bundled him off to Holland – and the proceedings had to be dropped.

Con's counsel advised her to remain in the marital home. Torn between his passion for his wife and parental pressure to part with her, Muilman was trying to persuade Con to acknowledge the nullity of the marriage but live with him as his mistress until his father died or he made his own fortune. Con was inflexible on the matter. As far as she was concerned she was Muilman's legally married wife and was determined to defend her position by going to law if necessary. He then conveyed her to a separate house, but unable to resist her sexual allure, could not stay away. If she refused his advances, he would beat her up. He would arrive in the night with his ruffians demanding admittance. On one occasion she scared them off by loading a pistol with firework powder and firing it. They fled, but Muilman went to Lord Chief Justice Pratt to swear the peace against Con. He had narrowly escaped with his life, he claimed, and had even felt the bullet fly through his hat. Con was summoned before Pratt. She assured him that Muilman's head was so thick he wouldn't know the difference if she did shoot him. He admired her wit and believed her story.

Con was on her way to the theatre one evening when Muilman

and six men waylaid her at the end of Downing Street. 'This bitch is my wife, and has run away from me with another man,' he told the chairmen as his men dragged her out of the sedan chair and into the back room of a tavern, where they robbed her of her jewels and stripped off her fine clothes. Without her 'trappings', he told her, she would find it much harder to pursue any legal action against him or in her own defence. Indeed, it was a setback, as she could have raised more than £1,000 on the jewels to fund her case. As it was, Muilman was giving her nothing to live on and prevented her from raising credit by publicly announcing that she was not his wife and that he was about to leave the country anyway.

Worn down and on the advice of her lawyer, she agreed on a compromise. A private agreement declared that she and Muilman were lawfully married but agreed to live apart, and that Muilman would give her a bond of £4,000, which would secure her an annuity of £200 a year for life, as well as £2,000 in cash, the return of her jewels, and plate and furniture to equip a house. He would also pay her legal fees. In return, Con's lawyer was to offer only a token defence against his nullity suit while, to avoid being examined in person under oath, she was to live abroad until sentence was granted. It was a clear case of collusion, with Muilman's lawyer advising against it, since the bond would offer Con a weapon to use against him if he ever reneged on his promises.

It was only by chance that Con discovered that the agreement, written in Latin, read £400, not £4,000. Muilman laughed it off as an honest mistake. Ever the opportunist, Delafield reappeared and blackmailed Muilman for £1,000. In February 1724 the court pronounced the marriage null and void. Con returned to London, only to be pressed by Muilman to sleep with him again. Advised by her lawyer not to do so, since a renewal of sexual relations would invalidate the nullity suit if it were ever appealed, Con decided to grant Muilman his wish. Who knew what the future held?

Unfortunately, she made one crucial mistake before her final parting from Muilman. Desperate for £700 to pay off her creditors, she asked him to lend her the money, naïvely agreeing to surrender to him the £4,000 bond as security until she repaid the loan. When she asked for it back four years later, he replied that she was a damned impudent bitch and he owed her nothing. Had he dealt with her fairly, he would not have been harried by her through the labyrinthine English legal system for the next eighteen years.

Con, still only sixteen, now took up with a Mr B, a young man with a fortune of £16,000 and excellent prospects. They spent five years together, some of them in Paris, where Mr B passed her off as his wife. In London she discovered that Muilman was planning to marry Anne Darnell, the daughter of his lawyer. She told Sir John Darnell, if he did not know it already, that she and Muilman were married, that the nullity suit had been based on lies. The marriage went ahead regardless, perhaps because Darnell was satisfied that Con was just a powerless woman and there would be no further case to answer and also, no doubt, because Muilman's father had now invested a great deal of money in his business, making him a rich man.

Having ruined Mr B with her extravagance, she left him. Enter Sir HP, a thirty-one-year-old baronet with a wife and children, who promised Con £500 a year to be his mistress. He took a handsome house for her and showered her with jewels, lace, fine clothes and all manner of luxuries. When the allowance did not materialize she told him she was leaving, at which he picked up a table knife and stabbed himself. Impatient with such melodrama, she took temporary refuge in a Ghent convent.

By 1732 Con was living in domestic bliss with Lord F in a country house in Hertfordshire when her marriage case with Muilman was unexpectedly reopened. Delafield, unwell and miserably poor, had been spurned by Muilman and now offered to testify for Con. Con's lawyers advised her that Delafield must make a public recantation of the false testimony he had given for Muilman in 1724 and that a proctor must take down his deposition on oath. Next she must begin a suit against Delafield to annul their so-called marriage on grounds of his bigamy, followed by a suit against Muilman to set aside the sentence of nullity of her marriage to him.

The case began well, with Delafield giving his evidence and even producing witnesses to his first marriage. Thanks to Darnell's legal acumen and use of personal contacts, the case then began to collapse. Somehow Delafield's court-assigned proctor was replaced by one favourable to Muilman, who submitted an affidavit that Delafield had died and that the case was therefore closed. It came as a terrible blow to Con. Delafield's disappearance was baffling. Con, who was never able to discover how or when he had died or where he was buried, believed that Muilman had arranged his murder. A story emerged of Delafield being made excessively drunk and carried to a common lodging house in the Strand, where the landlady was told he was a very sick man and subject to fits. Sure enough, next day he was dead, whether naturally or by the administration of poison is anyone's guess.

Despite the loss of her star witness, Con continued with her suit. She had to reconstruct her case all over again. The next hurdle was to prove Delafield's 1718 marriage to Margaret Yeomans. Was it even legal? Naturally, it had been clandestine, conducted in one of the Fleet's notorious marriage houses, the Hand and Pen up by Smithfield, by one of its more infamous parsons, the Reverend John Draper. Draper and the clerk Thomas Hodgkin and his nephew of the same name, who had signed the register on his uncle's behalf since he was blind, were all now dead, but the widow of Hodgkin Junior was still alive and making a good living from selling certificates copied from the register to people who needed to produce proof of their marriage.

Muilman almost pipped Con to the post. He had already approached Mrs Hodgkin and been caught red-handed trying to cut the page detailing Delafield's marriage out of the register. Then he had tried to suborn Mrs Hodgkin's landlord, to whom she owed money, to procure the book as security for his rent. Con outwitted him. She sent her footman to offer five guineas to Mrs Hodgkin to bring her book to a lady who wished to copy it. The fee was too handsome to resist. When she arrived at Con's house, it was to find a room full of the finest legal brains of Doctor's Commons. They examined the entry for Delafield's marriage and wrapped the register and sealed it, so that it could not be tampered with. Con gave Mrs Hodgkin twenty guineas for the loan of her register and next day deposited it with the judge.

Muilman's next resort was to deny the validity of the register as evidence, which sent Con on a mission to find someone who could verify Hodgkin's handwriting. This done, she was also able to provide Mrs Delafield's burial certificate, dated 1724, proving that she was alive three years after Con had 'married' Delafield, proving that her marriage with him was bigamous and therefore null and void. It was beginning to look as if her marriage to Muilman was valid, meaning that Muilman's to Anne Darnell was bigamous and their children illegitimate.

Muilman's team were sufficiently worried to approach Con with an offer of £5,000 to withdraw her suit. She refused it. The offer was increased to £6,000 and then to £8,000. She should have accepted and saved herself years of legal expense and hassle, but by now she was determined to have her pound of flesh. She proceeded with her suit to revoke the nullity sentence of 1724, since it was procured by fraud, and began a second suit against Muilman for restitution of conjugal rights, in order to pave the way for her claim to maintenance as his legal and much wronged wife.

Muilman and Darnell frustrated her every move, using delaying tactics to wear her down and drive up her legal expenses. Muilman's highly damning letters to her were to be read out in court and Con arranged to advertise the fact in the newspapers, so that there would be maximum public exposure. Muilman bought off the newspapers, so Con had handbills printed and distributed all over the City.

The case was drawing to a close in the London Consistory Court and Judge Henchman was just about to pronounce sentence when Muilman's proctor announced that he was going straight on to appeal in the Court of Arches, so he need not bother. Henchman was so angry at this usurpation of his role in his own court that he offered his services to Con free of charge. Eventually, after even more expense, the Court of Arches decided in favour of Con. Muilman immediately appealed to the ultimate authority, the Court of Delegates. This meant another delay of at least two years and even when the Delegates made a decision the case would only be sent back to the Court of Arches for re-sentencing. By that time, of course, many of the original witnesses would be dead, while less and less credence was being given to evidence supposedly supporting clandestine marriages in the courts.

Con's counsel advised her to hurry things along by inviting one of her creditors to sue her for debt for necessaries (beer) in the court of King's Bench. She could then plead her marriage to Muilman as a defence, the creditor would sue him, so challenging the validity of the marriage, and the issue would be brought to trial at common law. It seemed an ingenious plan, but Darnell was able to block the case as collusive and to turn the tables on Con's counsel for subornation of witnesses.

Chief Justice Hardwicke wanted to know which of her legal advisers had put Con up to this and summoned her to his chambers. Turning up unexpectedly one day, it was to find Hardwicke and Darnell having a cosy chat. She assumed the worst and, after an angry exchange with Hardwicke, swept out. 'I saw but too plainly that Darnell had a tongue – you an ear; that Muilman had money – you a hand,' she subsequently wrote to him.

The upshot of all this was that Con had to spend even more money defending herself against a charge of collusion and the subornation of witnesses. Refusing to name the counsel who had advised her – probably Henchman – which she saw as a dastardly plot to ruin him, she was found guilty, imprisoned pending her apology to Hardwicke – her lawyers did it on her behalf – and heavily fined. Nothing daunted, she began a new suit in Chancery to recover the bond for £4,000 which Muilman had refused to return to her, so preventing her from receiving the £200 annuity. By now Muilman had forty lawyers in his employ and had every incentive to delay, since the ecclesiastical court decided that the bond relieved him of the obligation to pay maintenance for the duration of the case, even though the bond was in his possession and useless to Con. Henchman, however, was right to raise the question, If Muilman could prove his case, why did he prevaricate so much?

Lord F, meanwhile, torn between his Connie and the lure of a stupendous dowry, reluctantly plumped for the latter: 'to be rich and wretched'. He was married with Con's blessing and she moved on to 'Mr Worthy', the son of a rich family with estates in Jamaica. She followed him there and spent the three happiest years of her life with him, but the climate did not agree with her and she was forced to return to England for her health. In 1741 she arranged to meet Worthy again in Boston, but the governor wanted Worthy to marry his daughter and sent him on a fool's errand to New York in winter, so that he would not have the chance to be reunited with Con. She returned to England and resumed her case against Muilman.

A case could be buried in Chancery for years and by now Con's funds were running low. She could no longer afford to keep cases running in several courts. If she lost and was left with costs to pay, she would be hideously in debt again. She would be arrested and Muilman would almost certainly contrive to keep her in gaol indefinitely. To add to her misfortunes, she had hired a new solicitor, who turned out to be careless, corrupt, greedy and expensive. She had no option but to concede defeat and settle out of court. Muilman offered her a derisory £500 – £300 down and a further £200 payable after she had withdrawn her case from the Court of Delegates. Not only was Muilman going to retain the original £4,000 bond that Con had surrendered to him – illegally, as it happened, since at the time she had been under age and the transaction should have been undertaken by a guardian – but he was now asking Con for a bond of £1,000 as a guarantee that she would never revive the Chancery suit.

Just as she was considering the awful consequences of signing the documents before her, her crooked solicitor rushed in with the bailiffs, demanding £300 which he claimed she owed him. Con had no time to think. She hurriedly signed the documents in order to collect the money and pay him off before she was arrested.

This left her in a tight corner, with her other creditors circling. Muilman extracted even harder terms. In return for the outstanding £200, she was to undertake never to claim to be Mrs Muilman again and to lose herself in France while her suits were withdrawn, uncontested, from the various courts. The judges were at first reluctant, but finally persuaded that Muilman must have reached a satisfactory settlement with Con. Since a 'marriage can never be at an end' the option was always there to revive the case, but as she was broke and had given a £1,000 bond to Muilman not to do so, Con was momentarily powerless. To make matters worse, all the documents relating to her numerous lawsuits – her original libel, Muilman's incriminating letters, affidavits and depositions from witnesses now dead – had been retained by her solicitor, to whom apparently she still owed money.

From shabby lodgings in Hoxton, Con wrote to Muilman begging for a small allowance. He refused, unless she returned to Jamaica, where hopefully the climate would kill her. Alternatively, he offered her £18 a year to go to some remote part of Ireland or Scotland. She seemed to have reached her lowest ebb when she was arrested for debt and sent to the King's Bench Prison. Since she was by now far too famous for Muilman to allow her to starve, he sent her small sums of money. For the next two years until she was released she occupied her time preparing a case against her corrupt solicitor, and won.

No sooner was she released than Muilman bought up one of her debts for twice its value, to hold it over her as a threat. He could have her arrested at any time. Con swiftly took up residence in the Verge of the Royal Court, where she could not be arrested except by the written consent of the Board of Green Cloth. Undeterred and desperate to forestall the second volume of her *Apology*, which would be highly damaging to him, Muilman obtained a warrant for her arrest. This is how Con came to be besieged by thirteen constables and fifty ruffians and was reduced to selling copies of the offending work through the window.

It was Con's case, almost more than any other, that convinced Lord Chancellor Hardwicke of the need for reform. He had wanted to tackle the marriage laws for the best part of his legal career, and indeed, various proposals had been debated and rejected in Parliament in that time, but he judged now that the time was ripe. The state had a vested interest in the proper regulation of marriage through the taxes it accrued from it, while a growing band of respectable people were becoming impatient with the anomalies in the system. Others, however, saw any change as an encroachment on their liberties or a threat to their vested interests.

Hardwicke encountered a surprising amount of resistance to his bill. He had to placate the peers by allowing the archbishops to retain the right to issue special licences for the nobility to be married at the time and place of their choosing. People of the middling sort were to be indulged in their preference for marrying by licence by the confirmation of the surrogates' right to sell licences, even though they had previously abused the privilege. With the end of the clandestine marriage trade, impoverished parish priests were promised a boost in the numbers of church weddings and an increase in income.

The propertied classes were appeased by the fact that they were given the legal right of veto over their children's marriages up to the age of twenty-one, although younger sons and lesser gentry in the Commons were less than pleased that it narrowed the chance of their marrying a rich heiress. It was ironic that just as young people were enjoying greater freedom to choose their marriage partners the law made it illegal to marry under the age of twenty-one without the consent of parents or guardians, but it did bring English law nearer to continental laws for the first time since the Reformation.

In deference to the Scots, they were omitted from the bill – which was to prove its Achilles heel.

In future, any marriage not preceded by the calling of banns or the purchase of a legitimate licence and conducted in a church by a regular clergyman according to the rites of the Church of England within the canonical hours was automatically null and void. Any clergyman conducting a clandestine marriage committed a felony, for which the penalty was transportation for fourteen years. Contract marriages were declared obsolete. Any marriage involving children under the age of twenty-one who had not obtained the consent of parents or guardians was invalid. Failure to record the correct date of birth of either of the parties rendered the marriage null and void, inadvertently creating a means of self-divorce, even years later. Only in 1823 was this loophole closed. No longer would lawyers have to depend on the evidence of fictitious registers in the hands of seedy clerks and ale-house keepers. Every marriage was to be entered into the register of the parish church and a copy of each register was to be sent to the bishop annually for its protection.

Among the losers were the dissenters, who since the Restoration had made their own arrangements, being married in their own chapels and meeting-houses. They were severely grieved by this forced submission to an Anglican ceremony, which, if observed, disturbed their consciences and, if ignored, the settlement of their property. Only the Jews and the Quakers were judged responsible enough to regulate their own marriages and were exempt from the Act. Not until the Marriage Act of 1836 were Nonconformist places of worship licensed for the celebration of marriage, while civil marriage before a registrar was re-established for the first time since the Commonwealth.

A church wedding was expensive and there was a feeling that the vast body of the poor, who had happily availed themselves of the cheaper option of a clandestine marriage, would simply cohabit. It was absurd that their children, who most likely would have been working away from home for a good seven years by the time they were twenty-one, could not marry without parental consent. Everyone recognized that this requirement was to protect the interests of the rich and powerful, but even in eighteenth-century England there could not be one law for the rich and another for the poor.

There was a last-minute rush of clandestine marriages before the Act came into force and the Fleet parsons and their brethren in the lucrative trade shut up shop.

It hardly affected Con at all. By the 1750s she was back in Jamaica, where she proceeded to make three more bigamous marriages in quick succession. In spite of extracting money from them all, she died in poverty in 1765. Witty and litigious to the end, she noted with satisfaction that it was a Saturday and since she would be buried on the Sunday, her corpse could not be held hostage for debt to her apothecary, since debtors were exempt from arrest on Sundays so that they could attend church.

INTERLUDE

The Hardships of the English Laws
in Relation to Wives

In 1735 *The Hardships of the English Laws in Relation to Wives* was written anonymously in the guise of a petition to the King and the House of Lords.

The Glorious Revolution of 1688 had confirmed the right of the 'freeborn subjects of England' to approach the sovereign with a grievance, without fear of retribution. The author of the petition hopes that this right extends to wives, 'our condition being of all others in his dominions the most deplorable and the most exposed to oppression.'

Since they have no legal identity of their own, and are their husbands' property to do as they like with just short of murder, wives are often equated with slaves. The author protests that 'the estate of wives is more disadvantageous than slavery itself'. That 'wives may be made prisoners for life . . . no other individuals, not even the sovereign himself, can imprison any person for life, at will or pleasure', since the Habeas Corpus Act provides for the condemnation of prisoners or their release.

The petitioner points out that 'wives have no property, neither in their own persons, children or fortunes'. The laws of ancient Rome were more favourable to wives, since in Rome a wife could retain her own property, whereas in England she is 'divested' of all her property.

As a woman places her whole happiness in her husband's hands, surely she has a right to his protection?

Since she belongs to her husband, he can recover damages of any man who shall 'invade' his property in her, but she cannot recover damages from a woman who takes him.

By the laws of England a woman whose husband has beaten or

Rome more favourable than [A kyle]

abused her may swear the peace against him and have him sent to gaol. 'This is if he does not confine her first, as he has the power to lock her up. She is exposed to his resentment if she reports him and she is still in his power.' If he is in gaol, she and her children will starve, and what justice is there in that?

A woman may place her fortune into the hands of trustees before marriage, if done with the consent of her intended husband. 'But if we reflect how extremely ignorant all young women are as to points in law, and how their education and way of life shuts them out from the knowledge of their true interest in almost all things, we shall find that their trust and confidence in the man they love, and inability to make use of a proper means to guard against falsehood, leave few in a condition to make use of that precaution.' Even those with money in trust are at the mercy of the husband, who can 'easily find means to bend her to his will'.

> Marriage with all its complicated hazards, appears more eligible than the solitary, unfriend'd, ridiculed condition of the single life; and no wonder, since the usual way of educating young women seems as if it were calculated on purpose to awaken all the affections of the heart, at the same time that it deprives them of their proper counter-balance, the strength of the head.

Marriage with an advantageous settlement is represented to young women 'as their highest advancement, and the end and design of all their attainments'.

It is true that the majority of wives have no reason to complain, but 'no thanks to the laws of our country for that exemption; let every particular woman who is well treated thank God and her husband for this blessing.' But let her not forget that in law she is no better than a slave!

12

'The causes must be grave and weighty'

LOVELESS ARISTOCRATIC MARRIAGES arranged solely on the basis of money were still all too frequent. In 1747 Lady Mary Campbell, youngest daughter of the Duke of Argyll and Greenwich, was married to Edward, Viscount Coke, heir to Thomas Coke, 1st Earl of Leicester, of Holkham in Norfolk, and they both had cause to regret it.

The marriage was 'conducted in the old-fashioned manner; overtures being made by Lord Coke's relations to hers, terms proposed and rejected, others acceded to and the bargain finally struck for two thousand five hundred pounds per annum jointure and five hundred pin-money, as the fair equivalent for her £20,000, which at that time was a larger portion than could often be met with outside the City.'

From the outset the Duchess of Argyll had doubts about the match, 'on account of Lord Leicester's notoriously dissolute and violent character'. Like father like son? The usual practice was for each family to make enquiries as to the character, reputation and, of course, financial position of the prospective partner, but in this as in so many cases the enquiries seem not to have been exhaustive enough. And it was all too easy to be deceived at the courtship stage. With the daughter's £20,000 portion in his sights, Lord Coke set out to disarm the mother: 'He dutifully attended her mother's tea-table, stroked Her Grace's cats, listened to her long stories, talked goodness and morality, and kept his countenance admirably throughout.'

Nor did he neglect the daughter, 'every now and then lowering his voice to its softest tone, and tenderly addressing the lady of his love'. But Lady Mary did not trouble to hide her contempt, 'bridling with ineffable disdain, turning away her head and hardly vouchsafing him an answer'.

Coke was enjoying his own performance, but those who knew his true nature could 'foresee that her airs of scorn would not go unpunished – for he was inwardly as haughty as herself, thoroughly unprincipled and profligate . . . and [had] not the smallest personal liking for her to counterbalance the secret resentment which such contemptuous usage inspired'.

As 'the lawyers' labours advanced, and the day of execution drew near', Lady Mary liked him less and less. She 'wept all the morning above stairs, and in the evening sat below stairs, a silent picture of despair'. Her sister begged her not to go through with the marriage, but matters took their inexorable course.

No sooner was the ring on her finger than Lord Coke dropped his act. He 'had a long score of insolence to pay off, and was predetermined to mortify the fair bride by every means in his power'. He refused to sleep with her on the wedding night, which probably came as something of a relief to her. He resumed his former habits of drinking and gambling, and 'used coarse language to her' when they were alone.

Lady Mary vowed never to cohabit with Coke, which earned her the hostility of her father-in-law, who wanted an heir to Holkham. She holed up in her room, feigning sickness. They consulted lawyers as to 'whether a wife's obstinately denying her husband his conjugal rights did not justify his placing her under unusual restraint'. The only surprise was that they bothered, since a husband had absolute power over his wife. He could force her to have sex, there being no such thing as marital rape, and he could confine or imprison her if he wished.

Coke did just that. He locked her up in an old house on the Holkham estate and deprived her of her maid. It could have been far worse. From the latter part of the seventeenth to the late eighteenth century, when Parliament at last passed legislation to prevent the abuse, there was a thriving business in private madhouses, where men could lock up their wives, no questions asked. Nobody enquired about their mental condition or who was committing them or why. Some wives who were perfectly sane found themselves stripped, whipped, starved, chained and fettered, and prey to sadistic keepers. Unless they had family and 'friends' to discover their whereabouts and secure their release, they might languish in the asylum for years. Daniel Defoe, scandalized by this 'vile practice so much in vogue among the better sort', concluded that if the women were not mad when they were confined, they soon became so by this 'barbarous' treatment.

From the relative comfort of her confinement on the Holkham estate, Lady Mary contrived to smuggle letters out to her family. Her mother, the duchess, now descended on Holkham demanding to see her, but was refused. She returned to London and applied to the court of King's Bench for a writ of habeas corpus, demanding that Lord Coke produce his wife. It offered her temporary release to appear before the court.

Lady Mary was duly brought up to town, swore the peace against her husband, and filed a suit for divorce *a mensa et thoro* – that is, a separation from bed and board, without permission to remarry during the lifetime of the other spouse – for 'cruel usage'.

The legal definition of cruelty shifted over time. Mental cruelty was not recognized at all. Physical cruelty had to be unjustified, frequent, and so extreme that it posed a threat to life itself. After the Restoration and in the course of the eighteenth century, this began to shift almost imperceptibly, from fear of life to 'grave and weighty' acts causing pain and suffering. In 1790 the eminent judge Sir William Scott, later Lord Stowell, made a landmark ruling:

> It is the duty of the courts, and consequently the inclination of the courts, to keep the rule extremely strict. The causes must be grave and weighty, and such as show an absolute impossibility that the duties of the married life can be discharged. In a state of personal danger no duties can be discharged; for the duty of self-preservation must take place before the duties of marriage . . . What merely wounds the mental feelings is in few cases to be admitted where they are not accompanied with bodily injury, either actual or menaced. Mere austerity of temper, petulance of manners, rudeness of language, a want of civil attention and accommodation, even occasional sallies of passion, if they do not threaten bodily harm, do not amount to legal cruelty; they are high moral offences in the marriage-state undoubtedly, not innocent surely in any state of life, but still they are not that cruelty against which the law can relieve.

Since it emerged that the only incident of physical violence in Lady Mary's marriage was Coke striking her on the arm and tearing a lace ruffle, she had evidently been very ill advised to file the suit. Threats of violence, unkindness and rude words, even her brief imprisonment, were not sufficient grounds for divorce.

With Lord Hartington acting as mediator, the couple agreed on a private separation. Informal private separation agreements were not recognized by the Church, nor did they hold any weight in law, but they were a handy form of self-divorce in a society where it was impossible to dissolve a broken marriage if it did not involve adultery or extreme cruelty. For the less affluent, it was also a cheaper way of ending a marriage without resorting to the courts, which had become progressively more expensive.

Private separations had come into being during the chaos of the Interregnum, following the abolition of the ecclesiastical courts and the failed attempt to transfer jurisdiction over marriage, adultery and fornication to the secular authorities. When the ecclesiastical courts were restored in 1660 there was a huge backlog of marital break-down cases to be dealt with, but for some the idea of making one's own, secular, arrangements, whether it be in marrying or dissolving a marriage, had taken hold.

The Glorious Revolution of 1688 had seen the triumph of the Whigs and Locke's theory of monarchy being a breakable contract between King and people. Some wondered why the same should not apply to marriage. As Lady Brute quipped in Vanbrugh's *The Provok'd Wife*, 'The argument's good between the King and the people, why not between the husband and wife?'

Unfortunately, it was not that simple. On marriage, a woman's legal existence was subsumed into that of her husband. They were one person in law. She could not testify against him. Nor could she make a contract with him, since legally they were one and the same person. Private separation agreements were not recognized in common law, but they offered the only relief for an unhappy, incompatible couple and the trade was flourishing.

It was agreed that Lady Mary must withdraw her suit and pay all the legal expenses herself. She could live separately, although not in London, and, as was standard in these agreements, her husband undertook not to 'molest' her. As her husband, he still had the power to seize her by force, take her home with him against her will, and keep her in confinement. She only had his word for it, in the agreement, that he would not do this. If he changed his mind and violated the agreement, the law offered her little protection. It was not until the late nineteenth century that a separated wife was safe from physical abduction by her husband.

Nor, in reality, did the agreement offer any real guarantee that the husband would not sue the wife if he subsequently decided to do so. Since a private separation was not recognized by the Church, there would be nothing to prevent the admittedly perverse Lord Coke from expressing a willingness for a reconciliation and applying to the ecclesiastical court for 'restitution of conjugal rights', forcing Lady Mary to resume cohabitation in the same house, although not, as is commonly believed, necessarily in the same bed.

A wife could be lulled into a false sense of security by a separation agreement. It was by no means safe for her to enter into another relationship. In the unlikely event of Lady Mary committing adultery, Coke would be able to apply to the ecclesiastical court for a separation from bed and board, in which case she would forfeit her common law right to maintenance. Having won his case in the ecclesiastical court, Coke might then apply to Parliament for a private Act enabling him to remarry to produce an heir for Holkham.

Conversely, if Lady Mary had had a justifiable case for separation from bed and board in the ecclesiastical court, she would have been entitled to maintenance amounting to one-third of her husband's income. As it stood, she was to have no maintenance, in spite of the £20,000 portion she had brought to the marriage, although since she was not divorced her jointure was not affected. She must live on her £500 a year pin-money.

When Lord Coke 'died of his excesses' only three years later, Lady Mary at twenty-six found herself in the rare, privileged position of an independent woman with a jointure of £2,500 a year, which was an excellent return on her portion. She was now at liberty to re-enter society. Labelled the 'White Cat' for her exceptionally blonde hair and streak of malice, she indulged her passion for gossip until her death in 1811. Wisely, she never remarried.

13

'What can equal the value of a virtuous wife?'

MARRIAGE WAS DISSOLUBLE only by death, but in early modern England the mortality rate was such that a marriage was unlikely to last more than twenty years and many far less than that. Over a third of all marriages were second marriages for at least one of the partners. Some married as many as five times. There can have been few cases like the men Daniel Defoe encountered in the malaria-infested Essex marshes, however, some of whom had had up to fifteen wives:

> The reason, a merry fellow told me, who said he had had about a dozen and a half wives, was this; that they being bred in the marshes themselves, and seasoned to the place, did pretty well with it; but that they always went up into the hilly country, or to speak their own language, into the uplands for a wife: that when they took the young lasses out of the wholesome and fresh air, they were healthy, fresh and clear, and well; but when they came out of their native air into the marshes among the fogs and damps, there they presently changed their complexion, got an ague or two, and seldom held it above half a year, or a year at most; and then, said he, we go to the uplands again, and fetch another; so that marrying of wives was reckoned a kind of good farm to them.

Thomas Turner, a shopkeeper living in East Hoathly in Sussex in the 1750s, had a more typical experience of marriage. He and his wife Peggy had been married only two years, but there were plenty of arguments, as he recorded in his diary: 'This morning my wife and I had words about her going to Lewes tomorrow; oh, what happiness must there be in the married state, when there is a sincere regard on both sides, and each party truly satisfied with each other's merits! But it is impossible for tongue or pen to express the uneasiness that attends the contrary.'

Surely marriage was not designed to make mankind unhappy, he reflected. He had married 'entirely to make my wife and self happy; to live in a course of virtue and religion, and to be a mutual help to each other'. And yet it had not turned out like that. There were interminable quarrels. He was even thinking the unthinkable, of separating: 'I have almost made a resolution to make a separation by settling my affairs and parting in friendship.'

A year later he marked their third wedding anniversary by recalling that 'many have been the disputes which have happened between my wife and myself during that time, and many have been the afflictions which it has pleased God to lay upon us,' yet at last 'we now begin to live happy.' So much so that he confesses, 'I am thoroughly persuaded that if I was single again, and at liberty to make another choice, I should do the same – I mean make her my wife who is now.'

It was often only when a man lost his wife that he was prompted to express his true feelings for her and incidentally to summarize the qualities that made a good wife.

In October 1760 Turner's wife fell ill. 'At home all day, and thank God, pretty busy, but my wife very ill,' he recorded. 'Oh, how melancholy a time it is that I, quite destitute of father and mother, am in all probability like to lose my wife, the only friend I have now in this world, and the centre of my worldly happiness.'

It was not until the following June that she died. She was only twenty-seven and had given birth to four children, who did not survive her. He paid tribute to her:

About five o'clock in the afternoon it pleased Almighty God to take from me my beloved wife, who, poor creature, has laboured under a severe though lingering illness for these thirty-eight weeks, which she bore with the greatest resignation to the Divine will. In her I have lost a sincere friend, a virtuous wife, a prudent good economist in her family, and a very valuable companion. I have lost an invaluable blessing, a wife who, had it pleased God to have given her health, would have been of more real excellence to me than the greatest fortune this world can give.

He was bereft. 'I hardly know which way to turn, or what way of life to pursue.' A year later, he was still mourning Peggy's loss. 'Oh, how does the memory of that ever-valuable creature, my deceased wife, come over my thoughts as it were a cloud in May! Who is that man that has once been in possession of all this world can give to make happy and then lose it, but must ever and again think of his former happiness?'

He regretted that his household was no longer well run, that everything that had been 'serene and in order' was now 'noise and confusion'. Most of all, he missed her comforting presence after a busy day: 'nothing to soothe the anxious mind, no pleasing companion, no sincere friend, no agreeable acquaintance, or at least amongst the fair sex'.

That was about to change. In the spring of 1765 he began courting Molly Hicks, who was working as a domestic servant. 'In the afternoon rode over to Chiddingly, to pay my charmer, or intended wife, or sweetheart, or whatever other name may be more proper, a visit at her father's, where I drank tea, in company with their family.'

He wished to marry again – 'marriage is a state agreeable to nature, reason, and religion' – and he esteemed this girl, and 'think she appears worthy of my esteem'.

This was no headlong romantic rush. He weighed up the pros and cons pragmatically. 'The girl, as far as I can discover, is a very industrious, sober woman and seemingly endowed with prudence, and good nature, with a serious and sedate turn of mind.' It was significant that 'industrious' came at the top of the list, since it was assumed that the wife of a tradesman would work alongside him and must be a good worker. 'She comes of reputable parents, and may perhaps, one time or other, have some fortune,' he continued. 'As to her person, I know it's plain (so is my own), but she is cleanly in her person, and dress . . . She is, I think, a well-made woman.' Her education had been indifferent, but 'she has good sense, and a desire to improve her mind'. And she treated him with courtesy and respect.

They were married in June 1765. 'Then the ceremony of receiving the visitors, and again the returning of them, has indeed, together with the business of my trade, taken up so much of my time,' he complained. However, it was all worth it, because, as he confessed before ending the diary six weeks later, he was happy in his choice of wife.

14

'He has often beat and kicked her when she has been big with child'

I N THE EARLY eighteenth century a Mr Veezey was tried at the Old Bailey after his wife found her life with him so intolerable that she threw herself out of the window. It was established that he had kept her confined in a garret for several years, without fire, proper clothing, or any of the basic comforts of life. He frequently horsewhipped her. Since food – one hard and mouldy piece of bread – was found in the garret and it was clear that Veezey had not pushed her out of the window himself, he was acquitted. He had as good as got away with murder.

The amount of cruelty husbands in all sections of society unleashed on the helpless women in their power was quite breathtaking. Wife-beating had become so common that Daniel Defoe noted that 'to hear a woman cry murder now, scarce gives any alarm'. Men did it because they could and because they were seldom called to account. Much of the violence was alcohol-fuelled – even by modern standards, they drank a prodigious amount. The wonder is just how much the women were prepared to endure, so deeply ingrained in their psyche was the doctrine of passive obedience.

Marital cruelty has to be seen in the context of the time. This was a hierarchical, brutal society in which relationships of dominance and submission were the norm and in which violence, or the threat of it, was the only means of maintaining order in the absence of a police force. Public punishments included the gibbet and the stocks; employers thought nothing of beating their servants; and, although the conduct books warned against it or regarded it as the very last resort, English husbands assumed it was their God-given right to beat their wives. As late as 1782 a judge confirmed that they were entitled to do so, provided the stick they used was no bigger than their thumb – hence, rule of thumb.

Domestic violence was probably all the more savage because there was no easy exit from marriage. It was a mark of frustration. New publications such as the *Spectator* and *Tatler* were calling for greater civility within marriage, but they were as yet running against the tide. It was demeaning for a man, who should be guided by reason, to lose control, they argued; with privilege came responsibility and the obligation to protect the weak and inferior. The courts, however, tended to uphold male authority, even while deploring its abuses. Men could play the system with confidence, accusing their wives of provoking them, knowing full well that such 'unwomanly behaviour' would not be condoned, while women generally were ignorant of the law and lacked the independent means to embark on expensive legal procedures. For a wife to leave her husband and seek a separation, to have all her dirty linen examined in court and to relive the humiliation, she had to be desperate.

Money was at the root of at least half the cases examined in the London Consistory Court. With money the motive for so many marriages, there was a corresponding resentment at the growing practice of women's separate settlements, to protect their interests against a husband's profligacy. A husband might use threats, blackmail, sustained mental torment and physical violence to make his wife rescind such a settlement. He could confine her to a madhouse until she gave in to his demands, or he could separate her from her children: legally, there was nothing to stop him because both his wife and his children were his property, to do what he liked with short of killing them.

If she still did not comply, he could make her life such hell that she would leave. Since even an abused wife did not have the right to leave her husband without his consent, this placed her legally in the wrong, while it was an offence to keep a man's wife from him by offering her refuge. She could swear the peace against him, but this exposed her to his resentment. If she had him sent to gaol, she and her children might starve. Unless she managed to obtain a judicial separation with maintenance in the courts, she was still his creature and at his mercy.

A husband might also mistreat a wife in order to force her family into paying an overdue dowry, or punish her for its non-payment.

Elizabeth Byfield was one such unfortunate case. The court heard

how Thomas Byfield 'being wholly unmindful of his conjugal vow
. . . hath for the most part behaved himself very barbarously and
inhumanly toward her'. Her libel stressed that it was 'without any
just provocation'. He was always shouting at her and 'he has often
beat and kicked her when she has been big with child and flung her
upon the ground and dragged her about the room by the hair of
her head.'

Not only had Thomas consorted with 'several lewd and scandalous women', but he had brought home one Sarah Williams to live
with them, ostensibly as some sort of companion. In 1706 Elizabeth
was pregnant and he sent her to her mother's in Herefordshire for
the confinement. During her absence, Sarah would apparently 'roam
into his bedchamber when he was in naked bed'. They would send
the maid to market early in the mornings and when she returned she
would find the door bolted.

When Elizabeth came home it was to find Sarah Williams installed
as her husband's mistress. She was imperious and disrespectful and
clearly had usurped Elizabeth's place in the household. Byfield locked
Elizabeth in her chamber and beat her 'day after day'. One day the
neighbours – who tended to act as a final safeguard in these situations,
intervening and expressing their disapproval of erring husbands –
heard her cry 'Murder' and ran to help.

Byfield dismissed the prying maid and had Elizabeth do the servant's work, which was considered far more demeaning then than it
would be now. He kept her and the child short of food and refused
to send for the apothecary when the child was ill. He routinely struck
and kicked her on the head, arms and legs, so that her body was black
and blue. He told her that if she didn't like it, she and her bastard
could leave. Courageously, one day she did just that.

Dorothy Arnold, described as 'a mild, sober, pretty sort of woman',
also claimed to have been a good wife to her husband John, a watch-
maker, who had 'at several times very cruelly beat and abused' her,
'using indecent and opprobrious language' and threats. He had taken
a mistress, Margaret Woods, whom he kept as his wife at a house in
Cold Bath Fields, Clerkenwell. At the same time, he withdrew from
his wife's bed and would not permit her to eat at table with him,
or to come into his presence, but kept her confined in a back room

'up two pair of stairs' in his house. The leftovers were taken up to Dorothy after he and the family had dined.

One night Dorothy went into his bedchamber and asked him 'by what means she was so unhappy as to have lost his affection, and what she had to do to regain it?' He jumped out of bed and 'knocked the said Dorothy down to the ground with his double fists . . . and continued to beat, kick and cruelly use her, till the persons in the house ran up to her rescue'.

Dorothy's position as mistress of the household had been belittled. In such a rigidly structured society, the courts took a dim view of this. John had ordered the servants not to pay her any respect or obey her orders. He frequently declared he would give £100 to any man who would 'debauch' her – allowing him to divorce her for adultery without maintenance – or £50 to any person who would bring him news of her death.

Dorothy was petitioning the court for a separation from bed and board with maintenance. Because of the sexual double standard, far fewer women than men tended to sue their husbands for adultery. Most wives quietly accepted it. A man could divorce his wife for adultery alone, but for a woman there had to be aggravating circumstances, such as life-threatening cruelty, unnatural practices – sodomy, the wilful transmission of venereal disease to the wife, although this was not as yet counted as cruelty, and the replacement of the wife by the mistress as head of the household, as in the Byfields' case.

Dorothy had to prove life-threatening violence; her petition said she was 'so bruised and battered that she was reduced to a very ill state of health', but her proctor, or lawyer, was also able to present the court with the written testimony of witnesses, who in turn would be interrogated individually by professional examiners.

James L'Argeau, a peruke maker, knew the couple and had observed her injuries. He had also seen Arnold give his wife some money to go and live in the country. Several months later she came home, but Arnold 'would not suffer her to go in, pushed her away, and shut the door upon her'. Dorothy stayed some time, knocking at the door, but could not gain admittance.

Mary Raitt of Crane Court, Fleet Street, was a servant who had lived with the Arnolds for four years. She had often heard Arnold call his wife 'a bitch' and heard him beating her and her calling out 'Murder'. On the night that Dorothy had entered his bedroom to plead with him, Mary Raitt had found her covered in blood. She appeared to have been 'much beaten about the mouth, which was so bruised and swelled, that for a day or two she could eat with nothing but a small teaspoon, and continued very bad for some time'.

On another night when Arnold was upstairs entertaining friends to supper, Dorothy came down to the kitchen crying. Raitt said that she appeared to have had a tankard of beer thrown over her and to have received a violent blow to her arm, 'which deprived her of the use of it for some time, and it looked so bad that she thought the arm in danger of mortifying'.

Adultery was often hard to prove, but at least two witnesses testified for Dorothy. Mrs Horsey, the landlady of the house in Cold Bath Fields where Arnold and Margaret Woods were lodging, stated that they pretended to be married, going under the name of Mr and Mrs Jackson. Elizabeth Hawkes, a servant, gave evidence that Arnold and Margaret Woods shared the same bed. Moreover, she used to wash Margaret Woods's linen, from which it was clear that she had miscarried.

Dorothy won her case and Arnold was ordered to pay her maintenance of £20 a year. Normally a man was responsible for his wife's debts, but not if they were legally separated and she was receiving maintenance. It was up to the husband to place an advertisement in the newspaper warning the local tradesmen that he was no longer responsible, as Arnold did in the *Daily Advertiser*. 'Whereas Dorothy Arnold, the wife of John Arnold, hath agreed to live separate and apart from me, and I do allow her a separate maintenance, this is to caution all persons not to give her any credit on my account, as I will not pay any debts she shall contract. John Arnold, Watch-maker, in Devereux Court, 23 September 1767.'

Martha Robinson's wifely credentials would seem to be impeccable. The court heard that she 'was and is a person of a mild, affable and obliging temper, of a very modest and sober carriage and behaviour, and of a religious and virtuous life, and conversation; and hath at all times, since her marriage, behaved herself towards her husband as a dutiful and indulgent wife.'

It was a pity, then, that Samuel Robinson, a cabinet maker, consorted with 'divers lewd, wicked, and debauched women, who were reputed to be common women of the town, and had carnal knowledge of them; by which he frequently contracted the foul distemper, or venereal disease; and did often apply to a physician or surgeon for a cure'. He readily admitted that he had caught the disease from 'his intercourse with common women'. He had twice infected his wife and threatened to 'murder her if she mentioned the nature of her disorder to the servants'. At first he appears to have tried a home remedy of some powder mixed with wine to cure his wife, but she had swelled up to such alarming proportions that he was obliged to call in the surgeon.

After this episode, Martha refused to live with him any more, saying she could not 'render him conjugal rights, without great danger of her life'. She left and took employment as a servant in Cheshunt under an assumed name. Like any married woman in this situation, she was still her husband's property and he could descend on her at any time, perhaps years later, and appropriate her business, the tools of her trade, and her earnings. Robinson tracked Martha down and insisted that she return home. She refused and 'begged that she might be at liberty to get her bread', but he dragged her back to his house at Houndsditch 'contrary to her own free will'.

A fellow cabinet maker, John Bisset, testified that Robinson 'hath several times in his presence abused and ill-treated his said wife, and knocked her down with his fist, and threatened to beat her brains out'. He also confirmed that Robinson kept a mistress, Peggy Walton, by whom he had four children.

Martha won her freedom, although we do not know how long she survived 'the loathsome distemper' which was the undeserved legacy of her marriage.

In the final irony, a wife who, provoked beyond endurance, murdered her husband committed high treason, just as if she had killed the King. If a husband killed his wife, it was a mere felony. The law decreed that she be dragged in a hurdle to the place of execution and burned alive. Not until 1790 was this horrendous punishment changed to death by hanging.

15

'The foul crime of adultery'

O N A SUMMER'S day in 1776 Elizabeth Smith, a servant in the household of the Reverend Crofts of East Bradenham, Norfolk, was looking out of the window when she noticed Mrs Elizabeth Lockwood, the vicar's married daughter, slip out of the house and make her way to the nearby bleach ground. Not far behind her was Simeon Knowles, a 'menial servant'. Her curiosity roused, Elizabeth Smith tripped out after them, taking up her position by the hedge and peering through it – it was 'not a thick one' – to see what was going on.

Her nosiness was well rewarded. She saw Simeon Knowles lay Mrs Lockwood down upon her back and lift up her petticoats, exposing her bare thighs. He lay on top of her and 'their bodies were in motion and they had the carnal use and knowledge of each other, and committed the crime of adultery together.' She was certain the man was Knowles because when he got up, she 'saw him very plainly, for he turned towards her, and his breeches were then down'.

Smith called out, 'Madam, dinner is ready,' and seized the opportunity for a bit of blackmail. She told her that she had been there all along. A few days later, Mrs Lockwood duly gave her 'an old gown of hers, and said, she gave it her, that she should not say anything'.

Smith had been aware of what was going on between the mistress and Knowles for some time. They were always 'toying and playing, and going into the pantry and other places by themselves'. Nor did they trouble to hide their infatuation. There had been many occasions in Smith's presence when Mrs Lockwood had 'put her hand into the said Simeon Knowles' breeches'.

In the age of servants, it was impossible to have an affair without them knowing. They seemed always to be listening at doors, peeping through keyholes, examining the sheets for tell-tale stains, catching the sound of bedroom doors opening and closing in the night and beds creaking, and gossiping. Since their employers hardly deigned to notice them or to tidy up after themselves, it was not difficult to accumulate evidence against them.

Servants' evidence was highly useful in court, although they were obviously susceptible to bribery. Since it was the master who held the purse strings and employed them, the odds were heavily stacked against an adulterous wife. Often witnesses repeated the same phrases, indicating that they had been rehearsed by the proctors in what they had to say, before appearing before the ecclesiastical court's professional examiners. These examiners were adept at getting to the truth.

Gossip was obviously rife in the Crofts household. Smith's fellow servant, John Secker, 'having heard that Mrs Lockwood and Simeon Knowles were very intimate with each other, and having observed them walking together like lovers, he determined to follow them; and in the dry ditch he plainly saw Mrs Lockwood lying on her back and Simeon Knowles was lying upon her.' Once more her naked thighs were exposed and Knowles had his breeches down. Secker 'told several people what he had seen'.

Mary Owen, a forty-six-year-old widow, did sewing at the vicarage. One day she found Mrs Lockwood in the garret, in bed with Simeon Knowles, 'and they were then in the very act of carnal enjoyment'. 'Lord have mercy, Madam!' she exclaimed. 'What are you doing? There will be murder when Mr Lockwood comes to know this!' To which Elizabeth Lockwood insouciantly replied, 'Why should he come to know this? If he was told of it, he wouldn't believe it.'

Her attitude obviously incensed Owen, who testified that Mr Lockwood had 'a vast love for his wife, and the highest opinion of her'. Mrs Lockwood was busy deceiving him and taking huge risks of being discovered, and yet she always got away with it, she recounted peevishly, behaving so well in front of her husband that 'he never had any suspicion of her'.

When Elizabeth gave birth to a boy and her husband had to go to London, it was perhaps telling that before her lying-in month was up, Simeon Knowles came to her room and had sex with her.

For Owen – jealous, resentful and outraged – this appears to have been the last straw. They 'seemed to glory in their wickedness, and in exposing themselves', she testified. Unable to tolerate such disgusting behaviour any longer, she was the one who betrayed the lovers. She told Elizabeth's mother and Mr Lockwood what was going on, which is how Elizabeth came to be in court, having 'been seduced by the devil and her own wicked lusts'.

The snooping of servants and clumsy attempts to bribe them also feature in the next tale of adultery. On 28 June 1775 Elizabeth Martha Chichely Harris went to Basingstoke races with her husband and sister. There they met the Reverend John Craven, described in court as a 'clerk, a gentleman of a very considerable fortune, and Rector of Woolverton near Southampton'. After the races Mr Harris was very drunk, but obviously they had had such a good time that the Reverend John Craven, who might also have been drunk, was invited back to their home. With her husband so inebriated, Elizabeth had no trouble in smuggling John Craven into her bedchamber.

And so the relationship started. Sarah Simmons, hired by Mr Harris as his wife's maid, testified that soon Mr Harris and Reverend Craven were so friendly that the latter spent weekends with them. Craven would rise early and walk in the garden. While Sarah was still dressing her mistress, Mrs Harris would lean out of the window with 'her breasts uncovered, and exposed to Mr Craven . . . she had only her shift, stays and petticoats on', to tell him that she would soon be down to join him.

When Mr Harris was away for three weeks in March 1776 the Reverend Craven came to stay. Mrs Harris asked her bedfellow, her kinswoman Catherine Burnford, not to sleep in her bed that night. Reverend Craven went to bed unusually early, while Mrs Harris went into the kitchen and ordered all the servants to have an early night. She even told her maid that she did not need her to undress her that night. About midnight, Sarah Simmons allegedly heard Reverend Craven leave his room and enter Mrs Harris's.

Avid with curiosity, Sarah went to the door of her mistress's room, standing in the passage with her ear pressed to the keyhole. The Reverend Craven and Mrs Harris were whispering together; she heard them kiss each other; 'but there was not any light in the room, and therefore she could not see anything that passed between them; but she heard the moving of the bedclothes, and curtains, and heard the bed crack; and the noise and shaking of the bed continued for about two or three minutes.' Then there was silence.

Sarah hung about to see what happened next. She checked that Reverend Harris was indeed absent from his own bed. Then she saw him leaving Mrs Harris's room at 2 a.m. Obviously the couple had had 'the carnal use and knowledge of each other's body, and committed the foul crime of adultery together'. Next morning, while Mrs Harris was at breakfast, Sarah recruited fellow maid Elizabeth Holden and they went to Mrs Harris's bedchamber to investigate.

The bed was 'very much tumbled, and they both observed several marks or spots upon the sheets; which were very visible, as the sheets were put on clean the night before'. Sarah believed 'such marks and spots were occasioned by Reverend Craven and Mrs Harris having lain together that night, and having had the carnal knowledge of each other.'

When Craven left that evening and Sarah helped him on with his coat, he gave her a guinea – the first time he had ever given her anything. Next day, Mrs Harris called Sarah into her dressing room and gave her 'a gown and a petticoat, and other things, and desired [her] not to tell tales, for that servants never got anything by it; or to that effect'.

The man-servant John Appleton testified that Craven was always made very welcome at the Harris' home. He had observed a familiarity between Reverend Craven and Mrs Harris, such as when he slid his hand 'into her bosom' or 'partly up her petticoats'. One day Mrs Harris ordered Appleton to 'take the sopha out of the little room adjoining to the middle parlour, and place it in the middle parlour by the fire'. Later, when he went in to make up the fire, he found Reverend Craven and Mrs Harris sitting on the sofa. He had his hand up her petticoats and her skirts were raised up, exposing the lower part of her legs. On seeing Appleton, Craven quickly snatched his hand away and they both looked embarrassed.

The upshot of all this was that Mr Harris sued Reverend Craven for criminal conversation, for trespassing on his property – the body of his wife – and depriving him of her company and comfort. He was awarded £3,000 damages. He also won his case for a separation from bed and board. Unfortunately, the record stops there; it does not tell us what happened to Mrs Harris or whether Craven was able to survive his financial misfortune and the stain on his reputation as a clergyman.

Bernard Brocas also sued his wife's lover. Bernard and Anna Brocas were married in 1753 but had not shared a bed for years, 'on pretence of her illness'. If he ever ventured into her bedchamber she complained. The servants noticed, however, that the arrival of William Matthew Burt on the scene, probably at a ball given by Brocas for the neighbouring gentry, quite transformed their mistress, so much so that they nicknamed him 'the Doctor'.

In October 1767 Anna went to stay at Buxton, ostensibly to take the waters for her health. Burt and his wife were lodging in the same house. Anna's maid testified that Burt would enter her mistress's bedchamber in the morning before she was dressed. Many 'amorous indecent familiarities' passed between them. One morning Burt came in with some black satin shoes, which Anna allowed him to slip on her feet, taking the opportunity to 'stroke his hand up her leg under her petticoats', complimenting her 'delicate leg'.

A year later and Burt was staying at the Brocas' home. Since it was 'public talk amongst the servants in the said Bernard Brocas' family', or household, that there was something going on between the mistress and Burt, two of the servants lay in wait to see what transpired. Sure enough, about quarter past one in the morning Burt 'opened his chamber door and passed from thence with a great coat over his shoulder and without any breeches on across the passage that parted his bedchamber from the said Anna Brocas''. There could be no doubt that they were lying in bed 'naked and alone together' and committing the 'foul crime of adultery' because the 'noise and motion of the bedstead was plainly and distinctly heard' by the inquisitive servants.

No one dared tell the master about his wife's infidelity, because of his 'passionate disposition', but somehow he learned about it. Brocas brought an action in the court of King's Bench against Burt for 'trespass and assault on the said Anna Brocas and for laying with her and carnally knowing her whereby the said Bernard Brocas lost the comfort of his said wife'. He asked for damages of £10,000. The jury awarded him £2,000, which probably indicates that they did not like him very much. We do not know whether Burt's marriage survived or whether he continued his liaison with Anna. The only certainty is that with her reputation ruined she had entered the twilight world of the separated wife.

Adultery was rife among the upper classes, partly because their marriages were based on money rather than affection, and partly as a diversion from idleness. When Richard, Lord Grosvenor, was trying to divorce his wife Henrietta for her adulterous affair with Frederick, Duke of Cumberland, she excused her adultery on the grounds that her marriage was not a match of her own choice, but strongly recommended to her by her parents. Similarly, when Lady Harriet Spencer married Lord Duncannon in 1780 it was very much to please her parents. 'I wish I had known him a little better first,' she told a friend, 'but my dear papa & mama say that it will make them the happiest creatures, and what would I not do to see them happy.' Like her sister, Georgiana, Duchess of Devonshire, she ended up having an affair.

The middling classes tended to ape their betters. Ever since the Restoration, when the promiscuity of the court provided such a bad example to the rest of the nation, there had been a steady decline in morals. Unlike in Scotland, where adultery was a criminal offence, by the eighteenth century the punishment of adulterers and fornicators in England had largely fallen into abeyance with the diminishing authority of the Church courts. The main concern now was not morality but money, to keep down the soaring poor rates by identifying fathers of bastards and either forcing them into marriage or paying for their upkeep.

It was left to the individuals themselves to pursue their erring spouses through the courts and to exact full retribution for adultery. Even though it was an increasingly expensive process, there are plenty of examples among people of the middling and lower middling sort.

Richard Draper, grocer, married Elizabeth Hartnell in December 1764. She was sexually voracious and soon tired of her husband. By 1771 Richard was suing her for adultery with a whole string of men, including his apprentice.

Draper had invited Edward Goode, a linen draper newly arrived from Gloucestershire, to live at his house in Bishopsgate Street in the City. Elizabeth Draper lost no time in luring him upstairs, ostensibly 'to see the pigeons', and pulling him into a room where there was a bed. Draping her arms round his neck, she began kissing him. Throwing her off, he left the room, with her shouting angrily, 'Blast your eyes!'

On another day, she sent for him to her bedchamber and asked him to 'come to bed to me'. He walked out, but she followed him downstairs and found him in the dining room. Sitting on his knee, she kissed him again and placed his hand on her breast. She then sat astride him and pulled up her petticoats, saying, 'Will you?' Goode could not help himself. After this she asked him to have sex with her many times, but he got cold feet.

Elizabeth had other fish to fry. William Penfold was her husband's apprentice. He testified that one day in the dining room after dinner Mrs Draper kissed him and 'put her hand to his breeches, and unbuttoned his breeches, and asked the deponent to enjoy her; and she pulled up her petticoats and he then had carnal knowledge of her'. For the rest of the time he resided in the house as Draper's apprentice, he 'very frequently (sometimes twice a week) and when the opportunity served, and the said Richard Draper was from home, had carnal knowledge of the said Elizabeth Draper in her own bed in her bedchamber'.

Both Goode and Penfold testified against Elizabeth – ungrateful wretches – but it was her affair with the leather merchant, John Lankester of Ely, that brought the testimony of a third party. Elizabeth was staying at the house of Joseph Marshall in St Ives, Huntingdon, a farmer and carrier, when the housekeeper's daughter, Mary Allen, witnessed her adultery. Lankester was having supper with Elizabeth and had sent Mary Allen downstairs for some wine. Something in their demeanour must have roused her suspicions, because when she returned she took off her shoes and crept up to the door to listen. There was a large keyhole, which afforded her a good view of the room. The couple were sitting by the fire and 'the bosom of the said Elizabeth Draper was quite naked'. John Lankester was touching and kissing her. The floorboard on which Mary was standing creaked and she hurriedly moved away, but, unable to resist, crept back to resume her spying.

By now Elizabeth's 'head was between John Lankester's legs'. Next Mary heard 'the bed to crack and make a noise . . . and the deponent heard them whispering and in motion upon the bed'. She could not see the bed, so went back downstairs and put on her shoes, making a great deal of noise when she returned with the wine. She found the door of the supper room locked until one of them opened it.

The next case is one of 'incestuous adultery', in which Sarah Oliver had no trouble in presenting herself as the deeply injured wife. She is described as being of 'an affable, mild, and easy temper, and of a very modest and sober carriage and behaviour; and also of a virtuous and religious life and conversation; and hath always behaved towards her husband with the utmost conjugal love and fidelity; and never was guilty of a breach of the marriage vow'.

She sounds almost too good to be true, in contrast to her adulterous husband. Samuel Euclid Oliver, 'a person of a lewd and vicious inclination, contracted and carried on a lewd and adulteress conversation to and with divers women; particularly with Elizabeth Hoskings, spinster, sister of the said Sarah Oliver.'

The Olivers were living in St Martin's Lane and had three children. Samuel and his father-in-law were in business together, which presumably gave him frequent access to the Hoskings' home. A fourteen-year-old servant there testified that she had often seen Samuel kiss Elizabeth 'and take indecent liberties with her'. On one occasion she went into Elizabeth's bedroom and found her 'sitting with her petticoats up, and Samuel Euclid Oliver close by her on a bench . . . with his breeches down and unbuttoned'. He ran into a corner 'holding his breeches up with his hands'.

According to Elizabeth's testimony, Samuel would enter her bedroom, catch hold of her on the stairs – there was nowhere she could escape to. She had 'resisted him all in her power', she told the court, but 'he debauched her and lay with her'. If it had just been the once, her testimony might have been credible, but the next day they had sex again and continued to do so over many months. Elizabeth must have been complicit.

When the inevitable happened and she experienced morning

sickness, Samuel visited Mrs Catherine Clarke, a midwife in Fleet Street, and obtained medicines to induce an abortion. 'All may be well if you will take things regular, and if you neglect now it must be discovered,' he urged in a note to Elizabeth, who was already three months gone.

Needless to say, having imbibed this rubbish, Elizabeth became very ill and was forced to tell her mother the truth. There was a huge family row, with Samuel taking his fists to his father-in-law. He was arrested for assault and committed to Bridewell. He did at least write the Hoskings a letter of contrition: 'I am sorry that I have been guilty of a crime so heinous in the sight of God and man, so contrary to nature and the solemn vow I made.' Sarah was granted a separation from bed and board.

Wives who committed adultery might also pass on venereal disease to their husbands. John Worgan, a music master living in the parish of St Andrew's Holborn, was suing his wife Sarah for 'the foul crime of adultery, fornication, or incontinency, with one or more strange men, particularly one Rowe, a married man, and she communicated the foul disease to the said John Worgan'.

Several of Worgan's servants came forward to testify against their former mistress. Katharine Bates noticed that Worgan's assistant, Robert Rowe, frequently came to dine alone with Sarah while Worgan was working. Sarah's three-year-old child had mentioned that she had seen Rowe kissing her mother. Her suspicions roused, Katharine scrutinized the room where Sarah had been entertaining Rowe and 'observed, on the floor, some matter, which comes from the man in the act of coition'. From this she deduced that Robert and Sarah 'had, on that day, carnal knowledge of each other, and did commit the crime of adultery'.

Another former servant, Anne Beckley, testified that one John Mully, a music pupil of Worgan's, was very close to Sarah and often dined and drank tea with her in Worgan's absence. Cross-examined, Beckley had to admit that she and Sarah had had a falling out – giving testimony in a court case was a sure way to pay off old scores.

Martha Homer of Salisbury Court near Fleet Street did the Worgans' washing. She noticed that Sarah's linen was 'very much stained', but since she had recently had a miscarriage, she put it down to the medicines she had been taking. But then she noticed that John Worgan's linen was also stained and 'began to suspect that he had got the foul disease'.

In August 1764 Worgan consulted a surgeon, William Bromfield of Conduit Street, who testified that he knew him to be 'a very honest, sober man, in every respect, and as a person no ways addicted to the company of loose women'. Worgan told Bromfield that he suspected he had the clap and concluded that he must have got it from his wife, whom he knew had been ill for some time and 'afflicted with a running from her private parts'.

To 'preserve the peace of the family', Bromfield told Worgan that his wife was suffering not from venereal disease, but 'the whites, which was common in women', and gave him some medicine – 'treating his complaint as venereal'.

Sarah in turn consulted Bromfield, admitting that she knew she had the clap and had passed it on to her husband, while recounting some ludicrous tale that she had 'caught it off a man who came over the garden wall and forced her'. She begged him not to disclose her secret to her husband.

Robert Rowe, meanwhile, had died in the Fleet, where he had been imprisoned for debt. His mother deposed that he had confessed his intimacy with Sarah and how they had 'frequently been out on parties of pleasure together, whereby they had expended great sums of money'. Ungallantly, he blamed Sarah for seducing him. Rowe's twenty-seven-year-old widow Elizabeth testified to the same effect.

Once imprisoned, Rowe had urged Sarah to do what she could to get him released. She responded by coming to his mother's house and offering to pawn her rings to pay one half of the sum required if his mother could provide the other half.

Apparently, Sarah had told Rowe at the outset that he was about to 'cuckold the honestest man in the world'. It seemed everyone was the loser in this sordid tale.

PART FOUR

1760–1827

16

'That part of the United Kingdom called Scotland'

IN MAY 1782 a young woman stole out of her father's house in Berkeley Square in the middle of the night into the arms of her waiting lover. Their destination was Gretna Green, Scotland.

She was Sarah Anne Child, daughter and sole heiress of the fabulously rich banker, Robert Child, and he was John Fane, 10th Earl of Westmoreland. At first glance there would seem to be no reason why these two should have been put to the extraordinary inconvenience and subterfuge of making a border marriage. He had a title, she would have money. But Child was unimpressed by Westmoreland's aristocratic credentials: 'Your blood, my lord, is good, but money is better.'

At eighteen, Sarah Anne needed her father's consent to a marriage in England. He wanted his only child to marry someone who would carry on his business. He had no intention of allowing her to marry an impoverished aristocrat, who not so long ago had gone cap in hand to Child's bank for a loan.

Westmoreland had organized their escape well, ordering horses to be in readiness all along the route. At one stage he hired every horse in the village in order to delay pursuit, but Child was no mean adversary. Throwing handfuls of largesse to the post boys, he was well supplied with horses. He caught up with the couple just short of the border, as they stopped to change horses at Hesketh-in-the-Forest, halfway between Penrith and Carlisle. The journey from London had done nothing to moderate Child's reaction. In his rage, he jumped out of his carriage and shot one of the other's leading horses. While one of Westmoreland's servants hurriedly untied the dead horse, another ran behind Child's carriage unobserved and cut the leather that suspended the body from the springs. The lovers' carriage took off with only three horses. Child had not gone far in pursuit when the body of his carriage fell upon the frame. He was stranded. By the time he clambered on to a post-chaise and caught up, it was too late. His daughter was married. He could only write her out of his will.

One of the unexpected loopholes in Lord Hardwicke's Act for the Better Preventing of Clandestine Marriage (1753) was provided by the exclusion of Scotland. Parliament had been keen to extend the Act for 'the more effectual preventing clandestine marriages in that part of the United Kingdom called Scotland', but such a move was seen to threaten the inviolability of the Scottish religion, which had been assured by the Union settlement of 1707. Left to decide their own course of action, the Scots had failed to agree to implement the provisions of the Act north of the border. The marriage laws of the two kingdoms diverged more sharply than ever, and any English couple who wished to marry in haste or in secret had only to go to Scotland to escape the restrictions of the Marriage Act.

Scotland had divorce with permission to remarry, England did not. Surprisingly for a country that had been so eager to bring its marriage laws into line with the rest of Protestant Europe at the Reformation, Scotland clung to contract marriage, a legacy of the medieval Catholic Church which, ironically, the Catholic Church ceased to recognize after 1563, when it stipulated that all marriages must take place in the presence of a properly ordained priest. While various Acts of the Scottish Parliament in the seventeenth century laid down that marriages must take place before a Church of Scotland clergyman to be legal, a contract marriage, abolished by Hardwicke's Marriage Act in England, was still valid in Scotland, if technically illegal.

According to this doctrine, consent made a marriage. Provided the couple were of lawful age (twelve for a girl, fourteen for a boy), were not within the prohibited degrees of kinship, and gave their full, free and mutual consent, they could be married by simply exchanging vows. The marriage did not have to take place in church, nor at any particular time of the day or night, nor even before witnesses, for it to be valid. A written record was not required, although it was advisable that a witness should be able to give evidence if later required to do so in court. Better still would be an interchange of letters between the couple confirming mutual consent.

Unlike in England, where property was paramount, the Scots did not seem to be concerned about the implications such a vague form of marriage would have for inheritance rights. One of the prime purposes of tightening up the marriage laws in England was to protect property, by preventing sons and daughters making clandestine marriages with persons of inferior rank and fortune-hunters. Indeed, the nobility were so concerned about it that they were very reluctant to allow their sons to attend Edinburgh University, given the ease with which they could make some rash and irrevocable marriage.

No sooner had Hardwicke's Marriage Act come into force in England than at least one of the notorious Fleet parsons paid off his debts and advertised his removal to Scotland, where he could continue his lucrative trade unhindered. However, the traffic in clandestine marriages north of the border only really took off after the construction of turnpike roads in the late 1770s and the coming of express coaches on the west coast highway leading up to Gretna Green. A tradition already existed in Scotland by which couples would go to be married by certain individuals who kept registers, witnessed their consent, and often pronounced some quasi-religious form of words over them. The most famous of these in the late eighteenth century was Joseph Paisley, 'a big, rough-drinking Borderer' so strong that he could 'straighten a horseshoe with his bare hands'. It was he who married Susan Anne Child and the Earl of Westmoreland. Once, in his haste to oblige two couples by marrying them simultaneously to beat their pursuers, he united the wrong bride and bridegroom. 'Awell,' he said, 'jest sort yersels.'

The most notorious Gretna Green marriage was that of the sixteen-year-old heiress, Miss Ellen Turner, who was abducted from her boarding school in Liverpool in 1826. Her abductor, thirty-year-old Edward Gibbon Wakefield, already had a track record in runaway matches, having previously eloped with Eliza Susan Potter, a ward in Chancery. There must have been something attractive about the rogue, because Eliza stayed with him, giving birth to two children before succumbing to tuberculosis. Wakefield now hatched a plot with his brother to kidnap the schoolgirl. On 7 March 1826 a barouche turned up at the school containing Wakefield's French servant, Edouard Thevenot, who carried a letter purporting to be from a doctor to say that Miss Turner's mother was very ill and that she must be taken home to Shrigley Park immediately.

Casually released by the school, Thevenot carried the girl to Manchester, where Wakefield informed her that her father had lost a great part of his fortune and was being pressed by his creditors. He had authorized the Wakefield brothers to bring her to him in Yorkshire. Either naïve or none too bright, she agreed to set off in the company of the two strangers. By dawn the next day they were at Kendal, where a letter from her father now asked her to meet him at Carlisle. The brothers told her that their uncle was a rich banker who had lent her father £60,000 to extricate him from his difficulties, caused by the failure of Ryle and Daintry's bank at Macclesfield.

Their uncle required security for his loan. Shrigley Park was his for the taking. However, if Miss Turner agreed to marry Edward Gibbon Wakefield, his uncle would turn over the property to her. 'Then our uncle will settle us in life handsomely and prevent your father being turned out of doors in his present circumstances,' Edward told her. The girl insisted on continuing to Carlisle to see her father. Once there, she was told that the inn where he was staying was surrounded by bailiffs, but that she should continue to Scotland to be married with all haste to relieve him of his miseries. Two days after her abduction Ellen Turner was married to Edward Gibbon Wakefield at Gretna Green, with every appearance of having given her consent freely.

The business done, it quickly became apparent that the game was up. Rather belatedly, the schoolmistress had become alarmed. The doctor's letter was exposed as a forgery. Then on 11 March an advertisement appeared in a newspaper announcing the marriage. The family lawyer went at once to the Secretary of State and procured warrants for the arrest of the Wakefields, who had fled with their prize to Calais. The lawyer, assisted by an officer from Bow Street, arrived in Calais on 15 March and arrested them. Miss Turner, or Mrs Wakefield as she was now, was taken home to her parents.

The trial Rex v. Edward Gibbon Wakefield and William Wakefield for conspiracy, abduction and forced marriage opened at Lancaster on 26 March. Unfortunately, the crimes had to be committed in England, so that they could only be tried for *conspiring* to commit the deed. As to the marriage, there was no evidence of force: the girl had not put up a fight or offered resistance, but the Wakefields pleaded guilty to abduction. Edward went to Newgate and William to Lancaster Castle Prison, each for three years. The marriage was annulled by Act of Parliament in April 1827.

By the mid-1850s the clandestine marriage business at Gretna Green was booming, facilitated by the expansion of the railways. There was a steady supply of customers, not least because in England attempts to abolish the parental veto for marriages of children under twenty-one had been defeated in Parliament. But was a Gretna Green marriage valid in England? Lord Mansfield argued that it was not, since the intention was clearly to flout the provisions of the 1753 Marriage Act. If not, were the children of these marriages illegitimate and so incapable of inheriting property? These were questions that remained unresolved until the introduction of Lord Brougham's bill in 1856, which declared that a Gretna Green marriage of an English couple was not legally valid in England unless it had been preceded by three weeks' residence in Scotland. This simple solution deterred the poor, who could not afford the long stop-over in Scotland, and allowed the parents and guardians of the rest to catch up with them before they had committed the irrevocable deed. It effectively put an end to the clandestine marriage business.

Not, alas, before one young lady followed in her grandparents' footsteps. Robert Child the banker never forgave his daughter Sarah Anne for her elopement and left his vast wealth to his granddaughter, Sarah Sophia Fane, who married the 5th Earl of Jersey. In November 1845 her daughter, Lady Adela Villiers, eloped to Gretna Green with a Captain Ibbotsen. Her parents were furious, but since Ibbotsen was highly regarded by his commanding officer, the Duke of Wellington, they had to make a virtue of necessity. How Child must have rolled in his grave!

17

'A match of her own making'

WHEN THE 1ST Duke of Richmond lost badly at cards to the Earl of Cadogan he agreed to settle the debt by marrying his son and heir, Lord March, to the earl's daughter, Lady Sarah Cadogan. The duke was forced to make out a receipt for £5,000, 'being part of the twenty thousand pounds given by the said Earl as a marriage portion in present with his daughter, Lady Sarah, to my son, Charles, Earl of March.'

No sooner was this sordid transaction completed than the eighteen-year-old earl was brought to meet the rather plump girl of thirteen. A clergyman was standing by and the couple were told they were to be married immediately. 'They surely are not going to marry me to that dowdy!' Lord March exclaimed. The deed was done and he was despatched to the Continent for his Grand Tour. Three years later he returned to London. He was in no rush to become reacquainted with his 'wife', so went to the opera. His eye was caught by the extraordinary beauty of one young woman and he asked who she was. 'You must be a stranger in London,' he was told, 'not to know the toast of the town – the beautiful Lady March.' He went straight to the box to reclaim the bride he had insulted three years before. From then on Lord and Lady March, soon to become the 2nd Duke and Duchess of Richmond, were the most conspicuously devoted married couple in London.

It was a coldly arranged marriage that succeeded against the odds, unlike that of their daughter, Lady Sarah Lennox, who in a more sentimental era married for love and scandalized society by her flagrant adultery.

The Lennox sisters – Caroline, Emily, Louisa, Sarah and Cecilia – were the great-granddaughters of King Charles II by his French mistress, Louise de Keroualle, Duchess of Portsmouth and Aubigny. Since their parents' marriage was so happy, the girls and their two brothers were a close and united family. Their family life was spontaneous and natural, in contrast to the frigid formality of many other aristocratic families. As one of the youngest, Lady Sarah, with her prettiness and vivacity, was a much petted and indulged child.

The only shadow on the Lennox family's serene existence had been the elopement of Caroline with the politician Henry Fox in the year of Sarah's birth. The duke strongly disapproved of Fox. His father, Stephen Fox, had begun life as a mere servant to Charles II, although he had ended up with the lucrative office of paymaster. His brother, Stephen, had had a suspiciously close relationship with another man. Fox himself was considered both too old and too poor for Caroline, who was nearly twenty years younger. He was not at all the splendid match the Richmonds had envisaged for their eldest child.

By the time of the duke's premature death in 1750 and his duchess's a year later, however, Caroline's elopement had been forgiven if not forgotten. By the terms of the duke's will, his younger daughters – Louisa, eight, Sarah, six, and Cecilia, one – were to be entrusted to the care of their elder sister, Emily, Countess of Kildare, in Ireland. As Emily's senior by eight years, Caroline was deeply affronted that her father did not consider her suitably responsible to take on the guardianship of her young sisters, but her earlier rebellion against parental authority told against her. Emily, whose marriage to Ireland's premier aristocrat was both suitable and happy, was considered a far safer influence on young girls. The only concession the duchess would make in her own will was that the three sisters should be returned to Caroline in London once they were of an age to be launched on the London marriage market.

It was not until she was fourteen, therefore, that Lady Sarah Lennox came to live with the libertarian Foxes at Holland House and made her debut in London society. As the sister-in-law of Lord Kildare, she was already well acquainted with Dublin society, which in the mid-eighteenth century enjoyed a brilliance and sumptuous gaiety rivalling the best of the European capitals. There was an easy spontaneity in Irish circles which was completely lacking in the stiffer etiquette of London. This influence, together with her natural flirtatiousness, would ensure that Sarah stood out among the more restrained English debutantes.

Everyone thought she was very pretty, although the gossip Horace Walpole discerned that this was due to the effervescent glow of youth rather than good features. Henry Fox said that her beauty was indefinable. She had 'the finest complexion, most beautiful hair . . . a sprightly air, a pretty mouth, and remarkably fine teeth, and excess of bloom in her cheeks, little eyes – but this is not describing her, for her great beauty was a peculiarity of countenance, that made her at the same time different from and prettier than any other girl I ever saw.' She was tall, but had a tendency to plumpness, and Caroline was disappointed to note that she held herself badly. Only after she had spent time in Paris and taken deportment lessons there did Sarah assume the gracious carriage appropriate to someone of her rank and beauty. Her undoubted fascination could be summed up by saying that she had sex appeal.

When Caroline brought Sarah to a 'Drawing Room' at Kensington Palace to present her to King George II he began to tease and play with her, just as he had when she was a charmingly naïve child of five and he had picked her up and deposited her in a large China jar and closed the lid. Instead of crying to be let out, Sarah had delighted her audience by her rendition of '*Marlborough, s'en va t'en guerre*'. In her confusion and embarrassment the adult Sarah now stood mute. 'Pooh! She's grown quite stupid,' he exclaimed dismissively. Standing behind him was his twenty-two-year-old grandson, Prince George, who being shy himself felt mortified on her behalf. He engaged her in conversation and was immediately smitten.

In October 1760 the old King died and Prince George succeeded as George III. By now Lady Sarah, together with her best friend, Henry Fox's niece Lady Susan Fox-Strangways, were court habituées, regularly attending the balls at St James's and the Drawing Rooms at Kensington Palace. The arduous search for a husband was not totally divorced from pleasure. Henry Fox noticed that the young King took 'every opportunity of conversing' with Sarah. His ambition was stirred. The King must marry and why should he not consider his pretty sister-in-law with her Stuart royal blood?

The Foxes were given every reason to hope, since George invariably focused all his attention on Sarah whenever she came to court, blushing when he spoke to her. At a ball at St James's in February 1761 he made a point of engaging Susan Fox-Strangways in a conversation that the family considered deeply significant. 'There will be no Coronation until there is a Queen,' he told her, 'and I think your friend the fittest person for it. Tell your friend so from me.'

It was a most oblique way to go about it. What was a fifteen-year-old girl to think? Why could the King not just say what he meant to Sarah herself in plain English? Or, more properly, speak to her guardians if his intentions were serious? For Sarah, it was all very flattering, but she had no feelings whatsoever for George, who was nice, but rather vacuous. She was far more excited by a flirtation with Lord Newbottle, who pursued all the pretty girls. Unfortunately, she had just found out what a cad he was when she paid her next visit to court. She was in far too bad a mood to parry the King's ambiguous questions.

As soon as she entered the Drawing Room, George rushed up to her to ask if Susan had relayed the message.

'Yes, Sir.'

'And what do you think of it?' he pressed.

'Nothing, Sir,' she replied, not hiding her indifference.

'Nothing comes of nothing!' he exclaimed impatiently.

Fox was furious with Sarah for letting her disappointment over Newbottle affect her response to the King. There was no opportunity to remedy the matter, as she was about to leave for Somerset. Here she had a riding accident and was laid up with a broken leg for two months. The King was all concern, wondering that 'she should be left to the care of a country surgeon'. Every time he saw one of her brothers-in-law he bombarded them with questions about Sarah's progress. Fox was elated by the King's evident infatuation. 'Don't tell Lady Sarah that *I am sure* he intends to marry her, for I am not *sure* of it,' he wrote to his wife. Of course Caroline would show the letter to Sarah in a calculated bid to inflame her ambition. Whatever her feelings for George, she would have been pleased enough to be Queen if that was her destiny. Under Fox's directions, Sarah spent the rest of her convalescence being coached on how to behave when she next saw the King.

Had they but known it, it was already too late. The Dowager Princess of Wales had no intention of furthering the ambitions of her old enemy, Henry Fox, who had opposed her regency, by allowing her son to marry Sarah Lennox. Nor did George's greatest confidant, his former tutor Lord Bute, to whom he had innocently confided his love for Sarah, relish the idea of losing his influence over the King, as he surely would do if he married her. In his letters to Bute, George abases himself, telling him, 'If I must either lose my friend or my love, I will give up the latter, for I esteem your friendship above every earthly joy.' While Sarah was convalescing in Somerset, George and his mother were spending their evenings combing through the *Almanach de Gotha* in search of a nice, biddable German princess.

When Sarah returned to court in time to attend the King's Birthday Ball on 4 June, he was obviously thrilled to see her, but it was still not clear what his intentions were. He repeated the ambiguous remark, 'For God's sake, remember what I said to Lady Susan before you went to the country, and believe I have the strongest attachment.' Was he going to propose or not? Flattering as it was to be the centre of the court's attention – for many were convinced that the King was going to marry her – Sarah was growing impatient. 'I won't go jiggitting forever,' she told Susan.

The blow fell on 8 July, when at a meeting of the Privy Council George announced his forthcoming marriage to Princess Charlotte of Mecklenburg-Strelitz. For most of the time George had appeared to be courting Sarah he had, in fact, been torn between his promise to his mother and Bute never to marry an Englishwoman, and his feelings for Sarah. When he had reminded her that 'I have the strongest attachment', it was a regretful goodbye.

Lady Sarah had been made to look a fool before the whole court, through no fault of her own. George was undoubtedly in love with her, but had been selfish in not disclosing his true intentions. He had, after all, monopolized her, using precious time she might have devoted to making a more attainable match. Henry Fox was culpable in that he had allowed ambition to override realism and as Sarah's self-appointed campaign manager had mishandled the whole affair. Too young to be ambitious, Sarah had not really bothered to play her cards properly at all.

She revealed her feelings in a letter to Susan. George had behaved without '*sense, good nature,* nor *honesty*'. She was determined to go to court at the earliest opportunity, to show the world that 'I am not mortified' and to snub him. Apart from 'this little revenge, I have almost forgiven him; luckily for me I did not love him, & only liked him, nor did the title weigh anything with me'. The worst of it was the knock to her pride and confidence. 'The thing I am most angry at, is looking so like a fool as I shall for having gone so often for nothing, but I don't much care; if he was to change his mind again . . . I would not have him, for if he is so weak as to be govern'd by everybody, I shall have but a bad time of it.'

She ended by begging Susan and her family not to speak of it to anyone, for to embarrass the King by reminding him of his bad behaviour 'might do a great deal of harm to all the rest of the family, & do me no good'.

Since her feelings were not really engaged, Sarah appeared to recover quickly, even – to Caroline's disgust – taking her place as chief bridesmaid at the royal wedding, which was her privilege as the eldest unmarried daughter of a duke. She conducted herself with such dignity that no one thought of her as poor, rejected Lady Sarah, but the collapse of her hopes with the King had been a setback and inwardly she was wounded. She was still only sixteen, but when she re-entered the fray of the marriage market she must have been all too aware of the barely suppressed hint of panic in the family that, after the best part of two years in London, she had still not secured a husband.

As Caroline confided fearfully to Emily, 'here are all the good matches going by her . . . some girls have all the luck'. Sarah had begun to fear that she was not liked and was somehow unmarriageable; if she was not married by the time she was seventeen, she told Emily, she would return to live quietly in Ireland.

No matter how eligible a young woman, she could not afford to let too many suitors pass her by. After a couple of seasons, she would look like tired goods or, as Caroline put it, 'I hope she may get married before her pretty face gets too common.' Caroline marked out the Duke of Marlborough as a possibility, but he seemed to prefer Lady Caroline Russell and married her. Feeling the pressure to get her sister married, not least because Emily had succeeded so spectacularly in securing Louisa's match with Tom Connolly, the richest man in Ireland, before even leaving those shores, Caroline then produced the Earl of Errol, a Scottish peer of distinguished pedigree, enormous height and modest fortune. Sarah, who dubbed him 'Ajax', failed to take him seriously.

There then appeared out of left field a 'Mr B'. With the words of her nephew Stephen Fox – 'Don't refuse a good match when you can get it, and don't go to plays and operas too often' – ringing in her ears, Sarah eagerly grasped this new possibility. Mr B, or Thomas Charles Bunbury to give his full name, seemed to follow her wherever she went, she told Susan. 'I have not put myself in his way, for at Leicester House (*en presence de ma soeur*) we changed places three times and he followed us.' At the theatre he came over to sit near them. 'This, you will allow, is *particular*.' One may gauge Caroline's desperation from Sarah's admission, 'My sister, who is quick at those sort of things, has settled it that he will make his declaration immediately.'

Charles Bunbury, MP for the County of Suffolk, had gained access to Holland House among the young Whigs who came to talk politics with Henry Fox, although as a politician he was singularly inept. It is not surprising that he began to pay attention to his host's lovely, unmarried sister-in-law, but Sarah, who had lost faith in her own judgement, was unsure about him. 'You will say I might find out what he thought by his conversation,' she wrote to Susan, 'but it's generally loud and of indifferent subjects, only broad hints now and then that he likes me, asking me constantly where I am to go, and when I shall be in town, and that he only comes to see me, and so forth.'

A dilettante, elegant, good-looking, rather languid, Bunbury's only true enthusiasm was for the turf. It was said that if his constituents had had four legs and a tail they would have been well served. The elder son and heir of the Reverend Sir William Bunbury, Baronet, he stood to inherit two good houses, Barton and Milden Hall in Suffolk, and an estate of about £5,000 a year. It was a competent enough fortune, but no match for the Richmonds and Foxes. He lacked Fox's political acumen, Kildare's title, and Connolly's fortune. Grateful that an eligible suitor seemed to be paying court to Sarah at last, however, Caroline began to make the usual enquiries, while Fox was to conduct the financial negotiations.

The Duke of Richmond was less than enthusiastic about the match, noting shrewdly that Sarah's mind was 'not so unalterable but that she might have done without him'. Indeed, Kildare, in London at the end of April, was perturbed by Bunbury's lack of ardour. Neither he nor Lady Sarah seemed 'to be much in love according to my notion of being in love', he told his wife. The pressure was all coming from Holland House. Sarah was probably telling herself she was in love with the young man because she knew that was what her guardians wanted to hear, while from Caroline's point of view there appeared to be no more suitors in the offing.

It was not as if Bunbury's financial prospects were so impressive as to make up for the shortcomings in his character, which were beginning to emerge. His father was willing to settle £2,000 a year on him and 'a house in town and country'. Richmond was offering an income of 5 per cent on his sister's dowry of £8,000 until the principal sum could be secured, presumably from his French estates, after the end of the war with France. Sarah was willing to forgo pin-money, but her family was insisting on a jointure of £1,000 a year rent charge. Fox and the duke feared that 'two people so very young can hardly be expected to have prudence enough to live within' these limits. For all her fine connections, Sarah would be comparatively poor. The family absolved themselves by telling themselves it was a love match.

The wedding of Lady Sarah Lennox and Charles Bunbury took place at the private chapel in Holland House in June 1762. It was a low-key affair, which was typical for the period, but the bridegroom's lack of enthusiasm may be gauged from the fact that he had postponed the ceremony by a week owing to some other engagement. Everyone agreed that with Sarah's radiant vitality and Bunbury's fine features and smooth elegance they made a very attractive couple, although Horace Walpole unkindly remarked that since Bunbury's beauty would outlast hers he would soon grow tired of her. Fox, who was largely responsible for his sister-in-law's haphazard journey to the altar, complacently noted in his memoir: 'not rich enough, but 'tis a match of her own making, and happiness don't depend on riches'.

The flaws in the marriage very soon came to the surface. The newly married Sarah's first letter from Suffolk to Susan Fox-Strangways neglected to mention Charles Bunbury at all. They 'let me go my own way here, and when they do that, I am very comfortable', she wrote. Charles's courtship ended abruptly with the marriage and he now reverted to type, preferring the company of his racing cronies to that of his bride. His indifference was puzzling and hurtful, but Sarah put on a brave front, protesting too much in a letter to Susan:

> Pray now, who the devil would not be happy with a pretty place, a good house, good horses, greyhounds, etc, for hunting, so near Newmarket, what company we please in ye house, and £2000 a year to spend? Add to this that I have a settled comfortable feel that I am doing right, that all my friends love me and are with me as much as possible; in short, that I have not one single thing on earth to be troubled about on my own account. Pray now where is the great oddity of that; or the wretch that would not be happy?

As the months passed, Sarah could not escape the dawning realization that Bunbury was unlikely to give her children. Just what the nature of the problem was – impotence, latent homosexuality, or just a lack of desire on his part – is unclear. Sarah wanted only to be a good wife, mother and homemaker. Instead, a lifetime of emptiness stretched before her. She began to crave excitement, to flirt with other men to prove that she was attractive and loveable, even if her own husband failed to acknowledge it. His lack of jealousy or concern, his sheer indifference, only spurred her on.

By the time the couple went on a prolonged visit to Paris in January 1767 Sarah was craving sexual adventure and fulfilment. Sir Charles Bunbury must be either an indulgent or an indifferent husband, the Parisians quickly surmised, since their party included his wife's young admirer, Lord Carlisle, who escorted her whenever Sir Charles was otherwise engaged. It was not long before the notorious seducer, Armand de Gontaut, Duc de Lauzun, scented a conquest, taking care to befriend the husband while lavishing on Sarah the adoration he denied her.

It was perfectly permissible for a married woman in society to have an affair, preferably after she had produced the heir and spare, and as

long as she was discreet. But Sarah was not discreet. She prided herself on her frankness. Her pent-up frustration meant that when she
strayed from the path of virtue, she would do so with flagrant abandon. It was all or nothing with her. Even before Lauzun had seduced
her, Sarah's behaviour had raised eyebrows. As Madame du Deffand
wrote to her friend and fellow gossip Horace Walpole:

> I find her very much a coquette . . . Monsieur de Lauzun sees her
> three times a day. No young woman of our world could behave as
> she does without being much talked about. However, the note among
> people here is rather one of astonishment than scandal. She pleases,
> has *naivete*, a caressing manner, is quite likeable. But she distinctly has
> not a sound good taste. Her Lauzun is a fool who plays the part of a
> giddy young man. He wouldn't ever have undertaken this affair with
> her except for the sake of telling all the world about it.

Before Lauzun could boast of his conquest, however, he had to
overcome the hurdle of Sarah's guilt. Aristocratic marriages bred
adultery because they were arranged and usually loveless. Sarah,
who had apparently made her own choice of husband, had no such
excuse. 'As we choose our husbands, it is less permissible to us not to
love them,' she told him, 'and the crime of deceiving them is never
forgiven us.'

When the Bunburys returned to England, Lauzun followed. Sarah
had no trouble in persuading her ever obliging husband to invite
their friend to stay with them in the country. Indeed, he was so
obliging as to return to town, leaving his wife alone with Lauzun for
three weeks. In his memoirs, Lauzun describes the seduction:

> At length, one evening, she told me that I might come down to
> her chamber when the household were gone to bed. I awaited this
> longed-for moment with the utmost impatience. I found her in
> bed, and supposed that I might take a few liberties. She appeared so
> offended and distressed by them that I did not persist. She allowed me,
> however, to lie down beside her, but she required of me a moderation
> and reserve of which I thought I should die. This charming torment
> continued for several nights. I had ceased to hope for consummation,
> when, clasping me on one occasion with the liveliest ardour, she
> gratified all my desires.

Sarah imagined herself in love with Lauzun and, ignoring the fact that he had a young wife, proposed a madcap scheme for them to run away to Jamaica together. He prevaricated, then tried to persuade her that such an arrangement would mean their social ostracism and ruin, so that they would soon hate each other. A romantic, Sarah had craved undying love more than sexual fulfilment. She now turned the tables on Lauzun so fast he did not know what hit him.

'You have not had sufficient confidence either in your own constancy or mine,' she told him. 'You have not found that I was necessary to your happiness, nor have you cared to bind yourself to me by ties which nothing could ever break. By rending my heart, you have dimmed your own image in it.'

It was over. Once again Sarah had misplaced her faith and her love. She now seems to have embarked on a series of indiscreet affairs, so that word got about that she was fast. She even seems to have had an assignation with an actor in a notorious Covent Garden bagnio, where her initials were inscribed on one of the windows. So low had she sunk that her name crept into the gossip columns of the gutter press, which could not have gone unchallenged if she were innocent.

Sarah had a streak of Stuart recklessness which made her fatally prone to sacrifice all for love. When she met Lord William Gordon at Richmond House six years into her marriage it seemed that she had met her match, for Gordon had all the dark, brooding, romantic and dangerous appeal that would subsequently make his younger kinsman Lord Byron so irresistible to women. He and Sarah were equally reckless in their passion for each other. By May she was pregnant.

To Charles Bunbury the news of his wife's pregnancy seems not to have come as a shock. Perhaps he was rather gratified to have paternity thrust upon him. He never hesitated to give the child – a daughter born in December – his name, so that little Louisa Bunbury began life like any other child born in wedlock and her mother was not forced to give her up, as other aristocratic women who bore their lovers' children had to do. Affecting ignorance of her infidelity, Sarah's family rallied round, delighted at the news. No doubt everyone was relieved that the child was a girl, so that there could be no question of Sir Charles's estates passing out of the legitimate line.

Sarah was no hypocrite, however, and she positively wallowed in her guilt. She simply could not bear to pass off her child as her husband's and to pretend to the world that she was a virtuous wife when she was not. It was unfair to Lord William to keep him apart from his child. She was delighted to find that he felt a similar impatience with the conventions. Six weeks after her confinement, she left London for Barton, away from the prying, anxious eyes of her sisters. Gordon followed. One morning in February she went out for a walk and did not return. She had eloped with Lord William.

The family was horrified, but it was still not too late, they decided, to save her. Louisa went in pursuit and brought Sarah back to Holland House, where they begged her not to destroy herself and, by extension, her innocent child. Sir Charles was offering his protection to them both, if only she would return to him and preserve appearances. She must think of the consequences for others. Her disgrace would impinge on the entire family. She had thoughtlessly jeopardized the reputation of her unmarried sister Cecilia, who had been staying with her at Barton and who would now be associated with her adultery. This threw Caroline and Emily into collision, since Kildare held Caroline and the lax atmosphere at Holland House responsible for Sarah's ill-advised marriage. Caroline, he implied, reopening the old wound, was not fit to have care of young girls.

Sarah was implacable. She would not return to Sir Charles. Taking her baby, she fled from Holland House and took lodgings at an inn near Southampton, where she told the landlady that she was waiting for her husband, Mr Gore. They had married without the consent of family and friends, she explained, and just wanted to live together privately in the country.

Society was titillated by such a delicious scandal, while Lady Mary Coke, who loved to chew over gossip, confessed that she was utterly shocked by the revelation from Sarah's aunt that she did not intend to marry her lover when Sir Charles divorced her. Apparently, he had too volatile a temper. Now that Sarah had irrevocably thrown in her lot with Lord William, Sir Charles lost no time in ridding himself of her. He had been willing to condone her adultery, if only she was discreet, but he would not be the object of ridicule. For someone who was normally so dilatory, the speed with which he acted must have come as a shock. He brought an action for criminal conversation against Lord William, although the latter was too poor to offer recompense, followed by a suit in the ecclesiastical court for a separation from bed and board.

'Lady Sarah Bunbury, being of a loose and abandoned disposition, and being wholly unmindful of her conjugal vow . . . did contract and carry on a lewd and adulterous conversation with Lord William Gordon,' the libel stated. Armed with the depositions of the couple's landlady, who could attest to the fact that they shared the same bed, and of his servants at Barton, it was an open and shut case.

Sarah's adultery meant the unravelling of the marriage settlement and the loss of her jointure. However, Sir Charles was not a mean or vindictive man. He generously returned her marriage portion of £500 a year, which he was not obliged to do, and as a matter of course he accepted that Louisa should continue to bear his name, as if she were his own child. It was up to him to refuse Sarah her freedom by leaving it at that, or to obtain a private Act of Parliament which would enable them both to remarry.

The lovers and their child had by now taken refuge in Scotland, but their solitary idyll could not last for long. Just before their elopement Lord William had resigned his army commission and he bitterly regretted it. Time hung heavy. At last there came a day when they could no longer pretend to themselves or to each other that they were happy. Lord William rode away alone. The break was permanent. Passionately as he had loved Sarah, he never tried to rekindle the affair. He never showed any interest in their child, just as if she did not exist, nor did he contribute to her upkeep. Eventually he married, for money.

It was left to Lady Sarah to pay the price of the disgraced woman. She was fortunate in that her brother the Duke of Richmond offered her a home on the Goodwood estate, but she could never resume her place in society. Ostracized, she must live in complete retirement and stay out of sight, while she had to work hard to regain the family's goodwill. Even within the relaxed atmosphere of Holland House, Sarah was seen as a social liability. Calling to see Caroline one day, Lady Mary Coke was put out that she was 'not at home', even though she had seen her with an unknown child on the balcony. 'All this appeared so extraordinary that at first I did not know what to make of it,' she recorded in her diary, 'but since I came home, I'm persuaded Lady Sarah Bunbury was at Holland House and that it was her child.'

As a fallen woman Sarah was the target of malicious scandal. In February 1774 the *Morning Post* blithely announced that she was with child by her nephew Charles James Fox. She was deeply upset by the allegation.

She took temporary refuge from her loneliness by returning to Ireland. The family had been slow to forgive her, but Kildare, latterly Duke of Leinster, who had been the main obstacle to her rehabilitation, was now dead. It had been Emily's turn to shock when she married her sons' tutor. Sarah resumed her old childhood closeness with Louisa. Irish society was a little less rigid. 'Some of my old acquaintance with the ladies have been more than civil to me, quite kind indeed, and some of Louisa's acquaintance have been very civil, but great part of both sorts have taken no notice of me . . . I always take the civilities I meet with from ladies as a *favour*.' It was a sad statement from the woman who might have been Queen.

In 1776 the petition of Sir Charles Bunbury in the House of Lords to dissolve his marriage with Lady Sarah Lennox and to enable him to marry again revived the scandal. Sarah shuddered as all the sordid evidence of the deponents was heard again, knowing that it would be reported in the newspapers and that her servants read those newspapers. A private bill required the royal assent like any other. Normally the King sat in the Lords in his crown and robes while the Clerk of the House read the well-known formula of royal assent, '*Le Roy le Veult*'. Sarah's case was considered too sensitive for her former admirer, George III, to witness in person. A distant precedent was found and the royal assent was given to the Bunbury divorce bill *in absentia*.

Sir Charles never did marry again. Three years after their parliamentary divorce he asked for a meeting with Sarah. She was glad to have the opportunity to ask his forgiveness. She was grateful, too, for the kindness he showed her daughter. Not only had he assumed paternity of the child born *during* the marriage if not *of* the marriage, but he now invited her into the Bunbury family circle. Acceptance by her putative father meant acceptance by society and it was an overwhelming relief to Sarah to know that her daughter would not suffer for her sins.

In August 1781 Lady Sarah Lennox and the Honourable George Napier were married in Goodwood parish church. She had met this career officer and younger son of an impoverished Scottish baron some years before. They liked each other instantly, but he had been married then. He was now a widower. Richmond and Louisa had watched the relationship unfold with disquiet. After so many years in quiet retirement was Sarah about to make another mistake? 'Why change when you are well off?' her brother demanded. 'You risk all, and may lose all.' Her friend Susan joined in the clamour to dissuade her. Poverty, she warned, was a constant irritant.

This time Sarah really was sure she was making the right choice. 'If you love me, Sarah,' Napier declared, 'I have not the least doubt of our being happy.' Two years later, on her thirty-eighth birthday, Sarah was able to answer Susan's objections definitively: 'I find I never knew what real happiness was, which from my marriage with Mr Napier till now is much greater than I had any idea of existing in human life.'

18

'A cruel, savage and abandoned disposition, as well as loose, wicked and lustful'

O N MARRIAGE A husband and wife became one and the woman ceased to have any separate legal existence. The man became responsible for any improper or illegal behaviour on her part, liable for all her debts, and even for any criminal behaviour committed by her in his presence, because he was supposed to be in command of her. As compensation for this heavy responsibility, and because as the man it was his duty to support the family, the law awarded him all her property and the power to chastise her. That was the law. It should in practice be mitigated by mutual respect, affection and kindness, but of course it was all too easy for the unscrupulous to exploit it.

Such a man was Andrew Robinson Stoney, a fortune-hunter whose surface charm quickly gave way to pathological violence. His victim was Mary Eleanor Bowes, Countess of Strathmore, the great-great-great-great-grandmother of Queen Elizabeth II. Mary Eleanor has been described as a 'silly woman' and certainly she was a bad judge of men. In her *Confessions* she also admitted she was a woman of loose morals, since at the time of the Earl of Strathmore's death she was already pregnant with her lover's child. Among her contemporaries her reputation suffered most, however, because she had tried to keep one hand on her fortune, when such a radical notion seemed to undermine the institution of marriage and, by implication, the very fabric of society.

Society's quarrel with Mary Eleanor was that she did not seem to know her place as a wife, but this was not altogether surprising. As the only child of George Bowes, whose fabulous wealth derived largely from iron and coal in County Durham, he had indulged her, giving her an education far beyond what was considered desirable for a woman. He instilled in her a passion for botany – later she would have hothouses full of exotic species – and she studied the classics, modern languages and music. It was enough to get her invited to become a member of the Bluestockings, an informal club of intelligent, well-educated women whose members scorned the usual female accomplishments, but all this learning did her no favours in the marriage market. Nothing Mary Eleanor learned from her father led her to believe that she was in any way inferior as a woman and she looked forward to enjoying the same close relationship with her husband. In this she was doomed to disappointment.

George Bowes died in 1760 when Mary Eleanor was only twelve, leaving her a fortune of £600,000 – well over £40 million in today's terms – and other property. Her mother retired from the world, leaving her daughter to the care of her unmarried aunt, Jane Bowes, who proved a most unsuitable chaperone. Practically an orphan, Mary Eleanor was given far more freedom than other girls of her age and status, spending her evenings at Almack's – today she would probably be seen falling out of Boujis in the early hours – and flirting with the Eton boys, first Campbell Scott, brother of the Duke of Buccleuch, and then the handsome Charles James Fox. Not only did she enjoy gossip, but as a flirt and a tease became an object of gossip. Although she was not particularly attractive, her fortune ensured that she received many offers of marriage. She would toy with them and dismiss them. It seems that she knew her value as an heiress.

When she was sixteen John Lyon, 9th Earl of Strathmore, whose family seat was Glamis Castle in Angus, Scotland, made her an offer of marriage. There was no question of love on either side. They had little in common other than the nearness of their estates. Known as 'the beautiful Lord Strathmore', his character was cold and deliberate, whereas Mary Eleanor's was passionate and volatile. He took no trouble to court her or to discover her interests. No sooner were they married than she was compelled to give up the Bluestockings, while he did nothing to encourage her love of botany. Whatever had that to do with a woman?

Mary Eleanor's mother was not particularly keen on the match, yet Mary Eleanor accepted his proposal. Perhaps she decided that his title was fair exchange for her fortune, or that it made good sense that their neighbouring estates should be joined. The matter was handed over to the lawyers, who spent eighteen months haggling over the settlement. One of the stipulations in George Bowes's will was that his daughter's husband and children must take the name Bowes. Strathmore was not pleased, but since there was a fortune at stake and his own was comparatively modest, he had no choice but to concede. He and his future progeny by Mary Eleanor would be known as Bowes-Lyon.

By the time of the wedding at St George's Hanover Square on her eighteenth birthday, Mary Eleanor was convinced she had made a mistake. 'I wished to retract . . . but my pride and sometimes my weakness would not let me.' As they journeyed to Gibside, her estate near Newcastle-upon-Tyne, after the wedding she suffered from a violent stomach ailment, which was probably psychosomatic. She was dreading living with this stranger. Nor did his family welcome her, making it clear that they thought their brother had married beneath him.

As it turned out, Strathmore was absent from home most of their married life. Mary Eleanor did her duty and bore him three sons and two daughters. After several years she was beginning to look for diversion elsewhere. She had already enjoyed a close relationship at Glamis with the gamekeeper's young son, with whom she may have been intimate. In 1774, however, she met George Gray, 'a gentleman from India, who had served under Lord Clive in no very high capacity, and purchased land in Scotland'. By the following year they were lovers. She used her footman, George Walker, who knew all her secrets, to arrange trysts and carry letters.

For Mary Eleanor, the affair was one of sheer wanton pleasure. Much of it was carried out in London, where Gray would spend alternate nights in the countess's bed in Grosvenor Square – the idea being that a night off in between would add to their pleasure – creeping out at dawn before the servants were up. Although 'precautions were taken' their mutual passion was such that she became pregnant 'even when I thought an accident scarce possible'. Gray procured some quack medicine which brought on an abortion on two occasions. By the third time, Strathmore was clearly dying of tuberculosis, and she kept the child.

In February 1776 Strathmore took ship for the warmer climate of Lisbon, but died at sea. It would have been hypocritical of Mary Eleanor to mourn and indeed she did not. She was still besotted by Gray. Shortly after her husband's death she promised to 'marry none but him' and placed his ring on her finger. They began to make plans for a wedding in April, which would be about four months before the baby was due. No sooner was she engaged to Gray, however, than she was thinking of reneging on her promise. An intriguing alternative had emerged.

Lieutenant Andrew Robinson Stoney, the younger son of a good Irish family, had to make his own way in the world. An army commission had been bought for him and although he later assumed the title of captain, his military career had been less than distinguished. With a stark, aquiline profile, he was attractive rather than handsome, but he could turn on the charm and seemed to exert considerable power over women.

When stationed in Newcastle he had married a local heiress, Hannah Newton, whose father, like George Bowes, had made his money from coal. He had married Hannah solely for her money and treated her with appalling cruelty, once locking her in a dark closet, clothed only in her shift, and feeding her one egg a day. On another occasion he threw her down the stairs. She had borne him three children, all of whom died, possibly owing to his ill-treatment of her. Before her marriage, Hannah had put £5,000 in a separate trust for any children she might have. By the time she died in 1775, however, Stoney had succeeded – no doubt by force rather than his legendary charm – in making her rescind the trust, so that he inherited her entire estate.

Stoney was now rich enough to come to London and behave as a gentleman about town. He quickly began to dispose of his late wife's fortune at the gaming tables. Having once succeeded in marrying for money, he was clearly on the lookout for another rich wife.

He did his research and laid his plans carefully. Only a truly evil mind could be as devious and calculating as his. He had heard about the widowed Countess of Strathmore and knew of her pregnancy and that she was due to marry in a month or so. Capturing the pregnant fiancée of another man would seem to be a challenge too far for most, but not for Stoney. Like the gambler he was, he studied the cards to hand. He knew of Mary Eleanor's difficult relationship with the Strathmores and their aversion to her. He would turn this to his advantage.

Next, he began to ingratiate himself with her circle. Mary Eleanor's governess, Mrs Parish, had threatened to tell the late earl's family that she was pregnant by her lover. Mary Eleanor, always liberal with her cash, had given her £2,000 to keep quiet and leave. She had been replaced by her equally poisonous sister, Eliza Planta, in whom the Reverend Henry Stephens, tutor to the children, took an interest. They were married, after Mary Eleanor had generously paid his debts. This was the ménage in the Bowes household that Stoney would engage to work for him.

He discovered, probably through Eliza, that Mary Eleanor was superstitious and liked to consult fortune-tellers. It was probably no coincidence that Eliza told her of a new 'conjuror'. They duly went along for a consultation. Here she heard of a new lover waiting in the wings – a handsome, Irish lover.

By this time Stoney had managed to secure an introduction to Mary Eleanor and was exerting all his considerable charm to make himself irresistible to her. He forged a series of letters from a fictitious fiancée in County Durham which mentioned that Gray was ingratiating himself with the late earl's family. Nothing was more calculated to raise Mary Eleanor's ire. It seemed that Gray was proving rather too interested in her affairs for Mary Eleanor's liking. She did not want another 'arranged' marriage. Meanwhile, she had heard rumours of Stoney's cruelty to his late wife, but she could not reconcile them with the kind, generous, charming man she knew and foolishly dismissed them as malicious fabrications.

It seems that Stoney and Mary Eleanor were now lovers, but he was not satisfied to leave it at that. How to get her to marry him? Attacks on Lady Strathmore inexplicably began to appear in the *Morning Post*, followed by letters defending her reputation. They were all written by Stoney. Unaware of the ruse, Mary Eleanor asked Gray to approach the editor, the Reverend Sir Henry Bate, to have publication of the letters stopped. It was an age when newspaper editors tended to fight a duel rather than settle in court. Why should Gray not throw down a challenge to Bate? He demurred. Exasperated,

Mary Eleanor told Eliza Planta that the man who challenged Bate would have her heart and hand.

Eliza duly informed Stoney, who challenged Bate to a duel – swords *and* pistols. But did he? Certainly a duel took place at the Adelphi Tavern in the Strand. Stoney was slightly wounded, Bate not at all. This is curious, as Bate, 'the fighting parson', was never known to miss his target. In the light of what transpired, it very much looks as if Stoney bribed Bate, who needed the money, to forge a performance as part of Stoney's plan to win Mary Eleanor's hand.

For someone of Mary Eleanor's passionate, romantic nature, hearing that someone had fought a duel on her behalf was bound to impress her. Stoney had taken on Bate to defend her honour and, apparently, had nearly lost his life in the process. While the honourable Gray visited Stoney to shake his hand in gratitude for defending the countess's honour, Mary Eleanor rushed to Stoney's side, all concern about his injuries. She begged him to give her the sword with which he had attacked her enemy. She duly placed it over her bed as a trophy.

Three days later she visited Stoney again. He seemed to be very much diminished, whispering that he was sinking fast. If only she would marry him, he confided, he would die happy. How could she deny a dying man? She agreed out of compassion and gratitude, without giving it a second thought. 'I married him without reflection,' she recalled, 'and without the advice and knowledge of any of my friends.' Always a mistake!

Four days after the duel Andrew Robinson Stoney was carried on a stretcher from his lodgings in St James's Street to the altar of St James's Piccadilly, where he married Mary Eleanor Bowes.

Andrew Robinson Stoney Bowes, as he was now pleased to call himself, celebrated the marriage by giving a formal reception in his rooms, lying dressed in full uniform on a chaise longue and bearing the pain of his injuries with the fortitude expected of a 'military' man. As soon as he was installed in Grosvenor Square with his bride he continued as he had begun, spending money with abandon, giving splendid receptions and dinners, the tables groaning with all sorts of exotic food, to be washed down with lashings of champagne or claret.

It did not take long for Stoney's veneer of charm to be stripped off. He was furious to learn that Mary Eleanor had given the Reverend Stephens £1,000 as a gift and promised him an annuity of £300. Clearly, Mary Eleanor had no financial sense – indeed, in a very considered farewell letter her former husband had warned her of this, suggesting she hire a good man to manage her finances – but as far as Stoney was concerned, she was being profligate with what was now *his* money.

His temper was not improved when he heard that Gray had also been paid off, as seemed only fair in the circumstances. Gray seems to have been the last to know of Mary Eleanor's new liaison, and he immediately threatened to sue her for breach of promise. Breach of promise suits had long been a civil matter, settled by financial compensation, but it was rare for a man to file one, since he would become a public laughing stock, and even if he won, the reward was likely to be derisory. Gray was obviously going to be a nuisance, so that Mary Eleanor paid him off, to the tune of £12,000. As usual, this was way over the top, but Gray retired satisfied, taking not the slightest interest in his daughter Mary, born at Gibside that autumn.

So far Stoney's progress had been unassailable, but now he made a very unpleasant discovery. Far from his wife's fortune belonging to him as unquestionably as her person, he found that he had no control over it whatsoever. Mary Eleanor was not entirely stupid. A few days prior to her marriage she had instructed her solicitor, Joseph Pride, to place all her worldly goods in trust for her children. Any financial transactions were to be carried out through her solicitor. The Ante-Nuptial Trust decreed that money paid to her was to be 'for her separate and peculiar use and disposal, exclusive of any husband she should thereafter marry with; and wherewith he should not intermeddle, nor should the same be anyways subject or liable to his debts, control or management'. She ordered two copies of the trust deed – one to be lodged with her solicitor, the other to be kept by her.

In her *Confessions* she says that it never occurred to her that Stoney, who supposedly had money of his own, would not be pleased to supply her with what sums she might need, whereas 'it struck me that having taken such precautions on my children's account . . . with a man I knew I could trust [Gray], I ought not to be less cautious with one whom I could not be so strongly assured of [Bowes]; but I would not tell you of the paper, lest it looked like mistrust.'

Certainly Bowes thought it looked like mistrust and in this he had the sympathy of a good many other husbands. It was the thin end of the wedge when a wife deceived a chap and presumed to keep control of her own fortune. Bowes determined to get his hands on the deed and destroy it. Doubtless already fearful of the terrible anger she had unleashed, Mary Eleanor told him that she had instructed her footman, George Walker, to destroy the deed, together with a mass of unrelated manuscripts. Nevertheless, Bowes would not rest until he had made her sign a deed revoking the Ante-Nuptial Trust.

The speed with which Bowes took control of Mary Eleanor and her household was breathtaking. He began to take precautions lest she took any more steps that might result in him being denied access to her money. He ordered the servants to bring the post directly to him; so frightened did Mary Eleanor become that she once told Walker, who brought her a letter, that she dared not open it and he must give it to Mr Bowes. Bowes asked his valet to give him the names of all those who entered the house, but he refused. It was none of his business, the valet told him, and beneath him to spy on his mistress. Bowes would have Mary Eleanor's coach followed, until eventually she was not allowed to go out without his permission. She rarely managed to see the hothouses of exotic plants she had set up at Chelsea and soon Bowes sold the property anyway.

Trust or no trust, it is likely that Bowes would have sloughed off the charm as soon as the ring was on Mary Eleanor's finger. Only days after the marriage he flew into a rage because he wanted champagne at dinner and there was none in the house. Hearing his wife holding a conversation in French and Italian with a guest, he forbade her to speak anything other than English, so that he could keep track of it. When Mrs Bowes asked permission to see her daughter in private, it was refused; they were never to see each other privately again. As far as Bowes was concerned, George Walker was far too close to Mary Eleanor and knew too much. He was dismissed on some trumped-up charge.

Quite how Bowes persuaded Mary Eleanor to revoke the trust deed is a mystery. It was too early for him to use physical violence

– although that would come soon enough. Possibly he threatened separation from her children, even though she was not particularly maternal. As a further guarantee of her good behaviour, Bowes forced Mary Eleanor to write her *Confessions*, an account of her 'imprudencies', presumably thinking of a time when he would use them against her. Certainly her conclusion – 'May I never feel happiness in this world, or the world to come; and may my children meet every hour of their lives in unparalleled misery, if I have, either directly or indirectly, told one or more falsehoods in these narratives; or if I have kept any thing secret, that even Mr Bowes could esteem a fault' – sounds as if the *Confessions* were extracted from a woman under some undisclosed threat.

He still shared her bed, but was already a serial adulterer. There was a mighty row when very early one morning Bowes's valet, Thomas Mahon, spotted Bowes coming out of Mrs Eliza Stephens's room. He was wearing the same clothes as he had the previous evening. The Stephenses were sent packing and only resurfaced to give evidence for Bowes when he was accused of adultery.

With Eliza gone, Bowes now entered the servants' quarters and had sex with them whether they liked it or not. Dorothy Stevenson, a seventeen-year-old nursery maid, shared a bedroom with Gray's child Mary, Mary Eleanor's new baby by Bowes, and the wet-nurse Mrs Houghton. Bowes would come into the room at night and slip into bed with Houghton. Soon she became pregnant and left. Bowes then told Stevenson that she was not to lock the door at night. Inevitably she woke up one night to find him in her bed. He stuffed a handkerchief into her mouth and raped her. She in turn became pregnant and about a week before the child was born he took her to lodge in a house in Hanover Square, telling the owner, Susannah Sunderland, that she had been seduced by his chaplain, a married man who did not want his wife to know. When Dorothy revealed to Susannah that Bowes was the father, he was so angry that he beat her up. No wonder that she later testified that he was a man of 'a cruel, savage and abandoned disposition, as also loose, wicked and lustful'.

In 1784 nineteen-year-old Elizabeth Waite saw an advertisement for a nursery maid at Grosvenor Square and applied. She was no ingénue. She had been working in a brothel. She was a bit disconcerted to be interviewed by Bowes, rather than the mistress of the house, especially as he made a pass at her. Later, when she returned for a final interview with the countess, she was confronted with Bowes again. He took her upstairs, plied her with wine, 'threw her down by force on a sopha' and raped her.

His mistreatment of his wife was obvious to all. Susannah Church, a middle-aged servant, later testified in court that she was shocked at the pitiful shabbiness of the countess's clothes. Her stays were in such a poor condition that Susannah would be ashamed to wear them. Dorothy Stevenson confirmed that she had heard the countess ask Bowes for a little money for clothes, only to be told she must wear what she had. The heiress who had once dressed in the height of fashion was reduced to borrowing the servants' clothes. When she went to buy shoes and gloves for the children it was to find that tradesmen would no longer extend credit to her.

Bowes also kept Mary Eleanor short of food. She was not to be given even a drink of water without his express permission. When Susannah Church took it upon herself to serve her mistress with some cold chicken she was instantly dismissed.

He had begun to abuse her physically. Dorothy Stevenson testified that 'she had frequently seen Mr Bowes pinch and beat the Countess, that he has frequently given her many violent blows on the face, head and other parts of the body; that he often kicked her, and that such treatment was without cause or provocation, except he sometimes complained she made too much noise by playing with the boy, or would give some such frivolous reason.'

In May 1784 the couple were dining at St Paul's Walden when he picked a quarrel with Mary Eleanor for walking in the garden without permission. His rage was so sudden and violent that he 'threw a dish of hot potatoes in the Countess's face'. He then made her go to the far end of the table where he made her 'eat potatoes till she was sick'. For good measure he threw a glass of wine in her face 'to wash off the potatoes'. Mary Eleanor was too shocked and terrified to utter a sound, yet Bowes used one hand to hold her by the hair while with the other he held a knife to her throat, telling her that 'he would cut her throat that instant if she spoke another word'. He left her face bruised and the underside of one ear slit and bleeding.

In the spring of 1784 Mary Eleanor had taken on a new lady's maid, Mary Morgan, who would prove loyal and supportive for the rest of her life. She quickly made some unpleasant discoveries. Bowes's behaviour towards his wife 'was one continued scene of abuse, insult and cruelty' and her mistress was 'seldom free from bruises upon face, neck or arms'. On a journey to Paris she noticed Bowes slyly pinch and kick Mary Eleanor when he thought he was unobserved. They had illegally taken Strathmore's daughter, Lady Anna, a ward in Chancery, out of the country and Bowes was constantly on his guard against pursuit. Locked in her hotel room while her husband dissipated her fortune on prostitutes and gambling, Mary Eleanor was forbidden to look out of the window. One day Morgan entered the room to find Mary Eleanor crying and holding a cloth to her face. She was bleeding from the nose and mouth and there was blood all over the top of her dress. Bowes told her the window had blown back and hit Mary Eleanor, but of course he had done it himself when he caught her looking out.

The violence was growing worse, so much so that Mary Eleanor was beginning to fear for her life – or wish it was over. Back in England, Bowes thrust a lighted candle into her face and burned her skin and on another occasion thrust a quill pen at her with such force it stuck in her tongue. He would beat her with his fists and a stick, shouting that he would do so until she learned not to cry out. Finally, he threatened to have her locked up for life. How easy that would be! Mary Eleanor could, quite literally, end her days in the madhouse with no one to hold Bowes to account.

Her spirit was not entirely broken. With the help of Mary Morgan and a couple of other loyal servants, she planned her escape. When Bowes left the house in the evenings, he would leave Mary Eleanor under guard. On 3 February 1785 she put her carefully contrived plan into effect. She asked her guard to nip round the corner and buy her a magazine, while her supporters lured the other servants to the far corners of the house, and she slipped out. Accompanied by one servant, Mary Eleanor made her way to a hackney coach stand in Oxford Street, narrowly missing Bowes coming in a coach the other way. That night she took refuge with a lawyer cousin in Lincoln's Inn Fields before taking lodgings under an assumed name in Holborn.

She wasted no time in swearing the peace against her husband and applying to the London Consistory Court for a divorce from bed and board on grounds of his adultery and cruelty: 'beating, scratching, biting, pinching, whipping, kicking, imprisoning, insulting, provoking, tormenting, mortifying, degrading, tyrannizing, cajoling, deceiving, lying, starving, forcing, compelling, and a new torment, wringing of the heart'.

Since she was destitute, she applied to Chancery for the re-establishment of the Ante-Nuptial Agreement, restraining Bowes from receiving any further rents or income from her estates, and the appointment of a receiver to collect and administer them. She also asked for a sum of £1,500 for her maintenance and with which to pursue her legal action, which would be prolonged, frustrating and painful. The request was granted, although Bowes protested bitterly that the Ante-Nuptial Trust had no validity, since as her future husband he had not been informed about it and as her husband he had every right to the possession of her fortune.

How Mary Eleanor must have been regretting her failure to make a proper settlement before her impetuous marriage to Bowes! She had always scorned such arrangements, but in neglecting to place her marriage on a proper business footing she had made herself vulnerable to abuse and exploitation.

Bowes swung into action, bribing servants past and present to supply evidence against his wife or not to disclose what they knew of his behaviour. He told the court to disregard the evidence of Dorothy Stevenson and Elizabeth Waite as they were 'common prostitutes'.

Bowes contended that Mary Eleanor was vicious, lustful, extravagant, insolent and disobedient and had only to produce her *Confessions* to prove her a flagrant adulteress into the bargain. By her own admission she had betrayed Strathmore with Gray, had brought off two abortions – a criminal offence – had a prior contract of marriage with Gray while carrying on an affair with Stoney, and had generally behaved in a flirtatious and improper fashion since her girlhood.

It was owing to this confession, he maintained, that 'he was induced to treat her with the strictest attention, and to lay such restraints on her conduct, as she appeared to want.' He denied that he had ever been cruel to her, but 'endeavoured to give her a proper sense and abhorrence of those vices, wherein she had so confessedly habituated herself'. He had discovered to his 'great astonishment and grief' that soon after their marriage 'Lady Strathmore was five months gone with child' by Gray and that to protect her reputation he had hired a house in Hammersmith where she gave birth to a daughter in secret. As her husband, he was only trying to protect her 'constitution, which by her former irregularities and vices, she had much impaired'.

Bowes's well-worn tactics of using the press were once more applied. Cruel and lascivious caricatures depicting the Countess of Strathmore by a young James Gillray excited public attention, making her a figure of infamy. Either the case was too scandalous an opportunity for Gillray to miss, or he was in Bowes's pay.

Unfortunately for Bowes, the ecclesiastical court ruled out the *Confessions* as evidence, on the grounds that everything they described had taken place before the countess's marriage with him. The court granted Mary Eleanor the separation she sought and Bowes was ordered to pay maintenance of £300 a year. Inevitably, he moved straight on to appeal at the Court of Arches.

If, pending the outcome of such a case, a wife returned to cohabit with her husband, even for a few days, her suit would collapse. Bowes began to stalk Mary Eleanor, waiting for the chance to seize her person. He would then be able to batter her into submission, to drop the divorce suit and cancel her request for the reinstatement of the Ante-Nuptial deed, which would deprive him of the income of £10,000 a year he was currently enjoying from her estates.

Mary Eleanor had wisely taken the precaution of writing to the Chief Justice, Lord Mansfield, to inform him that she feared that Mr Bowes was going to kidnap her.

> As a preparation against such accidents, I therefore beg to declare upon my oath . . . that I never will, except by force, return to Mr Bowes; and that if he should, after he has thus seized me, produce any paper signed by my name which contains a declaration that I am willing to live with him, it must either be an absolute forgery, or extracted by the immediate danger my life would be in, if I refused to comply; and your Lordship may be assured that I should joyfully snatch the first moment after I was produced in Court, or in your presence, to make

my recantation, and expose every fraud and violence which has been practised upon me.

Her request was all too prescient. Bowes and his group of ruffians would sit for hours in a carriage outside Mary Eleanor's Bloomsbury home and follow her whenever she ventured out. He now infiltrated her household, subverting a parish constable, Edward Lucas, to win the confidence of Mary Eleanor's coachman in order to gain access to Mary Eleanor herself. He had seen some suspicious characters lurking about, he told her, and had come to offer his services for her protection. A few days later the opportunity came to seize Mary Eleanor when she visited an ironmonger's in Oxford Street for garden seeds. She and Morgan had entered the shop when Lucas and one of his associates, who had procured a warrant for the arrest of three of Mary Eleanor's servants under false pretences, moved to take her coachman and footman. Hearing the fracas outside, Mary Eleanor and Morgan quickly dashed upstairs to a storeroom and locked the door, only for Lucas to come upstairs after them.

'Who's there?' she called out.

'My dear lady, here is your friend Lucas.'

'Oh Lucas – open the door!' she replied with relief.

No sooner had the two women accompanied Lucas downstairs than he turned and arrested Mary Eleanor, bundling her into a coach and leaving Morgan behind. She was taken to an inn in Highgate, where she was probably not altogether surprised to find Bowes waiting for her. While the men were drinking downstairs, Mary Eleanor was shouting 'Murder!' from an upstairs window. Bowes threw her into the coach again and they set off for the north at relentless speed. At one stage, Mary Eleanor succeeded in breaking the window and shouting 'Murder! Murder!' but again, no one came to her assistance. Bowes explained that she was a poor madwoman being taken to the asylum.

He wasted no time in producing a document for her to sign. When she refused he struck her in the face and threatened to kill her and as they drove off again he was observed hitting her on the breast with the watch-chain wrapped around his knuckles. After thirty-six hours they reached Mary Eleanor's Streatlam Castle, where once again Bowes produced the by now dog-eared document. Still she refused to sign, even under pain of death. He dragged her upstairs and, in the presence of the ruffians he had brought along after the kidnap, tried to rape her, but despite her exhaustion she somehow succeeded in fighting him off.

Word soon spread that Lady Strathmore was being held in the castle against her will and an angry mob of her tenants and the colliers who worked in her mines began to gather. By the time someone arrived at the castle with a writ of habeas corpus from the Lord Chief Justice at the behest of Mary Eleanor's solicitor, however, Bowes and his henchmen had made their escape with their victim. He took her to the cottage of one of his mistresses, and again tried unsuccessfully to rape her, resorting to beating her instead. Soon they were on the move once more, with Mary Eleanor mounted behind one of the ruffians, riding north through the freezing night. When they stopped briefly at a turnpike, the keeper and his wife were appalled at the state of the lady who was of the party. She was clearly exhausted, freezing cold and bedraggled.

A reward of £50 was offered by John Farrer, the countess's solicitor, for anyone who could bring Mary Eleanor to him at Carlisle and the same for Andrew Robinson Stoney Bowes and his crew of ruffians. At last a parish constable of Darlington and a small party caught up with Bowes, who had Mary Eleanor mounted behind him. Bowes drew his pistol, but while the men were parleying Mary Eleanor slipped off the horse and hurled herself towards her rescuers, shouting, 'I am Lady Strathmore – for God's sake assist me.' The men managed to unseat Bowes, knock him out and arrest him.

Back in London on 23 November 1786 Mary Eleanor once again swore the peace against Bowes and the court had no hesitation in supporting her. He was sent to the King's Bench Prison to await trial for abduction. But he was not beaten yet. He handed the court an 'allegation of mutual forgiveness' on the grounds that he and his wife had cohabited from 12 to 20 November. That had certainly been his intention, but he had been repulsed. How likely was it, the lawyers for the prosecution asked the court, that the couple had been reconciled while Bowes was dragging his wife about in the wilds, frozen, dazed with exhaustion and half-dressed? The court had no hesitation in sentencing Bowes to six years in prison, with the admonishment, 'let the faults of women be ever so great, they can be no extenuations of a man's cruelty.'

Nearly a year after Bowes's trial and imprisonment for abduction, the Lord Chancellor at last reviewed the countess's appeal to have the Ante-Nuptial deed she had revoked on 1 May 1777 reinstated. The case, which would be decided by a jury in the Court of Common Pleas, hinged on whether she had revoked the deed under duress.

While Mr Sergeant Adair, the Recorder of London, opened the case with a devastating summary of Bowes's career as a ruthless, vicious and cruel fortune-hunter, who had enticed a vulnerable woman to marry him by feigning a duel and other deceptions, Bowes's lawyer began to air all the allegations of Mary Eleanor's indiscretions that had already been presented to and dismissed by the ecclesiastical court. Again, it was irrelevant, but Bowes pursued this line hoping that the denigration of his wife's reputation would make his own appear in a more reasonable light.

Eliza Stephens duly testified that Lady Strathmore had signed the deed of revocation willingly, assuring her, 'I am sure Mr Bowes will never use me ill.' She told the court that she was 'vindictive, extravagant, in debt, irreligious and immoral, and much addicted to the gratification of her lust, drinking frequently to excess, until she became intoxicated' and she had 'a general levity in her behaviour, which was very unbecoming to her rank and sex'. Lady Strathmore had told her of her affair with Gray and that she had slept with him the night before she married Bowes. If her health was impaired, it was due to her excesses and abortions. Far from keeping his wife short of clothes, Bowes had treated her to 'a good stock of rich clothes fitting her rank' on their marriage. The Reverend Henry Stephens backed up his wife's statements and implausibly claimed that Bowes had always treated his wife with perfect propriety.

Neither witness impressed the court, particularly after the valet, Thomas Mahon, revealed that Eliza Stephens had been sexually intimate with Bowes and it was established that Bowes was paying Stephens's expenses during the trial. The jury took no time at all to reach its verdict, finding the deed of revocation to have been 'executed under duress'.

The case returned to the Court of Chancery, where the deed of revocation was set aside and Mr Justice Buller delivered the final verdict. If a man married a woman for her money and neglected to secure it with a proper marriage settlement, he had only himself to blame if he had to take her as he found her. Similarly, of course, Mary Eleanor had been negligent in not insisting on a proper marriage settlement. Bowes, after all, had money of his own when she married him and could well have afforded to make some contribution to the marriage.

In making a separate settlement to protect her fortune for her children, it had not been proved that the countess had set out to deceive her future husband – a deed could not be declared void just because he did not know about it. Bowes, the judge decided, had demanded that the Ante-Nuptial deed be set aside, while offering no alternative means for his wife's support. Too mean to offer a settlement, Bowes had lost the whole case. Naturally, he appealed to the House of Lords, rehearsing all the traditional arguments that the man was head of the wife and the family and as such was entitled to control of her fortune. He was found in contempt of Chancery for not immediately returning Mary Eleanor's plate and jewellery or paying the costs awarded her, and presented with a bill in excess of £10,000 he owed her for income he had accrued from her estates since the case was brought.

Not content to leave it at that, Bowes took the case to the High Court of Delegates. Once again the by now all too familiar story of Bowes's treatment of his wife and her lax morality were laid before the court. Previously dismissed as irrelevant to the case because her adultery with Gray had taken place *before* her marriage to Bowes, the court now heard that in the summer of 1777 the countess and her footman did 'very frequently commit the crime of adultery together' and so Bowes had sacked Walker. The Reverend Stephens testified that she had permitted Walker improper familiarities before and after her marriage to Bowes, although she did so after the marriage 'with more reserve'. He had no doubt that there had been 'a criminal intercourse' between them.

For good measure Bowes introduced a new allegation: that Lady Strathmore had had an adulterous relationship with a gardener at

Gibside and that in the spring of 1784 'the said Thompson and Lady Strathmore were several times seen and caught by the other servants in the family, and others, in the very act of carnal copulation together, in the green-house, garden-house and various parts of the garden adjoining and belonging to Mr Bowes' house at Gibside.'

Joseph Hill of Gibside, who had been employed by Bowes as a groom and gamekeeper, gave testimony that he and a fellow servant, Charles Chapman, had seen Lady Strathmore enter the garden-house followed by the gardener, Robert Thompson. They were suspicious and 'determined to see what was going forward'. They found that 'the gardener's blue apron had been rigged up to make a curtain across the window but there was a gap of one or two inches in one corner.' They invited the court to believe that they had crept on their hands and knees towards the window and raised themselves up gently, taking it in turns to peep through the gap left by the apron. They had been treated to the sight of 'Robert Thompson lying upon the body of the said Mary Eleanor Bowes, upon a bench placed against the wall' in the act of carnal enjoyment. Given that Hill and Chapman would never have been free to roam in the gardens of Gibside and that Thompson was lousy, decrepit and suffering from emphysema, it was most unlikely that he and Lady Strathmore would have been performing these athletic feats on a bench in the garden-house. The testimony was dismissed.

On 2 March 1789 the court delivered its verdict. Andrew Robinson Stoney Bowes was found guilty of several acts of cruelty and the 'heinous crime of adultery' and the court confirmed that he and Lady Strathmore 'be divorced, and live separately from each other'. Free from her hellish marriage, Mary Eleanor's reputation never recovered and she remained a figure of derision and scandal. Her fortune was restored to her, while the newly impoverished Bowes had to move to less salubrious quarters of the King's Bench Prison. He was still there when he heard of Mary Eleanor's death ten years later.

19

'A man may be the friend of another man, a *woman* alone can be his *companion*'

O N 17 MARCH 1791 a tiny wedding took place at Lambeth Church. Apart from the clergyman, there was the bridegroom, a working man of about nineteen years of age, the bride, a tall handsome young woman of not quite seventeen, and the man who gave her away, who was the bridegroom's brother-in-law. In a pew at the back of the church sat the solitary figure of a woman, who after witnessing the ceremony slipped out unobserved without congratulating the couple.

It turned out later that the mystery woman was the bride's mother. Having been tipped off about her daughter's forthcoming wedding, she had turned up at the church. Since the girl was only sixteen and marrying without her consent, the clerk told her that she might stop the ceremony, but she replied, No, they would only go somewhere else. She was right. It was all too easy in the overcrowded metropolis for a young couple to marry without their parents' consent by having the banns read in some busy parish where no one knew them. She just wanted to see them married, she told the clerk, who ushered her into the pew.

After the wedding the bridegroom escorted his wife home to tell her mother, only for her mother to retaliate that she knew all about it and wanted nothing more to do with her. She would certainly not be joining the couple for their small wedding supper. Not long ago she had taken a poker to her daughter's suitor, threatening to knock him down and telling him that he would not have her. It was this *fracas* that had precipitated the marriage. True, the couple were too young and he was nowhere near sufficiently established to support a wife, but Francis Place believed in early marriage. Poverty and fear of a large family were deterrents, but what should be repressed, he later argued in a groundbreaking work proposing the use of contraceptives, were poverty and fertility, not natural sexual instincts. Anyway, he did not intend to be a poor journeyman maker of leather breeches for long. One day, he promised the girl, he would be a master tailor.

Both their families had shared similar vicissitudes of fortune in the precarious world of eighteenth-century London. The bride's father was dead. He had been a coal porter who, 'exposed to all weathers and to the bad example of his fellow labourers, acquired the habit of drinking and was hurried to an early grave'. Her mother ran a lodging house and took in washing. Francis's father had been a master baker with a flourishing business in the Borough, but had lost it all through the national addictions of drink and gambling, leaving his wife to be turned out into the street. Eighteen months later he reappeared, set up in the bakery business again, saved £800, and blew the lot at the gaming table. This time when he disappeared he left his wife with a child. She eked out a living doing needlework. A year later he came home penniless, 'just as if he had returned from a walk'. Since it was all too easy for the poor and destitute to walk away from their wives and children, the wonder is that he returned at all.

By some stroke of luck he became the landlord of the King's Arms public house in Arundel Street, near the Strand. At fourteen, Francis was already bound apprentice to a master in the leather breeches trade when his father's final ruin began. A woman went to the overseers of his parish and claimed to have been married to him clandestinely at the Fleet forty years before. Knowing what we do of his character, it might well have been true. He was advised to pay the woman a small weekly sum, but he said he'd be damned if he would. She 'was no wife of his, nor ever had been, and he would have nothing to do with her'.

Enquiries were made, but how to prove or disprove a Fleet marriage so long ago? If the register survived at all, there was every chance its entries had been inserted, altered or expunged. The case dragged on in the London Consistory Court for three years, until finally Francis's father was excommunicated. A large sum of money had been expended on his defence. As Francis ruefully concluded, 'he saved the payment of four and sixpence a week at the cost of a thousand pounds.' Excommunication held no fear for him. 'A supper was given by him to commemorate the result.'

His next misfortune was to lose the pub. When the lease expired, his landlord, the Duke of Norfolk, did not renew it, preferring a Catholic tenant. Francis, not yet seventeen, managed to sell the fixtures and fittings for £250. His mother wanted to use the money to set up a shop; instead, Francis's father lost it all on the State Lottery. At fifty-seven, Mrs Place began to take in washing to support the family, while her elderly husband found lodgings within the Rules of the Fleet Prison.

Francis's fellow apprentices were 'all turbulent unruly fellows, scarcely under any sort of control'. Forbidden to marry during their seven-year apprenticeship, they would resort to 'the prostitutes who walked Fleet Street, spending their money with them in debauchery'. Francis would often spend an evening with them eating and drinking at 'the dirty public houses frequented by them', but 'I never had any connection or acquaintance in the day time with any one of these women.'

Besides their connection with the Fleet Street women, each of the apprentices had 'a sweetheart who was the daughter of some tradesman'. These girls tended to be handsome, well dressed and – important to Francis – 'in their general conduct respectable'. There was a free and easy atmosphere between the sexes. 'The sons and daughters of tradesmen and others were then under comparatively little restraint, and the boys used to knock at the doors of the parents to get the girls to go with them, as had been previously agreed, and out they went.' The girls were not expected to remain virgins till marriage; indeed, they and the young men 'were as familiar as we could be'.

Writing his *Autobiography* in the 1830s, Francis looked back from four decades to a time when 'want of chastity in girls of the class of which I am speaking was common, but it was not by any means considered so disreputable in master tradesmen's families as it is now . . . A tradesman's daughter who should now misconduct herself in the way mentioned would be abandoned by her companions, and probably by her parents . . . she would be prepared to quit her home without any thought of returning to it, and consequently her ruin would be complete.'

In his youth, being unchaste 'did not necessarily imply that the girl was an abandoned person as she would be now and it was not therefore then as now an insurmountable obstacle to her being comfortably settled in the world'. Indeed, he 'could name several of them now living long since married to young men who were as well acquainted with them before marriage as afterwards, and I never knew any one of them who made a bad wife'.

In the spring of 1790 Francis accompanied his master's sister, Miss Pike, to a dance at the pastry-cook's next door. Here he met the young woman who worked in the shop. 'I thought her a very fine and handsome person,' he recalled. 'I danced with her, and fell desperately in love with her. I therefore made it my business to see her again and again. I made enquiries about her and resolved to court her, at first I hardly knew on what terms, but in a little time for a wife.'

Young men and women had to save up for marriage, which is why they tended to marry no sooner than their mid- to late twenties. Francis's intended wife had been working at the pastry shop since she was twelve. Her education was minimal, which was all that was deemed necessary for a future servant; she could read and write and sew. But she had been 'taught to be industrious, was neat in her person, and beyond all comparison steady in her conduct'. Her wages were 'not more than sufficient to provide her with a good stock of clothes' – English women were noted for their love of clothes and enormous importance was attributed to a good appearance – 'and as she expended her money in the purchase of clothes she had no money by her.' Francis at eighteen had not even begun to save, but now he 'ceased to spend more than would suffice for a bare existence'.

As foreman to Mr Pike, Francis would have been able to save up to £1 a week, but unfortunately the Pikes had other ideas. Miss Pike needed a husband. Without troubling to consult Francis, they decided that he should marry her. She was several years older and Francis was well aware that she had had 'an intrigue or two before I was acquainted with her and was as intimate as she could be with Mr Piercey'. Indeed, the Pikes asked Piercey to put the proposition to Francis, 'as if he and the rest of the family were about to make a great condescension and do me a great favour'. Francis heard him out and then told him that he knew of his relationship with Miss Pike. This revelation caused embarrassment all round and Mr Pike was persuaded to discharge Francis. Miss Pike died unmarried in child-birth about a year later. It was rumoured that Piercey was the father.

Undeterred by this setback, Francis introduced his young lady to his parents, who liked her. 'I laid before her my whole scheme of life, and proposed that we should be married as soon as I was in a condition to earn as much money as would enable us to live. I had no doubt that I should improve my condition in life; but I saw clearly that it would be a very hard struggle through many difficulties.' True, he had no one to help him and nothing to fall back on, but he believed that if he worked hard and became his own boss, success would be 'pretty certain'. If she was 'willing to take her chance with me we should some day be well off in the world'.

Before his marriage in the spring of 1791, Francis found a new job at Mr Lingham's in the Strand, making leather breeches for a wage of not more than fourteen shillings a week. He began to save, rarely going out and eating and drinking very little. 'I was however able to pay for my washing and lodging and to save a trifle, not by any means enough to enable me to purchase many clothes, but I bought as many as I could.' His young bride, meanwhile, had left her employ and began to help his elderly mother with her washing and ironing. She would accept no pay – Mrs Place could hardly afford it – except her board, which was worth about three shillings a week. Out of an income of seventeen shillings Francis and his wife paid three shillings and sixpence a week rent for one furnished room, one shilling and sixpence for coal and candles, and the rest for food, clothes and other necessaries. They could save nothing, although 'contrived to dress ourselves respectably and were comfortable with each other'.

'We were poor, but we were young, active, cheerful, and although my wife at times doubted that we should get on in the world, I had no such misgivings,' Francis recalled. There was, however, a down-turn in the leather breeches trade. Gentlemen preferred corduroy and cashmere and leather was 'no longer commonly worn by any class of persons'. Francis's work became irregular and his earnings were considerably reduced.

His boss owed him money. 'We had been without money for a week, and payment of the seven shillings could not be obtained, it was in the depth of winter and we had neither food nor fire. In this state we remained so long that my wife was exhausted and was compelled to go to bed.' This was too much for Francis to endure. He went to Lingham to demand payment, expecting to be dismissed, only to be given an order that had just come in and needed doing in a hurry.

It was a temporary relief, but Francis realized that 'if I continued to make leather breeches I should be kept in wretched poverty'. His wife was 'far gone with child' and there was no hope of their being able to make any provision for the birth. He decided to try his luck making stuff breeches. Having applied to every breeches maker in London, he was soon rewarded with more work than he could handle and earning a guinea a week, which 'enabled us to live in comfort'. They moved to better lodgings. His wife gave birth to their first child. He even managed to buy some furniture: a bed, a table, three or four chairs and some bedding.

Just as they began to congratulate themselves on their good fortune, things took another turn for the worse. Francis was a member of the Breeches Makers Benefit Society. He had been too busy working to know that they were intending to strike for higher wages. The masters took a dim view of strikes and go-slows and discharged the lot of them. Francis found himself out of work. With nothing to do he began to take an interest in the organization of the strike. The society was intending to pay its members seven shillings a week. Francis calculated that at this rate the fund would be exhausted in three weeks, when as it turned out the strike would not be settled for three months. With the reformer's zeal for which he would become famous, he set about reorganizing the men so that none of them would starve. Some received a week's wages and were despatched to the provinces, where they could be sure of a charitable welcome from other members of the trade. Others would be engaged in making rag fair breeches, which would bring them in a few shillings a week.

The strike of 1793 marked Francis's entry into radical politics. The strike could not last indefinitely and eventually the men were compelled to return to work without any increase in their wages. For his part as an organizer, Francis was never to be employed again by any master breeches maker. For eight months he could obtain no employment and they plunged steadily towards abject poverty. They pawned or sold everything they had accumulated in their previous prosperity and used up their little savings. The three of them were living in one room when the child fell ill of smallpox and died. Too proud to let anyone know how poor they were, they rarely went out and suffered every privation, with little food and no fire. Francis's only solace was found in reading and studying, hoping and planning for the future.

The long period of unemployment took its toll on the marriage. 'My temper was bad, and instead of doing every thing in my power to sooth and comfort and support my wife in her miserable condition, instead of doing her homage for the exemplary manner in which she bore her sufferings, instead of meeting as I ought on all occasions to have done her good temper and affection, I used at times to give way to passion and increase her and my own misery.'

Poverty, he noted, could destroy a marriage: 'Nothing conduces so much to the degradation of a man and woman in the opinion of each other, and of themselves in all respects; but most especially of the woman; than her having to eat and drink and cook and wash and iron and transact all her domestic concerns in the room in which her husband works, and in which they sleep.'

At last after eight months a former employer, Mr Allison, sent for Francis. Fearing that the masters intended to prosecute him for forming a 'combination' of workmen, which was illegal, he refused to go. His wife determined to go instead. 'In a short time she returned, and let fall from her apron as much work for me as she could bring away. She was unable to speak until she was relieved by a flood of tears.' Mr Allison felt that Francis had been hard done by. Ignoring the other masters, he intended to send him as much work as he could handle.

Francis and his wife set to work with a will, working 'full sixteen and sometimes eighteen hours a day Sundays and all. We turned out of bed to work and turned from our work to bed again.' Once more they were able to buy clothes and household goods and moved to better lodgings. Soon they were able to help Francis's mother, who at sixty-four was now unable to work and near destitute. 'As we scarcely left our work for meals all the week we had a hot supper on the Saturday, a beef steak or mutton chops.' On Sundays they were able to reward themselves by putting on their best clothes and going for a walk in London's surrounding countryside. By now his wife was expecting her second child and they were even contemplating going to the expense of hiring a male midwife. 'Our neat place, the absence of want, and the expectation of continuing to do well, the persuasion that our days of suffering were at an end, and our mutual affection made us, perhaps, as happy as any two persons ever really were.'

In 1799 Francis opened a tailoring shop with his lodger, Richard Wild. For eighteen months they prospered. It looked as if their dreams of financial security were about to be realized. But then he learned that Wild was planning to break up the partnership. It was a devastating blow. After everything that she had endured, his wife, who by now had three children and another on the way, was in utter despair. 'She was sure we should all be turned into the street, industry was of no use to us, integrity would not serve us, honesty would be of no avail, we had worked harder, and done more than any body else, and now we were to suffer more than anybody else.' There was nothing he could say or do to comfort her. 'She dreaded the horrid poverty she now saw before her and she felt the more acutely, since she had thought that her troubles and difficulties were ended, and that abundance and happiness were before us.'

But the customers thought too highly of Place to let him go out of business. They loaned him £1,600 to start up again on his own. On 8 March 1801, three months after the end of his partnership, he opened a tailoring shop at No. 16 Charing Cross Road. He succeeded so well that in 1816 he made a net profit of £3,000. The following year, he handed the business over to his son and actively devoted himself to achieving some of the great reforms of the era: the repeal of the Combination Laws, the Anatomy Bill, the establishment of London University with his old friend Jeremy Bentham, the Reform Bill, the Penny Postage, the Chartist Movement and the Anti-Corn Law League.

Place and his wife were married for thirty-seven years and had fifteen children. She who had never aspired to her husband's great heights, who would have been content with a journeyman's wages for ever, never quite recovered from the reversals of fortune during their early marriage. She remained apprehensive, always expecting 'some catastrophe, something she used to say would happen to reduce us again to poverty, and her dread of being so reduced never left her'.

Nor did she derive much comfort from her nine surviving children, who were educated far beyond others of their rank. Naturally she found herself lagging behind them in knowledge and they 'became less and less respectful to her'. This was not true of her husband, however. 'The only relaxation I really either coveted or courted was her society,' he admitted. It was his greatest pleasure to have her 'as my *companion*, my delight was to see her and hear her voice'.

In 1827 she died of cancer. A grief-stricken Francis wrote that he had lost 'for ever my *friend* my long cherished *companion* in all my various changes of life, she who had my entire confidence, she who gave me hers, and had loved me most sincerely for thirty-seven years'. Writing to his son-in-law a few months after her death, he paid tribute to her:

> I loved my wife as well as ever man loved woman. I loved her as well at the close of thirty-six years of our marriage as I did on the day we were married. When young she was a most beautiful figure, my delight and consolation under all kinds of difficulties and privations. She was good tempered, kind, considerate, abstemious and singularly industrious. She was all in all that a man in my circumstances could wish she should be, and more than any man could reasonably expect to find. No wonder then that I loved her dearly. As we were very poor she endured more than I did, this in all such cases is necessarily the woman's fate. She seldom repined at her hard fate, she never made her condition matter of reproach to me, she was sometimes unhappy but this was transitory, and when we were not in actual want we were happy. At times we were supremely so, and but for her I never could have got forward in the world as I did.

In a sad little footnote to this story Francis Place remarried, out of loneliness. It was a terrible mistake and twelve years later he and his second wife separated.

INTERLUDE

Jane Austen, Fanny Knight and Clarissa Trant

A woman's whole happiness depended on choosing the right man to marry and yet she embarked on the quest with very little experience, within a limited social circle, and always under the pressure of knowing that her opportunities would be few. The temptation must have been to opt for the first presentable man who showed an interest, even if her feelings were not fully engaged. Either that, or rush headlong into a marriage without really knowing the man and find she had made a terrible mistake.

In 1814 Jane Austen was trying to advise her niece Fanny Knight in such a situation:

> I have no scruple in saying you cannot be in love. My dear Fanny, I am ready to laugh at the idea – and yet it is no laughing matter to have had you so mistaken as to your feelings – And with all my heart I wish I had cautioned you on that point when first you spoke to me; – but tho' I did not think you then so *much* in love as you thought yourself, I did consider you as being attached in a degree – quite sufficiently for happiness, as I had no doubt it would increase with opportunity. – And from the time of our being in London together, I thought you really very much in love. – But you certainly are not at all – there is no concealing it. – What strange creatures we are! – It seems as if your being secure of him (as you say yourself) had made you indifferent . . . And yet, after all, I *am* surprised that the change in your feelings should be so great. – He is, just what he ever was, only more evidently & uniformly devoted to *you*. How shall we account for it? . . . Oh! Dear Fanny, your mistake has been one that thousands of women fall into. He is the *first* young man who

attached himself to you. That was the charm, & most powerful it is.

At much the same time another young woman, Miss Clarissa Trant, was going through a similar experience. She was a character straight out of a Jane Austen novel. The daughter of an army officer, Sir Nicholas Trant, she was brought up abroad during the Napoleonic Wars, before returning to England. She had fallen for a Colonel Cameron, her '*preux chevalier*', who seemed to be devoted her. He had proposed and been accepted.

'The events of yesterday and today have crowded together so rapidly that I can scarcely persuade myself that the whole has been more than a happy dream. I am very *happy*,' she wrote in her diary on 30 January 1827. That evening Colonel Cameron left for Bath to discuss the settlement with his father, but promised to return in a fortnight.

As Jane Austen knew only too well, it all came down to money. 'Women have a dreadful propensity for being poor – which is one very strong argument in favour of matrimony,' she told her niece. Money was both a draw and an inhibitor in securing a marriage partner. Sure enough, on 13 February Clarissa reported: 'He has not returned because his father will not let him come back to London until he has written to my father about business arrangements.' Next day a letter from General Cameron enquired 'if my father can give me money'. He was prepared to settle £10,000 on his son and guarantee a jointure of £1,000 a year for Clarissa, if her father could put down a similar sum. Alas, Sir Nicholas could not.

17 February: 'The post has come and no letter from Bath. "Then he will surely come himself," I said to my father. But he is not here.'

18 February: 'No news of Colonel Cameron. . .'

19 February: 'The correspondence which has taken place between my father and General Cameron had prepared me for the termination of all future intercourse between the Colonel and myself, which from the knowledge I have acquired of his character within the last fortnight, I have but too much reason to think would have led to much future unhappiness,' Clarissa consoled herself.

Clarissa was obviously well rid of the colonel, whose love did not survive the first test, but it seems that Fanny Knight's admirer was a genuinely good man, making it all the more difficult for her to break off the relationship. Still, if her feelings were not truly engaged, Jane advised, she must not commit herself. 'Anything is to be preferred or endured rather than marrying without affection.'

Fanny's admirer was not in a position to marry her immediately and Jane did not think that her feelings were strong enough to survive a long engagement. Of course Fanny was concerned that she might not meet anyone else, but she should be equally wary of committing herself half-heartedly to one man, only to find that in due course she preferred another.

'It is very true that you never may attach another man, his equal altogether, but if that other man has the power of attaching you *more*, he will be in your eyes the most perfect,' Jane counselled. 'You like him well enough to marry, but not well enough to wait. – The unpleasantness of appearing fickle is very great – but . . . nothing can be compared to the misery of being bound *without* love, bound to one, and preferring another.'

Clarissa might have derived some comfort from Jane's final words of advice to Fanny: 'Do not be in a hurry; depend upon it, the right man will come at last; you will in the course of the next two or three years, meet with somebody . . . who will so completely attach you, that you will feel you never really loved before.'

Clarissa did indeed meet the right man. A year after Colonel Cameron's abrupt departure she met a young clergyman, John Bramston, on a crossing from Waterford to Bristol. They enjoyed each other's company during the voyage, but parted not expecting to meet again. Three years later, however, they did meet again, through a mutual acquaintance. Things moved swiftly from there and on 14 November 1831 she reported from Bath: 'We met this morning at my dear father's. A few words passed between us but those few said everything. He is all that my heart could desire in the guide, the friend, the protector of my future life. I feel such *repose*, such confidence in his affection, *quite different* from anything I ever felt before for anyone.'

Marriage, or love, was a woman's whole existence, so perhaps it was appropriate that with the wedding day fixed for the first week in January, Clarissa's last diary entry for 1831 should read: 'And thus ends a most eventful year of my life – the year that has decided my fate for ever.'

20

'Threatened with being sent to a lunatic asylum, only for asking for food'

ON THE EVE of her marriage in September 1814 Ellen Weeton wrote to her brother Tom:

> Dear Brother,
>
> In the midst of bustle and preparation you must not expect that I can say much to you. It is enough for the present to inform you, that on the day you receive this, I shall most probably have resigned my prospects of future happiness or misery for this life, into the hands of another . . .

It was indeed true that a woman's fate depended almost entirely on her choice of marriage partner, especially at a time when it was so difficult to extricate oneself.

Ellen Weeton barely knew the man she was marrying. Aaron Stock, a Calvinist cotton spinner and factory manager near Wigan, was a widower in his late thirties, only a year older than Ellen. There is no mention of a courtship in her journal. Only two weeks before the marriage she wrote to her brother Tom for his advice, since Tom had some acquaintance with Mr Stock through his mother-in-law, who rented a factory to him. Tom, a solicitor who stood to gain £100 by the terms of his mother's will on either the marriage or the death of his sister, unhesitatingly gave Stock a good character when in reality he was a blackguard. He effectively sold his sister for a legacy.

It is plain to see why Aaron married Ellen – he was virtually bankrupt and needed her investments and savings to rescue his ailing business – but unclear why she married him. She had managed to support herself for years, but presumably the insecurity and opprobrium attached to spinsterhood nudged her into marriage.

Ellen was the daughter of Thomas Weeton of Lancaster, a privateers-man who was killed at sea in 1782, and his wife, Mary Rawlinson. At twenty-one, on her mother's death, Ellen took over a small school her mother had opened at Upholland. Later, she became a governess and companion, filling that uneasy place in the household somewhere between the family and the servants. A careful manager of money and a shrewd investor, she had constantly denied herself in order to finance her adored brother's legal studies.

The Stocks embarked on married life in Aaron's house at the back of the Chapel Lane factory, but moved to a more salubrious area once his business, bolstered by his wife's capital, began to flourish. Ten months into the marriage she bore a daughter, Mary.

At a time when premature death meant that many marriages were second marriages, a wife might well have to negotiate the tricky path of mollifying stepchildren. Aaron's two daughters were ill-disposed to Ellen and neither they, nor the servants, gave her the cordial welcome that was her due as their father's wife and the new mistress of the house. Aaron persistently undermined her. Nor did he show her any kindness; she referred to the 'wayward humours', 'ill-treatment' and 'tyranny' that characterized Aaron's behaviour from the outset.

Perhaps her previous independence rendered Ellen incapable of the wifely submission that guaranteed harmony. She quickly discovered that Stock was not susceptible to any influence or persuasions she tried to exert. He was a bully, who ruled by fear and relished abject submission. He delighted to see 'everyone trembling around him', but Ellen would not give him the satisfaction of being cowed. For a time she believed she achieved a modest equilibrium by using a 'firm, judicious opposition' – surely not the right recipe. At any rate, Aaron quickly lost patience with her. Having appropriated her money, which was his right as her husband, he had no further use for her. He set out to break her will and drive her out of the home.

In her journal, written years later to set the record straight for her daughter, Ellen describes her situation:

Since then [the marriage] cruelty from a monster of a husband; my daily life in danger, attended with constant terror for many months, supposing each hour might be my last, and not knowing in what shape death might come – expecting at one moment to be poisoned, and therefore afraid to eat or drink anything that my husband could possibly have meddled with; obliged to be constantly on my guard against the deadly blows he would sometimes give me at the back of my ear unprovoked, and when I was least expecting it.

At the beginning of January 1818 Aaron turned Ellen out of the house. She sought refuge with her brother, who two days later accompanied her either to effect a reconciliation or a negotiated settlement with Aaron. If a husband withdrew his protection a woman only had her male kin to turn to, but Tom was half-hearted about defending his sister, primarily because it was not in his interest to upset the business arrangement between Stock and his mother-in-law, and Ellen simply could not accept Aaron's terms:

> Turned out of doors into the street! Mr Stock wants me either to remain at home penniless, as an underling to his own daughters, or to be kept by anyone who will take me. I cannot agree to such a reconciliation, or such a separation, whilst he has plenty of money. I am obliged totally to withdraw myself from any domestic affairs, in obedience to my husband's orders; to live in an apartment alone; not to sit at table with the family, but to have my meat sent to me; and amuse or employ myself as I can. When, and how, will this end?

None the less, penniless, Ellen had no choice but to return to her husband. She had lost all authority in the household: her stepdaughters were allowed to tyrannize her, jeering at her and often banishing her below stairs, and she was forced to eat the servants' food. The following year Aaron relegated her to the back quarters of the Chapel Lane factory and sent four-year-old Mary to boarding school. Ellen was confined to her room on a diet of bread and water. Aaron had long supplanted her by bringing his mistress into the house, but it was only after seven years of verbal and physical abuse that, fearing for her life, Ellen in 1822 finally agreed to a most unjust private deed of separation forced on her by her husband and brother, who perversely was acting as Stock's legal adviser.

She had already been 'threatened with being sent to a lunatic asylum, only for asking for food', and now Stock threatened her with starvation, further imprisonment, or a Lunacy Commission hearing if she would not sign. In a final betrayal, her brother advised Stock that Ellen should not be allowed to read the document, but have it read to her.

The separation deed banished her from Wigan and limited her access to her daughter to three annual supervised visits. Her compensation was her former governess's salary of £70 a year, an inadequate sum only irregularly paid. Ignoring the restriction on seeing Mary, Ellen would regularly walk the eight miles each way to Mr Grandy's Academy for Young Ladies to catch a glimpse of her in the school grounds or to join the file of children on their way to chapel. In 1827 Stock left Wigan and Mary, now twelve years old, was returned to her mother, possibly through the good offices of the local Hope Chapel, which she had joined.

Patriarchy, the combined force of husband, brother and lawyer, is seen here at its most cruel and crushing.

Wife-sale

For the rich there was parliamentary divorce; for the middling ranks, either a separation from bed and board granted by the ecclesiastical court or a deed of private separation; for the poor there was desertion or wife-sale. These were the options for those wanting to end their marriage prior to the 1857 Divorce Act and subsequent legislation.

The poor, unencumbered by property, tended to make their own rules. Those living in irregular unions could go their separate ways, free of any legal obligation; for the married, there had to be some form of 'closure'. In a period of almost continuous war between England and France between 1688 and 1815, it was easy for a man to desert his wife, disappearing into the army or being caught, willingly or otherwise, by the press gangs. And with desertion came its concomitant, bigamy. There were thousands of bigamous unions. Some preferred to place the end of their marriage on a more formal footing.

Wife-sale, by which a man sold his wife to another who had expressed a wish to buy her and take on responsibility for her, was a popular form of collusive self-divorce. A custom unique to Britain and New England, it had its origins in the late sixteenth century, but enjoyed a boost in popularity after Lord Hardwicke's Marriage Act of 1753, which had effectively pushed more of the poor into more formal, legally recognized unions in the first place.

Just as in the sale of an animal at Smithfield or any other cattle market, a shocked foreigner observed that the husband 'puts a halter about her neck and thereby leads her to the market place, and there puts her up to auction to be sold to the best bidder, as if she were a brood mare or a milch-cow'. The idea was to give the transaction maximum publicity, guaranteed on a busy market day, exonerating the husband from any future obligations towards the woman, including the payment of her debts and her rights to dower. She might cost anything from a few pence to a few guineas. A fee would be payable to the clerk of the market, as in any other sale.

In practice, the deal was usually agreed amicably beforehand between the husband and the man keen to take her, although there were the occasional impulse sales, such as the man who sold his wife for a lottery ticket: 'On Thursday last,' ran a notice in the *Public Advertiser*, 'a publican of Shoreditch sold his wife for a ticket in the present lottery, on condition that if the ticket be drawn a blank, he is to have his wife again as soon as the drawing of the lottery is over.'

Afterwards the trio might resort to an ale-house to toast the new arrangement, with some of the purchase money being spent on drinks all round. The woman tended to remove her wedding ring and return it to the man she now regarded as her ex-husband.

The fact that wife-sales were reported in the press probably indicates that the practice was comparatively rare and therefore of some sensational value. A Norwich newspaper in 1773 reported that 'A farmer of East Tuddenham bought for a guinea the wife of one Bushes. So elated was he at his purchase that the parish bells rang all day. The woman has one child, which he has given bond for maintaining.' Four years later the same newspaper noted that 'A butcher at Halstead in Essex sold his wife to a wealthy farmer for three guineas and a good supper: the woman acceding to the bargain, the farmer immediately took her home and seemed very well pleased with his purchase.'

As late as 1872 the *Western Times* was reporting, 'A man at Exeter has sold his wife for £50. It appears that the purchaser was smitten with the charms of his friend's wife, who did not live on the best of terms with her husband, having too much "dash" for him; negotiations were entered into, an offer of £50 was accepted, and the man took the woman to Plymouth, where the couple are now residing.'

Needless to say, wife-sale had no basis in law. When Thomas Hardy published *Jude the Obscure* in 1896, which included a scene depicting wife-sale, there was a public outcry. Respectable Victorian society was utterly horrified at the very notion. Even at its peak between 1753 and 1850 wife-sale had been rare, and its importance pales into insignificance compared with the thousands of desertions and elopements that were also taking place in the same period and the thousands of maintenance orders that would keep the courts so busy in the future.

PART FIVE
1820–1885

21

'I do not ask for my rights. I have no rights; I have only wrongs'

O N 18 AUGUST 1853 a woman stood in the witness box of a crowded courtroom at Westminster. The spectators swam before her eyes and her words stuck in her throat as if it were suddenly full of dust. 'What does the witness say? Let her speak up; I cannot hear her!' a bullying voice demanded. Impatient, he swept up his papers and moved to place himself directly in front of her, his eyes glaring with anger, a sneer of triumph on his dull features. Some of the lawyers in the court appealed to the judge not to permit the interrogator to sit so close to the witness, but the interrogator was oblivious of everything, except that at last he had the means to crush the woman who had taunted, plagued and bested him ever since their marriage a quarter of a century ago.

Victory was within his grasp as he produced with a flourish his final piece of evidence. He had broken the private separation agreement he had made with his wife in 1848, he told the court, and stopped her allowance, because when his lawyers examined her bank books they had discovered that she was receiving payments from another man, contrary to her promise never to take money from that source. That man was – the whole court waited in suspense – the late Lord Melbourne. There was uproar and Norton must have been delighted at the effect his bombshell had ignited. No matter that he was once more besmirching his wife's reputation and shadowing his sons' lives by his calculated revival of the former scandal. Money had always been his obsession, but he was motivated now by more than pecuniary interest. His wife Caroline's ruin was his vindication. The implication was clear. If Melbourne had left her money the couple *must* have been guilty of adultery all those years ago.

At the mention of Lord Melbourne's name a flaming surge of anger coursed through Caroline. How dare this gnome of a husband, who had falsely accused her of impropriety with Melbourne knowing it was not true, torn her away from her little children, letting one of them die through neglect, and consumed the best years of her life in misery, recrimination and litigation use the excuse of a disputed income to bring infamy upon her! As a married woman, she had never before been able to defend herself in court, not even when her reputation was at stake when Norton brought the case of criminal conversation against Lord Melbourne. Fury and indignation now replaced her former embarrassment and timidity and she rose to address the court with all the dramatic sense and oratorical skills she had inherited from her grandfather, the playwright Richard Brinsley Sheridan.

Lord Melbourne had left her nothing in his will, she stated, since his estate was entailed. She had never been his mistress – she was, after all, young enough to be his daughter. They were friends only. When he died, he had left a letter solemnly repeating his assurance that nothing improper had ever occurred in his relationship with Mrs Norton. Out of a sense of obligation to a woman who had been ruined through her innocent friendship with him, however, he had recommended her to the generosity of his brother, naming the sum of £200 a year, and his brother and sister, Lady Palmerston, had seen fit to honour his wishes. No one but her husband George Norton had ever accused Lord Melbourne of baseness.

When she finished this moving speech there was a brief silence before the court erupted into loud applause and wild cheers. Even Norton's solicitor felt impelled to jump up and deny his client's statement that there had been any clause relating to Lord Melbourne in the agreement of 1848. With public sympathy on Caroline's side, it looked like an open and shut case. Thrupps, a carriage maker, was suing Norton for a debt for repairs to Caroline's vehicle, which as her husband he was bound to pick up, since it appeared that the separation agreement between the couple had collapsed and he was no longer paying her allowance. In return for an annual allowance of £500 from Norton, Caroline had undertaken to pay her own debts, and she had done so scrupulously until on her receiving a small inheritance amounting to £480 a year on her mother's death Norton had decided to renegotiate the settlement.

No doubt Norton resented the fact that Mrs Sheridan had taken care to secure her legacy to her daughter for her own private use under the law of equity. It was no wonder she did so, because apart from years of cruelty he had meted out to Caroline, he had cheated her in their original marriage settlement, giving her to understand that his expectations were far greater than they were. By common law everything a woman owned became her husband's on marriage, but the law of equity relating to married women's property, administered through the Court of Chancery, was diametrically opposed to this. It took the view that the weak and vulnerable – women and children – needed protection and that, more often than not, the enemy was the husband.

As her husband, although long estranged from her, Norton was already in possession of all Caroline's worldly goods, including a life-interest in her father's estate, and it seemed so unreasonable that he would not let her enjoy the small augmentation in her income her mother's legacy afforded her without seeking to reduce the allowance she received from him. After all, her expenses were much greater now that she had access to her sons and was taking care of many of their expenses.

Norton had subpoenaed Caroline's maid, in the hopes of revealing that she was extravagant, her publishers and her bankers. John Murray had had to produce their royalty statements revealing Caroline's earnings from her literary activities, comprising poetry, plays and pamphlets, while her bankers had had to give Norton access to her bank statements, which was his entitlement as her husband. Norton's original purpose was to show that Caroline was quite capable of earning her own living without receiving anything from him; indeed, she was damned lucky he was not helping himself to her earnings, as he was entitled to do. The discovery of the Melbourne annuity, which had come to Caroline *after* the 1848 agreement, was an unlooked-for bonus. In his malevolent fervour Norton even subpoenaed Caroline, hoping that she would say something to incriminate herself, which is how she came to be standing in the witness box, for once given the opportunity to state her own case.

Her appearance in court rebounded on him, in that she drew the admiration and sympathy of the onlookers, but Norton won the case on a legal technicality. It seemed that Thrupps had presented his bill before Norton had withdrawn Caroline's allowance, so that, under the terms of their separation agreement, she was liable to pay it. Caroline had the last word, telling the court, 'I do not ask for my rights. I have no rights; I have only wrongs.' If her husband wanted to defraud her, there was nothing she could do about it. Once more, the court burst into applause, leaving an apoplectic Norton shouting above the din that it was all lies, everything she said was a lie, and angrily shaking his fists at her. Caroline was bundled out of the court by her lawyer, while the many journalists scurried off to file their reports.

Caroline may have felt powerless, but she was not defeated. She had already successfully contested a father's right to exclusive control over his children, denying their mother access. The Infants Custody Act of 1839 had been largely her achievement. Perhaps now she could change the law relating to divorce and married women's property.

There was nothing in Caroline Norton's background to suggest that she would become a law reformer and she was certainly no feminist. It was only her own sufferings under the law that taught her its many inconsistencies and injustices and propelled her to use her extensive political contacts and literary acumen to argue for drastic change.

One of the wonders of the fiercely competitive marriage market of the 1820s was the fact that Mrs Sheridan had managed to marry off all three of her daughters with virtually no money. Arranged marriages among the upper classes on the basis of money had ostensibly given way to marriages based on attachment, with young men and women free to make their own choice, if only from within the limited social circles in which they moved, but in reality money was as important as ever. That all three girls married well within a couple of years of their coming out was a tribute to their fascination, beauty and wit – attributes that outweighed their lack of money, their disconcerting tendency to swear, and unconventionality.

Long after the heyday of the great Irish dramatist Richard Brinsley Sheridan, the favourite of King George IV when he was Prince of Wales, the Sheridans were poor and operated on the edges of aristocratic society. With their theatrical background, not everyone considered them quite respectable. Mrs Sheridan, the widow of Sheridan's eldest son, was fortunate to have a grace-and-favour apartment at Hampton Court Palace, and she was determined to launch her girls. Their personal qualities, unblemished reputations and 'ton' (or fashion) were good enough to win them coveted tickets to Almack's, where they met all the most eligible young men. At the end of her second season Helen at eighteen married Captain Price Blackwood, the heir to Lord Dufferin. She was not in love with him and his family were opposed to the match, but it turned out to be a happy marriage. The fact that her sister had not married for love, but that it worked out well, influenced Caroline, who was at heart a romantic who dreamed of a marriage that would be happy ever after.

If Mrs Sheridan had stopped to think about it, there was something very odd about George Norton from the start. As an unruly sixteen-year-old Caroline had been sent to a young ladies' finishing school at Wonersh in Surrey. A party of girls had been invited to Wonersh Park, the home of Lord Grantley and the Norton family, and it was here that George Norton first set eyes on her. Caroline was striking, with luxuriant black hair, expressive dark eyes, voluptuous curves and a swanlike neck. Without even engaging her in conversation, Norton sent her mother a formal proposal for Caroline's hand in marriage.

Mrs Sheridan replied that Caroline was far too young, but Norton was prepared to wait. Caroline had no shortage of admirers during her first season, but it seemed none of them wanted to marry her. She was beautiful, intelligent, outspoken and unconventional – an unsettling combination. Perhaps they already detected disturbing elements in her character. She gave out the wrong signals, appearing much more sophisticated than she actually was. She was a flirt and a tease with a searing wit that she sometimes used to ridicule her would-be admirers. Older men enjoyed her company, but the more gauche among the young men often withdrew, offended or embarrassed by her. Only too aware that she had to snare a husband to shore up the faltering family finances, Caroline was beginning to panic. By her second season her younger sister, Georgiana, the most beautiful of the three, was pressing close on her heels. It would not do for Georgiana to be married before Caroline, but equally Caroline's tardiness could not be allowed to scupper Georgiana's chances.

It was now that George Norton renewed his suit. He had remained true to his determination to marry Caroline and was apparently very much in love with her, although how this could be when he contented himself with merely staring at her and had barely spoken to her is open to doubt. Obsession, or the urge to possess, would be a more accurate description of his feelings. Where formerly she might have dismissed the suit of the rather uninspiring young man from Wonersh, now she was prepared to entertain it. It was a relief perhaps that a moderately eligible bachelor was sufficiently 'in love' with her to overlook her lack of dowry. Given Norton's greed for money, it was a wonder.

On paper it was not a bad match. He was the younger brother and heir of a peer who was likely to remain childless. Seven years Caroline's senior, he was a lawyer by training, although he was naturally indolent and as a gentleman he considered it beneath him to work for a living. There was nothing known against his character and perhaps his slow, plodding temperament would complement Caroline's more mercurial one. No one at this stage gauged the depths of his coldly egotistical, devious, cunning and vicious personality.

On the Norton side there was no great enthusiasm for the match. Tories, they objected to Caroline's Whig connections and, of course, she had no money. Country gentry with no interest in the arts, the Nortons had little in common with the urbane Sheridans and Caroline did not trouble to ingratiate herself. Grantley disliked her intensely, while George's sisters, the butch Miss Augusta and hard-faced Grace, Lady Menzies, resented her for her youth and beauty and the fact that she was a great hit with Grace's husband, with whom she was unwise enough to flirt. Far from making herself acceptable to her new family, which was a bride's first duty, Caroline made enemies for life.

The auguries were not auspicious, therefore, when the couple married at St George's, Hanover Square, on 30 July 1827.

Caroline was quickly disillusioned. She did not love her husband and soon she did not like or respect him either. Quick-witted, intolerant, ardent and untamed, she had no control over her tongue and was too immature to conceal her contempt. On the contrary, she had a habit of ridiculing him in front of others, which was a cardinal sin for any wife. He was too dull to combat her biting wit, but he stored up resentment. If she was not taunting him, she was bombarding him with questions and trying to tell him what to do, and he hated clever, enquiring, argumentative women. It was not long before they had their first quarrel, during which Caroline made the alarming discovery that George, when provoked, became physically violent. On this first occasion he picked up a heavy ink stand and some law books and hurled them at her head.

To Caroline, who had been brought up in a close, warm, loving and civilized family, it came as a profound shock. She had never encountered violence before and was too ashamed to tell her family. If she thought it was an isolated incident, fuelled by brandy, she was quickly disabused. A visit to Lady Menzies in Scotland provoked a second attack when Caroline, in the privacy of their room, made a derogatory comment about an opinion he had expressed. There was 'a sudden and violent kick; the blow reached my side; it caused great pain for many days.' Caroline was too afraid to remain with him and spent the night in another room.

Not appearing to know her place as a wife, George was determined to subjugate her. A pattern quickly established itself. Caroline would argue or make some withering comment, which provoked George into a rage, in which he would not spare the kicks and blows. Afterwards he was full of remorse, begging her to take him back into her affections, to become her 'Geordy boy' again. What choice did she have? It would not be long until they fell to rowing again, with Caroline goading him ever further. In addition, she had to endure his forced attentions in bed, which must have disgusted her even more than the other violence.

Caroline was disconcerted to find that George always seemed to be short of money and, worse, he was mean. He had given Mrs Sheridan to understand that £30,000 was set aside for Grantley's siblings and that as the heir he would have the bulk of it. It was a lie. Mrs Sheridan bitterly regretted the betrayal and her own stupidity. Caroline was yoked to a man with no redeeming features, who abused her and who had no money into the bargain. George blamed Caroline for their poverty. He began to pester her mother to use her court connections to find him some sinecure. Very reluctantly she did so and George was made a Commissioner for Bankruptcy. When that expired, the onus was on Caroline to find some other source of income.

Ironically, it was Caroline's wish to help her husband that brought her into contact with Lord Melbourne, who was then Home Secretary. The general election of 1830 had swept the Whigs into power and Caroline began to write around and lobby her grand-father's old friends, asking for employment for George. One after-noon in the spring of 1831 Lord Melbourne called on the little house she and George were renting at 2 Storey's Gate, Westminster. He so much wanted to meet Sheridan's granddaughter. Melbourne was a suave fifty-one-year-old who delighted in the company and con-versation of a bright, intelligent and attractive young woman such as Caroline. As the widower of Lady Caroline Lamb, who had run off with Lord Byron, and the father of a disabled son, Melbourne's life was emotionally empty, as was Caroline's. They struck up an instant, affectionate friendship, with Lord Melbourne falling into the habit of calling in several times a week on his way back from the House of Commons.

As it was later pointed out in the press, George Norton made no objections to Melbourne's friendship with his wife and to his regu-lar visits to the house in the years 1831 to 1836. He must have been aware that there was gossip and speculation. Melbourne belonged to the more raffish Regency era and had a reputation with women, while Caroline was a notorious flirt. Favoured by the new King William IV and Queen Adelaide, who remembered her fondly as a child, and befriended by Melbourne, Caroline had swiftly become one of the most influential hostesses in London society. Everyone flocked to her drawing room to meet Melbourne and it was here she introduced her friend, the aspiring politician Benjamin Disraeli, to the great man. She was too conspicuous a figure and too indis-creet to have escaped censure and it was beginning to dawn on her that many women disliked and disapproved of her. And yet George appeared to encourage the friendship, no doubt because he stood to gain financially.

New posts were quickly found for George as Recorder of Guildford and as a magistrate in the Lambeth Division of the Metropolitan Police Courts, with an income of £1,000 a year. Much was later made of the fact that this took him out of the house three afternoons a week – the very afternoons that Melbourne chose to call. By now Caroline was also making a considerable contribution towards their income from her literary work and by editing some society magazines. George graciously allowed her to keep some of her earnings to defray the expenses of her first confinement.

George did not spare the brutality just because she was pregnant. By the summer of 1833 Caroline was within a few weeks of giving birth to their third child. On one occasion he came down to breakfast and demanded she get up from the chair where she was sitting as he wanted to sit there. When she refused he calmly picked up the scalding tea kettle and placed it on her hand, badly burning her. She could not bear the smell of George's hookah, which he insisted on smoking all over the house, so that after dinner one evening she announced she was going upstairs to work in the drawing room. The fact that she locked the door enraged him. How dare she show him such disrespect! He wrenched the door off its hinges and burst into the room, which he wrecked. He then fell upon her, hitting her and kicking her, and unceremoniously forced her down the stairs. Bruised and frightened, she spent the night in the nursery.

Seriously concerned about her welfare, the Sheridans intervened, but this brought the Nortons into the picture. They ignored Norton's faults and focused on Caroline's various defects, which caused additional strife. George was only too aware that the Sheridans despised him and took his resentment out on Caroline. To make matters worse, he had fallen under the influence of the spiteful, mischief-making Miss Vaughan, a cousin who promised to leave him all her property – the estate of Kettle Thorpe in Yorkshire and a house in Lower Berkeley Street. Like the Nortons, she loathed Caroline and began to make insinuations about her relationship with Melbourne to George. George's love of money forced him to ignore questions of honour and integrity and he put the question of Melbourne to one side, for the moment, while he allowed Miss Vaughan to gain total ascendancy over him.

In the summer of 1835 another violent quarrel took place, so that Caroline feared for her life. Even though she was pregnant again, she gathered up her children and sought protection at the home of her sister Georgiana, now Lady Seymour. The family begged her not to return to George, but what else could she do? She had three little boys and another child on the way and very little money. Separation from George would mean separation from her children, since they belonged exclusively to their father. Once more, George begged forgiveness and promised to mend his ways. In the eyes of the law, the fact that she returned to him on this occasion indicated that she forgave him, or condoned his behaviour, so that she would not be able to use the incident in any future case against him. Charges of cruelty were anyway difficult to prove.

On Caroline's second day back at Storey's Gate, George beat her again. She lost the baby and was seriously ill for a long time. Melbourne continued to visit her, spending afternoons in her bedroom. It was not quite proper, but George seemed neither to mind nor care. He was spending an inordinate amount of time with Miss Vaughan, so that Caroline began to wonder if they were having an affair. She was invited to spend Easter with her brother Brinsley Sheridan and his heiress wife at Frampton Court. All the Sheridans were going to be there. George was pointedly not invited, but he raised no objection to her going until Miss Vaughan insisted on the impropriety of his allowing his wife and children to stay at a house where he was not welcome.

Suddenly George announced that Caroline and the children would not be able to go to Frampton after all. Caroline retaliated that she had every intention of going, telling him that it was his own fault if he was not received by her family. He asked the servants to unload the children's luggage, as they would not be travelling next day, and went up to the nursery to repeat the command. Then they went to bed – the last night Caroline, her husband and children would ever spend under the same roof.

Next morning Caroline rushed round to consult the Seymours as to what she should do about Frampton. When she returned to Storey's Gate, it was to find that George had absconded with the children. Frantic with worry, she traced them to Miss Vaughan's, but by the time she arrived there they had already been taken off by her agent, Mr Knapp. At Mr Knapp's she found he had locked the children in a room with their nurse. Caroline could only beg the nurse not to leave them before being thrown out. She repaired to Frampton, alone, to seek solace and advice from her family.

George seized the opportunity to declare that she had left the family home, placing an advertisement in the newspapers advising trades-men that he would not be responsible for her debts. As a lawyer, he knew such an advertisement held no weight in law, but it did serve to tell the whole of society that the marriage was over. Scurrilous reports about Caroline and Lord Melbourne had frequently appeared in the newspapers, but as soon as it was known that Caroline had left Storey's Gate it was open house for the press to make the most vile and unfounded allegations.

George's terms for a separation were predictably mean and shabby. The children – Fletcher, six, Brinsley three and a half, and William not yet two – were to live with their father, where Caroline might see them occasionally; she was to have no allowance whatsoever and to live with her brother, since he had so often indicated that he would keep her. She could earn her living by her pen, although of course she must not forget that her husband was entitled to those earnings too.

George, who was busily searching for a co-respondent from among Caroline's many admirers, did not have to look far. Early in May 1836 he made known his intention of bringing a suit of crim-inal conversation against Lord Melbourne, for alienation of his wife's affections. To take on the Prime Minister on grounds George knew to be unfounded was an act of breathtaking audacity, but of course he was egged on by his fellow Tories, among them his brother Lord Grantley. The scandal was well calculated to unseat the government and George would be able to rid himself of his wife and at the same time have the glory of engineering a Whig defeat. That George was prepared to ruin the reputation of his wife and the mother of his children concerned him not at all.

Nor was he at all abashed by the fact that he had Lord Melbourne to thank for his employment, although the press expressed sur-prise that in the circumstances Norton had not resigned his post of stipendiary magistrate. If his fellow Tories were intent on destroying Melbourne's career and bringing down his government, Norton personally was motivated by the fact that he stood to win immense damages should he win the case.

Not since the trial of Queen Caroline, which had roused public sympathy for a wronged wife separated from her child, had a matrimonial case generated such excitement and speculation. London hummed with rumours about the sensational nature of the evidence that Norton would produce. The fate of the government hung on the verdict.

It was all the more surprising, therefore, that Norton, a lawyer by training, should present such a feeble case. He relied on the evidence of a drunken coachman who had been dismissed and a former woman servant. It was absurd, disgusting and quickly dismissed, especially when the court heard that the two had been comfortably accommodated and plied with drink courtesy of Lord Grantley and vigorously coached in what they had to say. All the written evidence Norton could produce were some innocent notes from Melbourne to Caroline, such as: 'I will call about half past four. Yours Melbourne.' Without even waiting to hear the witnesses for Lord Melbourne the jury returned a verdict against Norton.

Neither Melbourne nor Caroline had attended the court. As a married woman, one person in law with her husband, Caroline was not allowed to defend herself in the case he was bringing against Melbourne, even though it was her reputation that was being irreparably damaged. The jury had dismissed the evidence, but this did not stop the press reproducing it all for the gratification of its readers. Vindicated, Melbourne emerged from the trial with his popularity bolstered. Caroline was just as innocent, yet to all intents and purposes she was treated as if she were guilty. She could never hope to regain her former reputation or place in society. Sadly, too, Melbourne distanced himself from her. Just as it began to dawn on Caroline that she had been in love with him, she lost his friendship.

The fact that the case against Lord Melbourne foundered meant that there were no grounds for a divorce – that is, a separation from bed and board. Whether the impecunious George would have been able to afford the proceedings for a divorce with permission to remarry by private Act of Parliament is open to doubt. There had been no adultery between Melbourne and Caroline and her reconciliation with George after the brief separation in 1835 meant that she could not use cruelty as grounds for divorcing him. Excluded from her home and denied access to her children, unprotected yet legally tied, Caroline existed in the uneasy world of the separated wife. Later, she wrote a description of her situation and the restrictions women like her were to live under for many decades yet:

> Alone. Married to a man's name, but never to know the protection of this nominal husband, nor the joys of family, nor the every-day companionship of a real home. Never to feel or show preference for any friend not of her own sex, though tempted, perhaps by a feeling nobler than passion – gratitude for generous pity, that has lightened the dreary days. To be slandered, tormented, insulted; to find the world and the world's law utterly indifferent to her wrongs or her husband's sin; and through all this to lead a chaste, unspotted, patient, cheerful life; without anger, without bitterness, and with meek respect for these edicts which, with a perverse parody of Scripture, pronounce that it 'is not good for a man to be alone, but extremely good for a woman.'

No formal separation agreement had been reached, although even if it had been George would only have been honour-bound, not legally bound, to keep it. He could bar her from the house and he was at liberty to impound her jewels, books, clothes and other possessions, which he did. Financially she had no claim on him unless she could prove she had no other means of support, but of course she had her literary work. By far the worst injustice, however, was that for the next five years George indulged in a cat-and-mouse game with her, using the children as bait.

Caroline had blithely assumed that once the court case was out of the way she would be reunited with her children. She was shocked to discover that the laws of England afforded a separated mother no rights over her children. Access, if it was permitted at all, was purely at the whim or mercy of the husband. Caroline was a devoted mother and George knew that her vulnerability lay through her children. How he must have relished feeling superior and in control at last!

Of course, being George, it all came down to money. Access was to be conditional on Caroline entering into a financial agreement favourable to George. She in turn was urged by her relatives and friends to agree to nothing until the question of the children was resolved. 'They may bereave me of my beloved boys (since the law allows it), they may drive me mad, or wear me into my grave by the slow torture of that greatest of sorrows; but while I have the control of my reason, and strength to guide a pen, I will sign nothing, do nothing, listen to nothing, which has reference to any other subject – till it is decided what intercourse is to be allowed me with my children.'

When George initially offered her a meeting with the boys at his lawyer's chambers she had to decline. Meeting their mother in such an environment meant that she would be for ever associated in their minds with secrecy and shame. In the autumn of 1836 she was allowed to see them at her brother's house in Grosvenor Square for half an hour. It was a tearful occasion. Fletcher whispered that he had tried to get the servants to pass her a note, but they had refused. Caroline took to loitering outside the house where they were staying, trying to catch a glimpse of them, and once when George was out actually entered the house and made her way up to the nursery to see them. When she tried to do it again, she found her way barred by one of the male servants.

Possibly because of this incident, the children were to be sent to live with Lady Menzies in Scotland. Caroline wrote to George begging to be allowed to say goodbye to them, but there was no reply. She was terrified that Lady Menzies would ill-treat them, although this turned out not to be the case. They were still in Scotland the following March when Caroline heard by chance that the baby William had been dangerously ill. No one had bothered to let her know. She confronted George in a long and distressing interview. He said he would bring the children down from Scotland to see her, but only on condition she would sign an agreement accepting maintenance of a mere £200 a year.

It was particularly insulting since George was now comparatively well off: Miss Vaughan had died and left him the promised inheritance. Caroline refused. There would be no deal of any kind until she was granted access to her children. Several weeks passed before George responded, telling her he intended to sell her possessions. When her brother Brinsley offered to buy them, George at first agreed then changed his mind.

'Mr Norton may (as he has threatened) sell the jewels and dresses I have worn – the gifts made by my family on my marriage – the books which belonged to my father, and the presents of other friends. He may do this, to answer my personal debts – if my children are kept from me, all else is trivial and indifferent!'

It was now that a curious interview took place between Caroline and George. Seeing her in the flesh reminded him of the beauty that had never failed to move him. She knew he was sexually stirred and it made her uneasy to be alone with him. They were still married and marital rape was not an indictable offence. He broke down and begged her to return to him. He asked her to believe that the trial had been against his wishes, that he had been urged to it by family and friends and now regretted it. Caroline could see her boys at the first possible moment. Would she forgive the past and come to live with him again? She had only to write to Grantley to seek his favour and a new settlement covering themselves and the boys could be worked out. Out of exhaustion and desperation to see the children, she agreed.

No sooner had she done so than George began to backtrack, no doubt because Grantley and the rest of the family were not prepared to forgive and forget. George suggested that instead of bringing the boys to London she should go to them in Scotland. Caroline disagreed. She wrote:

> I do not consider it decent or fit that I should be sent to Lady Menzies' house; it is a cruel tyranny to tantalise me with such a permission to see my children, nor am I in a state of health to bear the journey. Altogether, it does amaze me that any human being should have the heart so to play upon the affection and sorrow of another as you do upon mine! This is the second time I have vainly trusted that you would recall my children. You promised it most heartily; you explained all your plans most fully; and how am I ever to believe anything again, or to what purpose can I see Grantley, if, while he tells me he is friendly to their coming, he opposes all in secret?

Experiencing first-hand the inhumanity of the law as it related to separated mothers and children, Caroline resolved to do something about it. Unlike Mary Wollstonecraft, the author of *A Vindication of the Rights of Woman* and mother of her friend Mary Shelley, she was no feminist, but she could appreciate that whatever had been done to advance the rights of man had done very little to safeguard the rights of mothers and children. Since men were held to be rational beings, morally superior to women, the law awarded fathers total power over their children. Yet the woman who had laboured nine long months and risked her life giving birth to them had no rights over them. Her husband could take them from her and give them to his mistress and there was nothing she could do about it. If Caroline did not hold with sexual equality, she did believe that a mother had 'natural rights' over her children. The law must be changed to accommodate these rights.

Caroline was uniquely placed to wage such a campaign. In spite of her disgrace, she still had first-rate political contacts; she was articulate and she could write. The Sheridans were horrified. As if Caroline were not held in enough disrepute, she was now threatening to interfere with what most people regarded as the sacred prerogatives of husbands and fathers.

In 1837 John Murray published Caroline's pamphlet, *Observations on the Natural Claim of a Mother to the Custody of her Children as affected by the Common Law Right of the Father*. As an indication of how sensitive the subject was Murray printed 500 copies for private circulation only. It argued that all children under the age of seven should reside with their mother and that the fate of older children should be decided by the Lord Chancellor, as a neutral arbiter. Her friend, the lawyer Serjeant Talfourd, MP for Reading, agreed to introduce a motion in the House of Commons to alter the law over the custody of infants.

To Caroline's subsequent shame, she lost interest in the progress of the legislation when it seemed that her troubles with Norton were over. In the summer of 1837 George did bring the boys down to London and she was allowed to spend some time with them. She told Talfourd she was no longer interested in the bill and he allowed it to lapse.

It was such joy to be with her boys, although she was distressed to see that Brinsley was not in good health and all three looked unkempt and neglected. Grantley was incensed that in spite of the privilege accorded her in being able to see her children she would not immediately sign a separation agreement. Nor would she do so unless regular rights of access were agreed.

While they were staying in London in the care of their aunt, Augusta Norton, Caroline was allowed to take them for daily outings, but they always had to be returned to Wilton Place for the night. One evening when she brought them back little Brinsley was unwell and begged to stay with his mother. A scene took place on the doorstep. Miss Norton started to abuse Caroline and upbraid the sick child, who was not quite five. A violent quarrel ensued. Caroline lost her temper and declared that she had never intended to return to live with Norton as his wife, whatever he might have hoped or expected. Next morning when she sent for the children she received a message to say that she would not be seeing them again. She hurried round to Wilton Place but the door was held against her by George and Augusta.

The boys were removed to Wonersh, where all three came down with measles. Caroline rushed down to Surrey and managed to bluff her way into the house and up to the nursery. When Grantley returned and discovered her presence he was furious. He burst into the room to find Caroline surrounded by her sick children, the smallest taking comfort on her knee. There was a terrible scene as he ordered her to leave, she refused, he laid hands on her and started shaking her, and she threatened to indict him for assault. Impervious to the screams of the children, a couple of servants were told to prise the smallest boy from his mother. They pulled his arms and legs with such force that Caroline gave way, frightened that they were going to injure him. Grantley ordered the by now hysterical children to be locked up and Caroline was ignominiously thrown out of the house, retreating down the drive under the triumphant, malevolent glare of her brother-in-law.

In her despair Caroline began to lobby unceasingly for the Infants Custody Bill, which now became her only hope of redress. She produced another pamphlet, *The Separation of Mother and Child by the Law of Custody of Infants, Considered*, in which she used real cases drawn from the court records to highlight the iniquities and anomalies in the system. In March 1838 the bill passed in the Commons, albeit on a very poor showing, but was thrown out in the Lords, where Lord Brougham, who had a personal axe to grind against Caroline, gave a powerful speech refuting it. If women suffered from legal hardships, they were necessary to protect the family unit. It was dangerous to tamper with the marriage laws, as any relaxation would encourage even the most devoted wives and mothers to rebel. Throughout it was assumed that any woman separated from her husband *must* be guilty of adultery, whereas a husband's adultery was irrelevant.

The cause seemed hopeless, but Caroline was nothing if not persistent. She wrote another pamphlet, *A Plain Letter to the Lord Chancellor on the Infant Custody Bill*, using the *nom de plume* Pearce Stevenson, Esq., to suggest it was the work of a male lawyer. She lobbied MPs and wrote letters to the press, gradually changing public opinion and winning sympathy for the plight of women separated from their innocent children. It worked. In 1839 the bill was reintroduced and passed by both Houses, the first alteration in the marriage laws as they related to women since the early Middle Ages. A mother now had the right to petition the Lord Chancellor for a hearing as regards access to her children. To achieve it, she had to prove her character to be unblemished. George, of course, was continually expressing concern about Caroline's 'immoral life' and demanding further proofs of her 'improved conduct', so that even proving her case before the Lord Chancellor would not be easy.

Caroline still hoped to settle matters by mutual agreement and wrote to George accordingly. 'The law now requires that a man shall prove he is justified in inflicting so great a cruelty. You have your choice of proving you were and are right in withholding access, or of granting it; but you have no longer the power of doing an unjust thing without being called to account by any human being.'

All autumn she waited on tenterhooks to see if Norton would co-operate. Now sharing a house in Mayfair with an uncle and a younger brother, she had bedrooms made ready for her boys' visit and the fires lit. But they did not come. Norton was a lawyer, familiar with every ruse and evasion, and he must have laughed up his sleeve at Caroline's wide-eyed optimism now that her wretched Infants Custody Bill had become law. Caroline's efforts had made a difference to countless separated mothers and children, but there was to be no redress for her. The Norton children's domicile in Scotland placed them out of the jurisdiction of the English courts. It was a crushing blow.

In 1841, however, Caroline discovered that the boys were to be sent to an English school. She turned up unannounced, but Norton had given explicit instructions that no one was to see them without his permission. She applied to his solicitor, only to receive a curt note refusing permission. There was nothing for it but to petition the Lord Chancellor. Rather than go to court, where Caroline would produce correspondence that did not put him in a good light, George yielded, grudgingly, and Caroline had her boys to stay for the first part of the Christmas holidays of 1841.

Access was limited, however, and it took a tragedy for George finally to agree an equal share. In September 1842 the boys were staying with their father in Yorkshire. The youngest, William, aged eight, was thrown from his horse, his injuries were neglected and he became gravely ill with septicaemia. Eventually Caroline was sent for, but it was far too late. When she arrived at the station she was met by Lady Kelly, the wife of George's lawyer. 'Is my boy better?' Caroline asked anxiously. 'No,' came the blunt reply, 'he is not better, he is dead.'

The child had already been placed in his coffin. As he lay dying, he had asked repeatedly for his mother. 'Half of what is now so lavishly expended in ceremony and decoration of the coffin would have paid some steady man-servant to be in constant attendance on their hours of recreation,' Caroline wrote in despair. 'My poor little spirited creature was too young to rough it alone, as he was left to do . . . It is a hard thing that I and my boys – that so many hearts should be in the absolute power of one who has no heart.'

After the court hearing of August 1853 the newspapers resurrected the Melbourne scandal. Caroline was so incensed at the slurs on her reputation that she foolishly wrote to *The Times*, giving a detailed account of her side of the story. Of course, Norton retaliated, not hesitating to accuse his wife of adultery with Melbourne and even throwing doubt on the legitimacy of two of their sons. When the newspapers grew tired of the argument Caroline replayed the account of her friendship with Melbourne and the difficulties of her marriage in another pamphlet, *English Laws for Women in the Nineteenth Century*.

In no other country in Europe were married women so

ill-protected by the law. Even in Scotland a wife kept all her property, whereas in England she must surrender everything to her husband on marriage – unless, of course, she was one of the fortunate few whose families were rich enough and sufficiently *au fait* with the law to preserve her separate property in equity. Of course, the intention of such trusts was not so much to enable a woman to have control of her property, as a guarantee to her father that his money should not be squandered by a son-in-law but preserved intact for his grand-children. Without the protection trusts and settlements afforded their upper-class sisters, middle-class wives were particularly vulnerable if the marriage turned sour.

After the case Caroline came to the unpleasant realization that George now knew everything about her financial affairs. He could appropriate her earnings and the law supported him. The time was ripe for a complete overhaul of the property laws as they related to married women. They were no longer relevant to the modern world. When the laws were formulated in the Middle Ages the only significant property was land and since land brought with it the duty to support the King in war and a woman could not fight, a married woman's land was accredited to her husband. With the establishment of banking and the stock market in the late seventeenth century and the dawn of the Industrial Revolution in the eighteenth, wealth was no longer pinned exclusively on land. Among the poor, mar-ried women had always worked, originally alongside their husbands when home and work functioned as one economic unit, but with the growth of industry, separately, in the factories. Lower middle-class women worked and now even some middle-class women were entering the workplace. Could it be right that their earnings automatically belonged to their husbands?

Legal reforms were long overdue and it was to be one of the great achievements of the Victorian age to make the law more relevant to economic and social realities and iron out some of the complexities in the system. For instance, no fewer than three courts had jurisdiction over marriage, divorce and married women's property, all following different, wearisome and repetitive procedures and likely to deliver contradictory verdicts. Not only was it desirable to set up one civil court for matrimonial causes, abolishing the Church's jurisdiction over marriage, which it exercised through the ecclesiastical courts, but Lord Chancellor Cranworth was also at work on a Divorce Bill.

The bill was the subject of intense debate, moving from a measure to rationalize the legal system to one affecting the rights and legal status of married women. Caroline was incensed to hear Lord Cranworth uphold the sexual double standard by maintaining that a husband could divorce a wife for adultery, but a wife must prove adultery with some other aggravating factor. To call a husband's adultery 'a little profligate' while making a wife's grounds for divorce, she said, was like refusing to prosecute a murder because it was not parricide.

As well as Parliament's general tolerance of the sexual double standard, the debates revealed an undercurrent of fear concerning the potential for disorder inherent in the unleashing of female sexuality. In vain, speakers drew attention to Scotland, where divorce for adultery was permitted to men and women equally, and which suffered no greater licentiousness than England.

Caroline was at first intrigued to learn that other women were engaged in the campaign; then piqued that she was not invited to join them. In 1854, the same year as she published her *English Laws for Women in the Nineteenth Century*, Barbara Leigh Smith's *A Brief Summary, in Plain Language, of the Most Important Laws Concerning Women, Together with a few Observations Thereon* described some horrendous cases of wives being robbed by their husbands. There were women whose husbands absconded with mistresses, taking all their money and leaving them destitute; deserted wives who had laboured for years to support themselves and their children, only to have a prodigal husband return and take their little business or savings; and another poor woman whose husband was imprisoned for assaulting her and whose inheritance was appropriated by the crown, since what was hers was legally his and the crown was entitled to the property of convicted felons.

Whatever Caroline's achievements, she was scorned by feminists such as Harriet Martineau, who believed she was motivated only by self-interest. That Barbara Leigh Smith and the Women's Committee did not ask Caroline to join them or to include her signature among those of the most prestigious women in the country on the 'Petition for Reform of the Married Women's Property Law', which was being presented to Parliament, was deliberate. Opponents of the principle that women should be allowed to retain their own property and earnings argued that it would only lead to the breakdown of marriage, to women taking lovers and leaving their husbands. The Women's Committee therefore chose only the most respectable married women to sign the petition, steering well clear of Caroline, although George Eliot, who in 1857 set up home with a married man, managed to creep on to the lower part of the list.

It was a pity, as Caroline's exclusion set her on a collision course with them, delaying the passing of Acts to safeguard the property and earnings of all married women for another decade and more. Caroline lent all her efforts to Lord Cranworth's Divorce Bill. When progress stalled she nudged it along by publishing *A Letter to the Queen on Lord Chancellor Cranworth's Marriage & Divorce Bill*. It was a clever device, written in the confidential tone of one woman to another in a world ruled by men. It is not known if Victoria even read the pamphlet, but she was well aware of the pitfalls of marriage for women. The bill did not go far enough, Caroline argued. Husbands and wives were not treated as equals. 'As the husband, he has the right to all that is hers: as his wife, she has no right to anything that is his.' She was particularly concerned with the economic vulnerability of the separated or divorced woman, advocating that she should have the same legal status as a *feme sole*, that above all her earnings should be protected.

A further delay in passing the Divorce Bill prompted her to write another pamphlet, *A Review of the Divorce Bill of 1856*. Among its proposals was the payment of alimony, desertion as a ground for divorce, the abolition of criminal conversation, and the restoration to a divorced or separated wife of all powers over her own property and earnings. Some of Caroline's suggested amendments were tacked on to the original bill word for word.

Measures originally intended for the benefit of the rich eventually filter down to the rest of society. Parliamentary divorce, which had offered full divorce with permission to remarry to a handful of the rich and privileged, was abolished. The new Court for Divorce and Matrimonial Causes had the authority to grant full divorce with permission to remarry to any husband for his wife's adultery and to any wife for her husband's adultery when combined with incest, bigamy, rape, sodomy, bestiality, cruelty or desertion for two years. Various bars to a petition included connivance, condonation, mutual guilt, and collusion – much as they had under the ecclesiastical courts. Powers to deal with child custody, use a jury, examine witnesses orally and order maintenance and alimony were given to the court.

The Act abolished *divortium a mensa et thoro*, or separation from bed and board, and substituted decrees for judicial separation. The grounds of such actions in the ecclesiastical courts had been adultery or cruelty of either spouse. To these the Act added desertion without cause for two years or more. Deserted and judicially separated wives had future earnings and property protected – as Caroline had wanted. Actions against a wife's seducer for criminal conversation were abolished, but a husband could still claim damages in the divorce court against the co-respondent. Anglican clergymen were given the right to refuse to marry a divorced person, with the proviso that such a marriage could take place in the parish church if another clergyman were willing to perform the ceremony.

Lord Cranworth's Divorce Bill was soon running neck and neck with Sir Erskine Perry's Married Women's Property Bill, being promoted by the Women's Committee and the Law Amendment Society. The crucial difference was that Caroline was concentrating on winning justice for divorced or separated women like herself, whereas the Women's Committee's proposals involved *all* married women. They were insisting that Parliament give statutory recognition to all married women's rights to hold property, to contract, to sue and be sued, just as if they were single women, and to enjoy a distinct legal personality from that of their husbands.

In July 1857 the bills were receiving second readings in the House. Gladstone and the High Anglicans were vigorously opposed to both bills, seeing any alteration in the marriage laws as an encouragement to divorce, while moderate opinion ranged cautiously behind Lord Cranworth's bill, which appeared to be more of a compromise. In redressing some of the problems of divorced or separated women, rather than interfering in the financial arrangements of other married couples, the bill was considered less threatening to the stability of marriage. Most peers and MPs simply could not conceive of a marriage in which husband and wife met as political and economic, as well as spiritual, equals.

The Prime Minister, Lord Palmerston, was determined to see at least some of this legislation through and so placed his full support behind the Divorce rather than the Property Bill. He made it plain to the Commons that they would sit there, through the stifling July heat with the stink wafting in from the Thames, until the work was complete. The bill batted back and forth between Lords and Commons until on 28 August 1857 'An Act to amend the Law relating to Divorce and Matrimonial Causes in England' received the royal assent. There was no time or energy left for the Property Bill, which was not presented for its third reading. Probably considering he had done enough for women for the time being, Palmerston let it lapse.

Perhaps unfairly, Caroline was held responsible for allowing the Divorce Bill to sabotage the Married Women's Property Bill, but her achievement in turning her personal misfortunes into something positive was immense. She lived long enough to see the first Married Women's Property Act in 1870, which allowed all married women to retain their earnings or property acquired after marriage. It would not be until the Married Women's Property Act of 1882, however, that the original intention of the reformers was realized and all married women were allowed to retain, as their separate property, the real and personal property they owned at the time of their marriage.

In the spring of 1875 George Norton died. Caroline was curiously upset and deflated. She had spent most of her life fighting this man. Lord Grantley died shortly afterwards. If George had lived a little longer, she commented acerbically, she would have been Lady Grantley, for they did not have sufficient grounds for divorce, even under the new Act, and were still married. The Nortons had cheated her to the last.

INTERLUDE

Bigamy sentence

In 1845 the self-reliant attempt of a labourer, Thomas Hall, to take the law into his own hands and provide a mother for his children by committing bigamy, and the judgement in the case, illustrates the yawning gap between the restrictive marriage laws and inaccessible legal system on the one hand and the practical realities of life for the ordinary man or woman on the other.

Mr Justice Maule's brilliantly sarcastic sentence is a classic:

Prisoner at the bar, you have been convicted before me of what the law regards as a very grave and serious offence: that of going through the marriage ceremony a second time while your wife was still alive. You plead in mitigation of your conduct that she was given to dissipation and drunkenness, that she proved herself a curse to your household while she remained mistress of it, and that she had latterly deserted you; but I am not permitted to recognise any such plea. You had entered into a solemn engagement to take her for better, for worse, and if you got infinitely more of the latter, as you appear to have done, it was your duty patiently to submit.

You say you took another person to become your wife because you were left with several young children who require the care and protection of someone who might act as a substitute for the parent who had deserted them; but the law makes no allowance for bigamists with large families. Had you taken the other female to live with you as your concubine you would ever have been interfered with by the law. But your crime consists in having – to use your own language – preferred to make an honest woman of her.

Another of your irrational excuses is that your wife had committed adultery, and so you thought you were relieved from treating her with any further consideration – but you were mistaken. The law in its wisdom points out a means by which you might rid yourself from further association with a woman who had dishonoured you; but you did not think proper to adopt it.

I will tell you what the process is. You ought first to have brought an action against your wife's seducer if you could have discovered him; that might have cost you money, and you say you are a poor working man, but that is not the fault of the law. You would then be obliged to prove by evidence your wife's criminality in a Court of Justice, and thus obtain a verdict with damages against the defendant, who was not unlikely to turn out a pauper. But so jealous is the law (which you ought to be aware is the perfection of reason) of the sanctity of the marriage tie, that in accomplishing all this you would only have fulfilled the lighter portion of your duty.

You must then have gone, with your verdict in your hand, and petitioned the House of Lords for a divorce. It would cost you perhaps five or six hundred pounds, and you do not seem to be worth as many pence. But it is the boast of the law that it is impartial, and makes no difference between the rich and the poor. The wealthiest man in the kingdom would have had to pay no less than that sum for the same luxury; so that you would have no reason to complain. You would, of course, have to prove your case over again, and at the end of a year, or possibly two, you might obtain a divorce which would enable you legally to do what you have thought proper to do without it.

You have thus wilfully rejected the boon and the legislature offered you, and it is my duty to pass upon you such sentence as I think your offence deserves, and that sentence is, that you be imprisoned for one day; and in as much as the present assizes are three days old, the result is that you will be immediately discharged.

22

'To soothe and not to vex or irritate her husband'

THE PROCEEDINGS OF the new Divorce Court in London opened a window on to the private hell of many Victorian marriages. Queen Victoria complained that it was no longer safe for a family to read the newspaper at the breakfast table, so heavy was the coverage of the most lurid cases. As soon as the court opened its doors in January 1858 the authorities were aghast at the avalanche of petitions. In the first year alone there were 253 petitions for divorce and 87 seeking judicial separation, in contrast to only 4 divorces by private Act of Parliament the previous year. Surely so much matrimonial misery could not have been stored up for so long?

More shocking still, many of the petitioners were women, confounding the assumption that the beneficiaries of the Act would be husbands ridding themselves of erring spouses. Few had envisaged wives enjoying the same dangerous privilege. Perhaps it was just as well that the Divorce Act came when it did, since a rise in life expectancy meant that marriages that would previously have been terminated by death after ten or twenty years would now have to be endured much longer. Even if the Act upheld the double sexual standard that had always prevailed, there was at least a chance of release.

The legal underpinnings of patriarchal power were being eroded. In the middle-class home particularly there was tension between the twin pillars of male authority and female subordination, as men began to feel their once unassailable supremacy under threat. The domestic idyll of the angel in the house – the obedient, submissive and dependent wife, imbued with the notion of self-sacrifice, who guarded the home and made it a haven, a refuge for her husband from the harsh realities of the outside world – often fell short of the dream. Behind the façade of respectability of many a Victorian marriage there was rottenness, a darker side of conjugal life which was increasingly exposed to scrutiny and correction.

Charlotte and Robert Chignell Bostock had married 'entirely out of affection' in 1827, when he was only twenty-one and she was sixteen. Such a marriage entailed higher emotional expectations and a corresponding degree of disappointment if it went wrong. Although her family appears to have been middle-class, she brought no money to the marriage. Robert's father was comfortably off and had set him up as a retail chemist in Kennington, much against his wishes, since Robert really wanted to work in the Stock Exchange. Perhaps this was at the heart of his evident unhappiness and frustration, which spilled over into his marriage and family life. He was determined to exert his mastery somewhere.

If Charlotte brought no money, she contributed to their livelihood by assisting him in the business. For many of the middle class, home and business were increasingly separate, with wives isolated in suburban villas and husbands going to work in the city, but the Bostocks continued to live above the shop. Considering their parental background, they lived a rather poor lower middle-class existence, employing no more than two servants and an assistant in the shop. The business failed twice, even after an injection of £10,000 from Robert's father. Money was often at the heart of their domestic strife, with Robert accusing his wife of extravagance and ignoring his plea to practise 'strict economy'.

Shortly after their marriage Robert began to treat her 'when alone and in the presence of others' with 'great harshness and violence and cruelty'. He would lose his temper on the slightest provocation. He called her 'a damned bitch, or damned devil', saying 'that she was worse than any woman that walked the streets'.

In spite of the fact that Charlotte bore him thirteen children in thirty years of marriage, of whom five sons and three daughters survived, and that she clearly had very little domestic help by Victorian middle-class standards, Robert accused her of idleness and dereliction of her domestic duties. She denied remaining 'in bed breakfasting therein and reading a novel, or that she in that or in any other manner neglected her family duties'. 'Family duties' in Robert's view also encompassed her role in the business, where he relied on her help. It is perhaps indicative of Charlotte's success as a mother that the children appear to have been close to her and increasingly took her side and supported her as they grew up.

Violence was followed by death threats. Robert pointed a loaded gun at her head, as he claimed so as to awaken her to a sense of her responsibilities. She began to pack to return to her mother, but he persuaded her to stay. However, she claimed that Robert declared that she and the children would not die a natural death but 'would be found some day with their throats cut or words to that very effect'. He denied threatening to kill her. What he said, he told the court, was that if he killed her 'he could show such provocation on her part that a jury would acquit him'. Since the turn of the century words of menace, rather than the deed itself, were enough; as Lord Stowell said, 'The law ought not to wait till the mischief is actually done.'

He struck her when her six-week-old baby was in her lap 'so violently on the head as to cut her face with her earring'. According to Charlotte, he struck her many times and, tellingly, she denied his accusation that she had provoked him with 'irritating language'. Unwittingly or otherwise, she had probably done exactly that. Certainly she insulted him.

Robert's version of the event was 'that his said wife had used very irritating language to him as she on many occasions did (sometimes calling him a dirty snuffy old man and saying he smelt like a labourer or words to that effect) and that he with his open hand boxed her ears – that he has no recollection whether by reason of his hand coming in contact with her earring her face or neck was cut but if it was so it was only in a very slight manner and that it did not call for any particular attention.'

Charlotte tried to juggle an acceptance of his authority with evasion and resistance. Occasionally she took refuge from his violence at her mother's house, but he always begged her to come home, where his 'unmanly' behaviour was soon resumed. One night he was so violent and abusive that she locked herself in another bedroom. Nothing was more likely to enrage the Victorian husband. He broke open the door with 'a sledge hammer which he got purposely from the coal cellar'.

A major row took place when Charlotte took it upon herself to stay over at her mother's house for a night to greet her brother, a major in the Indian Army who was returning after a twenty-year absence. When she came home at eight o'clock the following evening Robert struck her repeatedly and violently, although he denied that he did so to 'such a degree as to cause her face to be much swollen afterwards'. Later, he defended his action by saying that he 'was greatly annoyed and vexed at his said wife's frequently absenting herself from him . . . and at her neglecting her family duties'. Whatever his justification, Charlotte was less and less prepared to tolerate such treatment and she retaliated by throwing a tumbler at him. Infuriated at her resistance, he kept beating her and knocked her off the chair to the floor. She slept in the children's room for more than a fortnight afterwards.

The battle for mastery grew ever more desperate as the children grew up and began to take her side and defy Robert's authority as master in his own home. When Mrs Silva, a neighbour, called one night, Charlotte invited her upstairs to take tea. She sent the servant to bring the lamp Robert was using downstairs. Whether this was a calculated affront or just unwitting selfishness is unclear, but the effect was surely unlooked for. He dashed upstairs to retrieve it. When Chignell, their eldest son, protested, saying he had made the lamp as a present for his mother, his father knocked him down. The lamp was broken in the scuffle. Absurdly, Robert then repaired downstairs to fetch the staff he had been issued with as a special constable to deal with the riots of that year, 1848, to make a public arrest of his son for assault. In the ensuing fight, the blow with the constable's staff aimed at Charlotte was deflected by their hapless guest, who was badly injured. Robert's defence of his actions was that Charlotte had 'sided with her son and against her husband'.

The next day Charlotte's brother took her to consult a solicitor about a separation. His only advice was that she should return home and keep out of her husband's way. Once more she slept with her daughters, but Robert came to the door in the night claiming he was ill and his last hour had come. Concerned that he appeared to be 'of unsound mind', Charlotte sent for the doctor and subsequently sought the advice of several. It appeared that Robert was suffering from some sort of breakdown, threatening to kill his wife and injure his children. A 'keeper' was brought in to look after him for a week, before he was sent down to Brighton to recuperate. The doctors advised Charlotte that her duty as a wife was 'to soothe and not vex or irritate' him and she was sufficiently imbued with such thinking to write him affectionate letters while he was away.

In 1853 another incident took place when Charlotte and two of her daughters treated themselves to an evening at the theatre, escorted by Chignell. Robert complained 'of their not having treated him with proper respect in not having informed him of their intention nor asked him to accompany them'. A servant was instructed to serve his meal while they were out. On their return there was a row, in the course of which he struck his daughter. Their son Samuel intervened, using 'very disrespectful and insulting language towards his father and on his father threatening to chastise him for his insolence the said Samuel Peacock Bostock and his sisters rose up in a state of great passion and excitement and the said Katherine Elizabeth Bostock flew at her father and tore his coat nearly off his back'. Once more Charlotte took refuge for the night in her daughters' bedroom. Robert, in a very agitated state, broke open the door. According to his testimony, he did this only when she refused to open it.

The next morning Charlotte 'without any previous permission from or notice to him' left with the children and took lodgings in Greenwich. Robert apparently returned from visiting his sick mother to find the house 'empty and deserted' and had no idea where she and the family had gone. Tensions and quarrels over money, never far beneath the surface, exploded at this latest manifestation of Charlotte's extravagance, since now, Robert claimed, she was expecting him to pay rent as well. There had already been a quarrel about the doctors' bills she had run up 'without informing or referring to her said husband'.

Possibly some of these bills were accounted for by the fact that their eldest son had contracted venereal disease, which was all too common at a time when young men delayed marriage until they could afford to set up home with all the outward show and consumer goods deemed desirable by the aspiring Victorian middle class, and there was such a ready supply of prostitutes.

At any rate, Charlotte returned home, but in the summer of 1856 she left for good. Robert had referred to the recent Corrigan murder case, in which a husband had stabbed his wife to death and 'threatened to serve his wife as Corrigan had done his wife'. Whether he spoke in jest or in earnest, it gave Charlotte a reasonable apprehension that her life was at risk.

Bostock v. Bostock was one of the first petitions for judicial separation, based on a charge of cruelty, to be heard at the new Divorce Court in 1858. Since there was no adultery in the case there were no grounds for actual divorce. In court Robert went down the well-worn route of claiming his wife's behaviour had provoked him to violence, while the fact that she had left and returned to him so often indicated that she condoned it, or had forgiven him, so negating any legal cruelty that had been established. He denied her health had been impaired through his conduct or that she had any reason to dread violence from him, but the court decided otherwise. Robert had gone far beyond what were now considered to be reasonable limits of authority and subordination.

Extreme and unreasonable assertion of male authority features in the next case, Kelly v. Kelly, which became a legal landmark. It was a turning point in the law of matrimonial cruelty, establishing that non-violent cruelty, rather than physical violence alone, might justify a decree. It was not the nature of the respondent's actions – non-violent – that were relevant, Lord Penzance decided, but their consequences: the impairment of the petitioner's health. He did not go so far as to include mental cruelty in this definition.

Reverend James Kelly, the Anglican vicar of St George's Church in Liverpool, and his wife Frances were married in 1841. They had one surviving son, born in 1845. James had a 'very violent and passionate temper' and was extremely jealous. He would open his wife Frances's letters, break into her trunks and shout abuse at her. She became so ill as a result of his behaviour towards her that her doctor recommended she go away for a time. James complained that there was nothing medically wrong with her and that Frances had no business confiding their private domestic matters to the doctor. He rebuked the doctor for 'having elected to act the partisan, to champion . . . a wife's rebellion against her husband'.

He was adamantly opposed to Frances going away without him.

'I will not allow a liberty of absence from the protection and control which it is my duty to exercise over you, a liberty sure to be abused to the aggravation of the present misery which you have industriously brought about in our domestic relations,' he told her. 'In regards to change of air, it is possible you may have it. But it must be *with your Husband*, if I can secure a suitable place.'

Frances was just as determined to escape, taking refuge with her sister from June to October 1868, contrary to his express wish. She had had to steal out of the house, having taken the precaution the previous day, a Sunday 'while the respondent was attending to his sacred duties at church', of having her luggage removed.

It was nothing less than a 'rebellion against his due authority'. He regretted 'the inveterate, incorrigible, insubordination of spirit, by which you have been ruled, instead of by the ordinance of God and your marriage vow'. He immediately wrote to tell her that he would not put her up in a hotel or 'be answerable for any debts you contract, while living apart from me'. She should be grateful he was not putting a notice to this effect in the newspapers. He signed himself, 'Your irretrievably injured husband'.

At the core of their disagreements lay an argument about money. Kelly claimed that he had been upset to discover a correspondence between his wife and her brother-in-law, Nathaniel Henry Thornbury, a colonel in the Indian Army. Frances had been left a legacy of £5,000 by her sister, which Kelly, as was his right before the Married Women's Property Act of 1882, had taken possession of and lost.

'It is a melancholy thing to reflect that such a sum should have vanished in twelve years, and I do think it very wrong that I cannot get any information from my husband about what is left,' Frances wrote to Thornbury. 'Should there be any, can you tell me, have I any control over it now? I tried to get information from him about it, but he would tell me nothing. He has found out that someone has been looking at the Will, and is so indignant, that he has refused to take his meals with me; has them all sent up to his room, only comes down to prayers morning and evening, talks of *Treachery*, *Treason* and *Conspiracy*. My husband says that his offer some months ago, that I might go and have my own money, was an impulse which he now retracts.'

Colonel Thornbury confirmed that in law the money was her husband's to command and that neither she nor her son had any legal claim on it.

Frances confided her despair about her marriage to Thornbury, asking if she must show 'patient submission to this slow assassination for what else can you call it thus to live'. The servants were 'scandalized' by James's treatment of her, she told him, and were threatening to leave. One of them, George, 'says Master must be mad'.

What annoyed Frances was that James had not consulted her about what he was doing with her money. Kelly retaliated by accusing his brother-in-law of 'corrupting the petitioner into imparting to him the private affairs of her husband, therefore instigating her to act un-dutifully to her husband'. As to consulting her, he had this to say: 'I had hitherto suppressed the fact that owing to investments made for the best, but which had turned out disastrously, the resources in question were not to be looked to.' Instead of 'words of soothing comfort falling gracefully and graciously from you upon the spirit of your afflicted husband', she had reproached him and complained that she had not been 'consulted in my little monetary administration, as if that would have necessarily made a difference'. In other words, he suggested, Frances had been a little heartless. Nor had she shown any sign of repentance.

Wives were not expected to concern themselves with money, but Frances argued to the contrary: 'it is a wife's duty to know whether all the money is gone.'

'Just reflect on the spirit which this implies!' he noted sadly.

When she eventually returned home Kelly 'refused to allow me to act as Mistress of the house, told the servants not to obey me, kept the doors of the house locked to prevent me leaving it to see my friends, or for purpose of exercise, refused to allow me any money to permit me to buy my own clothes, to see my friends or to send or receive letters without his first reading them'. He had searched and examined the contents of her desk and wardrobe, taken his meals apart from her, and 'continually charged me with being a traitor and liar and possessed with the Devil'.

Nothing daunted, Frances had clambered out of the front window of the house, in broad daylight and full view of neighbours and passers-by. As far as James was concerned, it was an absolute scandal.

In December 1868 he hired a man and his wife and daughter to live in and take control of the household and its expenses, ordering them to watch Frances's movements and follow her closely on the rare occasions she was allowed out at all. They kept the keys, disobeyed her orders and treated her with contempt. This totally undermined Frances's position as mistress of her husband's house, a most serious matter which shocked the judge when the case came to court. After all, the Victorian husband and wife operated in separate spheres and the wife's was the domestic managerial role. Her husband had no business interfering in her wifely duties or humiliating her in front of the servants.

James was also determined to ruin any remaining pleasures she had. He threatened 'to destroy my birds and flowers and seized the cage'. When she tried to stop him, he wrenched her arm, leaving it bruised and painful. It was 'simply a little measure of discipline', he told the court. He refused to allow her to use her books and papers, except occasionally as a special favour.

James was constantly frustrated at Frances's failure to bow to his authority and to show abject repentance for her defiance of him. He recruited fellow clergymen to come to the house and lecture her on her duties as a wife and explain the religious basis of a wife's obedience. Not content with that, in the church where he officiated he referred to her in a sermon as 'a woman possessed with the Devil and as resisting her husband'. Frances had had enough. She left him in January 1869.

James Kelly was so convinced of his superior authority and the rightness of his actions that he wrote a fifty-page affidavit justifying his behaviour and conducted his own defence. It was a masterpiece of self-deception. His unswerving self-righteousness served only to convince Lord Penzance, the 'Judge-Ordinary' or president of the Divorce Court, of the inflexible and unreasonable regime under which Frances had suffered. He decided that James had used religion to sanction a 'harsh and cruel retaliation', while forgetting its 'leading precepts', humility and forgiveness.

When the case went against him, James Kelly moved to appeal and lost again. In the past women had been advised to secure their safety by controlling their tongues and tempers, to be eternally submissive and not offer any resistance to the will of their husband, who was their ruler, protector and guide. But when Kelly sought to use his wife's frequent loss of temper as an excuse for his own behaviour, the appeal judges countered with the affirmation that 'a wife does not lose her title to the protection of this court merely because she has proved unable to bear with perfect patience and unfailing propriety of conduct the ill-usage of her husband.'

Lord Penzance delivered a homily which was, in effect, a succinct statement of evolving judicial views on the limitations of male coercion and female submission in marriage. Yes, the law recognized the husband as the master – a position bolstered by established habits and customs – but with this privilege came responsibility. The 'law leaves the husband, by his own conduct and bearing, to secure and retain in his wife the only submission worth having, that which is willingly and cheerfully rendered'. If he failed in that he could not expect the law to 'recognize his failure as a justification for a system of treatment by which he places his wife's permanent health in jeopardy, and sets at nought not only his own obligations in matrimony, but the very end of matrimony itself, by rendering impossible the offices of domestic intercourse and the reciprocal duties of married life'.

In another case of contested authority and cruelty, Martha Ann Hewitt was married to Hosea Hewitt, a congregational minister, in June 1873 in Leeds. When the case came to court they had four children ranging in age from six to two. The violence started shortly after the marriage, when Hewitt struck her a violent blow and knocked her down, so that she hit the piano. In due course, he started calling her 'foul adulteress', 'strumpet', 'vile whore' and forced her to sign a confession that she had 'improperly looked at and thought about another man', although this was untrue. After she suffered a miscarriage he refused her a doctor. In July 1881 he knocked her down again, she was severely injured, and she left him. Unfortunately, she had to leave three of the children with their father, taking only the baby, Gertie.

Hewitt denied he was guilty of cruelty. His wife had provoked and attacked him. She had thrown a glass of water at his face. Worse, 'on the 9th day of June 1881 she seized the respondent by the beard and tore off his hair and bit him in the cheek.' A husband's wounded dignity did not readily recover from such an affront.

In September Martha went back 'to see if he was willing to receive and treat me kindly and to see my children, but he cruelly ordered me out of the home saying "Go, you cannot stay here innocent or guilty I won't have you . . . if I have to believe you innocent I make God a liar because the Lord has told me you are guilty . . . I only see one way for your salvation and that is by owning that you were tempted and overcome with the man."' Martha told him she would die first.

Hewitt then took two of the children, Willie and Florrie, one under each arm, into the study and locked them in, telling Martha she would not have them because she was guilty of 'deceit, lust, lying and hypocrisy' and that it would not be long before she was a 'street walker'. As she left the house he called after her, 'Go speak to the first man you meet and get him to go with you.'

A week later he turned up at her mother's house in Leeds. When Martha opened the door he shouted, 'You Devil, let me have Gertie!' before snatching the child from her. When she pleaded to see the little girl sometimes he cruelly replied, 'No, you shall never see her again!'

He was wrong. Thanks to the Infants Custody Act of 1839 custody of children under the age of seven was given to the mother, provided she could prove herself to be of unblemished reputation. Martha Hewitt apparently had no trouble convincing the court that her husband's allegations were unfounded, because she was awarded a judicial separation, and presumably custody of her children.

Contrary to popular belief, upper- and middle-class men were just as likely to hit their wives with pokers, throw them downstairs, threaten murder, beat them during pregnancy, enforce sexual intercourse during the late stages of pregnancy and after childbirth, and indulge in marital rape, sodomy and the wilful transmission of venereal disease, as those lower down the social scale.

Elizabeth Mellard Parker married John Newall in July 1841 in Staffordshire. There were five surviving children of the marriage and the family was sufficiently well off to employ a governess. In 1854 Newall struck his wife 'violently on the head, tore her hair, and boxed her ears and continued to do so until he had thereby rendered her insensible'. He did the same on another occasion and she was 'some days confined to her bed and required medical advice'. In July 1856 there was an argument in the summerhouse. He struck her 'several violent blows on her shoulders and breast . . . tore her hair, broke her combs and threw her violently to the ground'.

The following month he kicked her out of bed and compelled her to pass the night on the floor. When she was ill he denied her proper nourishment or medical assistance. He had a nasty habit of punching her violently on the back of the neck between the shoulders.

Fortunately for her, in July 1858 he left and took up with another woman. She was able to prove adultery aggravated by cruelty and the marriage was dissolved.

Many Victorian wives, Isabella Beeton among them, contracted venereal disease on their wedding night. Husbands who had been infected as young men assumed, or were told by ignorant doctors, they were cured when the symptoms disappeared. Some husbands, however, were so callous as knowingly to infect their wives with this ravaging disease. Young Victorian wives tended to be sexually ignorant and it was all too easy to deceive and manipulate them. It was not until the mid-1860s that the knowing and reckless communication of venereal disease by a husband to his wife was defined for legal purposes as cruelty.

Jane Lilly Rose married Bernard Brocas in November 1849. A daughter, Blanche, was born in August 1851. Jane claimed that he always treated her with great cruelty. Shortly after the marriage, knowing that he had venereal disease, he communicated it to Jane. She became seriously ill, but 'being ignorant of the nature and cause of her complaint was assured by the said Bernard Brocas that it arose merely from her being in the family way and that all women in that state suffered in the same way'. In consequence of this false assurance, the disease ran unchecked, until she was finally forced to consult a doctor. She spent several weeks under the care of Sir Charles Lacock. In spite of her illness and the fact that intercourse had been forbidden and was extremely painful for her, Brocas insisted on his 'marital rights'. Just as she seemed to be cured, Brocas contracted syphilis and passed that too on to his wife.

In the first year of their marriage he was 'frequently intoxicated, abusive and violent even when she was near her confinement'. He 'endeavoured in divers ways to terrify her and threatened to place her in a madhouse'.

Her father, Sir John Rose, afforded her some protection, but when he died in 1853 Brocas told her 'she should be obliged to bear whatever he chose to inflict on her as her father was dead, and that if she fancied her past married life had been unhappy he would now teach her something still more so, that he would in fact do all that he could to make her perfectly wretched.'

She begged him not to sleep with her as he was diseased, but he 'declared that he would "use" her as long as he chose. That no resistance of hers should prevent it for that he would tie her down – not that he cared for her but that he chose to make "use of her" and he treated her with the utmost cruelty and indelicacy in other respects which she forbears to mention.' In November 1853 she left him, since when he had committed adultery. The marriage was dissolved.

Mary Goodwin Norris of Teddington in Middlesex married George Goodwin Norris at Feltham in July 1860. They had a daughter the following March and at the time of the petition, 1862, she was expecting again.

Norris had sworn at and abused her in foul and offensive language and threatened to kill her. In February 1861, when she was in the last month of pregnancy, he had thrown her down 'violently on the bed and in order to terrify me, seized a razor and drew it across my throat as if about to cut it'. He kept loaded pistols in the bedroom and on one occasion held one towards her saying, 'By God, I'll shoot you.'

Violent assaults were frequent, but on two occasions in May and June 1861 he attempted to commit sodomy, despite her resistance, 'and thereby seriously hurt me'. The following month her cup of misery was complete when 'the said George Norris, knowing himself at the time to be infected with the venereal disease, communicated the same to me.'

If he had attempted sodomy but not succeeded he had not actually committed a crime. It was impossible to prove. Naturally, Norris denied it or treating his wife with cruelty. Mary Norris's petition was dismissed.

Army officers were often dissipated upper-class roués. Their wives lived in fear of their lives, or of what their husbands might inflict on them. Elizabeth Frances Denton was one of them. She had married Thomas Denton in 1881. He mistreated her from the outset. When she was ill, he hit her, and made her sleep on the floor. She told the court that he 'struck me on my breast and threw me down on a bed and threatened to throw me out of the window, smash my head and kill me'.

He had 'habitually insisted on having connection with men in an unnatural manner, and he has on numerous occasions attempted to commit and on divers occasions he has committed sodomy with me against my wish and notwithstanding my resistance and he thereby injured my health.' Petition granted.

Emily Norton Bower married Alan Henry Swatman at West Lynn in Norfolk in April 1856. They had two daughters, born in 1858 and 1859.

Swatman started to drink, becoming violent and abusive. He degraded her 'in her own home by contracting a familiarity with his servants and speaking to them in endearing terms' in her presence and 'encouraging them in disobedience to her'. He frequently kept her up until three or four o'clock in the morning carousing and 'indulging in habits of indecency which constantly shocked her'. He consorted with prostitutes and once, when she was away, he brought one home and into the marital bed.

When he came home in the early hours, he frequently 'committed acts of indecency by making water in the hall, on the kitchen stairs, and bedroom and over the toilet and washstand table'.

When she was lying in bed after a miscarriage 'he returned home about two or three o'clock in the morning in a state of intoxication . . . he made water in the hall and on the stairs and indecently exposed himself and remained clinging to the stairs until she went downstairs to his assistance.'

Finally, he returned drunk at nine in the morning, just as she was sitting down to breakfast. He 'made water through the passage into the dining room, where he sat down on a chair with his person indecently exposed until she arranged his clothes'.

Lord Penzance concluded that Swatman's behaviour had seriously impaired his wife's health and that she could not reasonably be expected to discharge the duties of married life in such circumstances.

A case of considered cruelty and adultery, it was enough to get the marriage dissolved.

Much of this marital behaviour could just as easily have taken place in the seventeenth or eighteenth centuries, but owing to the public exposure such cases were now receiving through the press reports from the Divorce Court, they were no longer going to continue unchecked. The accumulated evidence of case after case of marital cruelty and betrayal was bound to have its effect. Not only did the threat of publicity act as a salutary deterrent to marital misconduct, but a burgeoning newspaper industry and the spread of reading habits promoted discussion about marriage, and just what was and was not acceptable behaviour, and stimulated the reformers to greater efforts to curb abuses.

INTERLUDE

Charles Darwin's 'Marry' or 'Not Marry'

In the summer of 1838 the twenty-nine-year-old naturalist Charles Darwin – whose theory of evolution was to transform the scientific world and challenge the biblical view of the Creation – was trying to decide whether or not to marry. Torn between his intellectual discipline as a scientist and his desire for a wife, he methodically listed the pros and cons:

Marry:
Children – (if it Please God)
Constant companion, (& friend in old age) who will feel interested in one, – object to be beloved & played with. – better than a dog anyhow. – Home, & someone to take care of house – Charms of music & female chit-chat. – These things good for one's health. – *but terrible loss of time.* –
My god, it is intolerable to think of spending one's whole life, like a neuter bee working, working, & nothing after all. –
No, no won't do. – Imagine living all one's day solitarily in smoky dirty London House. –
Only picture to yourself a nice soft wife on a sofa with good fire, & books & music perhaps
Compare this vision with the dingy reality of Grt. Marlbro' St.
Marry – Marry – Marry Q.E.D.

Not Marry:
Freedom to go where one liked – choice of Society & *little of it.* – Conversation of clever men at clubs – Not forced to visit relatives, & to bend in every trifle. – to have the expense &

anxiety of children – perhaps quarrelling – Loss of time. – cannot read in the evenings – fatness & idleness –

Anxiety & responsibility – less money for books &c – if many children forced to gain one's bread. – (But then it is very bad for one's health to work too much)

Perhaps my wife won't like London; then the sentence is banishment & degradation into indolent, idle fool.

He came down, cautiously, on the side of marriage, but when and to whom? A year later he plucked up courage to propose to his cousin, Emma – their mutual grandfather was the renowned pottery designer and manufacturer, Josiah Wedgwood – who was so eminently suitable and accomplished that he need not have worried at all. They were married at the end of January 1839.

At the end of his life Darwin paid Emma the ultimate tribute when he told his sons: 'I marvel at my good fortune, that she, so infinitely my superior in every single moral quality, consented to be my wife. She has been my adviser and cheerful comforter throughout life, which without her would have been during a very long period a miserable one from ill-health.'

Without her, indeed, the author of *The Origin of Species*, published in 1859, might never have fulfilled his brilliant potential.

23

'There's no harm in it – everyone does it'

THE SUMMER OF 1868 was one of stifling heat. Even in Norway, where Sir Charles Mordaunt had gone for the fishing, it was unbearably hot. Having stared into the glassy water for some days and caught only a few salmon, he decided to cut short his holiday and go home to Warwickshire. How nice it would be to give Harriett a surprise. They were not due in Scotland for the shooting for another month, so that they would have some rare time to themselves at Walton. It would be like a second honeymoon.

Having missed the connection from Denmark to Hull, Sir Charles pressed on through Belgium and France, catching the ferry from Calais. He was on the train going up to London when he wrote Harriett a letter asking her to send the brougham to pick him up at the station at Warwick next day. He would stay overnight in London, and be home in time for luncheon. When he reached London, however, he changed his mind and decided to catch a train to Warwick straight away. Several hours later in the scorching afternoon, full of pleasurable anticipation at the thought of his reunion with his lovely young wife, his joy turned to instant displeasure.

There in front of the house was Harriett in her pony carriage, led by the two exquisite white ponies he had bought for her from the royal coachman, showing off her driving skills to no less a person than Albert Edward, Prince of Wales. He was incensed. He had warned his wife of the dangerous reputation of the Prince and expressly advised her not to see him, yet here she was flouting his wishes. It was a flagrant abuse of his trust, but he was even angrier at the Prince's callous exploitation of his absence.

He barely suppressed his rage as the two men made a cursory exchange and the Prince beat a hasty retreat. No sooner was he gone than Sir Charles called for the groom to bring the two ponies to the lawn in front of the conservatory. He grabbed Harriett by the arm and dragged her out of the house and down the steps, so that she could watch as he shot the two ponies dead. He then gave orders for the little pony carriage to be burned. Down at the local pub that night, two footmen from Walton Hall regaled their audience with the whole dramatic tale: the royal visit, Sir Charles's fury, the shooting and burial of the horses. Before long, the ripples of the Warwickshire scandal would spread wide and hold the entire nation riveted.

Sir Charles Mordaunt should not have been altogether surprised at his wife's behaviour. She was young, frivolous and heedless. When he had asked her to marry him she had agreed on one condition: that he would not hinder her pleasures, which encompassed her friendships with a good many men in the 'fast' set, the most notorious of whom, of course, was the Prince of Wales. Sir Charles had been so infatuated that he had acceded to her wish, but he was already beginning to regret it and soon would rue the day that he had asked her to marry him at all.

Sir Thomas Moncreiffe of Moncreiffe, Harriett's father, was a Scottish baronet with too many children and not enough money. As the fourth of eight daughters, Harriett knew it was her duty to marry soon and marry well. Throughout her girlhood a steady stream of suitable young men were invited to Moncreiffe, including the Prince of Wales, who was regarded as a family friend. One governess complained that there were so many interruptions in the girls' lessons that it made it very difficult for her to do her job properly, while others suspected that the Moncreiffe daughters were 'educated' to be flirtatious to help their father's task of matchmaking. Fortunately, they were all very beautiful. Friendships made during the Scottish season were cemented at balls and parties held later in the year in London and soon the eldest girl Louisa had married the Duke of Atholl; Helen, the second, Charles Forbes, the heir to a baronetcy and a very good castle; and Georgina, the elderly but fantastically rich Earl of Dudley.

In 1865 Harriett at sixteen had just emerged from the schoolroom. With her vivacious manner and lovely grey eyes she was already attracting admirers, including the Prince of Wales, who was, alas, married. In November, however, he invited Harriett to join him and the Princess at Sandringham. Surprisingly, given the Prince's reputation and her youth and inexperience, Harriett's parents let her go. Harriett was such a hit with the Prince that she rapidly became a member of the 'fast set'.

In London for her first season she stayed with her grandmother, Lady Kinnoull, at Belgrave Square. Harriett later described her grandmother as 'larky'; she was great fun and not too energetic a chaperone. Harriett was allowed to attend the Prince of Wales's intimate dinner parties without anyone enquiring too closely what went on. If her parents were careless of her honour where the Prince was concerned, her brother-in-law Lord Dudley was not. He was beginning to feel apprehensive of Harriett's behaviour, particularly about the fact that she seemed to be encouraging the Prince of Wales's attentions. At ball after ball she would be seen with his group of friends laughing and joking and placing bets. The Prince gave her a bouquet which she ostentatiously wore to the Dudley ball. It was after this that Dudley expressed his concern to the Moncreiffes, who ordered her abrupt return to Scotland before the end of the season.

In August that year, 1866, the Moncreiffes' visitors included Sir Charles Mordaunt of Walton Hall in Warwickshire. Thirty, slightly built, diffident, entirely conventional, he was a second cousin. He had known Harriett as an enchanting child; now she had grown into a beautiful young woman. He asked her father for permission to propose. With lands in Warwickshire, Northamptonshire, Norfolk and Somerset, he had an impressive rent roll and Sir Thomas could see no objection to the match. He set a very high price for his much admired but dowerless daughter, extracting a jointure of £2,000 a year in the event of her widowhood.

Later, Harriett told a friend, 'Never force your daughter to marry a man she does not like', but all the indications are that she accepted Sir Charles's proposal readily enough. True, he was virtuous and dull, but there would be compensations. Marriage to a landed gentleman brought considerable status as well as greater freedom. As a married lady she could dispense with chaperones and need no longer be dependent on her family. For Harriett, it would be a treat in itself not to be eking out the pennies as one of thirteen, soon to be fourteen and finally fifteen, children. Sir Charles had plenty of money and Walton Hall was reputedly splendid, with a conservatory full of hot-house blooms. They would be able to give wonderful house parties for her friends. Sir Charles was a countryman at heart, but as MP for South Warwickshire he would have to be in town while Parliament was sitting. Harriett need not be deprived of the society she loved. Life would be one long round of pleasure. 'I feel quite happy about it now it is all settled,' she wrote to her brother-in-law, Atholl.

In the weeks leading up to the wedding, Harriett raised eyebrows by flagrantly dancing and flirting with other men, putting Charles to the test. She blithely told him not to worry, as 'everybody did it'. Dudley had already taken him to one side to warn him about Harriett's intimacy with the Prince of Wales, which he considered imprudent, given the 'corruptness' of the Prince's character.

The wedding took place with due fanfare at St John's Episcopal Church in Perth. It was a cold December day and the bride wore a dress of white velour trimmed with Brussels lace and a Brussels lace veil held in place with a wreath of orange blossom. The eight brides-maids included her four younger sisters, Blanche, Frances, Selina and Mary, wearing dresses of white glacé silk trimmed with cerise velvet and white jessamine and bonnets of white tulle. It was tradi-tional for the bridegroom to give the bridesmaids a present and they each received a diamond-shaped gold locket with the initials H & CM in coloured enamel. The groom's wedding present to his bride was a huge pearl pendant on a necklace of diamonds and emeralds. The Prince of Wales, who was unable to attend as he was in Russia, sent Harriett a horseshoe diamond and emerald ring, which com-plemented the necklace perfectly. After the wedding breakfast, the couple spent a short honeymoon at Brechin Castle, before heading south to Walton, where loyal cap-doffing retainers unfastened the horses and dragged the carriage up the long drive to the house.

Charles soon found that his lovely treasure of a bride was an expensive acquisition. He was true to his promise, welcoming her friends to Walton, where they enjoyed lavish hospitality. Everyone commented on what an affectionate couple they were and, indeed, everything was just fine and dandy as long as Charles allowed Harriett her pleasures. To be fair, Harriett admitted she had grown very fond of Charlie and whenever they were apart they exchanged letters full of endearments.

In London he took a house in Chesham Place, just round the corner from her grandmother in Belgrave Square. Harriett did not intend to do the season by halves. A new footman, Frederick Johnson, was taken on especially to accompany Lady Mordaunt when she went out, keeping a diary which would prove very useful in due course. He was soon utterly exhausted by her frenetic round of social activity, waiting in the servants' hall until the early hours to escort her home. Night after night she went out, while her husband sat late in the House and retired to bed long before his wife came home.

Soon the servants noted that the Prince of Wales was coming to Chesham Place regularly for a couple of hours in the afternoons to take tea, alone, with her ladyship. This, in spite of Charles's explicit instruction to his wife to avoid being alone with the Prince. Albert Edward was a highly calculating adulterer, being careful never to leave a coach emblazoned with his arms waiting outside, but arriving in a plain hackney carriage. And when he wrote to Harriett – as he did frequently – his letters were carefully worded so that they could be construed to be entirely innocent. Whenever he was at Chesham Place, Harriett gave orders that they were not to be disturbed.

Sir Charles began to notice that Harriett was unstable, tending to become hysterical, especially when her periods were due. Later, her mother referred to her 'hysterics', indicating that it was a condition she was already suffering from prior to her marriage and which had been concealed from Sir Charles. Harriett was already consulting a Dr Priestley about 'irregularities'. Charles quickly learned that it was best to let his wife have her own way to avoid a scene, so that when in the winter of 1867 she announced that she was going to London, ostensibly to see the doctor, and would put up in a hotel with her maid Jessie Clarke, he raised no objection.

'My darling Charlie,' she wrote, 'I felt horribly dull all by myself yesterday evening.' She had not, in fact, been alone. After she had prepared her mistress for bed, Jessie had been surprised to find Captain Farquhar, one of Lady Mordaunt's more disreputable friends, outside in the corridor, and her suspicions were further aroused when the waiter asked her next morning if the gentleman who had dined in the room with her lady would also be taking breakfast. Jessie was convinced that her mistress had committed adultery.

Sir Charles had hoped that Harriett would accompany him on his fishing trip to Norway. After all, she had come with him to Switzerland the previous year and seemed to enjoy herself. When Harriett cried off at the last minute, he was disappointed. He advised her not to stay in London too long, but to go down to Walton. It was the Prince who encouraged her to linger in town. When she finally extracted herself it was with the comforting thought that she was going to throw a large house party at Walton in Sir Charles's absence. Her guests included many of her admirers: Lord Cole, the son and heir of the Earl of Enniskillen, who had almost married her younger sister but seemed to be irresistibly drawn to Lady Mordaunt instead; George Forbes; and her cousin George Newport, who was perhaps rather fonder of her than was strictly appropriate.

The servants were shocked at the goings-on. They spied their mistress in an embrace with one guest and disappearing into the shrubbery with another. A telegram from Norway, which Sir Charles despatched to advise his wife that he was thinking of leaving early, came as a shock and prompted an immediate exodus. It was only the Prince of Wales's unexpected appearance on the day of Sir Charles's return on 15 July that gave the game away. It was hardly her fault if he turned up uninvited, Harriett told her husband.

Charles was quick to anger but equally quick to forgive and Harriett was adept at winning him round. By the time they left for Scotland in August they were on good terms again. While Charles was out shooting she made a new friend in Sir Frederic Johnstone, a charming bachelor and one of the Prince's closest friends since their Cambridge days, when Johnstone had introduced him to the fast set. Johnstone was a racing man and his forthcoming visit to the September races at Warwick gave Harriett the excuse to invite him to stay at Walton. Perhaps because the Prince realized that he was *persona non grata* with Sir Charles, Sir Frederick soon established himself in the role of a 'darling', acting as the Prince's go-between, carrying letters between him and Harriett.

Harriett, who after two early miscarriages was now pregnant

again, was intrigued that someone titled, rich and handsome like Sir Frederic Johnstone should be unmarried at twenty-seven and asked her husband why he thought this should be. He seemed embarrassed and replied it was something to do with his health; he was said to suffer from a disease that prevented him from marrying. She pressed him to explain, which he did, telling her it was a venereal disease and that any children he had or were born to an infected mother could also be infected.

Harriett, whose fragile emotional equilibrium was already upset by her pregnancy, became unusually quiet and withdrawn. Charles was aware that she was suffering from some physical discomfort during the pregnancy and that she had a discharge, for which her London doctor, Priestley, gave her some remedies.

The baby was apparently due in mid-April, 1869. The intention had been for the confinement to take place in London under Dr Priestley's supervision, and Sir Charles had duly taken a house for their stay. Instead, Harriett's waters broke on 27 February while she was still in Warwickshire. The local man, Dr Orford, was called. She refused chloroform, on the plea that she might start talking 'all sorts of nonsense' under its influence, but he administered it anyway. She gave birth to a baby girl, which the experienced midwife, Mrs Hancox, judged to weigh about three and a half pounds.

The child was to be called Violet. Harriett was most insistent that the announcement of the birth in the *Morning Post* and *The Times* should include the word 'prematurely' and Sir Charles readily acquiesced.

Later that night she appeared very agitated, repeatedly asking Mrs Hancox if the baby was 'diseased'.

'My lady, do you mean deformed?'

'You know what I mean. Is it born with the complaint?'

Apart from the child's being so small, Hancox could see nothing wrong with her. She judged it to be an eight-month baby. When Harriett questioned her, asking why she thought eight months and not seven months, Hancox told her that the baby's nails were formed, which they would not have been at seven months.

The following night again, she kept on at the midwife. Surely she and the doctor could see that the child was diseased? When she asked Hancox if she herself would ever recover from the disease, the midwife was at a loss to know what she was talking about. Surely she could not mean venereal disease? It was rife, but an innocent young woman like Lady Mordaunt, married to a virtuous husband, should not know about such things.

As to the baby's being premature, she now casually told Hancox, 'I have been thinking it over and you are quite right for the baby comes from the last week in June when I was in London and Sir Charles was in Norway.' Although the Prince of Wales had called on her a number of times, she was sure it was the child of Lord Cole. Hancox told her not to talk nonsense.

A few days after the birth, the baby was indeed suffering from a discharge from the eyes. Harriett, who had never shown any interest in her or attempted to nurse her, was distraught. The child would surely be blind. Better to kill 'it' now, she told Hancox; why not give 'it' laudanum. It was all her fault, she told her, as Sir Frederic was 'a very diseased man'.

When Sir Charles next appeared at his wife's bedside she told him, 'Charlie, you are not the father of the child. Lord Cole is the father of the child, and I myself am the cause of its blindness.' Already alarmed at his wife's deteriorating mental state, he was dumbfounded. 'Charlie, I have been very wicked. I have done very wrong,' she continued. He asked with whom. 'With Lord Cole, Sir Frederic Johnstone, and the Prince of Wales, and with others, often and in open day,' she replied. She was crying, while he was overcome with horror.

Charles thought she must be delirious. She was talking nonsense, surely. He sent for Dr Orford, whose first thought was that she must be suffering from some kind of illness associated with child-birth – puerperal mania, perhaps. And yet she did not have the fever normally associated with that. Hearing from Sir Charles about her confession of adultery prompted Orford to view the baby's discharge in a different light. It was certainly severe enough to be venereal. Dr Jones of Leamington had been practising for far more years than he and he now sent for him to give a second opinion. They decided that Lady Mordaunt might be suffering from cataleptic hysteria.

Mrs Cadogan, the vicar's wife, came to visit and was shocked when Harriett, referring to her past behaviour, said there was no harm in what she had done because she knew lots of other ladies in London did the same. Anyway, she had only done it three or four times. Mrs Cadogan replied tersely that no matter how many times she had 'done it' she should show herself truly repentant and implore her husband's forgiveness. Harriett insouciantly replied, 'But I am not sorry.'

Hancox was of the opinion that Lady Mordaunt was only pretending to be ill and feigning mental disorder in order to win her husband's sympathy. Certainly Harriett believed that she would be able to win him round and that they could carry on as before. She clung to the belief that between them Charlie and her father would work everything out.

Charles sent urgently for Harriett's mother, Lady Louisa Moncreiffe, and her sister Helen Forbes. Neither of them appeared to be surprised by the allegations of promiscuity. Given that she always advised her daughters never to comment on a likeness when looking into the cradle of a newborn, adultery was something Lady Louisa took in her stride. The creed of the upper classes was that adultery was all very well, as long as one did not get found out. How could Harriett have been so stupid as to admit her infidelity to her husband! He would have been none the wiser about the baby's paternity. After all, he had cohabited with Harriett both before and after his holiday in Norway and the baby was certainly premature.

The main concern for the Moncreiffes was that Harriett's indiscretions would bring disgrace on the whole family and seriously jeopardize the marriage prospects of her younger sisters. Obviously Lady Louisa could not take Harriett back to live among her innocent, unmarried sisters; it would sully their reputation. She only hoped that Charlie would give Harriett enough money to keep her out of wickedness and keep her disgrace – particularly 'the disease' – as quiet as possible, arriving at some kind of private settlement out of the public eye. At all costs they wanted to avoid 'the ultimate nightmare of a divorce'.

They seriously underestimated Sir Charles, who was hell-bent on revenge. What angered him almost more than anything was the fact that these men had humiliated him; they had accepted his hospitality and abused his trust. Always very money-conscious, he reckoned his marriage had cost him a fortune and he would make damned sure to sue the lot of them for damages. The Divorce Act of 1857 had abolished criminal conversation as such, but a wronged husband was still entitled to sue his wife's alleged seducer for damages, any award being distributed between the husband, the wife and the children of the marriage at the judge's discretion. The wife was also now entitled to appear in court, to be represented by counsel, and to bring witnesses in defence of her good name, although whether Harriett would be in a fit state to do this remained to be seen.

As for the child, Sir Charles chose to believe she was not his. Lady Louisa and Helen coldly discussed her fate. Sir Thomas would not have her at Moncreiffe and Charles obviously did not want 'it', so 'it' would have to be put out to nurse until 'we can find a place for it'. Hancox expressed a wish to take the baby and bring her up as her own, but wanted money. How much? they asked. Thirty pounds, she replied. They demurred. Perhaps it could be agreed. Sir Charles, meanwhile, asked Helen to return the expensive baby clothes to the London shop where Harriett had bought them and send him the refund. The unwanted child would not need them in a poor cottage.

Nobody bothered to consult Harriett either about her fate or that of her child. They talked about her as if she were not there.

From the moment Sir Thomas arrived at Walton he maintained his daughter was mad. Even if what she told them was true, he failed to see what Charles would gain by dragging it out in the open. As it turned out, it was sensible advice. He had a brief meeting with Mr Haynes, Charles's solicitor, and left.

Harriett was very upset when her father left, realizing that she could expect no sympathy from him. Sir Thomas's concern was with the honour of his family and practical financial matters, not his lost daughter. As ever in marriage, money was at the heart of the matter. The Moncreiffes wanted to avoid a divorce because, apart from the disgrace, Charles would no longer be obliged to maintain her. If he succeeded in divorcing Harriett for adultery she would get nothing and lose her jointure and the Moncreiffes would have no choice but to support her, which they could ill afford to do. It was unlikely that under these circumstances another man would take her off their hands. They clung to the fact that whatever Harriett said, there was no proof of adultery – she had not been caught in the act – or that the child was illegitimate.

Instead of uniting to help a very unstable and bewildered young woman who had just given birth and desperately needed their love, support and care, the Moncreiffes and the Mordaunts lined up on opposing sides, and Harriett became a pawn in a legal game. Sir Thomas made one more attempt at a compromise. Admittedly his daughter had been imprudent, but no one, he warned, would take seriously the ravings of a woman 'suffering from the shock of a first confinement' who had just been told she had a blind baby. Haynes wrote back saying Sir Charles had no doubt whatsoever about her guilt and 'hopes that you as her parent and natural protector will take immediate steps for removing her from his house'.

To take her away would be tacitly to admit her guilt; Harriett would forfeit her rights as a wife by leaving her husband's house, so the Moncreiffes left her at Walton.

While she was out for a drive one day, Charles, aided by his brothers who were egging him on to get rid of her, searched Harriett's desk and removed her private papers. There were dozens of letters from the Prince of Wales. In her diary he found her entry for 3 April, in which she had written, '280 days from 27 June' – a date Lord Cole had been at Chesham Place with her and Charles had been in Norway. They also found the hotel bill for the night she had entertained Captain Farquhar, showing that dinner had been served for two. None of this was certain proof of adultery.

Harriett desperately wanted to be reconciled with Charles and reinstated to her rightful position as his wife, but his brothers – one of whom was a clergyman – were determined to prevent it. The marital vows, for better or for worse, in sickness and in health, held no sway here. Knowing that she had power over him still, they persuaded Charles to leave Walton. He was never to see her again. He left her surrounded by servants, including the footman Johnson with his incriminating diary, who had all vowed to testify against her, and an unchristianlike vicar, who owed the living to Sir Charles, who refused to church her while she was in such disgrace.

It seemed that Sir Thomas would rather have his daughter declared insane than branded an adulteress. He believed that the court would not let Sir Charles divorce his wife if she were a lunatic or temporarily indisposed. A long debate ensued as to whether Lady Mordaunt was actually mad or just pretending to be so at the behest of her father. Doctors brought in by each side to examine her could not reach a consensus. Dr Orford maintained she had never shown any sign of madness, whereas Dr Tuke, the eminent 'mad' doctor, believed she was suffering from puerperal mania with delusions. The problem was that her behaviour varied. Sometimes she was quite lucid, at others incoherent, and her behaviour peculiar. She would go into a trance, staring wide-eyed in front of her. Observers noticed that she was always worse after a visit from her father, as if he were tutoring her, and in front of the doctors.

The eminent Edinburgh doctor, Sir James Simpson, who had examined Lady Mordaunt and the baby, wrote a very reasonable, humane letter to Sir Charles giving his view that the child, now six weeks old, had just reached the size she could have expected to be had she not been born prematurely. There was no question that Lady Mordaunt was insane, although whether or not this was a permanent condition he could not tell. 'If the case is not arrested Lady Mordaunt will, I fear, be driven into a state of fixed and permanent insanity,' he predicted. 'I feel sure that no one and above all a husband would willingly and deliberately inflict so dreadful a result upon a fellow being and above all on his own wife. The world at large would revolt at such conduct as you well know.' Possibly because Sir James was a friend of the Moncreiffes, Sir Charles took no notice of the letter.

Dr Priestley also wrote to Sir Charles refuting the fact that he had ever treated Lady Mordaunt for a venereal infection. The remedies he had given her were those used to treat venereal discharge, but also perfectly innocent complaints such as thrush. 'Women often enough after delivering have accused themselves and others of faults never committed,' he added kindly, 'while under the effect of mental aberration.' The baby's discharge had cleared up now, revealing lovely grey eyes like her mother's; the infection would never have cleared up so quickly had it been venereal.

Charles refused to be moved and plunged ahead with the divorce.

The petition cited as co-respondents Lord Cole and Sir Frederic Johnstone. Much against his will, he had been advised to leave the Prince of Wales out of it for the present. Captain Farquhar, a notorious adulterer, was not worth pursuing in a suit for damages, since he was known to be broke. Apprehensive as all the others, including the Prince, he was urgently pressing for a posting to India.

It was Mr Haynes's sad duty to present the petition to Lady Mordaunt in person at Walton. He had never met her before and was filled with pity for the young woman who looked so beseechingly at him with such lovely, but sad, grey eyes, as she took the petition in her hand and read it:

> Victoria, by the Grace of God, of the United Kingdom of Great Britain and Ireland, Queen Defender of the Faith, to Dame Harriett Sarah Mordaunt, of Walton Hall, in the County of Warwick: Whereas Sir Charles Mordaunt, Baronet, of Walton Hall, in the County of Warwick, claiming to have been lawfully married to you, has filed for a dissolution of his marriage, wherein he alleges that you have been guilty of adultery: Now this is to command you that within eight days after service hereof on you, you appear in our said Court, then and there to make answer to the said Petition . . .

Harriett was in no fit state to go to court. Perhaps in a calculated bid to aggravate her condition and certainly as a delaying tactic, Sir Thomas had her sent down to a house in Worthing, where, at Sir Charles's expense, she was confined with keepers. Denied her freedom, she became profoundly depressed, not bothering to get out of bed or look after herself, relieving herself on the floor, crawling about on her hands and knees, and either refusing food or stuffing it into her mouth until she was sick. She was entirely cut off from the outside world. Her former so-called friends kept their distance. There were no longer any letters from the Prince of Wales. Forlornly, she asked if the postman was dead.

At the initial hearing the judge requested Dr Gull, ironically the Prince of Wales's doctor, and Dr Alderson to go to Worthing to examine Lady Mordaunt. They stood by the theory of puerperal insanity. Another posse of doctors, including Jones and Orford, followed. If they had not believed that she was insane before, they

The advent of divorce in 1857 and the accumulated evidence of case after case of marital abuse prompted an intense debate about marriage, which accelerated in the 1880s when feminists such as Mona Caird attacked patriarchal power and standards of masculine behaviour. The editor of the *Daily Telegraph* invited readers to comment and received 27,000 letters in response

A wife, accompanied by her Negro servant, spots her husband leaving a Soho brothel. With divorce virtually impossible in England, adultery was all too common

The Season was devised so that the children of the upper classes could socialise, and meet potential marriage partners, within a strictly prescribed milieu. Tickets to Almack's, open to only a select few, were highly coveted

Traditionally, brides rarely wore a veil or a white gown. These were part of the Victorian 'invention of tradition'. The bridal veil was possibly a substitute for the bride's long hair, which originally had been worn loose at her wedding as a symbol of her virginity

A glamorous white wedding was far beyond the reach of the poor, at least until the 1950s. In this wedding in London's East End in the nineteenth century several couples are being married simultaneously to save expense

Above left: In the late Victorian period the aristocracy were still selling their daughters to the highest bidder. Arranged marriages encouraged adultery; affairs were accepted in such circles, as long as one was discreet

Below left: The marriage of the 9th Duke of Marlborough and New York heiress Consuelo Vanderbilt highlighted a new trend, in which Old World titles were bartered for New World fortunes. It was a loveless match which ended in divorce

Above right: The wife's adultery ha been discovered. Her husband hold the incriminating letter. There can b no forgiveness. She will lose everything including her children, since the cour will judge her morally unfit to hav custody or access. In the background the children play with a house of card

Below right: The Divorce Cour opened its doors in January 1858 publicly exposing the hitherto privat hell of many marriages. There was a avalanche of petitions from women despite the horror of appearing in th witness box. All the shocking an salacious details were avidly reporte in the pres

With the advent of the motor car, this couple is taking a touring honeymoon

In the inter-war years the wife's place was in the home, the dutiful housewife

Right: Originally, a bride brought her trousseau – including lingerie she had sewn herself – to her husband's home in a coffer, which became a useful piece of furniture. She must never bring clothing of a value which her husband could not afford to replace in due course: a wife dressed to reflect her husband's status. Victorian and Edwardian trousseaus were sumptuous. It is surprising that the tradition endured into the 1950s, as seen here

Below: With clothes rationing and other shortages during the Second World War, it was considered unpatriotic to have a white wedding – unless you could secure a parachute from which to make a wedding dress. Most wartime weddings had this sombre appearance

Trousseau Specialists

This charming Nightdress is an example
of several specially designed for your
trousseau—expressed in white
pure silk Georgette and blue lace

PRICE £17·15·0

Lingerie—Second Floor

LANgham 4444
(Debenhams Ltd.) **Debenham & Freebody** WIGMORE STREET, LONDON, W.1

36   THE QUEEN, MARCH 15, 1950

The modern bride leaves the church – in the driving seat

The annual Wedding Show attracts thousands of visitors. Weddings are big business and everyone wants their day to be perfect, no expense spared. It's a long way from a simple ceremony 'at church door'

were certainly struck now by the deterioration in her mental state. Before he left, Dr Orford asked if there was anything he could do for her. 'Yes, you can ask Sir Charles to come and fetch me,' she said. Charles had married her to look after her and now he had sent her away. Pathetically, she still believed Charles would take her back if she promised to behave.

Lord Penzance was struck by the differences of opinion among the doctors. He agreed to postpone the hearing until the autumn. Perhaps by then Lady Mordaunt would have recovered. After all, adultery was a most heinous crime and it was only fair that she should be given the chance to defend herself against the charge and to make a counter-charge of cruelty or neglect on the part of Sir Charles if it applied.

Sir Charles was given custody of his wife and, to his credit, immediately removed her to a more civilized environment, installing her in a good house in Kent with his own staff to look after her. Of course, it was in his interest that she made a speedy recovery. Under these more normal conditions she did begin to improve, although Dr Wood, the visiting doctor, noticed how docile she was. When he asked her to write a cheque for £30 she did so without question. He felt she would have been equally acquiescent if he had asked for £30,000. Was she, perhaps, this docile when various men had suggested sex? After all, she had been easily led to believe there was no harm in it and 'everybody did it'. If that were so, it was the men who corrupted her who were at fault, not their innocent, or simple, victim.

At the subsequent insanity trial the Prince of Wales was subpoenaed to attend as a witness. His letters to Lady Mordaunt had been published in the newspapers and it was imperative he put in an appearance to defend himself. The courtroom was so packed that structural engineers had had to be called in to check that the galleries could take the weight. The Prince, under oath, was asked if there had ever been any improper familiarity or criminal act between him and Lady Mordaunt. The court collectively drew in and held its breath. 'There has not,' he replied in a firm voice. It was disappointing that he was allowed to leave after this brief avowal and that there were no further disclosures.

It was Sir Frederic's turn next. He was asked if there had ever been any improper familiarity or criminal act between him and Lady Mordaunt. 'Certainly not,' he said. He was asked if it was true he suffered from venereal disease. 'I say a more unfounded statement was never made by any man to the prejudice of another behind his back,' he replied.

'Utterly untrue, is it?' Penzance pressed.

'Certainly, for many years,' came the reply.

Sir Charles's counsel, Mr Serjeant Ballantine, tried to be more specific: 'You mean at this particular period at all events you were not suffering from any disease of any kind?'

'No, nor for many years previously,' Sir Frederic asserted.

To Sir Charles's impotent fury, the jury decided that Lady Mordaunt had been totally unfit both before and certainly after the citation of 30 April to instruct her solicitor for her defence. There was a reasonable assumption that if she had been insane on 30 April, she had also been so when the 'portentous confessions which are now too notorious to all the world' were made. Lord Penzance decreed that no further proceedings should be initiated against her until she recovered her sanity. *The Times* opined that it was a pity that all this had had to be dragged out in public, when it would have been so much better if the parties concerned had conducted a private investigation by mutual consent.

Whatever happened now, a cloud was cast over Lady Mordaunt's moral character: 'Whether the shameful revelations which she poured into her husband's ears during her illness were the ravings of a fevered brain or the guilty secrets of an overburdened conscience was surely a question which might have been submitted in confidential arbitration.' Sir Charles, who, according to the paper, seemed to have acted 'an honourable and straightforward part throughout has gained nothing by the exposure of his domestic unhappiness'.

Sir Charles announced his intention to appeal.

The point to be decided was whether insanity on the part of the wife was a bar to the further prosecution of a suit for divorce initiated by the husband. The Divorce Act had made no specific exception for insanity. The appeal was heard by three judges, including Lord Penzance, at Westminster. Of course a woman who had lost her mind could not be put in a position in which she recovered her senses, only to find she had been divorced. On the other hand, it was argued, it was unfair on the husband to be saddled with an insane alleged adulteress for a wife, whom he would be compelled by law to maintain suitably according to 'his own condition, rank, and fortune, liable to the risk of spurious issue, his legitimate children or natural heir despoiled of property as by the wife's claim to dower, and himself for ever precluded from contracting a marriage with another woman', with whom he could have legitimate issue.

It was argued that divorce was a civil procedure and could take place irrespective of the disabilities of either party. The lunacy of the plaintiff or defendant in a civil suit did not prevent the enforcement of the civil rights of the parties in a civil action. Similarly, had the legislature intended that a husband should have no remedy in the case of the lunacy of his wife in a divorce action, they would have said as much. The fact that an insane wife would be placed at a disadvantage did not mean that the husband should be denied his civil right which the Act of Parliament gave him. Before the Act, it was argued, divorce had been not a matter of right, but of grace. Yes, but that was when it was the preserve of the ecclesiastical courts; the new Divorce Court was secular. Moreover, the proceedings in the Divorce Court were not so much matters of individual rights or interest as of public concern. It was of the greatest public concern that marriages should not be improperly dissolved and that the person seeking a divorce should come to the court with perfectly clean hands. The real truth of the case could not be ascertained while one of the parties was insane.

After Sir Charles had spent a fortune on lawyers and doctors, the case seemed to have reached an impasse. On 15 May 1874 his appeal was considered again by a group of judges. By a vote of three to two it was decided that if a wife continued insane it was permissible for a husband to proceed in the Court of Divorce. The Prince of Wales and the named co-respondents now girded themselves for the final showdown. The Prince had not been named in the original divorce citation, but he could be now. Unlike in the insanity trial, the Divorce Court would put the co-respondents through a thorough grilling. Even if no one had witnessed Lady Mordaunt with any of the named men *in flagrante delicto* there was enough evidence of the Prince's romantic entanglement with a married woman, contrary to the express wish of her husband, to place him and the monarchy in opprobrium. There was already a widespread feeling among the public that the lax morals of the Prince and his set were to blame for the unfortunate Lady Mordaunt's plight. If such privileged people were vulnerable to drawing-room rape, what hope was there for the rest of society?

Male sexual conduct was increasingly coming under scrutiny and it was no coincidence that feminists such as Mona Caird were campaigning so vigorously against the double standard, by which a wife could be divorced for a single act of adultery while a husband was free to consort with any number of prostitutes, or that women should be the only targets of the Contagious Diseases Act – an iniquity that Josephine Butler's campaign had at last succeeded in having revoked.

In the New Year of 1875 Lord Cole suddenly announced that he would plead guilty, despite all his former denials. Sir Charles was granted his divorce on the grounds of his wife's adultery with Lowry Cole. He felt cheated. After five years of ruinously expensive litigation he believed that at last he would have the satisfaction of exposing the Prince of Wales. He had little doubt that the impecunious Cole had been heavily bribed to take all the guilt on himself. Had he announced his guilt five years ago, not only would Sir Charles have saved a fortune in legal fees, but the unfortunate Lady Mordaunt might perhaps have been spared the dreadful fate of being committed to an asylum, for by now there could be no doubt of her insanity.

A sum of £300 a year was agreed for the maintenance of the former Lady Mordaunt. As the child Violet would have to be regarded as the legal issue of the marriage, since she was born during the lifetime of the marriage when Sir Charles was still cohabiting with his wife, he had no choice but to pay child support of £100 a year until such time as she married. Ironically, the total maintenance of £400 was the sum he had originally offered Lady Louisa and the Moncreiffes and which they had rejected.

Sir Thomas had quashed the idea of giving Violet away to Mrs Hancox and she had been brought up at Moncreiffe alongside her younger uncles and aunts. As Violet Mordaunt, she was launched into society by her mother's sisters. In April 1890 she married Lord Weymouth, the son and heir of the Marquis of Bath. Sir Charles was piqued not to be invited to the wedding and realizing a few months later that he had mistakenly continued to pay her allowance when it should have ceased on her marriage, he had the effrontery to ask for a rebate.

The Prince of Wales, who had caused Lady Weymouth's mother such misery, steered well clear of Longleat, the seat of the Marquis of Bath. The Mordaunt case taught him to be more discreet, but he continued to have affairs with married women and ordered at least one of them to have an abortion. Selfish, self-indulgent, amoral, callous, idle and bored, he could always rely on the deferential to cover his tracks and get him out of a hole.

The once lovely and all too pliable Harriett Moncreiffe was condemned to a lunatic asylum, until released by death in 1906.

INTERLUDE

Mrs Henderson, *The Young Wife's Own Book, Her Domestic Duties and Social Habits*

In *The Young Wife's Own Book, Her Domestic Duties and Social Habits* (1857) Mrs Henderson stressed the importance of a bride taking care to integrate herself into her husband's family. Nothing was more calculated to mar a husband's happiness or to cause irritation than squabbles between his new wife and his relatives and she advises:

> A determination to be pleased herself, is half-way towards
> pleasing them; and this may be shown by her willingness to
> discover their agreeable traits of character, rather than with the
> critical penetration of ill humour, to mark their weaknesses
> and errors. By pleasing manners at first, she may secure herself
> a favourable reception into her husband's family; and, in time,
> when she has proved her worth, her footing among them will be
> on a surer foundation.

All the advice books warned young women to be very careful in their choice of husband, not to be too idealistic, and to prepare themselves for the reality of marriage: 'However discreet your choice has been, time and circumstances alone can sufficiently develop your husband's character: by degrees the discovery will be made that you have married a mortal, and that the object of your affections is not entirely free from the infirmities of human nature.'

Emphasis was always placed on 'managing' a husband and navigating a safe course through the shoals of his temper:

> Should your husband's temper be of the placid and gentle
> kind, endeavour to perpetuate it, even though your own
> may not naturally be of that description, and you will have a
> powerful incentive to imitation in observing the benign effects

of such dispositions on yourself and others: especially recollect, that nothing is more contagious than bad temper, and that a disordered mind, as well as a diseased body, may spread infection over a whole house. Should he be morose, fretful, or capricious, liable to sudden sallies, or the prey of constant irritability, the cure cannot be effected by opposing similar qualities; by these the evil would be increased and perpetuated.

Be positive:

Accustom yourself, in contemplation of your husband's character, to dwell on the bright side; let his virtues occupy your thoughts more than his failings; this will impel you to honour him in the presence of others, and may eventually produce the happiest effects on his character; for most probably he will feel the value of that estimation in which you hold him, and be solicitous in preserving it. Do not expose his failings; no, not even to your most confidential friend! His honour and yours are inseparably one.

A wife must never show up her husband in public and even in private she must never make him look a fool, even if he is one:

A woman can never be seen in a more ridiculous light than when she attempts to govern her husband: if, unfortunately, the superiority of understanding is on her side, the apparent consciousness of it betrays a weakness that renders her contemptible in the sight of every considerate person and may so fix in his mind a dislike never to be eradicated. In such a case, it would be wiser to let his defect appear unobserved, when he judged wrongly never flatly to contradict him; and to let the whole merit of every prudent determination rest on him, without indulging the foolish vanity of claiming any merit to herself.

Above all, always defer to his superiority: 'There cannot, indeed, be a sight more uncouth than that of a man and his wife struggling for power.'

24

'Wife-Torture in England'

SUSANNAH PALMER WAS a battered wife. Her husband had
habitually treated her to kicks and blows, given her a black eye
more than once and knocked out her front teeth. After years of
brutality, one day she gathered up her children and left him. She
managed to secure somewhere to live and earn enough to support
them. But her husband tracked her down. He seized and sold all the
possessions she had worked so hard to buy to provide a little comfort
for her family, since by law they belonged to him. Then he attacked
her. With the knife she was using to prepare the children's supper
she inflicted a slight cut on him while he was knocking her about
the head. He immediately summoned her for 'cutting and wound-
ing' him and she was sent to prison. For she was the criminal; not the
adulterous husband who beat and robbed her and failed to provide
for his family.

Two years earlier in 1867 John Stuart Mill gave a speech in
the House in favour of women's suffrage. Until women received the
vote, he argued, they could never hope to achieve equality before the
law and without this there could be no true harmony in marriage.

> I should like to have a return laid before this House of the number of
> women who are annually beaten to death, kicked to death, or tram-
> pled to death by their male protectors: and, in the opposite column,
> the amount of the sentence passed, in those cases in which the das-
> tardly criminals did not get off altogether. I should also like to have,
> in a third column, the amount of property, the unlawful taking of
> which was, at the same sessions or assizes, by the same judge, thought
> worthy of the same amount of punishment. We should then have an
> arithmetical estimate of the value set by a male legislature and male
> tribunals on the murder of a woman, often by torture continued

through years, which, if there is any shame in us, would make us hang our heads.

Male authorities considered theft a more serious crime than wife-beating, but of course it all came down to property in the end. A man mistreated his wife because he believed she was his possession to do what he liked with. 'The notion that a man's wife is his property, in the sense in which a horse is his property . . . is the fatal root of incalculable evil and misery,' wrote the feminist reformer Frances Power Cobbe. 'Every brutal-minded man, and many a man who in other relations of life is not brutal, entertains more or less vaguely the notion that his wife is his *thing*, and is ready to ask with indignation of any one who interferes with his treatment of her, "May I not do what I will *with my own?*"'

Very often for the working-class man his wife was the only underling on whom he could vent his anger and frustration, the most convenient human object to hand. It was the only power he possessed.

A society in which the male half was deemed superior to the female half, and in which the latter were placed in the same legal category as criminals, idiots and minors, had to expect a degree of domestic violence. In no other instance but wife-beating was an excuse made for a man taking the law into his own hands, bolstering the universal belief among the labouring class that a wife's chastisement was legally sanctioned and acceptable. Mill maintained that working-class wives were no better than slaves, while Cobbe believed that a wife's vow of obedience in the marriage service encouraged 'men's worst faults of selfishness and despotism'.

Wife-torture flourished in the overcrowded slums and tenements of the expanding urban industrial landscape, whose inhabitants were living at an intolerable level of degradation, plagued by disease, filth, crime and poverty. As ever, violence was fuelled by drink: 'the seas of brandy and gin, and the oceans of beer, imbibed annually in England'. 'He never laid a finger on me except when he was in drink,' was a common excuse. The women themselves, according to Cobbe, were often 'slatternly, coarse, foul-mouthed – sometimes loose in behaviour, sometimes madly addicted to drink'. A wife's nagging or insubordination was deemed to merit a beating.

Pecuniary dependence, aggravated by the notion of the male wage-earner as family breadwinner which industrialization had encouraged, and an ingrained habit of female submission, made wives easy targets. Where the 'polished profligate' of the upper class might 'with a smile break his wife's heart by polite cruelty', or take care to aim the blows where the bruises would not show, the labouring man was more likely to use his fists and his hobnailed boots to kick and jump on her. With good reason parts of London and Liverpool were known as 'the kicking districts'.

Frederick Knight, for instance, jumped on his wife's face, a month after she had given birth, with 'a pair of boots studded with hob-nails'. An hour after she had been confined, Richard Mountain beat his wife on the back and mouth and turned her out of bed. John Charnock was indicted for attempted murder after he had fastened his wife's head in a cupboard and kicked her with his iron clogs, and deliberately broken her arm.

John Harris, a shoemaker in Sheffield, found his wife and children in bed, dragged her out, and, after vainly attempting to force her into the oven, tore off her nightdress and turned her round before the fire 'like a piece of beef', while the children stood on the stairs listening to their mother's agonized screams. William White, a stonemason, threw a burning paraffin lamp at his wife and stood quietly watching her enveloped in flames, which killed her.

The wife of a drunk lay with many broken ribs, her shoulder and one arm broken, and her head 'so smashed that you could scarcely recognise a feature of a woman' when the police were called. In her last agony she told them that her husband had smashed her with a wooden bed-post. 'Yes, it is true,' he said, 'but I was in drink, or would not have done it.'

Many rows were about money. There was tension if a husband was unemployed while his wife was in work, or if a dependent wife asked for some of his wages to keep a roof over their heads and feed the family. One wife said, 'He earns twenty shillings a week, and out of that he gives me the odd seven shillings to keep house and find everything.' Then he would beat her because she could not provide him with a decent dinner.

James Styles beat his wife about the head when he met her in the

City Road, London. She had supported him for years by char-work and during the whole time he had been in the habit of beating her, and on one occasion so assaulted her that the sight of one of her eyes was destroyed. He was habitually drunk with the money she earned. James Lawrence, who had been supported by his wife's hard work for years, struck her in the face with a poker, disfiguring her. Thomas Paget, laundryman, knocked down his wife in the street and kicked her till she became insensible, because she refused to give him money to get drink.

Of course, there were the usual pleas on the part of men that their wives had provoked them. Mrs Brick's husband had insisted that she take off her wedding ring so that he could pawn it to get more drink. When she tried to stop him, he hit her on the head with a chopper and dragged her out of the house. He excused himself by saying 'his wife's action was so exasperating, he lost all control.' When a labourer killed his wife he retorted, 'If she had stopped at home, instead of going out drinking, it would not have happened.' Another man who beat his wife to death for helping herself to his wages told police, 'We had a few words about money matters . . . I never meant to kill her, she should have kept her hand out of my pocket.'

Some men were obviously psychopaths. James Mills cut his wife's throat as she lay in bed. 'He was quite sober at the time.' On a previous occasion he had nearly torn away her left breast. George Ralph Smith cut his wife to pieces with a hatchet in their back parlour. She died afterwards, but he was found Not Guilty, as it was not certain that her death resulted from the wounds.

There had always been marital conflict – hence the durability of puppet shows such as *Punch and Judy*, depicting the battle of the sexes. But industrialization, the squalor and isolation of urban living, and the secularization of society seem to have exacerbated it.

Traditionally an abusive husband was treated to a charivari, a noisy gathering of neighbours expressing their disapproval of his behaviour – just as they might do for nagging wives, adulterers or homosexuals. The steadfast belief that a man had the right to chastise his wife, especially if she had provoked him, had to be weighed against the extent of her injuries. If, in the last resort, the neighbours called the police, it was not because the man was beating his wife, but because they thought he might murder her.

Abused wives were hesitant about coming forward. Reporting a husband's violence was bound to bring retaliation. If he was prosecuted and sent to prison, she and the children would starve. They often felt guilty or that they had somehow 'earned' the beating, while they were fearful that the male legislature would take the view that they must have provoked their husband.

In May 1874 Colonel Egerton Leigh made a vehement plea in the House for some increased punishment for aggravated assaults on women. England, he reminded them, had been called 'the Paradise of Women'. He introduced the motion to prevent it becoming 'the Hell of Women'. Disraeli ordered an enquiry, which confirmed that the existing law was deficient, but no practical action was taken. It was hardly a priority for the male legislature.

The fact that the Divorce Court was in London put it out of reach of most, although not all, of the poor. It was expensive to travel to London and to stay there during the hearing. Something had to be done to bring justice within the reach of the whole community. Frances Power Cobbe's article, 'Wife-Torture in England', has been widely credited with being the inspiration for the Act to Amend the Matrimonial Causes Acts of 1878, giving magistrates the power to grant separation and maintenance orders to assaulted wives. By the end of the century local courts were granting over 8,000 separation and maintenance orders a year – 'the divorce of the poor'. Separation orders were not permanent – they lapsed if the couple was reunited, so that they were not an exact parallel with divorce – but since many of them did last for years it begged the question why not grant a divorce, the marriage clearly being at an end.

The latter part of the nineteenth century has been accredited with a decline in violence generally. Whether or not this was also true of marital violence, there can be no doubt that critical scrutiny of it intensified. Exposure of marital misconduct among men of all social classes had brought an unprecedented amount of attention to proper ideals of male behaviour in marriage. 'Unmanly' behaviour as opposed to female provocation came to be seen as the root cause of much marital misery. Abusive husbands increasingly appeared before the courts and were legislated against, although it is salutary to note that the Royal Commission on Divorce of 1910–12 provided ample evidence that wife-abuse continued to pose a profound social problem.

It remains true, however, that if Susannah Palmer's case had arisen twenty years later, the chances were that the court would have taken a more humane view of her situation. Nor, thanks to the Married Women's Property Act of 1870, would the beastly Mr Palmer have been able to help himself to her hard-earned property.

PART SIX
1880–1969

25

'A woman plotting the death of her husband . . . to follow her own degrading vices'

THE YOUNG WOMAN standing in the dock had the intense blue eyes of a china doll, a lovely face framed by blonde hair and soft curls, and a fashionable hour-glass figure. When she spoke it was with the soft, lilting tones of the Southern Belle. One could see that, in other circumstances, she would exude the sort of magnetic charm and feminine fragility guaranteed to win male protectiveness. Now, however, she was on trial for her life for the murder of her fifty-year-old husband, who appeared to have died from arsenic poisoning.

Florence and James Maybrick had been married for a little more than eight years. She had been born Florence Elizabeth Chandler in 1862 at Mobile, Alabama, and had met James Maybrick, a Liverpool cotton merchant with business connections in America, on a transatlantic voyage in 1880. Florence was impulsive and she and James became engaged after an eight-day acquaintance. They were married at St James's Piccadilly in July 1881, with Florie wearing a dress made of ivory satin which matched James's richly embroidered waistcoat.

At a time when American women with vast fortunes were infiltrating English high society, bartering their wealth for titles, Florie was glibly referred to as an 'American heiress'. Her thrice-married mother, a cousin of the immensely rich Mrs Cornelius Vanderbilt, had exaggerated Florie's prospects. Her much vaunted inheritance comprised thousands of acres in the Southern states, but the ownership of the land was disputed and much of it was swamp anyway. She was not the only one at fault. James had failed to mention that his cotton business was in trouble. Although he was no doubt attracted to his lovely eighteen-year-old bride, it seems to have been a case of each side marrying for money and deceiving the other.

Liverpool in the 1880s was a thriving commercial metropolis and the Maybricks enjoyed a busy social life. In spite of his precarious finances, James was intent on putting on a good show to impress the business community. They rented a substantial house, they travelled, they entertained lavishly and attended dinner parties, teas, card parties, balls and visits to the races, and he indulged Florie in her passion for gorgeous clothes. A son was born in 1882 and a daughter four years later, and Florie proved a devoted mother.

Only in 1887 did James confess to Florie that he was nearly bankrupt. She had absolutely no idea of the value of money and would be quite unable to follow the strict budget that James now imposed.

James's health appeared to be deteriorating. She noticed that he was taking a mysterious white powder and mentioned it to his doctor and to his brother Michael. Was she genuinely concerned, or did she have some ulterior motive? At the trial, the jury assumed the latter. For 1887 was also the year that Florie discovered that James had a mistress. Worse, he had kept this woman for twenty years and they had had five children together, two of them since his marriage to Florie. Naturally James was paying her an allowance. Through the whole of their marriage James had been living a lie.

Florie and James began to sleep in separate bedrooms. In 1888 she began an affair with Alfred Brierley, a tall, good-looking cotton broker from a wealthy family who was fifteen years James's junior. The sexual double standard was far from dead, however. When James found out he was furious and threatened to change his will, leaving Florie only her widow's third and the rest to the children.

At the trial James's adultery barely merited a mention, but much was made of Florie's. The fact that she was American did not help. American women were generally branded as 'fast'. Florie, partly in a bid to make James jealous, was too brazen about the affair. Either naïvely or to goad James, she arranged to meet Brierley for a week in London, booking a suite in the name of Mr and Mrs Maybrick at a hotel that was frequented by members of the Liverpool and Manchester cotton fraternity. Brierley, sensing trouble, began to withdraw, telling Florie that he had an attachment to another woman. They 'parted abruptly' and Florie did what women always do in such a situation: she went on a massive shopping spree, adding to James's financial woes. This same week she consulted solicitors and wrote a letter to James seeking a separation on the basis of his adultery.

Back in Liverpool they had an enormous row. Whether it was about her affair with Brierley, the separation she was seeking, or her debts, is unclear. He hit her, giving her a black eye. She threatened to leave and he retaliated that she would never see the children again. She stayed. The next day she consulted Dr Hopper, who testified to the black eye and the fact that he had advised her not to seek a separation.

There was plenty, then, to be angry about and, to the critical at least, there was no shortage of motives for murder. But it need not have come to that. With evidence of James's adultery and second family and his recent assault on Florie, she could have sued for divorce, or at least for a judicial separation. If she wanted rid of him, there was no need to murder him.

To his credit, James went to London to settle Florie's recent debts. In a fit of remorse she wrote to him, addressing him as 'My own darling Hubby' and pleading forgiveness:

> Darling, try and be as lenient towards me as you can. For notwith-standing all your generous and tender loving kindness, my burden is almost more than I can bear. My remorse and self-contempt is eating my heart out and if I did not believe my love for you and my dutiful-ness may prove some slight atonement for the past I should give up the struggle to keep brave. Forgive me if you can dearest and think less poorly of your wifey.

It was signed, 'Bunny'.

It was hardly the letter of someone about to poison her husband, unless she was extremely cold and calculating, and the impulsive, rather scatter-brained Florie was neither. Her attempts at reconcili-ation might have been more muted had she known that James had indeed changed his will, leaving everything in trust to his brothers Michael and Thomas for the benefit of the children, but stating that the furnishings of the house should remain intact for the use of Florie and the children and expressing the wish that 'my Widow shall live under the same roof as my children so long as she remains my Widow.' The new will was probably triggered by the fact that he had had to pay off Florie's substantial debts, amounting to at least £100,000 in today's money. It is not clear how he raised the money, but he seems to have been convinced that his wife was too irresponsible to manage the family's financial affairs if he should die. The will was timely, since James had only two weeks to live. There is no evidence to suggest that Florie knew anything about it.

In court Florie had to explain her purchase of arsenic-impregnated fly-paper. Florie and everyone in the household would have known from the publicity attending the 1884 trial of two Liverpool women, Flanagan and Higgins, for the murder of four people, that the arsenic could be extracted from the fly-paper and used to poison. But Florie claimed to have purchased the fly-paper for quite another purpose. It was a cosmetic treatment she had first used as a young girl in Paris; years later the original recipe from a Paris druggist fell out of her Bible, when it was far too late to convince a court of the veracity of her claim. She was going to a ball, she told the court, and the arsenic would be useful as a depilatory and to eradicate a spot. It is slightly suspicious that she felt the need to obtain the fly-paper on at least two occasions from two different chemists, but she had not concealed the purchases and at home she openly soaked the fly-paper in water to extract the arsenic.

James had already been complaining of headaches for two weeks before Florie bought the fly-paper and he had been confined to bed for a time with stomach pains and vomiting, but on 1 May he felt much better and returned to work. The doctor had given James a special concoction to take with him, but had Florie, on the pretext of sending the cook to get some wrapping paper for it, seized the chance to slip arsenic into it? James complained that it tasted strongly of sherry, and after taking it suffered a relapse, showing all the symptoms of arsenic poisoning: headaches, stomach cramps, vomiting and pains in the legs.

The Victorian wife was expected to be able to manage her servants. Through them she was supposed to run her home like a small company. Florie, whose youth had been spent trailing round Europe and America in her mother's wake rather than learning by example how to manage a well-run home, had problems exerting her authority and she had no supporters among the servants. The children's nurse, Mrs

Alice Yapp, was particularly hostile. Florie had come home one night to find her little daughter screaming unattended in the nursery while Yapp was living up to her name in the servants' quarters downstairs. Florie had given her a severe reprimand and threatened to fire her if it happened again. The malevolent Mrs Yapp was friendly with James's former fiancée, Mrs Briggs, whom Florie in her laid-back way continued to welcome to the house, failing to see that she was no friend. The two were only looking for an excuse to gang up on her.

On 8 May Mrs Briggs came to visit James in his sickroom, to be greeted by Mrs Yapp, who told her, 'Thank God you have come, Mrs Briggs, for the mistress is poisoning the master.' She told her that she had seen Florie fiddling with the medicine bottles the doctors had left for James, and also that she had been soaking fly-papers. Mrs Briggs telegraphed James's brother Michael warning him that 'something strange is going on here'.

Blithely unaware of the foul suspicions surrounding her, Florie gave Mrs Yapp a letter to post when she took the little girl out for her afternoon air. Claiming that she dropped the letter in the mud and read it inadvertently while transferring it to a clean envelope – a claim Florie's barrister, Sir Charles Russell QC, had no trouble disproving and so demolishing her character in court – Yapp read the letter. It was from Florie to Brierley:

> Dearest, Since my return I have been nursing M. day and night. He is sick unto death. The doctors held a consultation yesterday, and now all depends on how long his strength will hold out. Both my brothers-in-law are here and we are terribly anxious. I cannot answer your letter fully today, my darling, but relieve your mind of all fear of discovery now and for the future. M. has been delirious since Sunday, and I know now that he is perfectly ignorant of everything . . .

To those already ill-disposed to Florie, it sounded highly incriminating. Much was made of the words 'sick unto death' at the trial. In vain, letters poured in from Americans explaining it was simply a Southern expression for 'very ill'.

On 11 May 1889 James Maybrick died after what appeared to be an intestinal illness of two weeks. It might have been as a result of food poisoning, or he might have been poisoned. An autopsy showed traces of arsenic in his liver, kidney and intestines. The effects of small doses of arsenic produce symptoms very similar to food poisoning, making it the weapon of choice for murderers, particularly for women anxious to kill their husbands. On the other hand, James had been treated by several doctors, each of whom had prescribed a battery of medicines. A hypochondriac and drug addict, James had a habit of taking double the prescribed dosage. One of his doctors had even warned him that he was overloading an already impaired constitution.

James's doctor later admitted that he would have written a death certificate stating gastroenteritis as the cause of death, had not James's brothers alerted him to the fact that there might be cause for suspicion. The assumption was that Florie, in the role of concerned wife anxiously ministering to her husband on his sickbed, had slipped the poison into his drinks; the bitter taste and brown colouring agent which was used to prevent the fly-papers being used for nefarious purposes was easily disguised in strong tea or sherry. Servants and nurses brought in to look after James in the final days claimed to have seen her tampering with the medicine bottles and in his delirium James was alleged to have shouted out words to that effect. On the other hand, he was just as likely in his more lucid moments to have overdosed himself. While she was lying in her bedroom in a state of collapse, she was put under house arrest on suspicion of murder. Significantly, she was not allowed to attend James's funeral and the children had been taken away.

Thanks to the disloyalty of the servants to their mistress, James's brothers were already fully apprised of Florie's affair and other suspect activities. The day after James's 'suspicious' death, they searched the house without police authority or supervision. How gratifying it must have been for them to find large quantities of poison stashed about the place! There had been no attempt to hide or dispose of it. Surely if Florie had poisoned her husband she would not have left the evidence lying about. The 'poison' probably belonged to James as much as Florie, but the trouble was that in her room they found not only quantities of arsenic, but her love letters. How very tempting to put two and two together!

In the two months leading up to the trial, which opened at the

Crown Court in St George's Hall, Liverpool, on 31 July 1889, with the tall, red-robed figure of Judge Sir James Fitzjames Stephen presiding, the press concentrated all its energies on heaping opprobrium on Florie for the Brierley affair, so that public opinion was thoroughly convinced that she was a bad woman and therefore guilty before she even set foot in the courtroom. As she passed by on her way to court they hissed her in the streets. In court 400 eager spectators, who had won the frenzied battle for seats, waited for the show to begin. Florie noted that many of them were women, 'attired as for a matinee, and some brought their luncheons that they might retain their seats. Many of them carried opera glasses that they did not hesitate to level at me.'

The revelation at the trial that James had been an arsenic eater for years, a fact that one of his brothers had tried to suppress, came as an unexpected and startling shock. A black servant he had first employed in America testified that Maybrick was in the habit of taking arsenic in his beef tea – and that was years before he met Florie. A Liverpool druggist revealed that Maybrick had been a regular customer over the last ten years for an arsenic-laced tonic. Possibly he believed the tonic would give him sexual potency – after all, he did have a young wife *and* a mistress. A doctor confirmed that Maybrick had complained for years of symptoms characteristic of arsenic addiction.

Largely as an outcome of the Maybrick trial, the Criminal Evidence Act of 1898 allowed a person accused of murder to give evidence on his or her own behalf. When Florie was put on trial this was not permitted, but in an unusual departure the judge allowed her to make a statement from the dock. Unfortunately, she was not allowed to receive legal advice before she did so and her untutored statement was a hindrance rather than a help to the defence. Naïvely, she told the court that James had begged her to give him the medicine, or whatever was in the bottle. When she also told them that she had 'made a full and free confession' to her husband on his deathbed and 'received his entire forgiveness for the fearful wrong I had done him' everyone assumed she was referring to her affair, or worse. As she later revealed in her memoirs, her 'confession' to James was not about her affair, but the fact that she had been intending to divorce him.

The judge and the all-male jury, given access to the vitriolic newspapers every day of the trial, were determined on her guilt. She was a proven adulteress, so of course she was a murderess too. This is what happened when the ungovernable power of female sexuality was unleashed. This primordial fear of women as 'the dangerous sex' combined with the liberalization of the marriage laws was promoting profound male insecurity. It was disconcerting to know that of all the women convicted of murder in the last few years, 40 per cent of them had killed their husbands. This anxiety about female morality was reflected in the verdict.

In his summing-up for the defence, Sir Charles Russell tried to persuade the jury to put the matter of Florie's adultery to one side:

> I refer to that dark cloud that passed over her life and rests upon her character as a woman and a wife. But I would entreat you not to allow any repugnance resting in your minds against a sin so abhorrent as that to lead you to the conclusion, unless the evidence drives you irresistibly there, that, because a wife has forgotten her duty and faithfulness to her husband, she is to be regarded as one who deliberately and wickedly will seek to destroy his life.

Before the jury retired, the judge delivered a summing-up which for its prejudice must surely represent a milestone in legal history:

> You must not consider the case as a mere medical case, in which you are to decide whether the man did nor did not die of arsenic according to the medical evidence . . . You must decide it as a great and highly important case . . . involving in itself a most highly important moral question. For the person to go on deliberately administering poison to a poor, helpless, sick man upon whom she has already inflicted a dreadful injury – an injury fatal to married life – the person who could do such a thing as that must indeed be destitute of the least trace of human feeling . . . Then you have to consider . . . the question of motives which might act upon this woman's mind. When you consider that, you must remember the intrigue which she carried on with this man Brierley, and the feelings – it seems horrible to comparatively ordinary innocent people – a horrible and incredible thought that a woman should be plotting the death of her husband in order that she might be left at liberty to follow her own degrading vices.

No wonder his brother, Sir Leslie Stephen, father of Virginia Woolf, later described him as a 'moralist in the old school'. Eighteen months later Mr Justice Stephen died in the Ipswich asylum for the insane. Armed with his biased advice, meanwhile, the jury took only twenty-five minutes to reach a verdict. Florie was convicted of murder because she was guilty of adultery. The judge put on his black silk cap and sentenced her to death by hanging. As he drove away from the court, he needed a police guard to protect him from the indignant mob.

The Times was quick to denounce her 'treachery as a wife' – note the allusion to treason, since in the not too distant past a woman who killed her husband, her lord and master, committed treason rather than a felony. However, public opinion was at odds with the reactionary forces of the male establishment that determined the outcome of the trial. There was a massive outcry against the verdict.

First of all, it was deemed unsafe. To add to his other shortcomings, the judge, who had recently suffered a slight stroke, did not seem to be able to keep abreast of the evidence, dismissing or failing to explain some of the medical details to a jury of mediocre education and understanding, and he made several mistakes in his summing-up. There was reasonable doubt that arsenic had killed Maybrick – the medical men themselves could not agree on the cause of death – and the prosecution had not demonstrated that Florie had administered it with intent to murder him, if indeed she had administered it at all. Second, the women who attended the trial and who avidly read every detail of the case in the newspapers were outraged at the blatant upholding of the double standard of sexual morality. Women, who had become active and articulate, spoke out directly against the sexual prejudice of the verdict, signed petitions, wrote letters and even formed an organization in Florie's defence.

According to the law, three Sundays must pass before the condemned could be hanged. The date for the execution was set for 26 August. There was no criminal Court of Appeal – it was not created until 1908 – and Florie was relying on Sir Charles Russell and her legal team, her few friends and the growing mass of public protest at the outcome of the trial to save her from the gallows.

Queen Victoria wanted her to hang. For the grieving Widow

of Windsor, no punishment was too severe for a woman who had betrayed her husband in an adulterous relationship and then murdered him. The Home Secretary Henry Matthews had to take some notice of the thousands of petitions pouring in to the Home Office, however, and of the disquiet in the upper echelons of the establishment that justice might not have been served in this case. The judge seemed to be mentally impaired. Florie was listening to the sound of hammering as the gallows were being prepared when on 23 August Matthews issued the following statement:

> We are given to understand that the Home Secretary, after fullest consideration and after taking the best legal and medical advice that could be obtained, has advised Her Majesty to respite the capital punishment of Florence Elizabeth Maybrick and to commute the punishment to penal servitude for life; inasmuch as, although the evidence leads to the conclusion that the prisoner administered and attempted to administer arsenic to her husband, with intent to murder him, yet it does not wholly exclude a reasonable doubt whether his death was in fact caused by the administration of arsenic.

It was a cover-up masking an instance of judicial incompetence. Instead of releasing Florie or having her tried again on a charge of attempted murder, as he should have done, Matthews merely assumed attempted murder and sentenced her to life imprisonment – a term of twenty years. There could be no hope of a review or a pardon while Queen Victoria was alive. Even in the year of her Diamond Jubilee, when the American President himself suggested that this could be a good time to issue a pardon, Victoria did not relent. Eventually, in 1904 Edward VII's government released the prisoner.

Florie returned to America. She was never reconciled to her children, who had been brought up to believe in her guilt. She died in poverty and obscurity in 1941.

Whether Florie was guilty or innocent, we can never know. The significance of the case lies in what it tells us about attitudes to marriage and adultery at a critical turning point. The liberalization of the marriage laws created a minor social revolution – the revolution of rising expectations. The novels of the period dwelled on extramarital love, adultery, divorce and bigamy – and their terrible consequences.

It is no coincidence that Mrs Henry Wood's *East Lynne*, the harrowing tragedy of a woman who lost husband, home and children for one tiny lapse from marital fidelity, was a mega-bestseller. An obsession with divorce lit and bigamy lit implies dissatisfaction with the status quo. Female spectators at the Maybrick trial or those avidly following the case in the press derived the same vicarious fulfilment as they did from fiction. The accused had done what many of these women in their most secret thoughts had hardly dared imagine. Metaphorically at least, Florie had risen up and slain the monster who had betrayed her.

INTERLUDE

Wedding customs

In September 1873 Laura Troubridge attended the wedding of Lady Audrey Townsend of Raynham, Norfolk, and the Honourable Greville Howard, second son of the Earl of Suffolk:

> Lady Audrey wore a white satin gown, trimmed with Brussels lace, and a Brussels lace veil fastened with diamond stars, a diamond necklace and earrings, orange blossom in her hair, and a very large bouquet. She trembled dreadfully as she came up the aisle on Lord Bute's arm, followed by her eight bridesmaids. I did pity her so – she did look so *agitee*. Everybody, of course, was staring at her. Save me from ever having a grand wedding! The ceremony was very impressive. Soon after the service we walked up to the house and went into the salon, but there was such a crush there that we could not stay. The breakfast, which was in the large hall, was very good indeed.
>
> Lord Bute proposed the health of the bride and bridegroom and Mr Howard returned thanks, but they neither of them made speeches. For going away Lady Audrey had on a dark blue velvet gown with a very long train. They drove off in a regular shower of flowers and old satin slippers (one of which went straight into the bridegroom's hat as he was taking it off to bow). Everybody then said good-bye and drove off, and so ended the much longed for wedding day.

The marriage ceremony is a drama in which the bride, conspicuously dressed, passes from one kin group to the other. The bridegroom, who will remain the same, can be himself and is inconspicuous in his clothing. The transfer of the bride and the new alliance are symbolized by ceremonial and gifts.

The old practice of placing gold coins on the prayer book of the officiating priest, symbolic of dower, had died out by the late seventeenth century – as had the tradition of splitting an old coin in two and giving half to one's beloved, for the two halves to be reunited on the wedding day. Enormous importance was attributed to such tokens in the past, as becomes clear in the many cases of disputed contracts which came before the ecclesiastical courts, when the giving of a ring or an old coin was held as evidence of a promise to marry.

We must assume that the church bells rang at Raynham after Lady Audrey's wedding, to scare off evil spirits.

The 'traditional' white wedding was a Victorian invention, reflecting their obsession with everything old and 'truly' English. The majority of brides through the centuries married in their best dresses, which could be any colour and often did service for many years. In the Victorian era a white wedding dress indicated that the bride came from a certain class, rich enough to afford a one-day-only dress. It was also no accident that in a patriarchal society she should be 'given away' by her father in virginal white. To be married in white soon became the ambition of every girl, irrespective of wealth and class, but it was not until the 1950s, a boom time for marriage, that the big white wedding became universal.

From the earliest period until the seventeenth century it was the custom for a bride to be married with her long hair worn loose, a recognized symbol of virginity. The fact that bridal veils occasionally came to be worn in the seventeenth century may indicate that they were a substitute for the hair worn loose. Like the hair, the veil sometimes touched her feet. It was not until the nineteenth century that the fashion for wedding veils began in earnest, however; up until then the bride was just as likely to wear a hat rather than a veil, or a hat with a veil.

Lace was often a treasured family heirloom. Royal brides wore English lace from Honiton in Devon; among the nobility Brussels and Venetian lace was popular. English brides traditionally wore roses or wild flowers in their hair, making June a particularly popular month for a wedding, but around the 1830s the French custom of wearing orange blossom was adopted. Traditionally rosemary dipped in scented water was carried by the wedding guests, while the bridal path was strewn with rushes, herbs and flowers. At today's weddings the flowers are an important feature.

Favours such as coloured ribbons – the colour chosen by the bride – or gloves, scarves or garters, would be distributed to the guests and worn for many weeks. Today, favours take the form of a carnation or rose worn in the buttonhole of the bridegroom, best man and ushers, and sometimes of little tokens at the guests' place settings.

Until 1885 noon was the latest time for a wedding service, so that the reception that followed was the wedding breakfast – a sort of brunch. Bride cakes, which in the past had been broken over the heads of the newly married couple, were replaced by wheat and then by rice from India and eventually by confetti, symbolic of abundance – prosperity – and fertility.

In Aphra Behn's *Ten Pleasures of Marriage* in the seventeenth century we see the newly married couple embarking on a series of visits to announce their new status: 'all the world must see what a pretty couple they are, and how handsomely they agree together.' By the nineteenth century the 'wedding tour' had become 'the honeymoon'.

The slipper or old shoe thrown at the departing bridal pair represented the renunciation of authority over the bride by her father, and this was transferred to the bridegroom on receipt of the shoe. Throwing a shoe – preferably the left one – was also a lucky omen for travellers. In the seventeenth century stocking throwing was more prevalent than shoe throwing and symbolized good luck. The rather more reserved Victorians did not revive the boisterous practice of wresting the bride's silk garters from her.

Lady Audrey was wearing diamonds at her wedding and we must assume she had a diamond engagement ring. Diamond engagement rings made their first appearance 500 years ago when Emperor Maximilian of Austria was betrothed to Mary of Burgundy, but until the nineteenth century only royalty and the very rich could afford them. The brilliant-cut solitaire began to gain popularity and became a classic ring in the 1890s. Wedding rings date back to the thirteenth century and possibly earlier. The Romans and the Jews had used a ring to seal a bargain. A plain gold wedding band was highly symbolic: pure as gold and circular, that is, endless.

A bride must have her trousseau – a complete wardrobe of clothes that she brought to her marriage. Traditionally she sewed the under-clothes and nightclothes herself, but of course the affluent Victorians spared no expense on the trousseau, not least perhaps because it was laid out for inspection before the wedding. A wife's clothes must reflect her husband's status – a status she acquired on marriage; she must never include in her trousseau any item of clothing she would not be able to replace once married – in other words, her trousseau had to reflect her husband's means.

Women's magazines at the turn of the century were full of advice on the trousseau. In the 1930s *Bride's Book* warned: 'If men have one aversion that is fully and invariably justifiable, it is for the sight of a woman clad in pyjamas. Some women are misguided enough to wear pyjamas even on a honeymoon!'

26

'Coverture is dead and buried'

ONE SUNDAY IN July 1889 the parishioners of Clitheroe in
Lancashire were just emerging from church when a man
rushed up to two women, seized one of them, and unceremoniously
bundled her into a waiting coach. It hurtled away in the direction of
Blackburn. The next glimpse we have of the woman is of a rather
woebegone figure standing at a closed upper-floor window of a
private house trying to gesticulate to someone loitering in the street
outside.

The woman was Emily Jackson and she was the prisoner of her
husband, one Edmund Jackson of Blackburn. They had been married
on 5 November 1887 when Emily was forty-two years old. There
was something a little odd about the marriage because Emily deemed
it necessary to sneak out of the house in the morning without informing or consulting her sister that she was going to get married. How
had she met Mr Jackson; why did the family disapprove of him? The
court records do not tell us. It becomes apparent from the evidence
that Emily's family tended to dominate and make decisions for her.
Perhaps she was a little simple. She seems also to have been in a better
financial position than Mr Jackson, so perhaps the family considered
she was marrying beneath her.

On the evening of the marriage Mr Jackson brought her back
to the house she shared with her sister and returned to Blackburn.
The next day he went to London and on 10 November he sailed for
New Zealand. The couple kept up a correspondence for a time, with
Emily asking him to come home, but eventually they quarrelled and,
according to her sister, Emily wrote to tell him that she would not
live with him when he returned to England. It does sound as if Emily
was acceding to her sister's wish in this.

In July 1888 Mr Jackson returned and, true to her word, Emily refused to have anything to do with him. He began proceedings for the restitution of conjugal rights. This action had been part of canon law, but was transferred from the ecclesiastical courts to the Divorce Court by the Act of 1857; it was not abolished until 1970. The suit was intended to enforce compliance with the marital duty of cohabitation, in the same house if not in the same bed. Under the old canon law, the sanction for refusing to obey the order was 'admonition' – a mild form of ecclesiastical censure. The penalty for non-compliance in the Divorce Court was 'attachment' – imprisonment until the guilty party agreed to obey the court order. Non-compliance would be taken as an act of desertion, allowing the injured party to apply for a separation order immediately, rather than waiting two years. The deserter would be deemed the guilty party and would suffer pecuniary loss, and, if she was a woman with children, she was likely to forfeit custody.

In July 1889 Jackson was granted the decree for the restitution of conjugal rights, but Emily refused to obey it. He now took the law into his own hands, as it were, by seizing Emily as she came out of church and confining her in his house in Blackburn, placing his sister in charge of her. Emily's sisters started picketing the house, standing for hours in the street outside or keeping watch from the house opposite. As one of them told the court, 'I saw my sister at a window, and she seemed in great distress, and begged me to get her out and take her home.' She had tried to speak to her several times through the glass. On each occasion she said she was detained against her will and she was frequently in tears.

The house appears to have been in a state of siege. When Jackson emerged one day 'several men were let into the house to garrison it.' The sisters observed 'one young man let down by cords from one of the windows, and necessaries for the use of the inmates drawn up by cords through one of the upper windows.'

The sisters called on Dr Martin of Blackburn and asked Jackson if he could see Emily, but permission was refused. According to his later testimony, his own doctor was already attending his wife, who had suffered several bouts of rheumatic fever in the past and nearly died of severe inflammation of the heart, so that her heart was probably 'delicate'. Her sister told the court that Emily begged her to get her solicitor, Mr Weeks, 'to take proceedings to have her set at liberty', but it is more likely the sisters who took the initiative. Naturally Emily was unable to supply an affidavit, since she was under restraint, but the sisters readily did so.

Mr Weeks went to Jackson's house to try to gain access to his client. 'She was at an upstairs window, which was shut, and she beckoned me to her in an appealing manner,' he told the court. He was refused entry and 'someone in the room, seeing her motion to me, removed her from the window and drew down the blind.'

Jackson put his own solicitor, Mr Sanderson, on the case and he forwarded Jackson's terms:

> That Mrs Jackson's relatives and their agents withdraw from Blackburn, and so leave her absolutely free, in the sense of not being subjected to any influence which their presence may have over her. Her relatives and friends to be at liberty to communicate with her by letter on the understanding that they write nothing to her which may tend to weaken the influence of her husband. Mr Jackson will, of course, treat his wife with that kindness and consideration which every lady in her position has a right to expect from her husband, and he will also undertake not to remove himself or his wife outside the jurisdiction of the English courts . . . it is the wish of Mr Jackson that his wife should have the greatest happiness possible.

Weeks replied that the decision was Mrs Jackson's alone. Her sisters had no desire to influence her in any way, but 'wish her freely to make choice of that course which she considers will most conduce to her future happiness and well-being'. Of course they had no right to interfere, but 'as long as Mrs Jackson is forcibly imprisoned and detained by her husband against her will (as she informs her sister) . . . they would be wanting in natural affection if they deserted her.'

Emily's solicitor maintained that her 'seizure and forcible detention by her husband' were 'without justification in law' and accordingly her sisters applied to the Court of Queen's Bench to have her released on habeas corpus. No English subject may be forcibly detained by another. But did this apply to wives?

As Lord Mansfield expressed it in the late eighteenth century: 'The husband has in consequence of his marriage a right to the custody of his wife, and whoever detains her from him violates that right, and he has a right to seize her wherever he can find her.' Certainly no one else had a right to hold her, but did he? And, if so, were there any mitigating circumstances?

As recently as 1876 Mr Justice Coleridge had decided Cochrane's case in favour of a husband's right of forcible detention. 'There can be no doubt of the general dominion which the law of England attributes to the husband over the wife,' he said. However, 'the courts will interpose their protection whenever the husband attempts to abuse the marital power for any improper purpose, or by any wanton or excessive exercise of it.'

Husband and wife were one person in law and, as the weaker party, the wife was under her husband's coverture. Just as if she were a child or somehow incompetent, he could lay a restraint on her to preserve her honour and estate. He had a right to her body, but just what was the permissible extent of his control? The Jackson case would decide once and for all that the forcible seizure and detaining of a wife against her will was under all circumstances illegal. It was a major departure.

In their first application, Emily's family were unexpectedly rebuffed. Mr Justice Cave did not seem to think habeas corpus applied at all, suggesting that 'if she is ill treated she has a remedy by resort to a magistrate.' How could she do that, counsel argued, when she 'is kept under lock and key and she cannot even consult her solicitor?' The woman was in a most abject state. 'All that is asked in her behalf is that she shall be brought before this court that the court may determine whether she is entitled to be restored to her personal liberty.'

After all, there were plenty of precedents in which the writ had been granted 'when asked on behalf of women *illegally* confined by their husbands'. There was the case of Lady Strathmore, and what about the wife of Earl Ferrers in 1757? Cave objected that 'there was ill-usage in that case.' Certainly, but the ground on which the writ was granted was 'illegal confinement'. Earl Ferrers had forced his wife to say in the affidavit that she was 'content to remain with her husband', but the court still granted the writ because Lord Mansfield decided that 'the circumstances of the case, where delay may be dangerous, require it.' Countess Ferrers duly appeared before the court and, once out of his clutches, swore the peace against her husband.

Mr Justice Cave's next objection was that in the Jackson case the husband had already obtained a decree for restitution of conjugal rights, and the court would not have granted him that if there was any doubt about his probity. Maybe, counsel argued, but the Matrimonial Causes Act of 1884 enacted that such 'a decree for restitution of conjugal rights shall not be enforced by attachment' – that is, by arrest and imprisonment for disobedience to the decree. It was 'barbarous and monstrous to attempt to coerce a married woman to live with her husband by physical force and imprisonment'.

'All the authorities show that wherever the power of the husband has been *abused* the court will grant the writ to the wife,' counsel persisted. Surely such close confinement is an abuse of a husband's authority, especially since Emily's health was delicate and would suffer through lack of exercise, so that her very life could be endangered by continuing confinement.

Cave retaliated that it was no wonder that Jackson had had to resort to these extreme measures, since his wife's sisters were stalking the house in anticipation of her escape. It was clear from the affidavits that her sisters, 'annoyed because she had married him without consulting them', had influenced Emily against her husband. He had been well within his rights as a husband to take possession of her. The subsequent conduct of her sisters had been most unwise. 'Instead of having recourse to legal means or giving him the opportunity of trying to regain his wife's affections, they appear to have "picketed" the house to such an extent that he thought it desirable to have persons keep guard over her, and prevent her from being removed by force.'

He had seldom encountered 'more injudicious and unwarranted proceedings on the part of the wife's relatives'. It was they who were at fault, not the husband. 'They have never tried the experiment of leaving them alone for the purpose of enabling them to settle their differences and agree to live together as a husband and wife should do.' If Emily Jackson thought that the court would remove her from her husband's custody 'upon no ground whatsoever except that she does not like to live with him', she was very wrong indeed.

The application was refused since in Mr Justice Cave's opinion it failed to show there was anything illegal in the custody. Mr Justice Jeune, also presiding, concurred, stating the traditional view that marriage created a unique relationship giving the husband authority over his wife: 'It is necessary on such an application to show the detention is illegal; and though generally the forcible detention of a subject by another is *prima facie* illegal, yet where the relation is that of husband and wife the detention is not illegal.'

Emily's family immediately took it to appeal, where the decision was reversed.

The Clitheroe case, as it was labelled, was a sensation, but not everyone rejoiced at the outcome. The emancipated anti-feminist writer Eliza Lynn Linton protested indignantly, 'Marriage, as hitherto understood in England, was suddenly abolished one fine morning last month!' It had become 'a voluntary union during pleasure!' Women would now leave their marriages on a mere caprice. The Clitheroe case rested on nothing more substantial than Emily Jackson's 'I have changed my mind.' The Court of Appeal had a lot to answer for. The family would be destroyed 'by the virtual abolition of marriage' and then what hope was there for society itself.

The leading feminist Elizabeth Wolstenholme Elmy, on the other hand, was delighted. 'Coverture is dead and buried . . . it is the grandest victory the woman's cause has ever yet gained, greater even than the passing of the Married Women's Property Act.'

She exaggerated, since the decision of the Court of Appeal simply held that a writ of habeas corpus could not be issued against a wife who had of her own free will left her husband. But if a wife had the right to bodily autonomy, as the decision in Regina v. Jackson seemed to confirm, she argued, did that not also imply that she had the right to refuse her husband sexual intercourse? 'The wife submits to her husband's embraces, because at the time of marriage she gave him irrevocable right to her person . . . consent is immaterial,' Mr Justice Hawkins had pontificated in 1889. Why should a woman suffer 'enforced maternity'? she persisted.

No one in Parliament was prepared to discuss it. Failing the vote, the alternative was to give married women greater knowledge about sexuality and contraception, in both of which they were still woefully ignorant.

27

'The whole thing is so mysterious to me — how you could ever have found pleasure in what you knew I hated'

I N THE LATE summer of 1897 a pair of English honeymooners were to be seen on a beach in Holland sitting in bath chairs determinedly facing opposite directions. Hers faced the sea, which she loved; his, the land. Their unease in each other's company was down to what she later described as the difficulty of 'our married relations'. They loved each other and at the outset of the marriage she admitted to 'wanting you physically as much as you wanted me, every bit', yet something had gone badly wrong. She did not reproach him, she assured him, 'for what happened after because you were just selfish and I was silly too'. Yet for her the honeymoon had been 'a nightmare of physical pain and discomfort and you never left me alone'. Not only was she in pain, but she was tired. 'We tramped about all day sight-seeing when I ought to have rested and at night I lay beside you crying with pain, weariness and disappointment.' Years later, he begged her to 'try and forget the honeymoon . . . and remember I had anxieties and disappointments too', but she never could.

The marriage survived and produced five children, but Lady Emily Lutyens never reconciled herself to sex. Like other Victorian girls of her class, she had been brought up to be sexually innocent, if only because the 'perfect lady' was supposed to be sexually passive. That was as it should be, one eminent Victorian doctor declared, because

> the majority of women (happily for them) are not very much troubled with sexual feeling of any kind. What men are habitually, women are only exceptionally . . . The best mothers, wives, and managers of households, know little or nothing of sexual indulgences. Love of home, children, and domestic duties are the only passions they feel.

As a general rule, a modest woman seldom desires any sexual gratification for herself. She submits to her husband, but only to please him; and, but for the desire of maternity, would far rather be relieved from his attentions.

From the moment Lady Emily met the young architect Edwin Lutyens at the house of a mutual acquaintance in September 1896 they were the best of friends. He was not at all like the young men she so despised in her social circle. He was unconventional, creative and *fun*. Within a month of their first meeting he was writing to tell her that he loved her. 'Except my love I have nothing to offer you. I am poor, unknown, and little altogether.' But he offered her his life's work. 'All that I have is at your feet.' One word from her would turn his 'world to one great sphere of happiness'. He only wanted the chance to prove it.

Lady Emily's response was more cautious. 'My mind is too uncertain for me to say more one way or another, and I can only ask you to wait and give me time to think it over.' She assured him that she would always take an interest in his work. 'No one will be more pleased than I am to hear that you are getting on and making a name for yourself, as I am quite sure you will in time.' Far from rejecting his love, she invited him to visit for 'a day or two and we will talk about it'.

When Lady Lytton heard about Emily's suitor she was far from happy. For her daughter to marry an obscure young architect with no money was not part of her plan. Neither of them would have any money.

The Lytton fortunes had been in decline since the heyday of Lady Emily's grandfather, Edward Bulwer Lytton, later Lord Lytton. Since Lytton had married without his mother's consent, she had disinherited him, so he had turned to writing and become a hugely successful novelist. He was restored to maternal favour and inherited Knebworth. His early passion for his wife, the Irish beauty Rosina Wheeler, had soon turned to acrimony and recrimination when she caught him in an affair. Hell knew no fury like Rosina scorned. Everyone sympathized with her plight, but she was becoming a notorious embarrassment and no woman, it was felt, should speak publicly against her husband.

In the summer of 1858, when Lytton was running for Parliament, she climbed up on the platform to tell the Hertford electorate the truth about 'Sir Liar': his miserly treatment of her and the children, his adultery, and the rest, while distributing copies of her pamphlet, *Lady Bulwer Lytton's Appeal to the Justice and Charity of the English Public*, which elaborated on her grievances. The crowd loved it, cheering her and hissing him. Lytton was so angry that he obtained the signatures of two doctors and had her committed to a lunatic asylum, but there was a public outcry and he had to have her released after only three weeks.

Their son Robert, Emily's father, had inherited Knebworth and the baronetcy, later becoming 1st Earl of Lytton, and served as Viceroy of India and ambassador in Paris, but he died in 1891 when Emily was only thirteen. Knebworth was let and Lady Lytton and her three daughters moved in to a smaller property, the Danes, in Hertfordshire.

It was from here in October 1896 that Lady Emily wrote sadly to Edwin Lutyens telling him that her mother 'would rather we did not meet, or write or see each other again'. Of course it all came down to money. 'You probably do not know that I have no money of my own, and you tell me that you have nothing but love to offer.' Obviously, 'under these circumstances you will feel yourself that it is hopeless to consider the matter any further.' She hoped he did not think too badly of her and wished him all the best, promising to watch his career with interest.

Fortunately, Emily's married sister Betty Balfour worked hard to persuade Lady Lytton to relent towards the young couple. The family laid down stringent financial conditions: Lutyens was to take out a life insurance of £10,000 for Lady Emily, which would demand a hefty annual premium. It was a large undertaking which would mean that he could never let up his hard work, but he did not complain. As soon as her uncle was satisfied that Lutyens had agreed these terms, Lady Lytton gave her consent to the marriage.

Emily and Edwin could now write to each other as an engaged couple, although they barely knew each other. 'Oh Ned my darling! It is too wonderful to be true and I feel like a person in a dream,' she wrote. 'Oh Emy it's splendid. I may call you by name mayn't I?' Since they must always be accompanied by a chaperone – as Edwin described it, 'the stern fortress walls of Chateau chaperone' – they would not really begin to know each other properly until after the wedding.

Emily confessed how wretched she had been at the thought of losing him, 'because I loved you so – and I wanted your love more than anything in the world'. She was sure he would one day 'be a great and wonderful man, whom everyone would kneel to, and admire and praise', but had feared that by then 'you would have found someone else to love, and would have forgotten me, and another woman would have the right I longed for to be proud in your greatness and success.'

She might have been a little disconcerted to receive letters from him outlining his budgeting proposals for when they set up home together and, indeed, Lady Emily had little idea what anything cost and would be an indifferent household manager. 'I did sort of estimates yesterday for linen and kitchen things. Thought about £55 would do us in pots and pans, sheets and towels, dusters, napkins, etc. But I know nothing of quantity required or prices so it may be all wrong,' she explained with aristocratic vagueness for such mundane practicalities. Had she been a middle-class pupil in one of the many schools established for the education of girls during the Victorian period, she would have been given afternoons off school in order to learn household management. Nor was she ever to share Edwin's exacting standards of artistic perfection in his surroundings.

They were married on 4 August 1897 at St Mary's Church in the park of Knebworth House. After the honeymoon they returned to 29 Bloomsbury Square, a rented house they both loved and which would serve as the base for Edwin's architectural practice as well as their home. His meteoric success as a fashionable architect was attributed by some envious observers to his wife's social credentials rather than his genius, but Lady Emily had always steered clear of society. She was his confidante and adviser behind the scenes, but never overtly sought commissions for him. Years later she told him, 'If I don't help you by society touting and planning it is really because I know it is unworthy of us both, and you know it too in your real moments, and you would not really love me if I was the kind of wife you sometimes imagine I ought to be.'

Perhaps the fact that they spent so much time apart helped preserve the marriage. His work took him away from home frequently and for long periods and every summer she spent two months alone with the children on the Norfolk coast. When they were together, the problem with sex persisted. A year after the honeymoon he wrote to apologize for being 'brutal'. 'I hated to think of coming near you – it seems so cruel, only my angel when with you I can't help it.' But he did not want to hurt her. 'We are just one body Emy and Ned, and the health of neither is right unless both are well. D'you see?' It did not affect his love for her and his total commitment. 'The one great radiant spot is our love,' he assured her. But she could not help communicating her distaste of the sexual act to him. A decade later he was admitting, 'our rare encounters find my body self rampant, aggressive, horrid.'

After the birth of her fifth and last child in 1908 she sought an alternative outlet for her energies. Hitherto, the only permissible activity for upper- and middle-class married women outside the home had been charity work, but Lady Emily joined the struggle for women's suffrage by becoming an active member of the Women's Social and Political Union, alongside her sister, Lady Constance Lytton. As Mrs Pankhurst's militant wing stepped up the violence, however, she left to embrace a weird religious cult, the Theosophical Society, which drew heavily from Buddhism and Hinduism.

Unlike many husbands, Edwin tolerated all this and she was grateful to him. 'I know that we were made for each other even tho' we have such different tastes,' she wrote to him in 1911. 'I love you more than I can ever express, and tho' I fear you are worried at times at my oddities, you are really responsible for them, because it is your fostering love and care that have helped me to develop my nature in its own way.'

He worried that she was moving in a different direction to him, that one day she would pass him by. 'You are quite wrong in thinking that I am leaving you behind,' she wrote, 'I am only beginning very very slowly to grow up to you.' She wanted him to understand how much she loved him, 'only you will count by kisses, and lip kisses especially, and I can't pay in those coins. I can't even kiss my little baby on her lips, it is a horror to me.' All she wanted to do was to hold his hand and lean her head on his arm. Any closer physical contact was bound to lead to the Other: 'I should like so much better if it was just natural and occasional as it should be at our age, and not the intruding presence every time I hug you.'

Much as she dreaded sex, Lady Emily reminded Edwin that 'I have never refused you except when I was having babies. If I could not respond to your feelings at least I have let you come to me quite as often as any husband has a right to ask.' She loathed his pipe smoking and 'all I ask is . . . don't take your pipe out of your mouth and then ask me to kiss you, and wonder that I say no.' As for her interest in Theosophy, she knew he did not share it, but since she did not insist on his accompanying her to Theosophical meetings, he should not insist 'on my paying visits or going to dinner parties where I am hopelessly out of place'.

At the Durbar in 1911 George V had announced the plan to move the capital of India from Calcutta to Delhi. Lutyens was chosen to provide the Raj with a fitting seat of government. He was to be engaged in the task for the next twenty years, involving long spells away from home.

In September 1914 he received a letter from Emily severing their physical relationship once and for all. 'I have suffered intensely physically during all my married life,' she confessed. 'There were compensations when I wanted the children and had them. But now we are both entering upon middle age. I have done my duty to you and my country as regards children and I could never face another. With that incentive gone your coming to me has been increasingly difficult to bear.'

Once, there had been no question that a woman's body was her husband's to do what he liked with, but from the late 1880s there was a growing feeling among women that the present marriage system was nothing but a form of legalized prostitution, involving non-consensual sex and undesired childbearing. As the New Woman novelist George Egerton wrote in *Virgin Soil*, 'as long as marriage is based on unequal terms, as long as man demands from a wife as a right, what he must sue from a mistress as a favour . . . marriage becomes for many women a legal prostitution, a nightly degradation, a hateful yoke under which they age, mere bearers of children conceived in a sense of duty . . . until their love, granted they started with that . . . is turned into a duty they submit to with distaste.'

Reflecting this new thinking, Lady Emily wrote: 'I believe and hold firmly that a woman has the right over her own body. Where she gives it willingly the relationship is beautiful – where she gives it because she must it becomes prostitution whether in or out of marriage and is a degradation.'

She went on to tell him that he must decide what he wanted to do 'as regards sleeping arrangements'. Single beds for married couples were a relative novelty. 'I am sure a double bed will cause you constant torment and now is the moment when we could have single beds in a natural way.' She begged him not to be too miserable about it, adding tactlessly, 'The whole thing is so mysterious to me – how you could ever have found pleasure in what you knew I hated.'

Lutyens was devastated. She had 'put a pistol' at his head, and although he would accede to her wish because he loved her, 'the day may come when all I hold true may turn to dishonour and shame.' He had only ever been in love with Emily – 'which is dull of me I own and very boring' – and he had never been unfaithful. A wave of loneliness overwhelmed him and he dreaded returning to India.

He formed friendships with other women – mainly the socialites whose dinners and parties he attended – and a special relationship with Lady Sackville, who shared his passion for buildings, but nothing and no one could replace his love for Emily. 'I do not give you much comfort or happiness so if at any time you feel it would make you happier to bring another woman into your life I shall never reproach you or feel you have wronged me,' she wrote in 1924. 'If you can love another woman and be happy I shall only give you my blessing.' 'How could I afford it?' he replied jokingly. No, it would not do to ruin another life.

After 1930 the Lutyens did spend more time together. Lady Emily had become disillusioned with Theosophy. She realized, too, how her obsession with it had 'separated me from a very wonderful love'. Only Edwin's tolerance and forbearing had prevented their marriage falling apart. 'I now turned to him and found shelter and comfort in him as in no one else. He seemed to understand without words all that I was going through and welcomed me back without a single reproach or reminder of how much of our lives together I had wasted.' In their last years, she wrote: 'I like to think we were closer to each other than we had ever been before.'

INTERLUDE

Job Flower, *A Golden Guide to Matrimony*

In 1882 Job Flower's *A Golden Guide to Matrimony* advised a young man seeking a wife to 'mind where you pick her up' and 'select the daughter of a good mother'. As for the mutual duties of married life, he recommended:

1. Do not expect too much.
2. Continue courting.
3. Moderate your expectations.
4. Be prepared to be disappointed in each other.
5. Bear and forbear.
6. Be willing to make mutual concessions.
7. Try to hide one another's faults.
8. Study to adapt yourselves to one another.
9. Be mutually respectful.
10. Be ready to exercise self-denial.
11. Confide in each other.
12. Row together in the same boat.
13. Resolve to live within your means.
14. Seek the improvement of one another.
15. Have a family altar of your own.

Special duties of a husband:

1. To provide for the support of your wife.
2. Make your home your castle.
3. Prefer your wife's company to all others.
4. Love your wife sincerely.
5. Love your wife ardently.
6. Love your wife supremely.

7. Treat her with sincere respect.
8. Make yourself useful.
9. Remember that she is the weaker vessel.
10. Insure your life.

Special duties of a wife:

1. Learn to submit.
2. Strive to make home happy.
3. Set out with good intentions.
4. Be a keeper at home.
5. Preserve your health.
6. Dress neatly and not extravagantly.
7. Let your husband see that you desire to make home happy.
8. Study your husband's habits.
9. Study your husband's wants.
10. Study your husband's temper.
11. Don't talk about your husband's failings abroad.

Finally, remember Goethe's words: 'A wife is a gift bestowed upon a man to reconcile him to the loss of Paradise.'

28

'I shall be a better happier man and more useful soldier for being your husband'

IN THE EARLY days of the new century, January 1901, Francis Edward Bradshaw Isherwood took up a long-delayed challenge. After several false beginnings and a series of screwed-up paper missiles had been hurled to the far corners of the room, he began the fair copy: 'Dear Mr Machell Smith, I have for some time been wishing to write to you on the subject of my relations with your daughter, and as she tells me that you have spoken to her on the subject I feel that I ought to lay my position before you . . .'

Everything hinged on his financial prospects and he plunged on bravely. He had joined the York and Lancaster Regiment in 1892 and was now a lieutenant. He intended to apply for the Stockport Volunteer adjutancy, for which the pay and allowances amounted to about £300 a year. There would be a definite advantage in living near his parents at Marple Hall, Cheshire, and the chances were that they would offer him and his wife a home on the estate. He was the second son of the family, but 'my father allows me a hundred and fifty' a year. After being invalided home for a short time, he was about to return to South Africa, where the Boer War still raged, but in the meantime he would be very grateful if Mr Machell Smith would allow him a brief interview to discuss his plans in person.

It was a reasonable proposal from a gentle, kindly and even gallant young man who was devoted to the lady in question, but it met with a resounding rebuff:

> It is about eighteen months since you proposed to my daughter and I think it is now rather late in time to begin to talk of ways and means. Had you considered these beforehand you might possibly have considered yr position not sufficiently promising to think of marriage. You must remember that until now, except from hearsay of others,

the amount of yr income has not been mentioned to me, and when I spoke to you before you left England I expressed plainly to you my opinion that under yr circumstances you ought not to have proposed. You then told me there was no engagement between you and that nothing further would take place without informing me. I know you have not acted up to this promise as I find you have given my daughter a ring which is generally considered to indicate an understanding of an engagement. You have taken frequent opportunities of meeting and you write as if everything was arranged except what to live on.

There was no question of meeting to discuss the matter further. What was there to discuss? 'I certainly do not approve of the prospects you offer.' It was ludicrous even to think of marrying on an income of less than £600 a year and even then how would they manage in the case of illness or if they had a family? He was behaving as if 'what you are to live on is quite a secondary consideration'. He, Frederick Machell Smith, who had made his money in the cut and thrust of the wine business, had been around long enough to know the folly of such ideas. And he didn't think it was fair to his daughter to endeavour to gain her affection without having some reasonable income to offer. Of course, Kathleen was over thirty and was at liberty to do as she liked, but if she persisted with this mad scheme she could expect no help from him.

Perhaps her mother Emily would be more approachable, Frank Isherwood ventured when writing to Kathleen to report her father's response. If Frank, the landowner's son who had enjoyed a relatively sheltered existence, was a little vague about money, he was by no means a man to make rash and impetuous decisions and he urged Kathleen to think very carefully about the next step. 'You must make up your mind, if your father refuses to consent to our marrying, what you will do. I should be very loath indeed to persuade you to anything which would be a trouble to your mother and which could bring any discord between you and her or between her and your father.' He wanted her to think very seriously what marriage to him would mean. Not only would they have to live on a restricted budget, but he would be away a lot. 'I care for you too much my Kitty to want to marry you if it wouldn't make your life happier in every possible way.'

They could hardly be accused of hurrying to the altar. Frank and Kathleen, both in their mid-twenties, had met at the home of friends in the summer of 1895. Kathleen was slender, lively and attractive; her brown hair framed a face with lovely grey eyes that held just a hint of sadness. Frank resembled so many young English officers of the time: of medium height and good build, fair, with blue eyes and a moustache. A series of letters addressed to 'Dear Miss Machell Smith' followed. The friendship developed slowly. They discovered a mutual love of painting and were to enjoy visiting art galleries together. Almost a year after their first meeting Kathleen reported in her diary: 'Mr Isherwood called for me. We looked at his sketches.'

Frank was a sporadic correspondent and when he did write to say how much he would like to see her when he came to London it was with the caveat, 'I am so terribly impecunious!' In 1899 Kathleen was on her way to see friends in Scotland when she stopped off to meet Frank in York. They had not seen each other for over a year, but something between them ignited during this brief meeting. Soon Frank met up with her in Oxford, where she was taking a break with her mother, and they went sketching together. She still referred to him in her diary as 'Mr Isherwood'. In August Emily and Kathleen were staying with friends in Cheshire when they took the opportunity to visit Marple Hall. 'He asked me something unexpected,' Kathleen noted confidentially in her diary. No wonder, then, that on 20 August she 'spent a very reflective day'. The 'something unexpected' was a proposal of marriage, but Kathleen did not give him a definite answer for about three weeks, during a weekend staying at the home of mutual friends in Hexham.

They were in no position to announce it to the world. Frank's lack of money meant that there was, in reality, little chance of them getting married soon. He told her he had been busy 'scheming and devising', but that none of his schemes seemed to bring any promise of wealth.

Kathleen was far closer to her mother Emily than to her father. Emily, only eighteen years her daughter's senior, was a hypochondriac destined to live to a ripe old age. Before Frank came along, it looked as if Kathleen, thirty in 1898, might have to play devoted daughter-nurse to her mother for the rest of her life. Now, however,

Emily espoused the lovers' cause, probably gambling on the fact that she was likely to outlive her husband and Kathleen and Frank would look after her in her old age. Frank's mother, too, was in on the secret. Kathleen wisely went out of her way to secure this inconspicuous but important ally. After Kathleen had lunched with Elizabeth Isherwood in London Frank wrote approvingly: 'You have made quite a conquest of her.'

When Elizabeth invited Kathleen to stay at a hotel with her in order to see Frank off to the Boer War, however, Emily was unexpectedly opposed to the idea.

> It is, I know, very hard for you dear, it appears to me so very compromising – no mother would think of asking a girl to come unless she felt quite sure that the girl was engaged to and in love with her son, not a great friend only. It isn't as if you had been asked to Marple, but to an hotel . . . If you were really deeply in love for the first time, it would be quite different, but you are not and you might regret, oh so deeply, compromising and binding yourself in the hurry of the moment, stirred up to do so because he is going away.

Even if Kathleen did not love Frank, Frank and Elizabeth were under the impression she did, so Emily's attitude is difficult to explain.

Of course, the engagement or 'understanding' between Frank and Kathleen was not a formal one according to the conventions of the time. Frederick maintained that Frank had assured him before leaving for South Africa that there was no engagement and nothing would be done without informing him. This is why he took such a dim view of the situation when Frank wrote to him in January 1901. It was true that Frank had given Kathleen a ring, but it was not an engagement ring as such, more a symbol of private understanding and mutual reassurance. Frank wrote Frederick a grovelling apology, but he was not to be appeased. It was not just the money; Frank had given his word 'as an *officer and a gentleman* that nothing further should take place' without first informing him. '*You did not keep that promise* . . . I told you I thought that a man's word was his bond and I did not consider your bond cancelled by the apology.' Obviously as far as Frederick Machell Smith was concerned Frank was now branded a liar unworthy of Kathleen and nothing he ever did could absolve him.

Kathleen, too, seemed to be having second thoughts, asking Frank if he was absolutely sure. 'Of course the income doesn't sound to *me* so frightfully little but then I'm afraid I haven't had much experience how far money *does* go,' she told him. 'Then you see I'm not robust and strong like some people who could really do a lot of household work and things themselves. Please consider it well, too, because my happiness depends on *yours*.' If her father refused his blessing, she did not see what was to be done, except 'give it up altogether, or wait, and I am ready to wait if you are'.

Frank had at least told his father by this time and he 'rose nobly to the occasion and consented to give us two hundred pounds allowance and Wybbersley Hall to live in'. He was prepared to meet the considerable expense of having the place done up for them. Wybbersley had been the original home of the Bradshaws, of whom the most famous member, Colonel John Bradshaw, had presided at the trial of Charles I. 'I saw three magpies this afternoon which is always supposed to mean a wedding,' Frank continued cheerfully. 'I hope it referred to ours!'

Certainly his family were being very welcoming. On Frank's last evening at Marple before his second departure for South Africa it was Frank, rather than John Isherwood, who escorted Kathleen in to dinner. Normally, Frank would have escorted his mother and Frank's father Kathleen, while the rest of the family followed behind them in pairs. 'I went in with him as it was the last night,' Kathleen noted joyfully. It was a singular mark of recognition.

She continued to worry that she was not cut out for marriage. 'My dearest,' Frank wrote, 'I don't want anything in marriage but you – and a happy you. I have always envied the married people who were comrades, people who shared all their happiness and their work. We unfortunately are not artists, at least not professionally, but we can live in a great many ways as if we were. The last thing I want is to make a Hausfrau of you.' He assured her he was 'the most manageable person in the world' and that 'We shall be quite different to most married couples, and I can't think why you should now suddenly think otherwise.' Of course, if she felt that she did not like him well enough to spend the rest of her life with him, she must say so. She would be giving up a great deal to marry him.

Henry, as the eldest son and heir, would eventually inherit the Marple estate and his father's money, and he had to approve any settlement made for his younger brother. Younger siblings were expected to make their own way in life to keep the family inheritance intact, but some concessions were usually made to help them on their way. Henry initially approved of the proposed marriage between Frank and Kathleen, but he was not a soft touch. To compound their difficulties in reaching a settlement, Frederick Machell Smith now raised the stakes.

He wanted to know how the £200 that was to be settled on Frank and Kathleen would be secured and demanded that if at any time they were not occupying Wybbersley they should receive the equivalent in rent – about £50 a year. Henry Isherwood baulked at this. John wrote to Frederick to confirm that after his lifetime Henry would continue to allow the couple £200 a year and 'continue it in case of Frank's death to his widow and children'. He would also agree to them receiving the rent from Wybbersley, should they not be living there themselves, but only during his lifetime. 'This is all I have power to do, for, as you know, I only have a life interest in this estate.'

Frederick kept pressing the point that the £50 a year rent should be settled on Frank and Kathleen beyond John Isherwood's lifetime. He took the same condescending tone with John Isherwood as he did with Frank, which John thought quite amusing, but which was really very rude. He ended his letter to John: 'I presume that, in the event of your eldest son not marrying, your son Frank is the heir presumptive?'

All this squabbling and haggling was very trying, especially for Kathleen, who focused her frustration on Henry. For once, Frank was angry. 'What you said about my brother was a bit strong! Do you quite realise that my people are doing a great deal to help us to get married, indeed everything in their power. I don't quite understand why you are making such a point about the Wybbersley rent. I rather dislike pressing Henry about it personally. Don't think me unreasonable and cross, but you mustn't say things about my people till you really know them.'

Indeed, Henry, in Frank's view, had already 'done a great deal in allowing my future income to be increased and settled on my widow and children, and when you consider that he looks upon me only as one of his brothers and sisters who may all make like demands upon him, you can understand his hesitating to grant anything or everything I may ask.' The Isherwoods would have been quite justified in turning the tables on Frederick and asking what exactly he was prepared to settle on his daughter. Frank offered the refreshing view that he and Kathleen should do something to help themselves: 'if we want to be married we are the people to pay for it.' He looked enviously on his servant whose banns were to be read in church the following Sunday: 'I suppose he is not bothered with settlements.'

Finally, Henry made a concession. He agreed to Frank and Kathleen, or Kathleen the widow, receiving the Wybbersley rent 'until both your parents' deaths'. Surely Frederick would now be satisfied. 'It seems too good to be true that by next week we may be able to settle everything finally and tell people and begin again with furniture lists and even *fix the day*,' Frank reported with relief. 'You have had a long trying time and I can never thank you enough for sticking to me as you have done through it.'

The Isherwoods' compliance with his demands left Frederick with no place to retreat to. He could have been gracious, reconciling himself to the situation, but never did. In fact, he excluded Kathleen from his will, leaving his money to cousins, and by the time he decided to amend the will again in her favour it was too late. When Frank wrote asking if the engagement could now be officially announced, he replied sullenly that he must do as he pleased, it was really no concern to him for he could never approve or regard it with pleasure.

No sooner was the announcement of the forthcoming marriage made in the *Morning Post*, Kathleen noted wryly, than that very day 'advertisements from various firms began to arrive! Wedding orders solicited, bouquets, trousseaus. News offices offering to send cuttings, shops offering to print wedding cards, etc!' She was immersed in fittings for her wedding gown and her going-away outfit.

'My dear, a month today!' Frank wrote on 12 February 1909 in a letter full of anticipation and pre-wedding nerves. 'We shall have started off on our journey together. I do hope it will be a successful one for you and that we shall get to the end of it all the better for travelling together . . . Can you imagine that a month today it will all be over – the church, and the compliments and the jokes, and we shall really be ourselves again? I can't. I expect you have had some shivers over it.'

'I feel I shall be a better happier man and a more useful soldier for being your husband,' he confessed just prior to the wedding, 'and I hope most earnestly that you will find no reason to regret our joining forces.'

There were none whatsoever. Kathleen and Frank proved entirely compatible. For someone who had dreaded being stifled by marriage and bored by domestic tedium, Kathleen's fears proved unfounded. Frank was away a great deal, so that being with him was a pleasure to be enjoyed rather than a daily habit to be endured. He, too, was getting what he wanted: someone to come home to and to think about lovingly while they were apart. Marriage had given Kathleen a home of her own – she loved Wybbersley – and yet she was free to see Emily as often as she wanted. In August 1904 she had Christopher, the first of two sons. 'Mr Isherwood said I had done my duty and done it well,' she noted in her diary after the christening. 'I quite agreed.' She was now very much part of the family.

At the outbreak of the First World War in August 1914 Frank, who had been serving in Ireland, was sent with his regiment to France. 'I did so appreciate all your kindness. It makes it so different, leaving someone behind who really cares about you,' he wrote on his arrival at the front. 'I am writing in an awful din, so it is rather difficult to express myself.'

He thought wistfully about what they would do when 'the war is over' and hoped that his soldiering days were nearly done. 'Please thank Mama for her delightful parcel,' he wrote, ever appreciative of others' kindness. 'I should very much like to find in the next parcel you send me a tin of unsweetened condensed milk. It is very comforting in the night with a little rum in it, and sardines are rather nice things too. If father chooses to send me a pipe I shouldn't mind, I have only got one now. I am afraid this letter is all about things I want, rather like boys at school. It is very hard to be at school when you are 45, but I hope this is really positively my last go of it.'

With typical English *sangfroid* he played down the danger. 'We have in the last week dug or commenced to dig five different lots of trenches, and are going to dig another tonight. I think we have rather a reputation as diggers and certainly the men are very good,' he reported in November 1914. 'We got it rather hot last Sunday, as we advanced on a village rather prematurely, in fact I lost 60 killed and wounded in my company . . .' But she was not to worry, he urged her, 'I never do anything unnecessary or foolish, and I have got at the back of my mind the determination to get back to see you again.'

On 10 March 1915 he wrote:

> Isn't it twelve years ago today since we were married? We have had some ups and downs, haven't we, but I hope on the whole that you will be able to feel that it has been a happy time. I think you enjoyed the actual day itself a great deal more than I did, but I can never feel thankful enough now nor grateful enough to you for what you have been and are being. I don't think we have spent the day apart before and I hope it will be the last time that we do so. Anyhow I am with you in spirit, but that is nothing unusual. I am afraid I never realised quite what an easy person you were to live with until I had to live so closely with other people, and I shall be thankful when we can sit down together over the fire again in a home of our own. It is not that these people are particularly difficult or anything, but they are not you.

Kathleen noted the anniversary in her diary: 'such a sad and different day, no sun and one's mind full of dread and anxiety over this terrible war.'

Six weeks later he wrote her a quick line with the ominous news that he was being moved hastily in the middle of the night, north, towards Ypres. 'I am always thinking of you and my peaceful home and longing to hear from you again.'

On the night of 7–8 May 1915 Frank and his men were ordered to attack. He never came back and on 12 May Kathleen was informed that he was missing. There were various conflicting reports of him being wounded and rumoured sightings of him, all of which proved unfounded. Kathleen clung to the vague possibility that he might have been taken prisoner, while frantically searching the hospitals that had taken in the wounded who had been repatriated. Eventually, on 24 June the British Red Cross and Order of St John wrote with the chilling news that a disc bearing the inscription 'Isherwood,

F.E.B.Y & L Regiment, Siche 5. C of E' had been found on a dead soldier close to Frezenberg early in May.

'I don't know how the rest of the day passed, except that time seemed to have stood still and there appeared a vista of endless hopeless days of loneliness ahead,' Kathleen wrote in her diary, 'everything reminds me of him, the places we used to go together, our outings and the way he had of making everything nice and all his thousand kind and thoughtful ways . . . one could bear the parting when one had a future but now there seems nothing but the stabs of pain from each happy memory.'

It seems that Frank had been killed some time before midnight on the night of the attack. Like thousands of others, he had no known grave.

On 8 May 1918, the third anniversary of the Second Battle of Ypres, Kathleen had a vivid dream of Frank coming in again at the Marple gates.

Nearly three-quarters of a million British men were killed in the First World War, depriving thousands of women of their husbands and leaving around 2 million surplus women without the prospect of marriage. Kathleen remained Frank's devoted widow for the remaining forty-five years of her life.

29

'An avalanche of broken marriages'

L ATE ONE SATURDAY night in December 1942 in the blackout, tired and dishevelled after a long journey, a young officer stumbled up the steps to a tall London house, feeling for his key. He had carried the key to his front door in his pocket, as a sort of talisman, all through the fighting in the desert. He now put the key in the lock and, with a lump in his throat, opened the door, home at last. He later recalled that he had no thought but to give his wife Natalie a pleasant surprise, and the tiny gifts he had bought her. 'Who's there?' a startled voice called from upstairs. 'I called out who it was, and went up to greet her. She was not alone.'

He was introduced to a young French officer, who immediately gathered his things and beat a hasty retreat. The full significance did not immediately dawn on the home-comer until, left alone with his wife, without bothering with excuses or apologies she abruptly told him that she was going to leave him. Next morning she carried out her promise, taking the first instalment of her belongings. When she returned for the rest a few days later, he begged her to reconsider, to give their marriage a second chance. He was willing to forgive her indiscretions, even her affair with the Frenchman, which he chose to regard as the 'regrettable consequences of our enforced separation', but she would not hear of reconciliation. She wanted him 'to give her a divorce'.

In the twentieth century two world wars profoundly affected the English marriage. Wars tended to begin with a rush of hasty marriages and end with a flood of divorces; they both brought couples together and tore them apart. The Honourable Quintin Hogg's experience was one encountered by thousands of returning servicemen, each time sending the divorce rate soaring and prompting further liberalization of the divorce laws. As a committed Christian believing in the indissolubility of marriage, Hogg did not want a divorce. He could decline to take proceedings at all, leaving their marriage in a sort of limbo, or he could opt for a judicial separation, denying his wife the freedom to marry her lover, but also leaving himself tied to a dead relationship.

If Natalie had not expressed her determination to leave him, there would have been a third option: to accept the wife's adultery and live with it. It was a choice that Quintin Hogg's future political colleague, Harold Macmillan, had taken in 1929 when he realized that his adored wife of ten years, Lady Dorothy, had fallen passionately in love with his friend and political ally, Robert Boothby. Boothby was seen as a potential Prime Minister. He had all the assurance that Macmillan, diffident and affecting an old man's style and mannerisms even then, lacked. In contrast to Macmillan, he was bold, handsome, dashing and stylishly dressed; like Lady Dorothy, he appeared socially at ease wherever he went, although, as with her husband, it was Lady Dorothy, a Cavendish by birth, who opened doors for him and gave him social confidence.

Lady Dorothy seems to have entered on her adulterous affair, which was to last in one form or another until her death in 1966, with true aristocratic insouciance, careless of the hurt she inflicted on others. Harold was utterly devastated and it is perhaps indicative of her ruthlessness in getting what she wanted that Boothby's marriage to her cousin Diana Cavendish was to last only two years.

Proud, private and emotionally reticent, first Macmillan seriously considered divorcing her, but he could not bring himself to do it. He admitted he had never loved any other woman but her. She was too much part of his life. They had children together. He knew he owed everything to her; she had been an asset to his career and was to continue so in the future. It was true that their physical relationship seemed to have ended with the Boothby affair, Lady Dorothy confessing she was faithful only to Boothby. Her daughter Sarah, born in 1930, was suspected to be Boothby's child, although Macmillan brought her up as his own. Physical love was not everything, he believed. In spite of the deep hurt, he chose to stick it out, to find a *modus vivendi*. 'In doing what was difficult, I had my reward in the end,' he later affirmed. Gradually he and his wife reached a new understanding. They were affectionate and devoted and during his premiership his wife's support was to be invaluable. As her nephew Andrew, Duke of Devonshire, later remarked, 'I think their life was one of the greatest arguments against divorce.'

After much serious consideration and on the advice of his father, Viscount Hailsham, and his brother, Quintin Hogg reluctantly decided on the opposite course, opting for the clean break that only a full divorce could offer, leaving him free to form a new, legal and stable relationship in the future. Fortunately, there were no children of the marriage. Natalie obligingly provided the evidence he needed of her adultery and married her Frenchman and in 1944 Hogg made a second marriage that was to be supremely happy and produce five children, so bolstering the argument subsequently advanced by the pro-divorce lobby that the burial of dead marriages facilitated new ones, therefore keeping family life vigorous. Unwilling as he had been to divorce, the experience had a profound effect on him, one that was to influence his thinking on the subject in his later career both as a barrister and as Lord Chancellor, just as Macmillan's repugnance of and pain over his wife's adultery was to affect his tackling of the Profumo affair in 1963.

As the twentieth century dawned, lawyers at least realized that the divorce laws were deeply flawed, full of anomalies, inconsistencies, absurdities and injustices, but there was not much call from the nation at large for a further easing of the laws, at least before the end of the First World War. In 1912 the Majority Report of the Royal Commission on Divorce, based on hundreds of interviews highlighting marital misery and abuse, recommended that there should be equality of access to divorce for men and women, rich and poor, and, even more fundamentally, it advanced the radical notion that divorce was a secular affair, which should be regarded as a mere legal mopping-up exercise after the spiritual death of the marriage. The report was quietly shelved at the outbreak of war, but it set the agenda for a debate that was to last for the next sixty years.

It was only at the end of the First World War that the country realized with alarm the full scale of the increase in marital breakdowns caused by four years of mass mobilization. The divorce rate jumped sixfold between 1913, the last year of peace, and the post-war peak of 1921, before settling back to a figure that still represented a fourfold increase on the pre-war numbers.

During the inter-war years a stigma attached to divorce. This was most forcefully expressed during the abdication crisis of 1936 when the establishment and a large body of the public objected to their king marrying a twice-divorced American. And yet the divorce figures continued to rise, partly as a result of the growing emancipation of women and sexual awareness. In 1918 Marie Stopes's *Married Love* had been eagerly consumed by the troops at the front and the thousands of letters that she received over succeeding years revealed the extent of sexual ignorance in the nation at large. For centuries there had been an ingrained belief that marital sex was intended for procreation rather than pleasure and contraception was evil; now there was a dawning realization that sex within marriage should be enjoyed as a pleasure in itself. Knowledge of and access to contraception was slow to filter down to the working class, but thanks to the pioneering work of Marie Stopes sex manuals for newly married couples were more freely available by the 1930s. As the eminent physician Lord Dawson of Penn expressed it in the Lords, perhaps with some exaggeration, women were now demanding 'a sex-satisfied life' and asking for a divorce if they did not get it.

The recourse to divorce was nudged along by increasingly liberal legislation. In 1923 women – now part of the electorate – were at last given equality of access to divorce on grounds of adultery. By allowing a wife to divorce her husband because of a single act of adultery, Parliament had inadvertently made it easy for those who could afford it to divorce by mutual consent. It invited the farcical process of 'the hotel bill case', by which the husband obligingly provided the wife with evidence of his adultery by hiring a woman for a free weekend at an expensive seaside hotel, so as to be seen in bed with her when the chambermaid brought morning tea. She did not necessarily spend the night in the same bed and nor did sex take place. Detectives lurked, notebook at the ready, while the hotel bill mysteriously found its way into the wife's possession as another piece of evidence.

The ludicrous situation was neatly summed up in the opening sentence of A.P. Herbert's 1934 novel, *Holy Deadlock*: 'So here he was at last, travelling down to Brighton with a strange young woman in a first-class carriage', while in *Handful of Dust* Evelyn Waugh goes on to describe the comic absurdity of such a weekend, when to give his wife Lady Brenda the divorce she seeks, Tony Last finds himself in a Brighton hotel with a woman who insists on bringing her child along.

Rooms had been engaged for Tony by the solicitors in the name of Mr and Mrs Last. No mention had been made of a child, so that the reception clerk was rather taken by surprise and asked if they required a further room for her. Oh no, the woman blithely assured him, her daughter could come in with her. The two detectives lurking nearby exchanged disapproving glances.

Tony, meanwhile, wrote 'Mr and Mrs Last' in the register. 'And daughter,' the clerk insisted. Tony hesitated as if seeking inspiration. 'She's my niece,' he said, registering her as Miss Smith.

Next it was the detectives' turn to register. 'He got out of that all right,' one remarked to the other. 'But I don't like the look of this case. Most irregular. Sets a nasty, respectable note bringing a kid into it. We've got the firm to consider. It doesn't do them any good to get mixed up with the King's Proctor.'

It was the job of the King's Proctor to sniff out cases of collusion, which would prevent the granting of the divorce petition. Lawyers were disgusted at having to take part in these endless charades of collusive divorce. It was all so sordid. When the law was not in accord with public sentiment, Lord Dawson of Penn argued in the Lords, it was always systematically circumvented. It was time to amend the divorce laws accordingly. The backbench MP A.P. Herbert introduced a private member's bill which followed the recommendations of the Majority Report of the Royal Commission of 1912, in particular extending the causes of divorce beyond adultery to cruelty and desertion. His campaign resulted in the Matrimonial Causes Act of 1937, which led to a doubling of divorce petitions between 1937 and 1939, many of them by women seizing the opportunity to petition on grounds of cruelty and desertion.

The Act theoretically put an end to the charade of the hotel bill adultery cases, although the farce of proving adultery continued, as the barrister and novelist John Mortimer knew only too well when he tried similar tactics in the late 1940s, when his first wife, Penelope, had been trying to get divorced in order to marry him. They went 'at ruinous expense' to several Brighton hotels, but when detectives came round to question the staff later, they failed to remember them. They tried even more expensive hotels, and 'did our best, by burning holes in the sheets or screaming during the night' to make an impression on the staff, but totally failed to do so. Finally, they suggested a private detective. 'One afternoon we looked from the windows of the cottage we had then rented and saw a respectable-looking person in a bowler hat walking slowly up the front garden. He introduced himself as Mr Gilpin and we showed him up to our bedroom where he was delighted to find male and female clothing scattered.'

In a similar situation in the early 1950s, when the beautiful actress Valerie Hobson – the future Mrs John Profumo – and the actor Tony Havelock-Allan sought amicably to end their marriage, which had hitherto accommodated his mistress, his attempts to be caught officially with another woman failed miserably: 'The first night he spent in Brighton (with a lady conveniently hired for the purpose) was witnessed by a waiter, but by the time a detective had gone to collect the evidence he had returned to Spain. In an attempt to reprise this performance at Skindles Hotel (this time with a different *fille de joie*) their chambermaid tried to protect the hapless husband by refusing to identify him from the investigator's photographs.'

Just as at the end of the First World War, the end of the Second saw a surge in the marital breakdown figures. In a series of BBC broadcasts subsequently published under the title *Coming Home*, David Mace, Secretary of the National Marriage Guidance Council, which had been founded in 1938 – now renamed Relate – to promote marriage and family life, noted that 'The war has seen a widespread breakdown of fidelity. And the result has been an avalanche of broken marriages.' He warned about the effect this casual infidelity would have on family life, above all, on the children, which are 'the nation's most precious asset'.

Concurrent with marital breakdown was a rise in promiscuity and illegitimacy. By 1945 Mace estimated that one woman in six had abandoned the idea of premarital chastity. No fewer than 100,000 women were becoming pregnant outside marriage every year and one in four of all first babies were conceived before or outside marriage. A woman's needs, he argued, were best served within a stable marital relationship, while sexual fulfilment in marriage was the best guarantor of sexual morality.

'The outlook on the family isn't desperate by any means. But the danger signal *is* showing, and it would be folly to ignore it,' he warned. 'There's a job of work to be done; a vitally important job of work – the rebuilding of family life.'

The number of divorce petitions filed in England and Wales rocketed from about 9,970 in 1938 to 24,857 in 1945 and to a post-war peak of 47,041 in 1947. In addition, there were about 25,000 separation and maintenance orders in 1945–6, a 150 per cent increase over the pre-war level.

Just as at the end of the First World War, two-thirds of these immediate post-war divorces were initiated by husbands who had come home to find their wives had been unfaithful. At least, that was the ostensible reason; the figures could be slightly distorted. For the sake of morale, the Forces' Welfare Services enabled service personnel to obtain divorces cheaper and more expeditiously than civilians, so that it may be that some servicemen were only pretending they were the injured party to enable their spouses to save the full costs of the proceedings. Of course, many of the men, too, had been unfaithful, judging by the fact that during the First World War one in five servicemen contracted VD and by the numbers of condoms issued to the troops in both wars. A man's adultery was harder to prove than a wife's, however, which was more likely to come to the attention of relatives or neighbours or be irrefutable by the fact of a child born during her husband's absence.

A significant number were the result of hasty wartime marriages. David Mace explained to his audience that marriages ought to go through three stages. There was the honeymoon stage, which was carefree and would not last; the stage of mutual adjustment, necessitating a lot of give and take; and the stage of complete mutual understanding, which comes to people who have patiently resolved their differences and grown together out of conflict into harmony. In the war 'lots of couples never got past the honeymoon stage before being separated. Now, reunited, the glamour has faded and there are many difficult adjustments to be made. Many will simply cut their losses and get a divorce.'

With the experience of the post-war marital fall-out of the First World War before them, as the Second World War neared its end the BBC, the national press and the women's magazines swung into action to minimize the trauma of reunion. Servicemen who had retained a rosy picture of the wife and children just as he had left them waiting to welcome him home from the war were warned that the reality would be very different. The unprecedented war on civilians meant that their wives had spent six years under strain: they had had to cope with the terror of the bombing, with rehousing, with separation from their children if they had been evacuated, with shortages and rationing and wartime red tape, and endless queuing. Well over 2 million British women had been deprived of the company and support of their husbands during the Second World War: they had had to keep the home together in their absence, to take full responsibility for the children, and, more often than not, do some sort of war work.

No wonder, then, returning servicemen were shocked at the state of their wives. They looked tired, worn out, and so much older. 'The girl-wife had grown up, and perhaps become "tough" from factory life, while the husband may have acquired more refinement in the Officers' Mess. The housewife and mother, becoming a huntress for food, had given up glamour for a time-saving turban and stout-soled shoes. The charming baby is a boy with hostile eyes, very resentful at first of the much needed firmness of a father.'

Women, too, were targeted with advice. As if they were not tired enough, they were warned to prepare themselves for a reunion with a man whose war service might have left him deeply traumatized. It would take him time to adapt: she must be patient and prepared to compromise. 'There is always something strange and new in the eyes of a man who has come home from the wars,' the Reverend Elliott told women readers in the *Sunday Graphic*. 'Don't expect him to settle down in a month – or less. Don't expect him to look at life as he used to look at life. And don't worry if for a little time he seems disillusioned, even with his home, even with you. It will all come right, believe me, but it will need a lot of mutual adjustment – and a great love and a great patience.'

In the last months of the war the women's magazines were urging their readers to 'be like Caesar's wife, above suspicion'. During the war, with the ever present fear of death, there had been a 'live now' mentality. The temptation, particularly with the arrival of the Americans in 1943, had been to grab fun. Going out to dances, mixing with strangers of the opposite sex, it was all too easy for the lonely wife to become emotionally involved, a wartime marriage counsellor warned, even if her original intentions had been innocent enough. A Mass-Observation report had noted that evacuation and loneliness, as well as increased opportunity, had prompted promiscuous behaviour.

German propaganda about what the wives of British servicemen were getting up to with the Americans while their men were away and lurid statements concerning the morality of servicemen's wives made by judges, social workers and 'the eternal busybody' were criticized by the *Daily Mirror* as being exaggerated and inflammatory. The *Star* agreed: 'The exemplary conduct and courage of women in so many lonely homes fully justify the faith of the great majority of men overseas. Giddy and feather-brained women exist in war as in peace. War-time gives loose wives and loose husbands more opportunities for infidelity.'

But it was not just a question of infidelity. After six years of war husbands and wives who had endured long separations had grown apart. Even if their marriage had not been a hasty wartime affair conducted in the heat of the moment, before they really knew each other, couples found it extremely difficult, and in some cases impossible, to live together again. During the war the thought of the wife waiting at home or of the husband coming home at the end of it all had sustained many: the reality proved a shock and a disappointment. In one sad case, a repatriated prisoner of war, who had been badly wounded and kept alive largely by the thought of returning to his wife one day, told a WVS worker, 'It was as if we were strangers. We sat night after night facing each other across the fire. We seemed to have nothing to say. It was if a wall had grown between us. We couldn't go on like that. We're getting a divorce.'

Some returning servicemen complained that their wives had become 'uppity'. Women had experienced six years of independence and many of them had discovered a resourcefulness they did not know they possessed. Many of them had worked and earned money of their own for the first time. They had undoubtedly expanded their social circle, met people from other classes – as, indeed, had the men in the forces – and made new friends. Now, with the men coming home, they came under intense pressure to give up their jobs and return to their 'true place', in the home. Among the middle classes, it was still considered shameful to have a wife who worked – whatever she had done in the war. Wartime nurseries were closing, giving working mothers no option. It was not just men who were dissatisfied, although, as it turned out, women's retreat to the home was temporary.

Confronted with a wife's adultery, some trigger-happy servicemen took the law into their own hands and there was a spate of shootings. A Camberwell man who came home unexpectedly to find his wife *in flagrante delicto* shot her in the head, shouting, 'If I cannot have you, nobody else shall. You've had it.' Fortunately, she hadn't, she was only wounded and forgave him. The courts were surprisingly lenient in such cases, no doubt prompted by the age-old disapproval of the erring wife.

Not surprisingly with so much marital turmoil, before long there was a huge backlog of divorce cases and the courts were struggling to cope. Very cautiously, the Labour government embraced the idea, first mooted in the Majority Report of 1912, of establishing a series of decentralized divorce courts around the country, at least to hear undefended cases. These comprised the great majority, indicating that collusion was alive and well.

By the time the Denning Report was published in February 1947, acknowledging that the war had placed a severe strain on marriage, there was the additional problem of a desperate housing shortage, making post-war marital adjustment in the age of austerity even more difficult. The report recommended that divorce should be made easier and that marriage guidance and reconciliation services should be put in place around the country: they were to receive a substantial grant from the Home Office. After all, education for marriage was considered a crucial part of education for citizenship. In 1949 the Labour government started making legal aid for divorce proceedings, first introduced in a small way by Lloyd George in 1918, more widely available to the poor, something that would have had the legislators of the 1857 Divorce Act turning in their graves.

Not everyone rushed to the divorce court because the going was tough. One of the most remarkable features of the Second World War, which had disrupted family life on such a vast and dramatic scale, proved to be the social stability of the vast majority of families. Marriages were fractured, but not by any means always irredeemably broken. 'We've had to be tolerant, but in my day you were expected to stick it out,' Marguerite Patten told *Woman's Hour*. A London woman who had lost her home in the bombing recalls the difficulty of post-war adjustment when her husband came home from the war: 'When he came out it was very, very difficult to get to know him again. I think it was a time when we could have easily split up. He came home and no way did I feel I could settle down with him. You had to go all through a sort of courtship again. Four years is a very long time to be apart, but gradually we got together, though things were very, very difficult because we had nothing. Times were very hard.'

It was not only the less well-off people in poor housing conditions who were experiencing post-war trauma. In her memoir of her two marriages, the first to a member of the wealthy Courtauld family, the second to the politician and contender for the Tory leadership Rab Butler, Mollie Butler refers to her first husband's return from the war:

> And yet, behind the joy, I sensed, when the first weeks were over, that August was depressed. He was disillusioned and difficult to live with . . . Many men and women returning after years of great respon- sibility and strain found it difficult to adjust to so-called peace. They had been stretched to their fullest, there was no longer the tension to keep them taut, but relaxation was not yet possible. August was no exception, for life with no particular occupation to return to made him extra vulnerable.

In the 1950s the English marriage seemed to regain some of its former equilibrium. There was a steep rise in marriages and a plunge in the divorce rate, although it was still two and a half times higher than it had been before the war. The social stigma of divorce persisted. In 1955 the establishment lent its full weight against Princess Margaret's wish to marry the love of her life, Peter Townsend, because he was divorced. It would not do for the sister of the Queen, the head of the Church of England, to marry a divorcé, even though a large section of the public probably sympathized with her. Wives were firmly back in the home, for now, with the women's magazines exhorting them to ever greater feats of housewifely excellence. Yet another Royal Commission on Marriage and Divorce, which produced its report in 1956, was at pains to remind women that 'New rights do not release them from the obligations of marriage.'

Or so they thought: everything was about to change drastically. Two new pressures were soon placing marriage under strain again. Women were entering the job market in ever greater numbers and expecting husbands to take on their share of the chores and child-rearing. The freedom to work and earn their own living meant that married women were less afraid that divorce would mean financial disaster. The second factor was that women were making greater demands sexually.

The post-war booklet, *Living Together Again*, had implied that women had gained greater sexual knowledge and confidence during the war. They had their eyes opened to other possibilities: 'They had only a stereotyped experience to go upon, and in many cases had never so much as realised that their knowledge of sexual love was imperfect. Before the war they went on contentedly with their husbands, unaware that they were not really satisfied.'

It was a sexual revolution that was slow in coming, but quickly gathered momentum. Mass-Observation surveys on sexual habits conducted just after the war confirmed that married couples admitted to an average indulgence of twice a week. During the 1950s sex was still viewed as something men did and wives endured. In 1959 a *Woman's Hour* report showed that men expected their wives to be virgins, but not the other way round. Magazines were imploring young women to prize their virginity, since if they gave in to their boyfriends they would lose their respect. Where not so long ago wives were required to provide proof that they had their husband's permission for an inter-uterine contraceptive device to be fitted, by the early 1960s condom machines had appeared in university unions. By the end of the decade the Pill was being pressed on undergraduates during freshers' week. The implication was clear. Sex was for fun rather than the creation of a family within marriage.

More widely available contraception and the advent of penicillin encouraged greater promiscuity, and at the same time facilitated the ability of married women to have extra-marital affairs. Between 1950 and 1970 the proportion of divorces granted to men on the grounds of the wife's adultery rose from 48 per cent to 70 per cent.

The 1956 Royal Commission had identified what was perhaps the single most important factor in marital breakdown, namely the idealization of the individual pursuit of self-gratification and personal pleasure at the expense of a sense of reciprocal obligations and duties towards spouses, children and society as a whole. Mirroring this was a proposal, on the part of some members of the commission, that divorce should be regarded as no more than legal recognition of irremediable matrimonial breakdown. It was a revolutionary, but by no means novel concept. It had first been proposed by John Milton in the 1640s and revived by some of the more progressive in the debates of the inter-war period.

Nothing was done to amend the divorce laws until the late 1960s. Meanwhile, the establishment and its moral values had received a further knock in 1963 when the Secretary of State for War, John Profumo, married to the strikingly beautiful and elegant Valerie Hobson, who had given up her acting career to become a highly supportive political wife, was revealed to have had a sexual liaison with a notorious call-girl, Christine Keeler, while at the same time Captain Yevgeny Ivanov, nominally Assistant Naval Attaché at the Russian Embassy and probably a spy, was also enjoying her services. The immediate inference, which Harold Wilson and the Labour Opposition seized on with glee, was that Profumo's indiscretion posed a serious risk to national security. The security services, which had been shadowing the minister during his trysts with Miss Keeler, seem to have already satisfied themselves that there was no such risk. The minister's morals were none of their business. But, of course, the potential for blackmail was immense.

Ironically, 'the fateful weekend' at Cliveden was the first the

Profumos had spent with Bill and Bronwen Astor. As their son, David, later wrote, 'It was not somewhere my parents were especially ambitious to visit', although Cliveden's *louche* reputation was only generally applied after the goings-on of this particular weekend became public knowledge. The Profumos' fellow guests included President Ayub Khan of Pakistan, Lord Mountbatten, and the latter's daughter Pamela and her husband David Hicks. In a rented cottage on the estate a rather different set, comprising mainly pretty girls euphemistically calling themselves models, was gathering at the invitation of society osteopath, portraitist and pimp, Stephen Ward. In rather questionable judgement, Bill Astor was in the habit of inviting Ward and his friends up to enjoy the Cliveden pool; on a previous weekend, one of Astor's guests recalled, she and her husband 'were absolutely scandalised that Bill should allow this man Ward to go up to the pool with all these common tarts'.

It was on the Saturday night after dinner that Astor and Jack Profumo were the first of the house guests to arrive at the pool to find Ward and several girls already there. Astor slapped a very pretty girl, wet, topless and ineffectually clutching a towel in front of her, on the bottom and introduced her to Profumo. 'Jack, this is Christine Keeler.' Although Profumo officially maintained that this was their first meeting, it seems he may have met Christine some time before, at Murray's Club off Beak Street, where she earned a living posing topless and stationary – as the law then prescribed – on stage. Certainly after the Cliveden weekend he lost no time in catching up with her again in London, even, while his wife and family were away on holiday, bringing her to his house at Chester Terrace and into the marital bed.

When rumours of Profumo's escapades with Christine Keeler began to emerge two years later after her unfortunate embroilment with two trigger-happy West Indian drug pushers in seedy and notorious Notting Hill, his immediate instinct was to deny any involvement with the girl, possibly because he knew he was already skating on very thin ice with Valerie. The wife is often the last to know, but her husband's infidelity probably came as no great surprise to Valerie Profumo. As she later ruefully told her son, 'He thought he could get away with it – after all most of his friends did.'

The problem was that Profumo lied and lied again, thinking he could brazen it out. Lord Hailsham, Lord President of the Council, took a dim view of it: 'It is intolerable for Mr Profumo in his position to have behaved in this way, and a tragedy that he should not have been found out, that he should have lied and lied and lied; lied to his family, lied to his friends, lied to his solicitor, lied to the House of Commons.'

In his statement to the House in March 1963 Profumo had admitted that he knew Miss Keeler but categorically denied that there was any impropriety whatsoever between them. The story refused to die, however, particularly as the police decided to charge Stephen Ward with pimping. Ward then made a misguided attempt to blackmail the government: he was tired of covering for Profumo, he said, and if the charges against him were not dropped he would expose the minister. For good measure, he wrote to the Leader of the Opposition and Wilson did not hesitate to exploit the security angle when passing a copy of Ward's letter to Macmillan.

On 31 May Profumo took his wife for a holiday in Venice, staying at the Cipriani. Here, over a Bellini cocktail before dinner on the first night, he finally told her the truth, that he *had* had a sexual involvement with Keeler. We do not know what her reaction was – although as she had a fiery temperament we might guess – but the upshot was that together they decided to return to London and face the music.

Perhaps it need not have gone so far if the Prime Minister, Harold Macmillan, had paid attention to the rumours at the outset and questioned Profumo personally. Profumo later said that he would have been unable to look Macmillan in the face and tell him a lie. It was Macmillan's deep loathing of adultery, deriving from his wife and Boothby's betrayal of his trust, and instinctive shying away from a world in which it was no longer possible to 'go to a restaurant with your wife and not see a man that you knew having lunch with a tart', that had made him close his eyes and ears to the unfolding scandal which would be largely responsible for his government's defeat at the next election.

There is nothing quite as ridiculous as the British public indulging in one of its periodic bouts of moral indignation. Continental Europe looked on with amazement at the fuss the British were making, just because a government minister was enjoying a little *cinq à sept* with a pretty girl. The public were both titillated and riveted by the Profumo affair, which toppled the rich and privileged from the moral high ground, introducing a new climate of disrespect for authority. This was best exemplified by the pert reply of Keeler's erstwhile flat-mate, Mandy Rice-Davies, in court to the news that Lord Astor had denied ever sleeping with her: 'Well, he would, wouldn't he?'

One redeeming feature of the whole business was that, despite her feelings of hurt and betrayal, Valerie Profumo decided to stick by her husband. It was an emotionally turbulent period and she apparently consulted a lawyer about her position. There were also external pressures. The Profumos had once enjoyed a glamorous, high-profile lifestyle; now they were social pariahs and Valerie found there were few friends she could call on in her distress or who wanted to become involved. It was a lonely and isolated existence. But ultimately, she loved her husband, despite his infidelity and the likelihood of more in the future, for Profumo was a party animal who loved beautiful women. On their tenth wedding anniversary, New Year's Eve 1964, Valerie found it in her heart to write to him 'of my joy in being married to you'. Joy was to be found 'in the relief after pain shared, in the good news following bad, in the knowledge of greater closeness after disaster. And so it is for me, with you.'

The Profumo marriage had survived where so many others would have foundered. How to remedy those marriages that were irretrievably beyond repair? In 1969 a private member's bill was introduced into the Commons by a Labour backbencher, Leo Abse, to convert the idea of no-fault divorce into the law of the land.

Hitherto divorce had always been a legal response to a specific marital fault, such as adultery, cruelty or desertion. Now, the proposal was to abolish the concept of 'matrimonial offence' and with it the public attribution of moral blame. It would be necessary to prove only 'irretrievable marital breakdown': adultery, desertion and cruelty would all be taken as sufficient proof. The bill also proposed that a separation for two years should be grounds for divorce if both parties agreed, or separation for five years even if one of the parties did not agree. The definition of cruelty was stretched to encompass any behaviour because of which the petitioner 'cannot reasonably be expected to live with the respondent'. It was a far cry from the seventeenth century when the definition of cruelty stopped just short of a man killing his wife.

The 1969 Divorce Reform Act made clear that its first aim was to uphold the institution of marriage and support those that had a chance of survival and only then to 'give a decent burial with minimum embarrassment, humiliation and bitterness to those that are indubitably dead'. Perhaps the most striking aspect of the bill was that, for the first time in the long debate about the English marriage and in its thousand-year history, no speaker so much as mentioned the theological arguments about the sanctity of marriage, according to the words of Christ.

The most prescient question was posed by Lord Hailsham, who was to become Lord Chancellor when the Tories were returned to power the following year. He expressed his fears about the rising tide of divorce and questioned the wisdom of making divorce any easier than it was already, which might encourage parties to enter marriage without a real intention of making it permanent, or end it over some temporary quarrel or casual act of infidelity. However, his own experience and his professional career at the Bar, during which he had witnessed so much marital misery, inclined him to take the liberal view that priority should be given to the pursuit of individual self-fulfilment. The divorce rate had risen tenfold over the previous thirty-five years. 'Are we sure how much human happiness has increased during those thirty-five years?' Hailsham asked the House. 'Would anyone care to dogmatise?' There was an uneasy silence.

Epilogue

F OR THE FIRST time in our history married couples will soon be in the minority, as more couples choose to live together without tying the knot. Just under twenty-three men in every thousand and just over twenty women in every thousand were married in 2007, but the fact that 240,000 couples a year opt for marriage and more than half of them will stay together is impressive. For better for worse, marriage continues to impinge on all our lives and provides a topic of endless fascination, interest and debate.

Just as in past centuries when the preferred option of many was to live together in irregular, but stable, unions, so now two-thirds of the population do not think there is much difference between being married and living together. There is no stigma to having a child outside marriage and just over a quarter believe married couples make better parents than unmarried pairs, despite clear evidence to the contrary. Again as in the past, when many families were of a hybrid nature through death and remarriage, step-families have become the norm and they are considered to be doing a good job.

A national survey reveals that weddings, which in a society obsessed with celebrities and aping their excesses cost the average couple somewhere in the region of £20,000, are believed to be more about celebration than life-long commitment. Quiet contemplation of the meaning of the vows they are about to exchange seems to be lost somewhere amid noisy stag nights and hen nights, focus on the dress and other external appearances, and the reception. The wedding, as the author of *The Wives of England* warned in the early nineteenth century, is only the beginning, not the summit of achievement or the end in itself, but then, as far as her readers were concerned, marriage was an irrevocable step that bound them for life.

For many in our non-religious society, a wedding in a pretty country church answers their romantic idea of marriage, rather than the sacred nature of it. It is one of the few occasions, other than christenings and funerals, that they will ever set foot in a church. Others prefer to take up the new option of being married in licensed premises, from castles to stately homes, to golf clubs, and even to foreign beaches – just as once they married impulsively 'in a field, in the night time, by moon light', and not necessarily 'at church door'.

It has taken only a century and a half for England to move from a non-divorcing to a divorcing society, although we must not forget that there were plenty of instances of marital breakdown before the advent of divorce with permission to remarry in 1857, with forms of self-divorce, private and judicial separations, and desertions common enough. In the past when marriage was for life adultery was common, whereas today it might be the signal for divorce and remarriage. It is heartening in an age of omnipresent sexual temptation and opportunity that the majority of those questioned in a recent survey disapprove of extra-marital affairs.

Most people today think that divorce is a normal, if regrettable, part of life, with two-thirds saying that it can be 'a positive step towards a new life'. The thirty-something generation getting married today is the first to have personal experience of their parents' or their classmates' parents' broken marriages, so that they are apt to be more cautious.

Just as in the past when marriage was terminated by death rather than divorce, the average marriage lasts only eleven years. Living as many of us do into our eighties, perhaps we are setting unrealistic goals in expecting marriage to be for life when such a time span is the equivalent of three marriages in past centuries.

Marriage is seemingly under greater strain than ever before, while much of the former support system of Church, family, 'friends' and a close-knit community has been removed. Nor does the government do anything to encourage marriage any more. It is not that the pressures on marriage are so much greater than in the past, when war, civil war, poverty, disease, economic uncertainty and the precariousness of life were equally burdensome, but there is less incentive to work at marriage when it is all too easy to end it. Where in the past and at least as recently as the Victorian era the maintenance of the family unit was considered vital for the good of society as a whole, now we live in an age of self-gratification when the happiness of the individual is paramount. It does not fit easily with marriage, which demands at the very least forbearance, consideration for another, and unselfishness.

The demand for emotional and sexual fulfilment from marriage has risen to unrealistic levels, while there is less tolerance of boredom or a partner's shortcomings. With parity in education between men and women, the emergence of women as equals in boardroom and workplace, salaries on a par with or exceeding men's, and women's control over their own bodies to limit their families or not have them at all, the dynamic between the sexes has totally altered and men and women have had to find a whole new way to live together in partnership.

In a throwaway society we ignore the wisdom and experience of our forbears at our peril. For them marriage was for life. They had to work at it and find the means of living together in harmony. The companionate ideal propounded by John Milton and Daniel Defoe, and the principle that one's spouse should be one's best friend, companion and confidant, are surely as valid today as they were in the past.

England has distinguished itself in having the highest rate of divorce in Europe, while London has become the divorce capital of the world for wives. In recent years the focus on celebrity divorce pay-outs and even the sums bartered between relatively obscure but wealthy couples have sent a chill down the spine of any man of means contemplating divorce and confirmed the impression that the English marriage is all about money. It does not help that these agreements, which should surely be private, are bandied about the press like a footballer's signing-on fee.

In 2007 observers of the English marriage identified a new phenomenon. The 'toxic wife' is about as far from Margaret Paston, Mary Verney, Emma Darwin, Mollie Butler and all the other loyal and devoted wives of the past few centuries as it is possible to imagine. Neither career woman nor domestic goddess, all she seems to do is shop, lunch and be pampered, secure in the knowledge that if the marriage ends she can take her husband to the cleaners in the divorce court. Fortunately, the toxic wife is in the minority and is hopefully on the way out along with bankers' bonuses.

After centuries in which women's rights were so hardly won, it is disappointing to see women in their thirties and forties, quite capable of working to support themselves, apparently treating marriage as a cash cow. Legal rulings made in big money cases apply to all of us; it is only the figures that differ. In 2005 an £85,000-a-year PR executive, Melissa Miller, took £5 million of hedge-fund manager Allan Miller's £17.5 million fortune after less than three years of a marriage that had produced no children. The court's decision, based on the new principle of equal division of assets rather than the 'reasonable needs' of the wife, was upheld by the House of Lords, sending a powerful message that divorce is a bonanza for women and prompting some to question the sanity of the legal system.

One of the most notorious recent cases of naked greed was the divorce of Sir Paul McCartney and Heather Mills McCartney. She claimed that her 'reasonable needs' amounted to £3,250,000 a year and that she was 'entitled to compensation', as her marriage to Sir Paul had 'restricted the development of her career'. The judge found her a 'less than impressive witness' and scaled back her exorbitant demands considerably. The public, meanwhile, was treated to the unedifying spectacle of Heather Mills voicing her grievances, ranting at the lawyers and, most damaging of all, vilifying her husband and trying to blacken his name by alleging abuse. Having upended a carafe of water over Sir Paul's solicitor, she emerged from the courtroom many millions of pounds adrift, but £24.3 million was still a hefty return for four years of marriage by any reckoning.

The English divorce court has become a notoriously frosty place for the male breadwinner, unlike, say, France, which is not nearly so generous to wives, or even Scotland, where the courts do not take bonus payments into account in dividing the assets. The acrimonious nature of so many divorces is not doing marriage any favours. As one aggrieved company executive who recently emerged from the bear pit of the London courtroom £48 million worse off said, 'Unless there is a fundamental realignment of the law to the concept of fairness and common sense, my advice is quite simply, I regret, not to get married.'

England, which has been adrift from the rest of Europe for so long in matrimonial matters, may yet have to bring its divorce laws more into line with those of the rest of the EU.

Stripped of much of its sacramental aura in a secular society, marriage is beginning to look more than ever like a mere contract – rather as, three centuries ago, the same was argued in the wake of the Glorious Revolution. The English marriage has always been mercenary. The marriage settlements of the past will be replaced by pre- and post-nuptial agreements, which are increasingly being taken account of in the divorce courts. Indeed, a German heiress who filed for divorce in London when domiciled in England recently made legal history when her pre-nuptial agreement was recognized by the Court of Appeal. We may even take it a step further. As one matrimonial lawyer cynically put it recently: 'Marriage is basically a deal, a money-based transaction. In twenty-five years' time there'll be renewable agreements; it's happening already and it will soon have to be recognized.'

Marriages are made in Heaven, according to an old English proverb. Whatever pragmatic arrangements are put in place in the future, marriage is still there to be celebrated. Over the thousand years the English marriage has evolved, standards of behaviour within marriage have changed and the laws that govern it have shifted, but the players are not so very different. Love triumphs and hope springs eternal.

Notes

Abbreviations

GLRO Greater London Record Office
TNA The National Archives

Introduction (pp. 1–12)

1. 'Now the women'. Thomas Platter and Horatio Busino, *The Journal of Two Travellers in Elizabethan and Early Stuart England in 1599*, p.xvii.
1. 'Wives in England'. Emmanuel van Meteren quoted in William Brenchley Rye, *England as Seen by some Foreigners in the Days of Elizabeth and James I*, ii, pp.73–3.
1. a paradise for wives. Platter and Busino, p.46.
2. 'By marriage'. Sir William Blackstone, *Commentaries on the Laws of England, The Rights of Persons*, p.442.
3. 'Chastity in women'. Dr Johnson quoted in Judith Schneid Lewis, *In the Family Way. Childbearing in the British Aristocracy, 1760–1860*, p.39.

3. sumptuous porches. Christopher N.L. Brooke, 'The Church Porch: Marriage and Architecture', in his *The Medieval Idea of Marriage*, pp.248–57.
5. *Utopia*. Thomas More, *Utopia*, chapter on Marriage.
5. Isabella Wakes . . . 'in the month'. Frederick J. Furnival, *Child Marriages . . . in the Diocese of Chester*, p.140.
5. vicar of Tetbury. E.A.Wrigley, 'Clandestine Marriage in Tetbury in the Late Seventeenth Century', pp.15–21.
6. an island carrying. Alan Macfarlane, *Marriage and Love in England. Modes of Reproduction 1300–1840*, p.339.
7. 'What will she'. Mary Astell, *Reflections Upon Marriage*, p.12.

8. 'Dear Heart'. Frances Parthenope Verney and Margaret M. Verney, eds., *Memoirs of the Verney Family during the Seventeenth Century*, i, p.348.

8. 'I have tried'. Dorothy Gardiner, ed., *The Oxinden Letters 1607–1642 Being the Correspondence of Henry Oxinden of Barham and His Circle*, Part III, pp.261–3.

9. 'Men should'. Richard Allestree, *The New Whole Duty of Man*, pp.229–30.

9. 'a strong inclination'. Quoted in Mary Abbott, *Life Cycles in England 1560–1720*, pp.101–2.

9. Darwin. Quoted in Edna Healey, *Emma Darwin, the Inspirational Wife of a Genius*, pp.146–7.

10. Francis Place. Francis Place, *The Autobiography of Francis Place (1771–1854)*.

10. 'very industrious'. Thomas Turner, *The Diary of a Georgian Shopkeeper*, p.75.

10. 'We that have'. Quoted in Maureen Waller, *1700: Scenes from London Life*, p.37.

10. Nottinghamshire parish. Peter Laslett, *Family Life and Illicit Love in Earlier Generations. Essays in Historical Sociology*, p.58.

10. Daniel Defoe. Daniel Defoe, *A Tour Through the Whole Island of Great Britain*, pp.54–5.

10. 'only friend'. Turner, p.46.

10. 'for ever my'. Place, p.254.

12. John Stuart Mill. Mary Lyndon Shanley, 'Marital Slavery and Friendship: John Stuart Mill's *The Subjection of Women*', pp.230–40.

12. 'a glimpse'. Mona Caird, 'The Morality of Marriage', p.324.

Epigraph

13. 'And although their'. Quoted in Charlotte Augusta Sneyd, *A Relation, or Rather a True Account of the Island of England . . . About the Year 1500*, p.24.

PART ONE 1465–1645

Chapter 1 (pp.17–24)

17. 'Marry thy daughters'. Old English proverb.

17. dictate a letter. Although she was well educated for a woman of her time, Margaret Paston could only read, not write. Even her expensively educated husband wrote a poor hand. It was customary to have a clerk do the writing.

17. 'a goodly young . . . marriage'. Alice Drayton Greenwood, ed., *Selections from the Paston Letters*, p.6.

18. 'for we be either'. Quoted in Helen Castor, *Blood and Roses, The Paston Family in the Fifteenth Century*, p.214.
18. a cousin remonstrated. Greenwood, p.95.
18. 'that my master'. Ibid., p.106.
19. 'To my right'. Ibid., p.273.
20. 'the coming'. Ibid., p.3.
20. 'And as for'. Ibid.
20. 'Right worshipful'. Ibid., p.5.
21. 'our ungracious'. Ibid., p.272.
21. 'never have'. Ibid.
21. 'Mine own Lady'. Ibid., p.274.
21. 'we that ought'. Ibid.
22. 'I understand'. Ibid.
22. 'I suppose'. Ibid.
22. 'for they had'. Ibid., p.277.
23. 'her demeaning'. Ibid.
23. 'that he would'. Ibid., p.278.
23. 'rehearsed'. Ibid.
23. 'her words'. Ibid.
23. 'I was with'. Ibid.
23. 'were dead'. Ibid., p.279.
24. 'As for the divorce'. Ibid.
24. 'she shall'. Ibid.
24. 'he would have'. Quoted in Castor, p.270.

Chapter 2 (pp.25–9)

25. 'Upon Friday'. Greenwood, p.384.
26. 'she will in no wise'. Ibid., p.380.
26. 'I shall give you'. Ibid., p.382.
27. 'I am yet'. Ibid., p.388.
27. 'Ye have'. Ibid., p.384.

27. 'it is but'. Ibid.
27. 'Right reverend'. Ibid.
27. 'my Lady'. Ibid.
27. 'But if'. Ibid.
27. 'the young gentlewoman'. Ibid., p.386.
27. 'And I heard'. Ibid.
28. 'And Cousin'. Ibid., p.391.
28. 'I will depart'. Ibid.
28. 'trouble me'. Ibid., p.398.

Interlude: The Form of Solemnisation of Matrimony, Book of Common Prayer

Chapter 3 (pp.35–47)

35. 'My Lord hath'. Anne Somerset, *Unnatural Murder, Poison at the Court of James I*, p.82.
35. 'For here is'. Quoted in Lawrence Stone, *Road to Divorce*, p.49.
36. 'When I came out'. Quoted in Somerset, p.36.
36. 'divers times attempted'. Ibid., p.38.
36. 'when he was willing'. Ibid.
36. 'desirous to be'. Ibid.
36. 'penetrate'. Ibid.
37. 'he drinketh'. Ibid., p.83.
37. 'the bed's head'. Ibid., p.51.
38. 'Sweet Turner'. Ibid., p.82.
39. 'although he did'. Ibid., p.99.
39. 'the Earl had no'. Ibid.
39. 'We all agreed'. Ibid., p.114.
40. a survey of the poor. John

F. Pound, ed., *The Norwich Census of the Poor*, 1570.

42. 'perpetual'. Ibid., p.119.
43. 'She saith so'. Ibid., p.121.
43. 'in naked bed'. Anon, *The Cases of Impotency and Virginity Fully Discuss'd*, p.9.
43. 'was at Hampton'. Ibid., p.16.
44. 'a woman able'. Somerset, p.122.
44. 'expert in the matter'. Ibid., p.123.
44. 'fit for carnal'. Ibid.
44. 'That since'. *The Cases of Impotency and Virginity Fully Discuss'd*, p.9.
45. 'some secret'. Somerset, p.138.

Interlude: William Gouge, Of Domesticall Duties

Outlined in the introduction to the 1634 edition.

Chapter 4 (pp.52–60)

52. 'Teach her'. Quoted in Linda Pollock, '"Teach Her to Live under Obedience": The Making of Women in the Upper Ranks of Early Modern England', p.1.
52. 'a notorious riot'. Quoted in Laura Norsworthy, *The Lady of Bleeding Heart Yard, Lady Elizabeth Hatton 1578–1646*, p.50.
52. 'If WE'. Ibid., p.45.

52. 'clam et secrete'. Ibid., p.48.
52. 'without the consent'. Ibid., p.48.
52. 'intending to bestow'. Ibid., p.49.
53. 'Although I would'. Ibid., p.30.
54. 'would not buy'. Ibid., p.39.
54. 'I vow before'. Ibid., p.43.
56. 'I resolve to be'. Ibid., p.64.
57. 'My lord'. Ibid., p.125.
59. 'wherewith to buy'. Ibid., p.151.
59. 'had been married'. Ibid.

Interlude: Henry Oxinden of Barham in love

61. 'I do now'. Gardiner, ed., *The Oxinden Letters*, Part III, pp.261–3.

PART TWO 1642–1734

Chapter 5 (pp.65–75)

65. 'Good men'. Miriam Slater, *Family Life in the Seventeenth Century, the Verneys of Claydon House*, p. 91.
65. 'I am afraid'. Verney, i, p.416.
65. 'I pray mistake me'. Slater, *Family Life in the Seventeenth Century*, Ibid., p.91.
65. 'I must let'. Verney, i, p.241.
66. 'Let no respect'. Gardiner, Part III, p.87.

66. 'Those good'. Verney, i, p.241.
66. 'When her husband'. Ibid., p.249.
66. 'my sister'. Ibid.
67. 'Since I am'. Ibid., p.421.
68. 'a bad husband'. Duchess of Newcastle, *CCXI Sociable Letters*, p.184; Jerome Nadelhaft, 'The Englishwoman's Sexual Civil War', p.568.
68. 'My brother Thomas'.Verney, i, p.417.
68. 'she is resolved'. Ibid.
68. 'is very ready'. Ibid., p.418.
69. 'although I know'. Ibid.
69. 'if she have him'. Ibid.
69. 'Sure it would'. Ibid., p.420.
69. 'a pretty gentleman'. Ibid., p.423.
69. 'will have clothes'. Ibid., p.420.
69. 'I was never'. Ibid., p.425.
69. 'It is no prison'. Ibid.
69. 'poor Pegg'. Ibid., p.423.
70. 'I wish with all'. Ibid., p.424.
70. 'to keep much'. Ibid.
70. 'Now for my'. Ibid.
70. 'good furniture'. Ibid.
70. 'On my word'. Ibid., p.426.
70. 'had she stayed'. Slater, *Family Life in the Seventeenth Century*, p.94.
70. 'sensible her portion'. Verney, i, p.427.
71. 'that I may'. Ibid.
71. 'for I believe'. Ibid.
71. 'received her'. Ibid.
71. ''Tis a very'. Ibid., p.429.
71. 'studies nothing'. Ibid., p.430.
71. 'If you did'. Ibid.
71. 'hath so ill'. Ibid.
71. 'is a fit'. Ibid., p.431.
71. 'as wild'. Ibid.
71. 'much the worst'. Ibid., p.433.
71. 'pestilent wench'. Ibid.
72. 'too much frequency'. Quoted in Lawrence Stone, *The Family, Sex and Marriage in England 1500–1800*, p.313.
72. 'Because you write'. Slater, 'The Weightiest Business', p.35.
73. 'Women were never'. Slater, *Family Life in the Seventeenth Century*, p.66.
73. 'I long for nothing'.Verney, i, p.346.
73. 'Dear Heart'. Ibid., p.348.
74. ''Tis only'. Ibid., p.365.
74. 'Believe me'. Ibid., p.357.
74. 'As thou lovest'. Ibid., p.353.
74. 'I will be governed'. Ibid., p.355.
74. 'I cannot see'. Ibid., p.384.
74. 'My dearest heart'. Ibid., p.382.
75. 'extraordinarily warm'. Ibid., p.391.
75. 'When I was'. Ibid., p.458.
75. 'not to delight'. Ibid.

Chapter 6 (pp.76–85)

76. 'Women must'. Marquis of Newcastle, *The Phanseys of William Cavendish, Marquis of*

Newcastle, addressed to Margaret Lucas and Her Letters in Reply, p.107.

76. 'Let me ask'. Dorothy Osborne, *The Letters of Dorothy Osborne to Sir William Temple 1652–54,* p.97.

77. 'an old decayed'. Marquis of Newcastle, *Phanseys,* p.xix.

77. 'for the most'. Duchess of Newcastle, *CCXI Sociable Letters,* p.50.

77. 'A happy'. Quoted in Kathleen Jones, *A Glorious Fame, The Life of Margaret Cavendish, Duchess of Newcastle 1623–1673,* p.51.

77. 'Where there is doubt'. Ibid.

77. 'though I did dread'. Quoted in Jones, p.41.

78. 'but being as'. Marquis of Newcastle, *Phanseys,* p.112.

78. 'if you cannot'. Quoted in Jones, p.44.

78. 'those that marry'. Duchess of Newcastle, *The World's Olio,* p.80.

78. 'My lord'. Marquis of Newcastle, *Phanseys,* p.99.

79. 'was constant'. Ibid., p.97.

79. 'for though I love'. Ibid., p.99.

79. 'the fear you'. Ibid.

79. 'Though I give'. Ibid., p.106.

79. 'I am a little'. Ibid., p.107.

79. 'There is nothing'. Ibid., p.124.

79. 'There is a customary'. Ibid., p.111.

79. 'afraid to lie'. Quoted in Jones, p.54.

80. 'Pray, my lord'. Ibid., pp.115–16.

80. 'and thereby'. Marquis of Newcastle, *Phanseys,* p.xxix.

80. 'the state of'. Ibid.

80. 'I desire nothing'. Ibid., p.119.

81. 'I will write'. Quoted in Jane Dunn, *Read My Heart: Dorothy Osborne and Sir William Temple,* p.74.

81. 'Can there be'. Ibid., p.17.

81. 'I am apt'. Dorothy Osborne, p.16.

81. 'I can never'. Ibid., p.73.

82. 'I had no quarrel'. Ibid., p.28.

82. 'Yet he protested'. Ibid., p.29.

82. 'be as acceptable'. Ibid., p.71.

82. 'a debauched'. Ibid., p.66.

82. 'If I had been'. Ibid., p.80.

82. 'two of the finest'. Ibid., p.162.

82. 'I find I want'. Ibid., p.41.

83. 'I have lived'. Ibid., p.179.

83. 'any woman'. Ibid.

83. 'He must not'. Ibid., p.172.

83. 'must not be'. Ibid.

83. 'What an age'. Ibid., p.184.

83. 'I think I shall'. Ibid., p.51.

83. 'though he be'. Ibid.

83. 'With what reverence'. Ibid., p.61.

83. 'She has lost'. Ibid., p.53.

83. 'broke loose'. Ibid., p.130.

83. 'She is old'. Ibid., p.130.

84. 'He loves her'. Ibid., p.174.

84. 'all such as intend'. Ibid., p.185.

84. 'You undo me'. Ibid., p.123.
84. 'that you have'. Ibid., p.218.
85. 'it will fright'. Ibid., p.147.
85. 'the old one'. Ibid.

Interlude: Hannah Woolley, The Gentlewoman's Companion or, a Guide to the Female Sex

86. Extracts taken from the Complete Text of 1675, pp.134–7.

Chapter 7 (pp.88–103)

88. 'Lay long'. Robert Latham, ed., *The Shorter Pepys*, 26 May 1663, p.279.
88. On this particular January morning. Ibid., 9 January 1663, pp.251–2.
88. 'we have been'. Ibid., 24 October 1662, p.229.
88. 'was so piquant'. Ibid., 9 January 1663, pp.251–2.
89. 'I pulled'. Ibid.
89. 'The best of husbands'. Francis Osborne, *Advice to a Son*, p.66.
91. 'My wife hath'. Latham, 31 October 1660, p.90.
91. 'a dirty slut'. Ibid., 31 August 1661, p.150.
92. 'What a mind'. Ibid., 30 June 1662, p.209.
92. 'I was in hopes'. Ibid., 1 August 1662, p.217.
92. 'but I dare not'. Ibid.
92. 'Dined at home'. Ibid.

92. 'when she dresses'. Ibid., 19 June 1666, p.633.
92. 'was very pleased'. Ibid., 27 September 1662, p.226.
93. Lady Castlemaine. Ibid., 21 May 1662, p.196.
93. 'who ought'. Ibid., 6 November 1660, p.192.
93. 'At night to'. Ibid.
93. earrings. Ibid., 4 July 1664, p.401.
93. Lady Sandwich. Ibid., 9 November 1661, p.163.
93. 'I find she'. Quoted in Claire Tomalin, *Samuel Pepys, The Unequalled Self*, p.196.
94. 'I went up'. Latham, 19 August 1660, p.72.
94. 'Home to dinner'. Ibid., 22 and 25 December 1661, pp.167–8.
94. 'Lay long'. Ibid., 5 October 1662, p.228.
95. 'neglecting the keeping the house clean'. Ibid., 2 May 1663, p.270.
95. 'She reproached me'. Ibid., 3 May 1663, p.271.
95. 'not dancing'. Ibid., 15 May 1663, p.275.
95. 'So that I'. Ibid., 21 May 1663, p.276.
95. 'I espied Pembleton'. Ibid., 24 May 1663, p.278.
95. 'lay long in bed'. Ibid., 26 May 1663, p.279.
95. 'and I am led'. Ibid.
95. 'This is my . . . content me'. Ibid.

96. 'took occasion . . . great discontent'. Ibid.

96. 'sad for want'. Ibid., 15 June 1663, p.288.

96. 'towse her'. Ibid., 29 June 1663, p.291.

97. 'vexed me'. Ibid.

97. 'I could love'. Ibid., 20 March 1667, p.743.

97. 'full liberty'. Ibid., 18 July 1663, p.294.

97. 'I did so'. Ibid., 5 August 1663, p.300.

97. 'I must have . . . pleasure of her twice'. Ibid., 21 July 1664, p.406.

98. 'Strangers'. Osborne, p.60.

98. 'I did there'. Latham, 20 October 1664, p.435.

98. 'I did arrive'. Ibid., 20 December 1664, p.453.

98. 'a decent interval'. Ibid.

99. 'touching'. Ibid., 17 February 1667, p.728.

100. 'she is already'. Ibid., 15 October 1667, p.841.

100. 'yo did take'. Ibid., 31 March 1668, pp.898–9.

100. 'occasioned the'. Ibid., 25 October 1668, p.950.

100. 'endeed I was'. Ibid.

101. 'with inconstancy'. Ibid.

101. 'mightily troubled'. Ibid.

101. 'in a mighty'. Ibid., 27 October 1668, p.951.

101. 'the poor girl'. Ibid., 28 October 1668, p.952.

101. 'for my wife's'. Ibid., 1 November 1668, p.960.

102. 'I have a great'. 13 November 1668, p.960.

102. 'with more pleasure'. Ibid., 14 November 1668, p.961.

102. 'for fear of'. Ibid., 18 November 1668, p.963.

102. 'yo did besar her'. Ibid.

102. 'threats and vows'. Ibid., 19 November 1668, p.963.

102. 'no curse'. Ibid., 19 November 1668, p.964.

Interlude: Henri Misson on English marriage customs

104. 'And when bed'. Extract from Henri Misson, *Memoirs and Observations in His Travels Over England* (1719 edition), pp.352–3.

Chapter 8 (pp.106–10)

106. 'The bargain'. Quoted in Bridget Hill, *Women, Work, and Sexual Politics in Eighteenth-Century England*, p.175.

106. 'I was married'. Walter Calverley, *Memorandum Book of Sir Walter Calverley, Bart*, p.115.

106. 'I never saw'. Hill, p.175.

107. 'dined'. Calverley, p.113.

107. 'the match'. Ibid.

107. 'What will she'. Astell, p.12.

107. 'Ask the ladies'. Daniel Defoe, *Conjugal Lewdness*:

or, Matrimonial Whoredom,
pp.27–8.

107. 'Men rather'. Donald F.
Bond, *The Spectator*, no. 268,
7 January 1712, p.546.

107. 'When a girl'. Ibid., no. 66,
16 May 1711, pp.282–3.

108. 'The market'. Daniel Defoe,
*The Fortunes and Misfortunes of
Moll Flanders*, p.44.

108. 'he had hardly'. Anon, *The
Hardships of the English Laws in
Relation to Wives*, p.33.

108. 'Separate purses'. Bond, *The
Spectator*, no. 295, 7 February
1712, p.53.

108. 'Furnishing'. Ibid., p.52.

108. 'that it is'. Ibid.

109. I could therefore'. Ibid.

109. 'to assist'. Calverley, p.113.

109. 'staid most'. Ibid.

109. 'advice about'. Ibid.

109. 'seemed to advise'. Ibid.

109. 'obtain a decree'. Ibid.

110. 'for the trouble'. Ibid., p.115.

110. 'My Lady'. Ibid.

110. 'were at cost'. Ibid.

Chapter 9 (pp.111–16)

111. 'My circumstances'. William
Matthews, ed., *The Diary of
Dudley Ryder*, pp.251–2.

111. 'the sorrows'. Quoted in
Mary Abbott, pp.101–2.

111. 'I wish'. Ibid.

111. 'to see my mother'.
Matthews, p.38.

111. 'I pity him'. Ibid., pp.53–4.

111. 'Such a temper'. Ibid.

112. 'passed the afternoon'.
Quoted in Mary Abbott, p.97.

112. 'played at'. Ibid.

112. 'His talk'. Ibid.

113. 'ten shillings'. A.E. Goodwyn,
ed., *Selections from Norwich
Newspapers 1760–1791*,
p.24.

113. 'I was so raised'. Quoted in
Mary Abbott, p.98.

113. 'But there was'. Matthews,
p.278.

113. 'Read law'. Ibid.

114. 'not proper'. Ibid., pp.251–2.

114. 'I thought my'. Ibid.

114. 'It gave me'. Ibid., p.287.

115. 'so deeply'. Ibid.

115. 'I enquired'. Ibid., p.367.

115. if 'she has'. Ibid.

115. 'anything at all'. Ibid.

116. 'I look upon'. Ibid., p.20.

Chapter 10 (pp.117–24)

117. 'Nothing but'. Anon, *Cases
of Divorce for Several Causes*,
p.32.

117. 'put to bed'. Ibid.

117. 'he would'. Ibid.

117. 'contracted an'. Ibid.

117. 'dissolve'. Ibid.

118. Roos case. Stone, *Road to
Divorce*, pp.309–11.

119. 'A better man'. Ibid.

119. 'Cuckolds'. Ibid.

119. 'for illegitimating'. Ibid.

120. Norfolk case. Ibid.,
pp.313–17.

122. 'It seems so'. Anon, *Cases of Divorce for Several Causes*, p.37.

122. 'My Lords'. Anon, *The Cases of Impotency and Virginity Fully Discuss'd*, p.10.

122. 'give the use'. Ibid.

122. 'since nothing'. Anon, *Cases of Divorce for Several Causes*, p.32.

123. 'The said Edward'. Anon, *The Cases of Impotency and Virginity Fully Discuss'd*, p.8.

123. 'nor could they'. Ibid., p.7.

123. 'he was seized'. Ibid., p.31.

123. 'her parts'. Ibid.

123. 'carnal conversation'. Ibid.

123. 'he *believed*'. Ibid., p.34.

123. 'if the gentleman'. Ibid.

123. 'strengthening'. Ibid., p.30.

Interlude: Lord Halifax, The Lady's New Year's Gift: or Advice to a Daughter

125. 'I have seen so many'. Lady Mary Wortley Montagu, *The Complete Letters of Lady Mary Wortley Montagu*, 28 April 1711, i, p.105.

125. Mary Astell advises resignation. Astell, pp.56–7.

125. Extracts from George Savile, Marquis of Halifax, *The Lady's New Year's Gift: or Advice to a Daughter*, pp.25–68.

PART THREE 1706–1780

Chapter 11 (pp.131–47)

131. 'For ten guineas'. Teresia Constantia Muilman, *An Apology for the Conduct of Teresia Constantia Phillips*, i, p.59.

132. 'Tears and prayers'. Ibid., p.25.

132. 'though no ceremony'. Ibid.

133. 'should procure'. Ibid., p.59.

134. Tetbury. Wrigley, pp.15–21.

134. 'To proclaim'. Misson, p.183.

135. 'given to understand'. Muilman, i, p.61.

136. 'he might not'. Ibid., p.63.

136. 'the business'. Ibid.

136. 'all the people'. Ibid.

136. 'in which case'. Ibid., p.66.

136. 'Mr Cook'. Arthur Vincent, ed., *Lives of Twelve Bad Women*, p.170.

137. 'contracted a'. Ibid.

137. 'she had'. Muilman, i, p.99.

137. 'Pray, Sir'. Ibid.

137. 'too much a'. Ibid., p.127.

139. 'This bitch'. Ibid.

143. 'I saw but'. Ibid., Appendix, iii, p.4.

143. 'to be rich'. Ibid, ii, p.70.

Interlude: The Hardships of the English Laws in Relation to Wives

148. Extracts from the anonymous work.

Chapter 12 (pp.150–4)

150. 'The causes'. Quoted in Stone, *Road to Divorce*, p.203.
150. 'conducted'. Mary Coke, *The Letters and Journals of Lady Mary Coke*, i, p.ix.
150. 'on account'. Ibid.
150. 'He dutifully'. Ibid.
150. 'every now'. Ibid.
150. 'bridling'. Ibid., i, p.x.
151. 'foresee'. Ibid.
151. 'the lawyers'. Ibid.
151. 'wept'. Ibid.
151. 'had a long'. Ibid.
151. 'used coarse'. Ibid.
151. 'whether a'. Ibid., i, p.xvi.
152. 'vile practice'. Daniel Defoe, *Augusta Triumphans: or, The Way to Make London the Most Flourishing City in the Universe*, pp.30–1.
152. 'It is the duty'. Quoted in Stone, *Road to Divorce*, p.203.
153. 'The argument's'. Quoted in Lawrence Stone, *The Family, Sex and Marriage in England 1500–1800*, p.164.
154. 'died of his'. Coke, i, p.xvi.

Chapter 13 (pp.155–7)

155. 'What can equal'. Turner, p.51.
155. 'The reason'. Defoe, *A Tour Through the Whole Island of Great Britain*, pp.54–5.
155. 'This morning'. Turner, p.3.

156. 'entirely'. Ibid.
156. 'I have almost'. Ibid.
156. 'many have'. Ibid., p.9.
156. 'At home'. Ibid., p.46.
156. 'About five'. Ibid., p.50.
156. 'I hardly'. Ibid., p.51.
156. 'Oh, how'. Ibid., p.46.
157. 'serene'. Ibid.
157. 'nothing to'. Ibid., p.70.
157. 'In the afternoon'. Ibid., p.73.
157. 'marriage'. Ibid.
157. 'The girl'. Ibid., p.75.
157. 'She comes'. Ibid.
157. 'As to her'. Ibid.
157. 'she has good'. Ibid.
157. 'Then the'. Ibid., p.76.

Chapter 14 (pp.158–63)

158. 'He has often'. GLRO/DL/C/154/51–57.
158. Veezey. Anon, *The Hardships of the English Laws in Relation to Wives*, p.1.
158. 'to hear a'. Daniel Defoe, *The Great Law of Subordination Consider'd*, pp.6–7.
159. Elizabeth Byfield. GLRO/DL/C/154/51–57.
160. 'being wholly'. Ibid.
160. 'he has often'. Ibid.
160. 'several lewd'. Ibid.
160. 'roam into'. Ibid.
160. 'Murder'. Ibid.
160. Dorothy Arnold. Anon, *Trials for Adultery: or, The History of Divorces*, iii, pp.2–23.
160. 'a mild'. Ibid., p.2.
161. 'by what means'. Ibid., p.3.

161. 'knocked the'. Ibid.
161. 'so bruised'. Ibid., p.4.
161. 'would not suffer'. Ibid., p.15.
162. 'much beaten'. Ibid., p.19.
162. 'which deprived'. Ibid., p.20.
162. 'Whereas Dorothy'. Ibid., p.4.
162. Martha Robinson. Anon, *Trials for Adultery*, iv, pp.2–9.
162. 'was and'. Ibid., p.2.
163. 'divers lewd'. Ibid.
163. 'his intercourse'. Ibid.
163. 'murder her'. Ibid.
163. 'render him'. Ibid., p.8.
163. 'begged'. Ibid., p.9.
163. 'hath several'. Ibid.

Chapter 15 (pp.164–73)

164. 'The foul crime'. Anon, *Trials for Adultery*, ii, p.1.
164. Elizabeth Lockwood. Anon, *Trials for Adultery*, v, 1–17.
164. 'their bodies'. Ibid., p.5.
164. 'Madam'. Ibid., p.7.
164. 'an old gown'. Ibid.
164. 'toying'. Ibid., p.4.
164. 'put her hand'. Ibid.
165. 'having heard'. Ibid., p.10.
165. 'told several'. Ibid., p.11.
165. 'and they were'. Ibid, p.13.
165. 'Why should'. Ibid.
165. 'a vast love'. Ibid., p.15.
166. 'seemed to glory'. Ibid., p.17.
166. 'been seduced'. Ibid.
166. Elizabeth Martha Chichely Harris. Anon, *Trials for Adultery*, i, pp.10–54.
166. a 'clerk'. Ibid., p.10.
166. 'her breasts'. Ibid., p.13.
166. 'but there'. Ibid., p.20.
167. 'the carnal use'. Ibid., p.23.
167. 'very much tumbled'. Ibid., p.24.
167. 'such marks'. Ibid., p.25.
167. 'a gown'. Ibid.
167. 'into her bosom'. Ibid., p.41.
167. 'take the sopha'. Ibid.
168. Bernard Brocas. GLRO/ DL/C/555/79/2.
169. Grosvenor. Paul-Gabriel Bouce, *Sexuality in Eighteenth-Century Britain*, p.131.
169. Lady Harriet Spencer. Henrietta Bessborough, *Lady Bessborough and Her Family Circle*, p.31; Judith Schneid Lewis, pp.18–19.
169. 'Richard Draper. Anon, *Trials for Adultery*, i, pp.1–21.
170. 'to see the pigeons'. Ibid., p.4.
170. 'Blast your'. Ibid.
170. 'come to bed'. Ibid., p.5.
170. 'Will you?' Ibid.
170. 'put her hand'. Ibid.
170. 'very frequently'. Ibid., p.20.
170. 'the bosom' Ibid., p.15.
171. 'head was'. Ibid., p.16.
171. 'the bed'. Ibid.
171. Sarah Oliver. Anon, *Trials for Adultery*, iii, pp.3–4.
171. 'an affable'. Ibid., p.3.
171. 'a person'. Ibid.
171. 'and take indecent'. Ibid., p.4.
171. 'sitting with'. Ibid.
171. 'resisted'. Ibid.
172. 'All may be'. Ibid.
172. 'I am sorry'. Ibid.

172. John Worgan. Anon, *Trials for Adultery*, ii, pp.1–49.
172. 'the foul'. Ibid., p.1.
172. 'observed, on the'. Ibid., p.18.
172. 'very much stained'. Ibid., p.28.
173. 'began to'. Ibid.
173. 'a very honest'. Ibid.
173. 'preserve the peace'. Ibid., p.30.
173. 'caught it of'. Ibid., p.32.
173. 'frequently been'. Ibid., p.34.
173. 'cuckold'. Ibid., p.49.

PART FOUR 1760–1827

Chapter 16 (pp.177–81)

177. 'That part . . . Scotland'. Quoted in T.C. Smout, 'Scottish Marriage, Regular and Irregular 1500–1940', in R.B. Outhwaite, ed., *Marriage and Society: Studies in the Social History of Marriage*, Chapter IX.
177. 'Your blood'. Meliora C. Smith, alias 'Claverhouse', *Irregular Border Marriages*, p.852.
179. 'a big, rough-drinking'. Smout, p.43.
179. 'Awell'. Quoted in Elizabeth Laverack, *With this Ring: 100 Years of Marriage*, p.15.
180. 'Then our uncle'. Smith, p.82.

Chapter 17 (pp.182–96)

182. 'A match of'. Quoted in Stella Tillyard, *Aristocrats, Caroline, Emily, Louisa and Sarah Lennox 1740–1832*, p.137.
182. The Duke of Richmond's story is recounted in E.R. Curtis, *Lady Sarah Lennox, An Irrepressible Stuart, 1745–1826*, pp.113–14.
182. 'They surely are'. Ibid.
182. 'You must be'. Ibid.
184. 'the finest'. Quoted ibid., p.46.
184. 'Pooh!' Ibid., p.40.
184. 'every opportunity'. Ibid., p.44.
185. 'There will'. Ibid., p.49.
185. 'Yes, Sir . . . nothing!' Ibid., p.53.
185. 'she should'. Ibid., p.58.
185. 'Don't tell'. Sarah Lennox, *The Life and Letters of Lady Sarah Lennox 1745–1826*, p.102.
186. 'If I must'. Curtis, p.73.
186. 'For God's'. Ibid., p.67.
186. 'I won't go'. Lennox, p.104.
187. 'sense, good . . . good'. Ibid., pp.104–6.
187. 'here are all'. Quoted in Tillyard, p.135.
187. 'I hope she'. Ibid.
188. 'Don't refuse'. Lennox, pp.114–15.
188. 'I have not . . . immediately'. Ibid., p.115.
188. 'You will say'. Ibid., p.116.

189. 'not so unalterable'. Quoted in Tillyard, p.138.
189. 'to be much'. Ibid.
189. 'two people'. Curtis, p.108.
189. 'not rich enough'. Tillyard, p.137.
190. 'let me go'. Curtis, p.111.
190. 'Pray now'. Ibid., p.117.
191. 'I find her'. Ibid., p.138.
191. 'As we choose'. Ibid., p.146.
191. 'At length'. Ibid., p.154.
192. 'You have'. Ibid., p.157.
194. 'Lady Sarah'. Tillyard, p.284.
194. 'All this appeared'. Curtis, p.188.
195. 'Some of my'. Ibid., p.192.
196. 'Why change'. Ibid., p.211.
196. 'If you love'. Ibid., p.210.
196. 'I find I'. Ibid., p.216.

Chapter 18 (pp.197–214)

197. 'a cruel, savage'. Anon, *A New Collection of Trials for Adultery: or, General History of Modern Gallantry and Divorce*, p.10.
199. 'I wished to'. Countess of Strathmore, *The Confessions of the Countess of Strathmore, written by herself, carefully copied from the original, lodged in Doctors Commons*, pp.65–6.
199. 'a gentleman'. Quoted in Derek Parker, *The Trampled Wife: The Scandalous Life of Mary Eleanor Bowes*, p.31.
199. 'even when'. Strathmore, p.23.

202. 'I married him'. Quoted in Parker, p.51.
203. 'for her separate'. Ibid., p.59.
203. 'it struck me'. Strathmore, pp.29–30.
205. 'May I never'. Ibid., p.99; Anon, *A New Collection of Trials for Adultery*, p.55.
205. Dorothy Stevenson. Anon, *A New Collection of Trials for Adultery*, p.10.
205. 'a cruel'. Ibid.
206. 'threw her down'. Ibid., p.6.
206. Susannah Church. Parker, p.74.
206. 'she had frequently'. Anon, *A New Collection of Trials for Adultery*, p.17.
206. 'threw a . . . word'. Ibid.
207. 'was one'. Ibid., p.26.
208. 'beating'. Parker, p.88.
208. 'he was induced . . . impaired'. Anon, *A New Collection of Trials for Adultery*, p.56.
209. 'As a preparation'. Quoted in Parker, pp.93–4.
210. 'Who's there? . . . door!' Ibid., p.106.
211. 'I am Lady'. Ibid., p.117.
212. 'let the faults'. Anon, *A New Collection of Trials for Adultery*, p.68.
212. 'I am sure'. Ibid., p.63.
212. 'vindictive'. Ibid.
212. 'a good stock'. Ibid.
213. 'very frequently'. Ibid., p.60.
213. 'with more reserve'. Ibid.
214. 'the said Thompson'. Ibid.
214. 'determined . . . wall'. Ibid.

Chapter 19 (pp.215–23)

215. 'A man may'. Place, p.256.
215. Wedding description. Ibid., p.104.
216. 'exposed to all'. Ibid., p.105.
216. 'just as if'. Quoted in M. Dorothy George, *London Life in the Eighteenth Century*, p.303.
216. 'was no wife'. Place, p.85.
216. 'he saved'. Ibid.
216. 'A supper'. Ibid.
217. 'all turbulent'. Ibid., pp.74–5.
217. 'the prostitutes' Ibid., p.75.
217. 'the dirty'. Ibid.
217. 'a sweetheart'. Ibid.
217. 'in their general'. Ibid.
217. 'The sons'. Ibid., pp.76–7.
217. 'were as'. Ibid., p.75.
217. 'want of'. Ibid., p.73.
217. 'did not necessarily'. Ibid., pp.75–6.
218. 'could name'. Ibid., p.76.
218. 'I thought'. Ibid., p.96.
218. 'taught to be . . . money by her'. Ibid., p.100.
218. 'ceased to'. Ibid., p.96.
218. 'an intrigue'. Ibid.
218. 'as if he'. Ibid.
219. 'I laid before'. Ibid.
219. 'willing to'. Ibid., p.101.
219. 'I was however'. Ibid., p.102.
219. 'contrived to'. Ibid., p.106.
219. 'We were poor'. Ibid., p.109.
219. 'no longer'. Ibid., p.110.
219. 'We had been'. Ibid.
220. 'if I continued'. Ibid., p.111.
220. 'enabled us'. Ibid.

221. 'My temper'. Ibid., p.115.
221. 'Nothing conduces'. Ibid., p.116.
221. 'In a short'. Ibid., p.119.
221. 'full sixteen'. Ibid., p.123.
221. 'As we scarcely'. Ibid., p.124.
222. 'Our neat place'. Ibid.
222. 'She was sure'. Ibid., p.205.
222. 'She dreaded'. Ibid., p.218.
222. 'some catastrophe'. Ibid.
223. 'became less'. Ibid., p.255.
223. 'The only relaxation'. Ibid., p.256.
223. 'for ever my'. Ibid., p.254.
223. 'I loved'. Ibid., p.255.

Interlude: Jane Austen, Fanny Knight and Clarissa Trant

224. 'I have no scruple'. Jane Austen, *Jane Austen's Letters*, p.279.
225. 'The events of yesterday'. G.C. Luard, ed., *The Journal of Clarissa Trant 1800–1832*, p.222.
225. 'Women have a dreadful'. Austen, p.332.
225. 'He has not returned'. Luard, p.222.
225. 'if my father'. Ibid.
225. 'The post . . . future unhappiness'. Ibid., p.223.
226. 'Anything is'. Austen, p.280.
226. 'It is very true'. Ibid., p.286.
226. 'Do not be'. Ibid., p.332.
226. 'We met'. Luard, p.304.
227. 'And thus ends'. Ibid., p.308.

Chapter 20 (pp.228–33)

228. 'Threatened'. Miss Weeton, *Journal of a Governess 1811–1825*, p.176.
228. 'Dear Brother'. Ibid., pp.133–4.
229. 'everyone trembling'. Quoted in Amanda Vickery, *The Gentleman's Daughter, Women's Lives in Georgian England*, p.79.
229. 'firm, judicious'. Ibid.
229. 'Since then'. Weeton, p.140.
230. 'Turned out'. Ibid., p.159.
230. 'threatened with'. Ibid., p.176.

Interlude: Wife-sale

232. 'puts a halter'. Quoted in Stone, *Road to Divorce*, p.144.
233. 'On Thursday last'. George Ryley Scott, *Curious Customs of Sex and Marriage*, p.137.
233. 'A farmer of'. E.A. Goodwyn, *Selections from Norwich Newspapers 1760–1790*, p.20.
233. 'A butcher'. Ibid., p.21.
233. 'A man at Exeter'. Anon, *The Newgate Calendar and the Divorce Court Chronicle*, p.47.

PART FIVE 1820–1885

Chapter 21 (pp.237–60)

237. 'I do not ask'. Quoted in Alice Acland, *Caroline Norton*, p.198.
237. 'What does'. Ibid., p.197.

238. 'gnome'. This was Lord Melbourne's description of George Norton in a letter to Caroline.
240. 'I do not ask'. Acland, p.198.
243. 'a sudden'. Alan Chedzoy, *A Scandalous Woman, The Story of Caroline Norton*, p.53.
249. 'Alone'. Quoted in Acland, p.163.
249. 'They may'. Chedzoy, p.146.
250. 'Mr Norton'. Acland, p.99.
251. 'I do not consider'. Ibid., p.107.
254. 'The law'. Ibid., pp.130–1.
255. 'Is my'. Ibid., p.134.
255. 'Half of'. Ibid., p.135.
255. 'My poor'. Ibid.
258. 'As the husband'. Chedzoy, p.249.

Interlude: Bigamy sentence

261. Quoted in Owen McGregor, *The History of Divorce in England*, pp.15–17.

Chapter 22 (pp.263–77)

263. 'To soothe'. Bostock v. Bostock, TNA/J77/2/B3.
264. Bostock v. Bostock. TNA/J77/2/B3.
265. 'The law ought'. Quoted in Stone, *Road to Divorce*, p.204.

267. 'to soothe'. Bostock v. Bostock, TNA/J77/2/B3.
268. Kelly v. Kelly. TNA/J77/91.
272. 'a wife does'. Quoted in James Hammerton, *Cruelty and Companionship: Conflict in Nineteenth-Century Married Life*, p.129.
272. 'law leaves'. Ibid.
272. 'recognize'. Ibid.
272. Hewitt v. Hewitt. TNA/J77/275/8083.
273. Newall v. Newall. TNA/J77/39.
274. Brocas v. Brocas. TNA/J77/3.
275. Norris v. Norris. TNA/J77/39/N17.
276. Denton v. Denton. TNA/J77/276.
276. Swatman v. Swatman. TNA/J/77/53.

Interlude: Charles Darwin's 'Marry' or 'Not Marry'

278. Darwin's pros and cons of marriage are quoted in Edna Healey, *Emma Darwin, The Inspirational Wife of a Genius*, pp.146–7.
279. 'I marvel at'. Ibid., p.342.

Chapter 23 (pp.280–97)

280. 'There's no'. Quoted in Elizabeth Hamilton, *The Warwickshire Scandal*, pp.24, 120, 220.
283. 'I feel quite'. Ibid., p.22.
283. 'corruptness'. Ibid., p.24.
284. 'My darling'. Ibid., p.54.
286. 'My lady . . . complaint'. Ibid., p.102.
287. 'I have been'. Ibid., p.105.
287. 'a very diseased'. Ibid., p.107.
287. 'Charlie, you'. Ibid., p.111.
287. 'Charlie, I'. Ibid.
288. 'But I'. Ibid., p.121.
288. 'the ultimate'. Ibid., pp.130, 138.
289. 'we can find'. Ibid., p.131.
290. 'suffering from'. Ibid., p.139.
290. 'hopes that'. Ibid.
291. '280 days'. Ibid., p.144.
291. 'If the case'. Ibid., pp.164–5.
291. 'Women often'. Ibid., p.177.
292. Victoria, by'. Ibid., p.182.
293. 'Yes, you'. Ibid., p.225.
293. 'everybody did it'. Ibid., p.220.
294. 'I say a more'. Ibid., p.353.
294. 'Utterly . . . years previously' Ibid., p.353.
294. 'portentous'. *The Times*, 28 February 1870, p.9.
294. *The Times* opined. Ibid.
294. 'Whether the shameful'. Ibid.
295. 'his own condition'. Ibid.
295. not a matter. Ibid.
295. greatest public. Ibid.

Interlude: Mrs Henderson, The Young Wife's Own Book, Her Domestic Duties and Social Habits

298. Extracts taken from 1857 edition, pp.10–16.

Chapter 24 (pp.300–5)

300. 'Wife-Torture'. Frances Power Cobbe, 'Wife-Torture in England'.

300. Susannah Palmer. Cobbe, 'Wife-Torture in England', p.69; Lee Holcombe, *Wives and Property, Reform of the Married Women's Property Law in Nineteenth-Century England*, p.3.

300. 'I should like'. Quoted in Carol Bauer and Lawrence Ritt, '"A Husband Is a Beating Animal" – Frances Power Cobbe Confronts the Wife-Abuse Problem in Victorian England', p.101.

301. 'The notion that'. Cobbe, 'Wife-Torture in England', p.62.

301. 'Every brutal-minded'. Ibid.

301. 'men's worst'. Ibid.

301. 'the seas of'. Ibid., p.65.

301. 'slatternly'. Ibid., p.60.

302. 'with a smile'. Frances Power Cobbe, 'The Law in Relation to Women', p.700.

302. 'the kicking'. Cobbe, 'Wife-Torture in England', p.61.

302. Frederick Knight. Ibid., p.74.

302. Richard Mountain. Ibid.

302. John Charnock. Ibid., p.75.

302. John Harris. Ibid., p.74.

302. William White. Ibid.

302. 'so smashed'. Ibid., p.75.

302. 'Yes, it is'. Ibid.

302. 'He earns'. Nancy Tomes, 'A "Torrent of Abuse": Crimes of Violence Between Working-Class Men and Women in London, 1840–1875', p.331.

302. James Styles. Cobbe, 'Wife-Torture in England', p.74.

303. James Lawrence. Ibid.

303. Thomas Paget. Ibid., p.75.

303. Mrs Brick's husband. Tomes, p.329.

303. 'If she had'. Ibid., p.331.

303. 'We had a'. Ibid., p.332.

303. James Mills. Cobbe, 'Wife-Torture in England', p.74.

303. George Ralph Smith. Ibid.

304. In May 1874. Ibid., p.78.

PART SIX 1880–1969

Chapter 25 (pp.309–19)

309. 'A woman'. Quoted in Mary S. Hartman, *Victorian Murderesses*, p.217.

311. 'Darling, try'. Quoted in Victoria Blake, *Mrs Maybrick*, p.25.

311. 'my Widow'. Ibid., p.27.

313. Thank God'. Ibid., p.35.

313. 'something strange'. Ibid.

313. 'Dearest'. Ibid., p.68.

315. 'attired as for'. Ibid., p.50.

315. 'made a full'. Hartman, p.217.

316. 'I refer to'. Ibid., p.60.

316. 'You must not'. Ibid., p.217.

317. *The Times*. Ibid.

318. 'We are given'. Blake, p.82.

319. vicarious . . . fiction. See

Elaine Showalter, 'Family Secrets and Domestic Subversion: Rebellion in the Novels of the 1860s'.

Interlude: Wedding customs

320. 'Lady Audrey'. Jacqueline Hope-Nicholson, *Life Amongst the Troubridges: Laura Troubridge*, pp.60–2.
321. For the best overview of wedding dress through the centuries see Phillis Cunnington and Catherine Lucas, *Costumes for Births, Marriages and Death*.
323. 'If men have'. Quoted in Elizabeth Laverack, *With this Ring: 100 Years of Marriage*, p.40.

Chapter 26 (pp.324–9)

324. 'Coverture is'. Quoted in Mary Shanley, *Feminism, Marriage and the Law in Victorian England 1850–1895*, p.182.
325. 'I saw my'. Law Report, *The Times*, 16 March 1891.
325. 'several men'. Ibid.
325. 'one young'. Ibid.
326. 'to take proceedings'. Ibid.
326. 'She was at'. Ibid.
326. 'someone in the'. Ibid.
326. 'That Mrs Jackson's'. Ibid.
326. 'wish her freely'. Ibid.
326. 'as long as'. Ibid.

326. 'seizure'. Ibid.
326. 'The husband has'. Ibid.
327. 'There can be'. Ibid.
327. 'if she is'. Ibid.
327. 'is kept under'. Ibid.
327. 'All that is'. Ibid.
327. 'when asked on'. Ibid.
327. 'there was ill-usage'. Ibid.
327. 'the circumstances'. Ibid.
328. 'a decree for'. Ibid.
328. 'barbarous and'. Ibid.
328. 'All the authorities'. Ibid.
328. 'annoyed because'. Ibid.
328. 'Instead of having'. Ibid.
328. 'more injudicious'. Ibid.
328. 'They have never'. Ibid.
328. 'upon no ground'. Ibid.
329. 'It is necessary'. Ibid.
329. 'Marriage, as hitherto'. Shanley, *Feminism, Marriage and the Law in Victorian England*, p.182.
329. 'Coverture'. Ibid.
329. 'The wife submits'. Ibid.

Chapter 27 (pp.330–7)

330. 'The whole'. Edwin Lutyens, *The Letters of Edwin Lutyens to his Wife, Lady Emily*, p.303.
330. 'wanting you'. Ibid., p.223.
330. 'for what happened'. Ibid.
330. 'a nightmare'. Ibid.
330. 'We tramped'. Ibid.
330. 'try and forget'. Ibid., p.224.
330. 'the majority'. William Acton quoted in Steven Marcus, *The Other Victorians*, p.31.

331. 'Except my love'. Edwin
    Lutyens, p.18.
331. 'All that'. Ibid.
331. 'world to'. Ibid.
331. 'My mind'. Ibid., p.19.
331. 'No one will'. Ibid.
331. 'a day'. Ibid.
332. 'would rather'. Ibid., p.20.
332. 'You probably'. Ibid.
332. 'under these'. Ibid.
332. 'Oh Ned'. Ibid., p.21.
332. Oh Emy'. Ibid., p.22.
333. 'because I loved'. Ibid.,
    p.29.
333. 'be a great'. Ibid.
333. 'I did sort'. Ibid., p.35.
333. 'If I don't'. Ibid., p.215.
334. 'I hated to'. Ibid., p.62.
334. 'We are just'. Ibid.
334. 'The one great radiant'. Ibid.,
    p.137.
334. 'our rare encounters'. Ibid.,
    p.220.
334. 'I know that'. Ibid., p.215.
334. 'I love you'. Ibid.
334. 'You are quite'. Ibid., p.221.
334. 'only you will'. Ibid.
335. 'I should like'. Ibid.
335. 'I have never'. Ibid., p.223.
335. 'all I ask'. Ibid.
335. 'on my paying'. Ibid.
335. 'I have suffered'. Ibid., p.302.
335. 'as long as'. Bridget Bennett,
    ed., Ripples of Dissent,
    Women's Stories of Marriage
    from the 1890s, p.136.
336. 'I believe'. Edwin Lutyens,
    p.302.
336. 'I am sure'. Ibid.

336. 'The whole thing. Ibid.,
    p.303.
336. 'the day may'. Ibid.
336. 'I do not'. Ibid., p.399.
336. 'If you can'. Ibid., p.400.
336. 'How could I'. Ibid.
336. 'separated me'. Emily Lutyens,
    Candles in the Sun, p.186.
336. 'I now turned'. Ibid.
337. 'I like to think'. Ibid.

Interlude: Job Flower, A Golden
Guide to Matrimony

338. Extracts taken from 1882
    edition, pp.43–58.

Chapter 28 (pp.340–9)

340. 'I shall be'. Christopher
    Isherwood, Kathleen and Frank,
    p.175.
340. 'Dear Mr'. Ibid., p.101.
340. 'It is about'. Ibid., p.102.
341. 'what you are'. Ibid.
341. 'You must make'. Ibid., p.103.
341. 'I care for'. Ibid.
342. 'Mr Isherwood called'. Ibid.,
    p.33.
342. 'I am so'. Ibid., p.42.
342. 'He asked me'. Ibid., p.44.
342. 'spent a very'. Ibid., p.45.
343. 'You have made'. Ibid., p.49.
343. 'It is, I know'. Ibid., p.52.
343. 'You did not'. Ibid., p.145.
344. 'Of course the'. Ibid., p.104.
344. 'rose nobly'. Ibid., p.105.
344. 'I saw three'. Ibid.
344. 'I went in'. Ibid., p.111.

344. 'My dearest'. Ibid., p.132.
344. 'the most manageable'. Ibid.
345. 'This is all'. Ibid., p.149.
345. 'I presume'. Ibid., p.150.
345. 'What you said'. Ibid.
345. 'done a great'. Ibid., p.151.
346. 'if we want'. Ibid.
346. 'I suppose he'. Ibid., p.153.
346. 'It seems too'. Ibid.
346. 'advertisements'. Ibid., p.158.
346. 'My dear'. Ibid., p.171.
347. 'I feel I'. Ibid., p.175.
347. 'Mr Isherwood'. Ibid., p.195.
347. 'I did so'. Ibid., p.294.
347. 'Please thank'. Ibid., p.300.
347. 'We have in'. Ibid., p.299.
348. 'We got it'. Ibid.
348. 'Isn't it twelve'. Ibid., p.317.
348. 'such a sad'. Ibid.
348. 'I am always'. Ibid., p.324.
349. 'I don't know'. Ibid., p.335.

Chapter 29 (pp.350–66)

350. 'An avalanche'. David Mace, Coming Home, p. 21.
350. 'Who's there?' Lord Hailsham, A Sparrow's Flight, The Memoirs of Lord Hailsham of St Marylebone, p.203.
350. 'regrettable'. Ibid., p.205.
351. 'In doing what'. Alistair Horne, Macmillan, 1894–1986 The Official Biography, i, p.90.
352. 'I think their'. Ibid.
352. Lord Dawson. Quoted in Stone, Road to Divorce, p.400.
353. 'So here'. Ibid., p.398.
354. 'He got out'. Evelyn Waugh, A Handful of Dust, p.134.
355. 'at ruinous expense'. John Mortimer, Clinging to the Wreckage, p.125.
355. 'One afternoon'. Ibid.
355. 'The first night'. David Profumo, Bringing the House Down, A Family Memoir, p.114.
355. 'The war has . . . broken marriages'. Mace, p.21.
356. 'The outlook'. Ibid., p.23.
356. 'lots of couples'. Ibid., pp.26–7.
357. 'The girl-wife'. Quoted in Maureen Waller, London 1945, p.380.
357. 'There is always'. Ibid., p.382.
358. wartime marriage counsellor. Barbara Cartland.
358. A Mass-Observation. 'Sex, Morality and the Birth Rate', February 1945.
358. 'The exemplary'. Waller, London 1945, p.403.
358. 'It was as'. Ibid., p.381.
359. 'If I cannot'. Ibid., p.405.
360. 'We've had'. Jenni Murray, The Woman's Hour: 50 Years of Women in Britain, p.234.
360. 'When he came'. Quoted in Waller, London 1945, p.437.
360. 'And yet'. Mollie Butler, August and Rab, A Memoir, p.32.

361. 'They had only'. Phoebe D. Bendit and Laurence J. Bendit, *Living Together Again*, p.76.

361. Woman's Hour. Murray, p.242.

363. 'It was not'. Profumo, p.156.

363. 'were absolutely scandalised'. Ibid., p.159.

363. 'Jack, this is'. Ibid., p.157.

363. previous meeting at Murray's Club. Ibid., p.158.

363. 'He thought he'. Ibid., p.167.

364. 'It is intolerable'. Ibid., p.193.

364. Profumo took his. Ibid., p.188.

364. Profumo later. Ibid., p.183.

364. 'go to a restaurant'. Horne, ii, p.495.

365. consulted a lawyer. Profumo, p.212.

365. likelihood of more. Ibid., p.219.

365. 'of my joy'. Ibid., p.235.

366. 'give a decent'. Quoted in Jane Lewis, 'Public Institution and Private Relationship, Marriage and Marriage Guidance, 1920–1968', p.233.

366. Hailsham's fears. Hailsham, pp.412–18.

366. 'Are we sure'. Quoted in Stone, *Road to Divorce*, p.409.

Epilogue (pp.367–71)

367. twenty-three men in every thousand. Figures taken from *The Times*, 28 March 2008.

367. two-thirds of the population . . . just over a quarter. Figures taken from National Survey released by the Office of National Statistics, January 2008; *Daily Telegraph*, 23 January 2008, p.21; *The Times*, p.9 and times2 section pp.4–5, 29 January 2008.

367. The wedding, as the author. Sarah Stickney Ellis, *The Wives of England: Their Relative Duties, Domestic Influence, and Social Obligations*, Chapter 1, 'Thoughts Before Marriage'.

369. toxic wife syndrome. Tara Winter Wilson, *Daily Telegraph*, 2 March 2007, p.22.

370. McCartney v. Mills McCartney. Law Reports.

370. Scotland. Niznick case reported in the *Daily Mail*, 16 February 2008, p.3.

370. 'Unless there'. John Charman quoted in the *Daily Telegraph*, 1 March 2007, p.30.

371. a German heiress. Katrin Radmacher. See interview, *Sunday Times*, 5 July 2009.

371. 'Marriage is basically'. Raymond Tooth quoted in the *Sunday Times*, 15 March 2009, p.15.

Bibliography

All books published in London unless otherwise specified

Abbot, George, *The Case of Impotency as Debated in England in that remark-able trial anno domini 1613 between Robert, Earl of Essex and the Lady Frances Howard*, 2 vols. (1715)

Abbott, Mary, *Life Cycles in England 1560–1720, Cradle to Grave* (London and New York, 1996)

Acland, Alice, *Caroline Norton* (1948)

Allen, Grant, *The Woman Who Did* (1895)

Allestree, Richard, *The New Whole Duty of Man* (1744)

Anon, *Cases of Divorce for Several Causes* (1715)

Anon, *The Cases of Impotency and Virginity Fully Discuss'd* (1732)

Anon, *The Hardships of the English Laws in Relation to Wives* (Dublin, 1735)

Anon, *Trials for Adultery: or, The History of Divorces. Being Select Trials at Doctors Commons for adultery, fornication, cruelty, impotence, etc, from the year 1760 to the present*, 7 vols. (1780)

Anon, *A New Collection of Trials for Adultery: or, General History of Modern Gallantry and Divorce*, 3 vols. (1796)

Anon, *How to Woo; How to Win; And How to Get Married* (Glasgow, 1856)

Anon, *The Newgate Calendar and the Divorce Court Chronicle* (1872)

Anon, 'Why We Men Do Not Marry. By One of Us', *Temple Bar* (October 1888)

Astell, Mary, *Reflections Upon Marriage* (1706)

Austen, Jane, *Jane Austen's Letters*, collected and edited by Deirdre Le Faye (Oxford, 1995)

Baker, Margaret, *Wedding Customs and Folklore* (Newton Abbot, 1977)

Balsan, Consuelo Vanderbilt, *The Glitter and the Gold* (Maidstone, 1973)

Bauer, Carol and Ritt, Lawrence, '"A Husband Is a Beating Animal" – Frances Power Cobbe Confronts the Wife-Abuse Problem in Victorian

England', *International Journal of Women's Studies*, vol. 6, no. 2 (March/April 1983)

Beckwith, Lady Muriel, *When I Remember* (1936)

Beddoe, Deirdre, *Back to Home and Duty: Women between the Wars 1918–1939* (1989)

Behn, Aphra, *The Ten Pleasures of Marriage and The Confession of the New Married Couple* (n.d.)

Bell, Lady F.E.E., *At the Works: A Study of a Manufacturing Town* (1907)

Bendit, Phoebe D. and Bendit, Laurence J., *Living Together Again* (1946)

Bennett, Bridget, ed., *Ripples of Dissent, Women's Stories of Marriage from the 1890s* (1996)

Besant, Annie, *Marriage, As It Was, As It Is, and As It Should Be* (New York, 1879)

Bessborough, Henrietta Frances Spencer Ponsonby, *Lady Bessborough and Her Family Circle* (1940)

Biggs, John M., *The Concept of Matrimonial Cruelty* (1962)

Blackstone, Sir William, *Commentaries on the Laws of England, The Rights of Persons* (Philadelphia, 1900)

Blain, Virginia, 'Rosina Bulwer Lytton and the Rage of the Unheard', *Huntingdon Library Quarterly* (Summer 1990)

Blake, Victoria, *Mrs Maybrick* (Kew, 2008)

Bland, Lucy, 'Marriage Laid Bare: Middle-Class Women and Marital Sex c. 1880–1914', in Lewis, Jane, ed., *Labour and Love: Women's Experience of Home and Family, 1850–1940* (Oxford, 1986)

Blodgett, Harriet, *Centuries of Female Days, Englishwomen's Private Diaries* (Stroud, 1989)

Bodichon, Barbara Leigh Smith, *A Brief Summary, in Plain Language, of the Most Important Laws of England Concerning Women* (1854)

Bond, Donald F., ed., *The Spectator* (Oxford, 1965)

Bonfield, Lloyd, *Marriage Settlements 1601–1740: The Adoption of the Strict Settlement* (Cambridge, 1983)

Bossy, John, ed., *Disputes and Settlements: Law and Human Relations in the West* (Cambridge, 1983)

Boucé, Paul-Gabriel, *Sexuality in Eighteenth-Century Britain* (Manchester, 1982)

Branca, Patricia, 'Image and Reality: The Myth of the Idle Victorian Woman', in Hartman, Mary and Banner, Lois W., eds., *Clio's Consciousness Raised, New Perspectives of Women* (New York, 1974)

Branca, Patricia, *Silent Sisterhood: Middle-Class Women in the Victorian Home* (1975)

Braybon, Gail and Summerfield, Penny, *Out of the Cage, Women's Experiences in Two World Wars* (1987)

Brooke, Christopher N.L., 'Marriage and Society in the Central Middle Ages', in Outhwaite, R.B., ed., *Marriage and Society: Studies in the Social History of Marriage* (London, 1981)

Brooke, Christopher N.L., *The Medieval Idea of Marriage* (Oxford, 1989)

Butler, Mollie, *August and Rab, A Memoir* (1987)

Caine, B., *Destined to be Wives: The Sisters of Beatrice Webb* (Oxford, 1986)

Caird, Mona, 'The Morality of Marriage', *Fortnightly Review* (1890)

Calder, Jenni, *Women and Marriage in Victorian Fiction* (1976)

Calverley, Sir Walter, *Memorandum Book of Sir Walter Calverley, Bart,* in *Yorkshire Diaries and Autobiographies in the Seventeenth and Eighteenth Centuries*, Surtees Society, vol. LXXVII (Durham and Edinburgh, 1886)

Castor, Helen, *Blood and Roses, The Paston Family in the Fifteenth Century* (2004)

Chandrasekhar, S., *'A Dirty Filthy Book', The Writings of Charles Knowlton and Annie Besant on Reproductive Physiology and Birth Control and an Account of the Bradlaugh-Besant Trial* (Berkeley, 1981)

Chedzoy, Alan, *A Scandalous Woman: The Story of Caroline Norton* (1992)

Clark, A., *Women's Silence, Men's Violence: Sexual Assault in England, 1770– 1840* (1987)

Cobbe, Frances Power, 'Wife-Torture in England', *Contemporary Review*, vol. 32 (1878)

Cobbe, Frances Power, *The Duties of Women. A Course of Lectures from Frances Power Cobbe* (Boston, 1881)

Cobbe, Frances Power, 'The Law in Relation to Women', *Westminster Review*, vol. 128 (1887)

Cobbett, William, *Advice to Young Men, And (incidentally) to Young Women, in the Middle and Higher Ranks of Life: in a Series of Letters Addressed to a Youth, a Batchelor, a Lover, a Husband, a Father, a Citizen, or a Subject* (n.d.)

Coke, Mary, *The Letters and Journals of Lady Mary Coke*, vol. 1, *1756–1767*, ed. J.A. Home (Bath, 1889–96)

Cressy, David, *Birth, Marriage and Death: Ritual, Religion, and the Life-Cycle in Tudor and Stuart England* (Oxford, 1977)

Cunnington, Phillis and Lucas, Catherine, *Costumes for Births, Marriages and Deaths* (1972)

Curtis, E.R., *Lady Sarah Lennox, An Irrepressible Stuart, 1745–1826* (1947)

Davidoff, Leonore, *The Best Circles: Society, Etiquette and the Season* (1973)

Davidoff, Leonore, 'Mastered for Life: Servant and Wife in Victorian and Edwardian England', *Journal of Social History*, vol. 7, no. 4 (Summer 1974)

Davidoff, Leonore and Hall, Catherine, *Family Fortunes, Men and Women of the English Middle Class, 1780–1850* (1987)

Davis, J., 'A Poor Man's System of Justice: The London Police Courts in the Second Half of the Nineteenth Century', *Historical Journal*, vol. 27, no. 2 (1984)

Defoe, Daniel, *The Fortunes and Misfortunes of Moll Flanders* (first published 1722; this edition, Harmondsworth, 1984)

Defoe, Daniel, *The Great Law of Subordination Consider'd* (1724)

Defoe, Daniel, *Conjugal Lewdness: or, Matrimonial Whoredom* (1727)

Defoe, Daniel, *Augusta Triumphans: or, The Way to Make London the Most Flourishing City in the Universe* (1728)

Defoe, Daniel, *A Tour Through the Whole Island of Great Britain* (1986)

Devey, Louisa, *Letters of the Late Edward Bulwer, Lord Lytton, to His Wife. With Extracts from Her Ms Autobiography and Other Documents. In Vindication of Her Memory* (1884)

Dunn, Jane, *Read My Heart: Dorothy Osborne and Sir William Temple: A Love Story in the Age of Revolution* (2008)

Dyhouse, Carol, 'Mothers and Daughters in the Middle-Class Home, c.1870–1914', in Lewis, Jane, ed., *Labour and Love: Women's Experience of Home and Family, 1850–1940* (Oxford, 1986)

Ellis, Sarah Stickney, *The Wives of England: Their Relative Duties, Domestic Influence, and Social Obligations* (1843)

Evelyn, John, *The Diary of John Evelyn*. Edited from the original manuscript by William Bray, 2 vols. (1901)

Fletcher, Anthony, *Gender, Sex and Subordination in England 1500–1800* (New Haven and London, 1995)

Flower, Job, *A Golden Guide to Matrimony* (1882)

Forster, Margaret, *Good Wives? Mary, Fanny, Jennie and Me, 1845–2001* (2002)

Foyster, Elizabeth A., 'A Laughing Matter? Marital Discord and Gender Control in Seventeenth Century England', *Rural History: Economy, Society, Culture*, vol. 4, no. 1 (April 1993)

Furnival, Frederick J., *Child Marriages, Divorces and Ratifications in the Diocese of Chester, A.D. 1561–6* (1897)

Gardiner, Dorothy, ed., *The Oxinden Letters 1607–1642 Being the Correspondence of Henry Oxinden of Barham and His Circle* (1933)

Gardiner, Dorothy, ed., *The Oxinden and Peyton Letters, 1642–1670* (1937)

George, M. Dorothy, *London Life in the Eighteenth Century* (1925; this edition, 1992)

Gibson, I., *The English Vice: Beating, Sex and Shame in Victorian England and After* (1978)

Gill, R., *A New Collection of Trials for Adultery: or, General History of Modern Gallantry and Divorce* (1799)

Gillis, John R., *British Marriages, 1660 to the Present* (Oxford, 1985)

Goodwyn, A.E., *Selections from Norwich Newspapers 1760–1791* (Ipswich, 1972)

Gouge, William, *Of Domesticall Duties, Eight Treatises* (1634)

Gough, Richard, *The History of Myddle* (Harmondsworth, 1981)

Greenwood, Alice Drayton, ed., *Selections from the Paston Letters. As transcribed by Sir John Fenn* (1920)

Hailsham, Lord, Quintin Hogg, *A Sparrow's Flight, The Memoirs of Lord Hailsham of St Marylebone* (1990)

Halifax, Lord. *See* Saville, George, Marquis of Halifax

Hall, Ruth, ed., *Dear Dr Stopes, Sex in the 1920s* (Harmondsworth, 1978)

Hamilton, Cicely, *Marriage as a Trade* (Detroit, 1971)

Hamilton, Elizabeth, *The Warwickshire Scandal* (2000)

Hammerton, A. James, 'Victorian Marriage and the Law of Matrimonial Cruelty', *Victorian Studies*, vol. 33, no. 2 (Winter 1990)

Hammerton, A. James, 'The Targets of "Rough Music": Respectability and Domestic Violence in Victorian England', *Gender and History*, vol. 3, no. 1 (Spring 1991)

Hammerton, A. James, *Cruelty and Companionship: Conflict in Nineteenth-Century Married Life* (1992)

Hardy, Edward John, *How to Be Happy though Married* (1885)

Hartman, Mary S., *Victorian Murderesses* (1975)

Healey, Edna, *Emma Darwin, The Inspirational Wife of a Genius* (2002)

Helmholz, R.H., *Marriage Litigation in Medieval England* (Cambridge, 1974)

Henderson, Mrs, *The Young Wife's Own Book, Her Domestic Duties and Social Habits* (Glasgow, 1857)

Herbert, A.P., *Holy Deadlock* (1934)

Heywood, Oliver, *The Reverend Oliver Heywood, 1630–1702. His Autobiography, Diaries, Anecdotes and Event Book*, 4 vols., ed. J. Horsfall Turner (1881–5)

Hill, Bridget, *Women, Work, and Sexual Politics in Eighteenth-Century England* (Oxford, 1984)

Hill, Bridget, *The First English Feminist. Reflections Upon Marriage and Other Writings by Mary Astell* (Aldershot, 1986)

Holcombe, Lee, 'Victorian Wives and Property: Reform of the Married Women's Property Law, 1857–1882', in Vicinus, Martha, ed., *A Widening Sphere* (1980)

Holcombe, Lee, *Wives and Property, Reform of the Married Women's Property Law in Nineteenth-Century England* (Oxford, 1983)

Hope-Nicholson, Jacqueline, ed., *Life Amongst the Troubridges: Laura Troubridge* (1966)

Horne, Alistair, *Macmillan, 1894–1986, The Official Biography*, 2 vols. (1989)

Horstman, Allen, *Victorian Divorce* (1985)

Houlbrooke, Ralph A., *The English Family 1450–1700* (London and New York, 1984)

Hunt, Margaret, 'Wife Beating, Domesticity and Women's Independence in Eighteenth-Century London', *Gender History*, vol. 4, no. 1 (Spring 1992)

Ingram, Martin, 'Ridings, Rough Music and the Reform of Popular Culture in Early Modern England', *Past and Present*, 105 (1984)

Ingram, Martin, *Church Courts, Sex and Marriage in England, 1570–1640* (Cambridge, 1987)

Isherwood, Christopher, *Kathleen and Frank* (1971)

Jalland, Pat, *Women, Marriage and Politics 1860–1914* (Oxford, 1986)

Jeaffreson, John Cordy, *Brides and Bridals* (1872)

Jones, Kathleen, *A Glorious Fame, The Life of Margaret Cavendish, Duchess of Newcastle 1623–1673* (1988)

Knyvett, Thomas, *The Knyvett Letters, 1620–1644*. Transcribed and edited by Bertram Schofield (1949)

Laslett, Peter, *Family Life and Illicit Love in Earlier Generations. Essays in Historical Sociology* (Cambridge, 1977)

Latham, Robert, ed., *The Shorter Pepys* (1985)

Laverack, Elizabeth, *With this Ring: 100 Years of Marriage* (1979)

Le Faye, Deirdre, ed., *Jane Austen's Letters* (Oxford, 1995)

Lennox, Lady Sarah, *The Life and Letters of Lady Sarah Lennox, 1745–1826*, ed. the Countess of Ilchester and Lord Stavordale, 2 vols. (1901)

Lewis, Jane, *Women in England 1870–1950, Sexual Divisions and Social Change* (Brighton, 1984)

Lewis, Jane, ed., *Labour and Love: Women's Experience of Home and Family, 1850–1940* (Oxford, 1986)

Lewis, Jane, 'Public Institution and Private Relationship. Marriage and Marriage Guidance, 1920–1968', *Twentieth Century British History*, vol. 1, no. 3 (1990)

Lewis, Judith Schneid, *In the Family Way. Childbearing in the British Aristocracy, 1760–1860* (New Brunswick, 1986)

Lindley, David, *The Trials of Frances Howard, Fact and Fiction at the Court of King James* (1993)

Linton, Eliza Lynn, *The Girl of the Period and Other Social Essays*, vol. 1 (1883)

Luard, G.C., ed., *The Journal of Clarissa Trant, 1800–1832* (1925)

Lutyens, Lady Emily, *Candles in the Sun* (1957)

Lutyens, Edwin, *The Letters of Edwin Lutyens to his Wife, Lady Emily*, ed. Clayre Percy and Jane Ridley (1985)

Lytton, Lady Bulwer, *Lady Bulwer Lytton's Appeal to the Justice & Charity of the English Public* (1857)

Lytton, Lady Bulwer, *The Collected Letters of Rosina Bulwer Lytton*, ed. Marie Mulvey-Roberts (2008)

Mace, David, *Coming Home* (1946)

Macfarlane, Alan, *Marriage and Love in England. Modes of Reproduction 1300–1840* (Oxford, 1986)

Marcus, Steven, *The Other Victorians* (1964)

Martin, Joanna, *Wives and Daughters: Women and Children of the Georgian Country House* (London and New York, 2004)

Masterman, Lucy, ed., *Mary Gladstone: Her Diaries and Letters* (1930)

Matthews, William, ed., *The Diary of Dudley Ryder 1715–1716* (1939)

Maybrick, Florence Elizabeth, *Mrs Maybrick's Own Story, My Fifteen Lost Years* (New York and London, 1905)

McGregor, O.R., *Divorce in England: A Centenary Study* (1957)

Milton, John, *The Doctrine and Discipline of Divorce* (1645)

Misson, Henri, *Memoirs and Observations in His Travels Over England*, translated by R. Ozell (1719)

Montagu, Lady Mary Wortley, *The Complete Letters of Lady Mary Wortley Montagu*, ed. Robert Halsband, 2 vols. (Oxford, 1966)

More, Sir Thomas, *Utopia*, translated by Raphe Robynson, edited by J. Rawson Lumby (Cambridge, 1940)

Mortimer, John, *Clinging to the Wreckage* (Harmondsworth, 1982)

Muilman, Teresia Constantia, *An Apology for the Conduct of Teresia Constantia Phillips*, 2 vols. (1748)

Murray, Jenni, *The Woman's Hour: 50 Years of Women in Britain* (1996)

Nadelhaft, Jerome, 'The Englishwoman's Sexual Civil War: Feminist Attitudes towards Men, Women, and Marriage 1650–1740', *Journal of the History of Ideas*, vol. 43, no. 4 (Oct.–Dec. 1982)

Newcastle, Margaret Cavendish, Duchess of, *The World's Olio* (1655)

Newcastle, Margaret Cavendish, Duchess of, *CCXI Sociable Letters Written by the Thrice Noble, Illustrious, and Excellent Princess, The Lady Marchioness of Newcastle* (1664)

Newcastle, William Cavendish, Marquis of, *The Phanseys of William Cavendish, Marquis of Newcastle, addressed to Margaret Lucas and Her Letters in Reply*, ed. Douglas Grant (1956)

Nicholson, Virginia, *Singled Out, How Two Million Women Survived Without Men after the First World War* (2008)

Nicolson, Nigel, *Portrait of a Marriage* (1975)

Norsworthy, Laura, *The Lady of Bleeding Heart Yard, Lady Elizabeth Hatton 1578–1646* (1938)

Osborne, Dorothy, *The Letters of Dorothy Osborne to Sir William Temple, 1652–54*, ed. Edward Abbott Parry (1888)

Osborne, Francis, *Advice to a Son* (Oxford, 1658)

Outhwaite, R.B., ed., *Marriage and Society: Studies in the Social History of Marriage* (1981)

Outhwaite, R.B., *Clandestine Marriage in England, 1500–1850* (1995)

Oxinden, Sir Henry. *See* Gardiner, Dorothy

Parker, Derek, *The Trampled Wife: The Scandalous Life of Mary Eleanor Bowes* (Stroud, 2006)

Pepys, Samuel, *The Shorter Pepys*. Selected and edited by Robert Lathan (1990)

Perkin, Joan, *Women and Marriage in Nineteenth-Century England* (1989)

Peterson, M. Jeanne, 'No Angels in the House: The Victorian Myth and the Paget Women', *American Historical Review*, vol. 89, no. 3 (June 1984)

Place, Francis, *The Autobiography of Francis Place (1771–1854)*, ed. Mary Thale (Cambridge, 1972)

Platter, Thomas and Busino, Horatio, *The Journal of Two Travellers in Elizabethan and Early Stuart England in 1599* (1995)

Pollock, Linda, '"Teach Her to Live under Obedience": The Making of Women in the Upper Ranks of Early Modern England', *Continuity and Change*, vol. 4, part 2 (August 1989)

Porter, R. and Hall, L., *The Facts of Life: The Creation of Sexual Knowledge in Britain* (1995)

Pound, John F., ed., *The Norwich Census of the Poor, 1570, Norfolk Record Society*, XL (Norwich, 1971)

Profumo, David, *Bringing the House Down, A Family Memoir* (2006)

Quilter, H., *Is Marriage a Failure?* (1888)

Raine, J., ed., *Depositions and other Ecclesiastical Proceedings from the Courts of Durham Extending from 1311 to the Reign of Elizabeth*, Surtees Society, 21 (London and Edinburgh, 1845)

Roberts, Elizabeth, *A Woman's Place: An Oral History of Working-Class Women, 1890–1940* (Oxford, 1984)

Roper, Michael and Tosh, John, *Manful Assertions: Masculinities in Britain Since 1800* (1991)

Rose, P., *Parallel Lives: Five Victorian Marriages* (1985)

Russell, Bertrand, *Marriage and Morals* (1961)

Rye, William Brenchley, *England as Seen by Some Foreigners in the Days of Elizabeth and James I*, 4 vols. (1865)

Savage, Gail, '"The Wilful Communication of a Loathsome Disease": Marital Conflict and Venereal Disease in Victorian England', *Victorian Studies*, vol. 34, no. 1 (Autumn 1990)

Savile, George, Marquis of Halifax, *The Lady's New Year's Gift: or Advice to a Daughter* (1699)

Scott, George Ryley, *Curious Customs of Sex and Marriage* (1953)

Shanley, Mary Lyndon, 'Marital Slavery and Friendship: John Stuart Mill's *The Subjection of Women*', *Political Theory*, vol. 19, no. 2 (May 1981)

Shanley, Mary Lyndon, '"One Must Ride Behind": Married Women's Rights and the Divorce Act of 1857', *Victorian Studies*, vol. 25, no. 3 (Spring 1982)

Shanley, Mary Lyndon, *Feminism, Marriage and the Law in Victorian England 1850–1895* (Princeton, 1989)

Sheehan, Michael M., 'The Formation and Stability of Marriage in Fourteenth-Century England: Evidence of an Ely Register', *Medieval Studies*, vol. 33 (1971)

Shillito, Joseph, *Womanhood: A Book for Young Women. Its Duties, Temptations, and Privileges* (1877)

Shorter, Edward, *The Making of the Modern Family* (1976)

Showalter, Elaine, 'Family Secrets and Domestic Subversion: Rebellion in the Novels of the 1860s', in Wohl, Anthony S., ed., *The Victorian Family: Structure and Stresses* (1978)

Slater, Miriam, 'The Weightiest Business: Marriage in an Upper-Gentry Family in Seventeenth-Century England', *Past and Present*, vol. 72 (August 1976)

Slater, Miriam, *Family Life in the Seventeenth Century, The Verneys of Claydon House* (1984)

Smith, Meliora C., alias 'Claverhouse', *Irregular Border Marriages* (Edinburgh, 1934)

Smout, T.C., 'Scottish Marriage, Regular and Irregular, 1500–1940', in Outhwaite, R.B., ed., *Marriage and Society: Studies in the Social History of Marriage* (1981)

Sneyd, Charlotte Augusta, tr., *A Relation, or Rather a True Account of the Island of England . . . About the Year 1500* (1847)

Somerset, Anne, *Unnatural Murder, Poison at the Court of James I* (1997)

Stenton, Doris Mary, *The English Woman in History* (1957)

Stone, Lawrence, *The Family, Sex and Marriage in England 1500–1800* (1977)

Stone, Lawrence, *Road to Divorce: A History of the Making and Breaking of Marriage in England* (Oxford, 1995)

Stone, Lawrence, *Uncertain Unions and Broken Lives: Marriage and Divorce in England 1660–1857* (Oxford, 1995)

Stopes, Marie, *Married Love* (Oxford, 2004)

Strathmore, the Countess of, *The Confessions of the Countess of Strathmore, written by herself, carefully copied from the original, lodged in Doctors Commons* (1793)

Swinburne, Henry, *A Treatise of Spousals or Matrimonial Contracts* (1686)

Taine, Hyppolite Adolphe, *Notes on England*, translated and with an introduction by W.F. Rae (1872)

Thomas, Keith, 'Women and the Civil War Sects', in Aston, Trevor, ed., *Crisis in Europe 1560–1660* (1965)

Thomas, Keith, 'The Puritans and Adultery: The Act of 1650 Reconsidered', in Pennington, Donald and Thomas, Keith, eds., *Puritans and Revolutionaries, Essays in Seventeenth-Century History Presented to Christopher Hill* (Oxford, 1978)

Tillyard, Stella, *Aristocrats, Caroline, Emily, Louisa and Sarah Lennox 1740–1832* (1995)

Tinniswood, Adrian, *The Verneys, A True Story of Love, War and Madness in Seventeenth-Century England* (2007)

Tomalin, Claire, *The Life and Death of Mary Wollstonecraft* (1985)

Tomalin, Claire, *Samuel Pepys, The Unequalled Self* (2002)

Tomalin, Claire, *Thomas Hardy, The Time-Torn Man* (2007)

Tomes, Nancy, 'A "Torrent of Abuse": Crimes of Violence Between Working-Class Men and Women in London, 1840–1875', *Journal of Social History*, vol. 11, no. 3 (Spring 1978)

Turner, Thomas, *The Diary of a Georgian Shopkeeper* (Oxford, 1979)

Verney, Frances Parthenope and Verney, Margaret M., eds., *Memoirs of the Verney Family during the Seventeenth Century*, 2 vols. (1925)

Vicinus, Martha, ed., *Suffer and Be Still: Women in the Victorian Age* (1980)

Vicinus, Martha, ed., *A Widening Sphere* (1980)

Vickery, Amanda, *The Gentleman's Daughter: Women's Lives in Georgian England* (London and New Haven, 1998)

Vincent, Arthur, ed., *Lives of Twelve Bad Women. Illustrations and Reviews of Feminine Turpitude set forth by Impartial Hands* (1897)

Walker, Sue Sheridan, *Wife and Widow in Medieval England* (Ann Arbor, 1993)

Waller, Maureen, *1700: Scenes from London Life* (2000)

Waller, Maureen, *London 1945* (2004)

Waugh, Evelyn, *A Handful of Dust* (Harmondsworth, 1973)

Weeton, Miss, *Journal of a Governess, 1811–1825*, ed. Edward Hall (1939)

Williams, C., tr., *Thomas Platter's Travels in England* (1937)

Wilson, Elizabeth, *Only Halfway to Paradise, Women in Postwar Britain: 1945–1968* (1980)

Wohl, Anthony S., ed., *The Victorian Family: Structure and Stresses* (1978)

Women's Co-Operative Guild, *Working Women and Divorce: An Account of Evidence Given on Behalf of the Women's Co-operative Guild Before the Royal Commission on Divorce* (1911)

Wood, Mrs Henry, *East Lynne* (1984)

Woolley, Hannah, *The Gentlewoman's Companion or, a Guide to the Female Sex. The Complete Text of 1675* (Totnes, 2001)

Wrigley, E.A., 'Clandestine Marriage in Tetbury in the Late Seventeenth Century', *Population Studies*, vol. 10 (Spring 1973)

Picture Acknowledgements

Index